Self-
governing
Socialism

VOLUME ONE

A READER

Self-governing Socialism

VOLUME ONE

Historical Development
Social and Political Philosophy

_____

Edited by
BRANKO HORVAT

MIHAILO MARKOVIĆ

RUDI SUPEK

Helen Kramer, *Assistant Editor*

INTERNATIONAL ARTS AND SCIENCES PRESS, INC.
WHITE PLAINS, NEW YORK

Contents | Volume One

Part I   Historical Development

Visionaries

Movements

Syndicalism

Industrial Unionism

Guild Socialism

Revolutions

Paris Commune

Russia

Comintern

Establishment

Germany

Yugoslavia

Bolivia

Peru

Chile

Part II   Social and Political Philosophy

The New Society

Preface

There is increasing need for serious study of problems of self-government. The idea of self-government and the organization of society as a federation of workers' and citizens' councils is one of the most interesting and challenging concepts in modern history. Great liberal-democratic revolutions in the eighteenth century brought to life the principles of freedom, equality, and brotherhood in the very limited form of civil liberties, equality before the law, and solidarity within nuclear social communities only. It is a natural extension and radicalization of these principles to demand that all individuals be equally free to take part in decision-making on all matters of general social importance, and that all monopolies of economic and political power be abolished.

This demand became a part of the program of the international socialist movement in the nineteenth century, and spontaneously emerged in all workers' revolutions and uprisings in the twentieth century. Recently, there has been a very significant shift in the priority goals of the labor movement in most advanced European countries from higher wages and mere amelioration of working conditions toward more participation, workers' control, and workers' self-management. There is a growing awareness that self-management is not just one among alternative roads to and models of socialism, but a defining characteristic of the new classless, non-authoritarian society.

Capitalism, for its part, has manifested a considerable capacity for modification and adjustment during the last four decades. In the interest of its self-preservation and inner stability, and to the extent to which it is still able to maintain some measure of political and economic democracy, capitalist society has incorporated some initial forms of workers' participation in management. In fact, it is clear by now that in every modern society at a high level of technical, economic, and political development, there is a growing need to overcome the traditional hierarchical and authoritarian forms of social organization and to introduce new forms which provide for some degree of autonomy and participation in decision-making for all citizens in processes that are of general social concern. Precisely from the standpoint of rationality and efficiency, a very advanced bourgeois society can no longer afford to keep the worker and ordinary citizen in the position of apathetic, positive, reified creatures—mere objects of the historical process.

The immediate motivation for the beginning of work on this Reader was the awareness that the rapidly growing interest in problems of self-government has far outstripped the existing literature. In the last ten years, on many occasions and in a number of countries, we have been asked by listeners or hosts to provide them with literature on self-government. That proved to be difficult because the important relevant texts are not very numerous and are scattered in various books and journals, in various countries. Some of the valuable works—such as certain writings of G. D. H. Cole—were not accessible, and a large proportion of available material of direct practical relevance had been written in languages not widely known, as, for example, Serbo-Croatian studies on the Yugoslav experience. Only recently has the great demand for literature on self-government been partly satisfied by a certain number of translations of Yugoslav studies, by the appearance of the French specialized journal *Autogestion,* and by several readers focusing on workers' control (in Britain, Coates and Topham, *Workers' Control: A Book of Readings and Witnesses for Workers' Control;* in other countries, Mandel, *Contrôle ouvrier, conseils ouvriers, autogestion;* Hunnius et al., *Workers' Control: A Reader on Labor and Social Change;* and others). Valuable material was provided by the First International Conference on Self-management held in Dubrovnik in December 1972.

However, no single study or collection of material approaching self-government as a worldwide phenomenon and dealing with all its important aspects has been produced so far. The purpose of the present Reader is to fill this gap.

This Reader traces the development of self-government from its beginnings as an apparently utopian idea of a handful of visionaries a century and a half ago to its implementation on a national scale in the contemporary world. All fundamental aspects of this development are dealt with—historical, philosophical, sociological, political, and economic. Contributions from some twenty countries are included. Several synthetic papers have been written especially for this book; because of their inclusion, as well as the comprehensiveness of the book's coverage, this work transcends the usual confines of a reader.

Such an undertaking greatly surpassed the professional competence of a single person. The Reader had to be a collective work. However, while its preparation involved numerous discussions among its editors, each of them is fully responsible for his own part of the book. Branko Horvat, who is also the initiator and *spiritus movens* of the entire project, has prepared the parts on history and economics; Mihailo Marković, on philosophy; and Rudi Supek, on sociology. The reader will note certain differences in approach and interpretation among the editors. This is not a matter of chance or of insufficient coordination. Self-governing socialism is not a monolithic, absolutely uniform system. It is, in fact, the reverse: assuming a consensus on some fundamentals, such as equity as a basic principle of social organization, it presupposes an unrestricted diversity of individual opinions. The editors, being firm believers in self-governing socialism, followed the same principle.

The Assistant Editor, Dr. Helen Kramer, an American economist whose long residence in Yugoslavia gave her a thorough acquaintance with the theory and practice of self-government, rendered an invaluable service in translating most of the material from Serbo-Croatian, French, and German into English and in helping to make the appropriate selections. If it were not for her efficient work, the manuscript would not have been completed.

Our goal was to assemble *all* important contributions of historical and theoretical value in one book. Several years of research have been spent to accomplish this goal. The following three provisos are in order, however.

First, the editors could not agree on the place of anarchists in the development of self-government. According to one view, the anarchist theory properly belongs to the mainstream of the development of self-governing socialism. The opposite view holds that anarchism represents a utopian deviation from self-governing socialism, just as state socialism represents a bureaucratic deviation. As a consequence, the Reader contains only a rather limited selection of anarchist texts.

Second, a few texts (Spanish, Swedish, Russian, and others) which we have reason to believe are important could not be located or could not be obtained in time for publication. Third, there was the irremovable constraint of available space. The material originally collected had to be reduced by about one-fourth. In doing so, we eliminated primarily historical and informational-descriptive material and the more technical contributions. The latter consisted exclusively of economic papers, and thus the economic analysis of a labor-managed firm may appear somewhat incompletely represented. (The interested reader is referred to a specialized collection edited by Jaroslav Vanek.)

Belgrade, October 1973

Branko Horvat
Mihailo Marković
Rudi Supek

PART I

Historical Development

Introduction

1. A New Social System in the Making: Historical Origins and Development of Self-governing Socialism

BRANKO HORVAT

The world in which we live is very imperfect. We may try to improve it. If we do, it is very natural to attack the problem in the following way: by producing a blueprint for a good society in which the manifest evils of the present society will be eliminated; by introducing national central planning into the affairs of the society; and by asking society's members to follow certain rules designed to increase their welfare. That is why socialist thought has had a distinctly centralist orientation throughout its history: from Thomas More (1478–1535) and Tommaso Campanella (1568–1639) to Comte de Saint-Simon (1760–1825) and Étienne Cabet (1788–1856) in its utopian phase; and from the Internationals and social democratic parties in the nineteenth century to Lenin, the Comintern, and Communist parties in the twentieth century in its second phase, when practical applications were attempted.

It was only in the nineteenth century, in connection with the advent of liberal capitalism, that social reformers began to question the desirability of a centralist order. If the good society means maximum freedom for each individual, then clearly the elimination of the state and complete decentralization is the goal for which one should strive. William Godwin (1756–1836), to a certain extent Pierre Joseph Proudhon (1809–1865), Mikhail

Bakunin (1814–1876), Prince Kropotkin (1842–1921), and modern anarchists developed this line of thought.

So far, anarchists have not succeeded in implementing their ideas on a national scale, and thus their teaching may be considered as remaining in the utopian phase. Centralists, or state socialists, have been successful in a number of cases. However, the resulting social systems tended to deviate considerably from what had been expected: instead of socialism, centralizers produced etatism.

Elitism is to a certain extent connected with, though by no means identical to, the centralist orientation. If you know what is good for the people, you are entitled to tell them what they should do. Saint-Simon, like Plato, believed that knowledge should rule; but for him, the great industrialists, rather than the philosophers—who did not appear of great avail in an industrial setting—are the natural leaders of the industrious poor. Lenin and modern communists vest all power in the vanguard party, which is to lead the less conscious majority into a better society. (In a backward society with a large percentage of illiterates—to mention just one dimension of retarded development—elitism may make good sense.) Anarchists, on the other hand, rely largely on the goodwill and sense of justice of individuals guided by the ultimate rule of reason.

The third dichotomy in socialist thinking relates to the means by which the new society is to be achieved. In the first half of the nineteenth century, trade unions were illegal in most of the then developed countries and universal suffrage existed in none of them. The working class was subject to brutal exploitation and suffered the needless misery which capitalism inflicted upon it. It was hopelessly naive to believe that the ruling class would voluntarily abdicate its privileged position and allow a classless socialist system to be built. Thus the only realistic way to carry out social reforms was to force the ruling class by violent means to undertake changes or to overthrow the entire system by one single blow through an eruption of the revolutionary energy of the exploited masses. In fact, nineteenth-century Europe was passing through an unending series of violent social upheavals and revolutions. The first theoreticians and practitioners of revolution were Gracchus (Francois Émile) Babeuf (1760–1797) and Louis Auguste Blanqui (1805–1881). Since legal paths to radical social change were barred, they held, illegal ones had to be used. Well-organized, small conspiratorial groups, representing a conscious minority, would seize power at an appropriate moment and lead the oppressed masses into a fight for the overthrow of the present exploitative order. The doctrine of *minorité consciente* was later widely accepted by revolutionary syndicalists. In its mature form, it was elaborated into the theory of a clandestine workers' party to prepare the revolution and establish a dictatorship of the proletariat. The Russian October Revolution represents the most successful application of this theory. Che Guevara and the contemporary Latin American Tupamaros are the latest practitioners of a more primitive version of Blanquism.[1] It remains to be added that some groups of anarchists—who often had nothing to do with socialism—believed in the necessity of violence. They would indulge in individual terrorism, carrying out "propaganda by deeds."

In the second half of the last century, political liberties in the developed countries of Europe were substantially extended; trade unions were legalized, and the first mass workers' parties emerged. It appeared possible to reform society nonviolently. Soon peaceful reformism, as distinct from the earlier ideology of revolutionary violence, came into being. Louis Blanc (1811–1882) and Ferdinand Lassalle (1825–1864) were among the first political figures to rely on the state for carrying out reforms. In the later years of his life, even Engels became a convinced reformist (at least regarding Germany—he acknowledged a possible need for revolutions in some other countries): "The irony of world history turns everything upside down. We, 'revolutionaries,' 'rebels,' we advance immensely better using legal means than illegal ones or by a rebellion."[2] By social inertia, the social democratic parties of the Second International (1889–1914) continued to profess ideas of revolutionary violence, but they were already completely reformist. More than that, they became part and parcel of the establishment and, when World War I broke out, all of them that entered the parliaments voted for war credits in support of the war efforts of their national bourgeoisie. That clearly was in complete contradiction with their professed socialist ideals. As a result, a split occurred in the world working class movement. A new, Communist International was established, reformism was declared a treason, and the necessity of violent revolution was again proclaimed as the only acceptable tenet of socialist faith. Thus the exclusive insistence on either reform or revolution became the basic distinction between social democrats and communists. Bitter political fights ensued, and in the process the two approaches developed into articles of faith, completely divorced from historical circumstances that might render one or the other approach practically relevant. The confusion is further increased by the frequent current use of the terms *revolutionary* and *reformist* in the sense of *radical* and *gradual,* or *progressive* and *reactionary.* Greek dictatorship calls itself "revolutionary," while the Swedish government would no doubt apply the description "reformist" to its affairs.

The three theoretical and tactical dichotomies—centralization versus decentralization, the state dominated by a conscious minority versus anarchy (in its original sense as a society without government), and revolution versus reform—reflect the trial-and-error nature of the development of socialist thought and socialist movements. Ex ante, all of the six naive extreme alternatives appear very natural approaches to be tried out. Ex post, after two centuries of experimentation, none of them appears to be leading to the proclaimed goal. Clearly a more sophisticated theory is required. It is likely that it will include all six alternatives as components, though not in an eclectic fashion. It is of great importance to find out what history can teach us in this respect.

The text which follows is not intended to be a condensed history of socialism with all its detours, frustrated attempts, and mistaken ideas. Its purpose is rather to distill from such an indiscriminate history only those ideas and developments that seem to be leading to socialism conceived as a self-governing society.

In the making of the self-governing society, we can distinguish four waves of events, waves that are partly successive and partly superimposed upon each other. First come the visionaries, whose dreams of a better society, though utopian in terms of practical implementation, are realistic and relevant in terms of later historical development. Next, people associate into groups and social movements emerge. The third wave produces practical attempts to establish a new society. Finally, a new establishment is gradually built up.

The visionaries

The second half of the eighteenth century witnessed the advent of a new, capitalist society. The new society generated a new class conflict, and very soon the exploited class obtained its first intellectual defenders. Not quite conscious defenders, to be sure, because, as Engels observes, they at first did not claim to emancipate a particular class, but all humanity at once. The most developed countries of that time, Britain and France, supplied the most remarkable among them.

Robert Owen (1771–1858), the first and perhaps the most outstanding of the reformers, conceived of the future society as a federation of cooperative communities governed by producers. He evolved to this view after two decades spent as the manager of a large cotton mill in the Scottish village of New Lanark, where he improved the housing conditions of his workers, organized education for their children, reduced working hours from fourteen to ten and one-half hours per day, abolished child labor, introduced some sort of unemployment insurance, and, in general, anticipated by more than a century the treatment that workers would later receive on a national scale. In 1824, Owen went to the United States; he bought an estate in Indiana and established New Harmony, the first experimental cooperative village, whose statute reads like that of a contemporary Israeli kibbutz. The experiment did not prove a success—though in the next few years eighteen more such communities were formed—and Owen left his sons in New Harmony while he himself returned to Britain. There he became involved in the trade union movement, which had just emerged from illegality and which came to stimulate the formation of cooperative workshops. Owen's ideas inspired the cooperative movement and later, in 1844, a group of his disciples founded the Rochdale Pioneers' Co-operative Society. In the meantime, Owen induced the just-formed Builders' Union to lay plans for taking over the entire building industry through a Grand National Guild of Builders, thus eliminating private contractors. This action anticipated future schemes of French syndicalists and British guild socialists. However, after the Grand National Consolidated Trade Union had been formed (1833–1834) in an attempt to unite the entire working class for a direct onslaught on the capitalist system, which was to be replaced by a system of management by the workers, employers and government acted quickly, and in a few months Owenite unionism came to an abrupt end.[3] Even before that event, the once popular "philanthropic Mr. Owen," as he was called in establishment circles, was expelled from "good society" as a sinister individual who intended to destroy the established order of Church and State.

On his deathbed Owen told the minister who visited him that his ideas had not been accepted because they had not been understood and because he had come before his time.

Charles Fourier (1772–1837) came from a middle-class merchant family and was himself a clerk and commercial traveler. He lived in a less industrialized environment and so he lay more stress on the proper organization of agriculture. In contrast to Owen, he considered human nature to be unchanging. Therefore, he felt, a social environment must be created to fit it. For this, it is best to establish self-governing *phalanstères* in which around sixteen hundred persons will cultivate some five thousand acres of land. The main cause of all the wrongs in agriculture is private ownership of land, and thus land must be collectivized in a phalanstery. Industrial establishments ought to be widely dispersed and located in agricultural phalansteries in order to eliminate the differences between the city and the village. Work must be transformed from an unpleasant necessity performed for fear of hunger into an attractive activity. This can be achieved if workers change occupations, attaching themselves to an occupational group according to current interests. In addition, hired labor is abolished. The bulk of the income of a phalanstery will go to cover costs of production and social overheads (board and lodging, medical care, education, etc.) , and the remainder will be used to remunerate talent, capital, and labor. Phalansteries will be federated under a coordinating governor called the omniarch.

Fourier was very much concerned about individual freedom. The French Revolution proclaimed political liberties but did not provide the poor with material means to make use of them. When a poor man expresses an opinion contrary to the opinion of a rich man, he will be persecuted regardless of whether or not his opinion is justified. It appears that freedom is reserved for the small minority possessing the wealth. Freedom is illusory if it is not universal. There cannot be full freedom if people are economically dependent. That is why the phalanstery guarantees the right to work and provides material security for its members. Once this is achieved, the state may disappear, since the absence of opposing interests makes coercion unnecessary.

Fourier advertised for rich philanthropists to finance the establishment of phalansteries and every day expected the unknown guest at the lunch table in the restaurant where he took his meals. None ever came. Yet, after his death, his disciples did raise money and set up a number of cooperative communities, most of them in the United States, where the social climate was very favorable for this sort of venture. Between 1843 and 1853, forty phalansteries were founded. In Owenite communities, income was distributed in equal shares; in Fourierist communities, members who brought more capital or showed greater ability received more of the income of the community. Both types of communities disintegrated with equal speed, the most successful surviving a decade or so.[4]

Another Frenchman, *Louis Blanc* (1811–1882), a lawyer and journalist, decided to explore a different possibility. A moderate and a disbeliever in violent revolution, he thought that the state could be used for carrying out social reforms. In his famous book *L'organisation du travail* (1840), he argued that only the state could protect the weak members of society. Key industries, banks, insurance, and railways ought to be nationalized. The government must undertake to regulate national production. It will supply capital for the creation of *ateliers nationaux*—national workshops—in the most important industries. The government will appoint the director in the first year, and afterward workers will choose their own directors. The capital subscribed is to be interest bearing and there will be no profit. Blanc accused the Fourierists of capitalism for assuring a permanent share in product to suppliers of capital. In Blanc's system, the distribution of income, at first inequitable, will gradually become more and more equal. Blanc's ideal was an egalitarian society with personal interests merged in the common good. This he summed up as "à chacun selon ses besoins, de chacun selon ses facultés," (to each according to his needs, from each according to his abilities), the idea which later became famous in Marx's hands as the formula of communism. National workshops ought to establish a real fraternity within the country and by gradual evolution transform international relations and lead to a peaceful organization of humanity.

The revolution of 1848 brought Blanc unexpectedly into government. His colleagues were unsympathetic to his projects, but they had to tolerate his presence because they hoped that he would help to keep the workers quiet. Soon, however, they tricked him out of the government and made him the president of the Commission de Gouvernement pour les Travailleurs, known as the Luxembourg Commission, which was to study workers' problems and report on what was to be done. Needless to say, the commission had neither money nor power to act. In a speech in March 1848, Blanc asked for a true social revolution which would lead to the achievement of the ideal "de produire selon ses forces et de consommer selon ses besoins" (to produce according to their powers and consume according to their needs) .[5] The commission prepared the draft of a law which stipulated that one-quarter of profits ought to be accumulated in a reserve fund. Various reserve funds would form a fund of mutual assistance to be used in case of need. In this way, large capital would be accumulated, capital which would belong not to any one person but to all. The distribution of this capital would be controlled by a council.[6] In the meantime, the government acted on its own and discredited Blanc's chief project by establishing national workshops as relief agencies in which unemployed workers were assembled to do useless work or even no work at all, the main idea being to keep them off the streets in those turbulent days. After the Assembly declined to consider Blanc's proposal for the creation of a Ministry of Labor, he resigned. His commission disappeared. He was accused of a rebellion against the Assembly and soon sentenced to deportation. Thus, in the same year of 1848, Louis Blanc was compelled to leave his country and could not return for more than twenty years.

When Blanc became a member of the government, another associationist, Philippe Buchez (1796–1865) , became the president of the Constitutional Assembly, although he was soon removed from that post. Buchez, a doctor of medicine, anticipated Blanc's main idea. In 1831 he founded an association of cabinetmakers which served as a model for later producer cooperatives. Buchez thought that associations would provide means of creating the new society within the womb of the existing society.[7]

Blanc demanded universal suffrage in order to enable workers to compel the state to set up national workshops. In the 1860s, the reasoning of the German workers' leader, *Ferdinand Lassalle,* was the same. Lassalle expected the state to provide capital and credit which would enable workers to organize production cooperatives, dispense with employers, and appropriate for themselves the whole product of their collective work. The appearance of self-governing workshops in France, associated with Louis Blanc, influenced a group of English Christian socialists, who formed the Society for Promoting Working Men's Associations and succeeded in establishing several workshops. In Hungary, Blanc was followed by Jozsef Kritovics, who advocated the introduction of manhood suffrage and the establishment of self-governing national workshops whose initial capital was to be provided by the state. Lassallean influence was considerable in Hungary in the late 1860s. All this was severely criticised by Marx, who considered it both absurd and treasonable to expect an emancipation of the working class from the bourgeois state. Given the historical conditions of the time, Marx was right, as the complete failure of Blanc's and Lassalle's attempts amply demonstrates. And yet, somewhat more than a century later, the Chilean government was providing capital for self-managing agricultural cooperatives, and the Peruvian government was also supplying capital to worker-managed agroindustrial and industrial enterprises. Blanc's mutual reserve funds, administered by industrial councils, were introduced in the Yugoslav economy under the same name and were used to cover the losses of collectives encountering difficulties.

A complete system of self-governing society was described for the first time in the voluminous writings of *Pierre Joseph Proudhon* (1809–1865). Proudhon, the only proletarian among the visionaries, was a man of great intuition but very little formal education. His father was a cooper and a domestic brewer, his mother a peasant woman. He was apprenticed to printing, became a press corrector, and educated himself by studying the volumes he corrected. Later he taught himself bookkeeping and engaged in various business ventures. The revolution of 1848 brought him into the National Assembly. But he soon found himself in jail, and remained there several years. In 1858, he published the book *De la justice dans la révolution et dans l'église,* for which he was charged with "attacking the right of the family, outraging public and religious morality and disrespecting the law." To avoid persecution, he emigrated to Belgium, where he lived until 1862.

Like Fourier, Proudhon set for himself the task of completing the unfinished work of the French Revolution. The French Revolution failed, he thought, because it was limited to political reforms; what should be done was to extend liberty and equality to the economic sphere, to establish economic democracy. Also, in a way like Fourier, Proudhon derived the institutions of the good society from the characteristics of human nature. The supreme principle is justice. Justice is given together with labor, and together they represent an unchanging feature of human nature. From the principle of justice are derived the ideals of liberty and equality. Liberty is the fundamental precondition of justice. Thus the social order should be such as to enable every individual to enjoy full freedom. People, endowed with identical reason and eager to preserve dignity, are equal before justice. Consequently, the development of consciousness determines the pace of social development and also relations among men. When a man comes to know his true nature, external coercion for the maintenance of discipline becomes unnecessary. If wealth is approximately equally distributed, people can cooperate in the society without the interventions of an authoritarian state. The way to abolish the state is to dissolve its economic organization and to decentralize it by transferring all power to local units, the communes. In both these steps, the principal instrument is a contract as a basis for reciprocal justice, which precludes the violation of an individual's freedom. This means that each man is free to make arrangements with other men as he pleases, provided this is done in a situation of free bargaining.

Economic organization based on free contracting leads to *mutuellisme*. This means an equitable exchange, equalization of business conditions, and an equitable cooperation of individuals with personal freedoms preserved. The institution responsible for such an economic organization is the *banque d'échange,* the only central institution which remains in Proudhon's society. The bank determines the labor value of commodities and issues the appropriate receipts to producers. (One recognizes the old naive idea of labor money suggested earlier by Owen, and by anticapitalist economists John Gray [1799–1850] and J. F. Bray [1809–1895]). There is no money and credit is reduced to "exchange in which one partner gives his product at once, while the other supplies it in several installments, all without interest."[8] Since production is carried out at the order of the consumer, supply and demand are in equilibrium. Large private productive properties are clearly incompatible with the system of reciprocal justice and ought to be abolished. But small private property is acceptable. When technological conditions require employment of many workers, private property is to be replaced by collective property of workers' associations. Workers form associations to set up enterprises on the basis of contracts stipulating mutual rights and obligations. The initial capital is provided by the exchange bank. When a worker leaves an enterprise, he takes with him a certain amount of money, corresponding to his past labor. Individual producers and associations federate themselves into industries and into a national economy on the basis of contracts. The national economy is an agroindustrial federation. Contrary to

Louis Blanc's formula, reciprocal justice, reflected in equitable exchange, requires that the reward for work be proportionate to service.

Mutualism in the political sphere is federalism. A commune is created through a contract among a certain number of family heads. Communes are federated into provinces and states. The decisions of central organs become obligatory only when accepted by the communes. Proudhon considered traditional representative democracy unsatisfactory because it represents the rule of the majority, which restricts the freedom of the minority. Also, no man can really represent another. Thus all individuals should participate in political decision-making and there can be no hierarchy in the political organization of the society. The most important central political organ is the Assembly of the confederation. It is composed of the provincial delegates, who are at the same time representatives of communes. The delegates elect an Executive Commission which carries out the decisions of the Assembly. Political parties are superfluous in such a system in which citizens retain their sovereignty.

In short, the new social order is based on mutualism in economics and federalism in politics. In this way, nonearned incomes and exploitation are eliminated, social classes are abolished, and social revolution is carried out. An equilibrium of various individual interests, brought about by mutualism, represents a new social order which needs no coercion for its maintenance. Looking back a century later, one can conclude that Proudhon's vision was a remarkable anticipation of a modern—still, to a certain extent, future—self-governing society. Proudhon touched on all important aspects of this society. But his handling of the problems was hopelessly naive, confused, and often just plainly wrong. The idea of labor money was economically untenable, and when an exchange bank was created, it soon went bankrupt. Collective ownership is incompatible with income based on labor only. And so is gratuitous credit. Equilibrating supply and demand is an immensely more complicated affair than Proudhon even suspected, as is the functioning of the state. Free bargaining does not automatically eliminate the inequality in and the abuse of political power, and so forth. Proudhon's solutions to the problems were inadequate or wrong partly because inherently it was extremely difficult to solve problems of a late-twentieth-century society in the mid-nineteenth-century environment. But it is also true that many mistakes were at least partly avoidable and were due to his deficient and unsystematic training. Proudhon extensively discussed questions of economics, political organization, philosophy, and law without having been trained in any of these disciplines. It is therefore hardly surprising that Karl Marx happened to be the first and one of the most outspoken critics of Proudhon. At first, Marx and Proudhon were friends. They held in common certain fundamental ideas such as the withering away of the state, the elimination of unearned incomes and exploitation, the disappearance of money, and the creation of a classless society. However, Marx, a man of great learning, soon found Proudhon's professional ignorance—and the intellectual arrogance that usually goes with it—utterly irritating. In 1847, Marx produced a book-length critique (*Misère de la philosophie*) of Proudhon's views, particularly of the economic views expressed in the latter's *Philosophie de la misère,* published a year before. Marx complained that Proudhon treated economic categories as eternal ideas instead of approaching them as theoretical expressions of historical conditions in production corresponding to a certain level of development of material production. He found Proudhon's knowledge of political economy—whose critique he undertook—incomplete and totally insufficient. In an article written in 1865, after Proudhon's death, at the request of the newspaper *Social-Democrat,* Marx scathingly described Proudhon's "self-boasting and conceited tone, particularly that always unpleasant chatter about science! . . . This is accompanied by a clumsy and disgusting pretention to scholarship of a self-taught person."[9]

What Marx found wrong about Proudhon's confused and unprofessional writings must have appealed to other, less learned men (apart, of course, from the inherent values of his ideas). Proudhon's influence was predominant among Parisian workers in the 1850s and 1860s. In the early days of the First International, Proudhonists controlled its French section. French cooperative and trade union movements were also affected. The Paris Commune of 1871 was dominated by Proudhonists and Blanquists; the former were responsible for the economic decrees of the Commune. Proudhon was first to introduce the word *anarchism,*[10] and his international influence was greatest among anarchists. Proudhon's ideas can be traced in the guild socialist thinking at the time of World War I. It is also of some interest to record the revival of Proudhonism a century later in a completely different environment. Although in Yugoslavia Proudhon is practically unknown—except in the utterly negative version presented by

Marx—the official thinking of the 1960s and 1970s and some in-stitutional solutions bear striking resemblance to some of Proud-hon's ideas. The enterprise is conceived as an association based on a contract among workers. Mutualism at higher levels is reflected in bargaining among associations, called *samoupravno sporazumi-jevanje* [self-management agreement] when bargaining is sec-toral and *društveno dogovaranje* [social contract] when bargain-ing is general and involves state authorities. The "right to past labor," proclaimed recently by a constitutional amendment, en-visages a worker's stake in the enterprise capital apart from the current wage. In political thinking, the withering away of the state and of political parties is accepted as a goal. Federalism is the main principle of political organization. The communes enjoy great autonomy and the relatively small federal states retain sovereignty in principle. The federal government is an Executive Committee of the Assembly and is so called. It cannot act before the constituent states have agreed about a particular decision. In the constitution ratified in early 1974, directly elected representa-tives are replaced by the delegates of work associations and of local political bodies.

After Proudhon's death, at the beginning of the last third of the nineteenth century, the time for writing utopias had already passed. The problems to be solved were of an immediate and very practical nature. Yet utopias continued to be produced. Two in-teresting books deserve to be briefly mentioned: *News from No-where* (1891), by William Morris, and *Freiland* (1890), by Theodor Hertzka.

William Morris (1834–1896), an artist and activist in the Brit-ish socialist movement, described in his book—as he himself put it—the kind of society in which he would feel most at home. In-stead of just commodities produced for the market in an alienat-ing environment, everything made ought to be "a joy to the maker and a joy to the user."[11] The state will wither away when the minds of a sufficient number of people have been changed to enable them to lead the masses toward a free association. Social and economic life will be based on the spontaneous activities of relatively small groups.

Theodor Hertzka (1845–1924), an Austrian Jew born in Bu-dapest and a journalist by profession, is the only alien in the An-glo-French company of visionaries. Like others, Hertzka detested capitalism. But the way to destroy it lay, in his opinion, neither in engineering violent revolutions nor in appealing to the government to carry out reforms. The former repelled him, the latter he found futile. He would lead a group of pioneers into an area not yet infested by capitalism—in his novel *Freiland,* he chose the highlands of Kenya—where they would set up self-governing communes. Perfectly free movement of labor and capital would eliminate all unearned incomes and exploitation. Each worker would be free to choose where to work, which, due to diminishing returns, would equalize incomes and eliminate rent and profit. The system would be closed by the introduction of gratuitous credit provided by the community, which would eliminate interest. The prosperity of Freiland would induce one country after another to adopt the same social system. It hardly need be mentioned that the economics—and politics—of Hertzka are utterly naive. Yet in his insistence on the perfected market as one of the instruments of social organization, Hertzka foreshadowed the so-called market socialism that appeared in the next century. In his own day, he attracted a considerable following, chiefly among intellectuals. Freeland Associations were formed in a number of Continental countries, in Great Britain, and in the United States. His book is said to have influenced the Australian labor leader William Lane to lead five hundred pioneers to Paraguay, where in 1893 they established the colony New Australia. After six years, internal dissensions and the unfavorable climate brought this experiment to an end.[12]

The movements

By the middle of the nineteenth century, the primitive accumulation of capital had already been accomplished in the most advanced countries, the Industrial Revolution had been carried out, and the development of a new social order was in full swing. In the ideological sphere, isolated individuals were to be replaced by broad movements. The new social order, capitalism, generated a new exploited class, the industrial proletariat. Numerous strikes, industrial warfare, and illegal trade unions were evidence of the gradual emergence of its class consciousness. There was a pressing social need to provide a theoretical explanation of the dynamics of the new order and a moral need to provide a defense for its victims. Both were superbly accomplished by *Karl Marx* (1818–1883) and *Friedrich Engels* (1820–1895). Thus, historically, Marxism appears as a theory of emancipation of the emerging working class. Since the proletariat is the exploited class, by emancipating themselves workers will emancipate the society at large; they will destroy the class society and establish socialism. Consequently, socialist movements appeared to be essentially working class movements, with "working class" meaning primarily an industrial proletariat.

Around the middle of the century, political democracy was still in its infancy, voting rights were severely restricted, and trade unions were not legal. The state was completely dominated by the propertied classes, which showed no desire to allow their privileges to be infringed upon in the least. Thus no political channels existed even for small social reforms to be carried out, not to speak of radical reforms. Radicals could see only one instrument of social transformation: a violent revolution, as foreshadowed by the great French Revolution. And indeed, the history of the nineteenth century in Europe is characterized by a great number of revolutionary upheavals in many countries.

Very naturally, Marxism is primarily a theory and ideology of a revolutionary emancipation of the working class, as a result of which "the proletariat will be organized as a ruling class" (*Communist Manifesto*). The latter idea goes back to Gracchus Babeuf and also contains the latter's notion of the dictatorship of the proletariat. In order to fight the bourgeoisie successfully, the proletariat ought to be well organized. Hence the need for political centralization and for disciplined political parties. Once workers' parties were formed in the second half of the last century, they mostly accepted Marxism as their ideology.[13] As a consequence, the first two Internationals were dominated by Marxist thinking.

Yet Marxism is a critical theory of capitalism and its destruction, not a theory of socialism. As early as his first writings, Marx declared: "If building a future and completing it for all time is not our affair, then it is all the more certain what we should do right now. We are thinking of reckless criticism of everything existing, certainly reckless in that the criticism does not fear its results, and also that it does not fear a conflict with the existing forces." Marx rarely and unwillingly—mostly when pressed to do it—wrote on socialism. He thought that it was utopian to write on a society which did not exist. Besides, it was unnecessary. Since capitalism could be replaced only by socialism, all that mattered was to find the ways and means to destroy capitalism. The men of the future will be no less intelligent than we, Engels added, in deciding what to do next. There were pressing current problems to be solved, which implied that idle speculation about the future could be positively harmful by distracting attention and energy from the important daily tasks. The latter pragmatic attitude was prevalent among the political leaders of the social democratic parties. As a consequence, the organized socialist movements were very little concerned with socialism; their energy was absorbed fighting capitalism and exacting small improvements when possible. Even worse, fighting a stronger enemy, they unwittingly adopted his attitudes. And when the great day eventually arrived, the day after a victorious revolution, they could do no better than simply turn the bourgeois society upside down. They did not know how to replace it by a basically different society. Instead of socialism, etatism turned out to be the next social system.

These historically determined contradictions have caused great confusion in the evaluation of Marxian socialist thought. It is therefore necessary to clarify this point by allowing Marx to speak for himself.[14] As a twenty-five-year-old youth, then a bourgeois radical, Marx was enthusiastic over the idea of human liberation: "Man, who would be a spiritual being, a free man—a republican. Petty bourgeoisie will not be one or the other. . . . What they want is to live and multiply . . . that's what animals want. . . . Man's feeling of his own values, freedom, should be awakened in the breast of these people. Only this feeling . . . can again make of society a community of men for the realization of their greatest aim: a democratic state." The same idea appeared seven years later in its mature form in the *Communist Manifesto*, written together with Engels: "In place of the old bourgeois society, with its classes and class antagonisms, we shall have an association in which the free development of each is the condition for the free development of all." Many years later, Marx explained that "freedom is when the state is transformed from an organ that is dominant over society into an organ that is completely subordinate . . ." (*Critique of the Gotha Program*, 1875). Engels naturally agreed, and elaborated: "When there is no longer any social class to be held in subjection; when class rule and the individual struggle for existence based upon our present anarchy in production . . . are removed, nothing more remains to be repressed, and a special repressive force, a state, is no longer necessary. The first act by virtue of which the state really constitutes itself the representative of the whole of society—the taking possession of the means of production in the name of society—that is, at the same time, its last independent act as a state. State interference in

social relations becomes, in one domain after another, superfluous, and then dies out by itself, the government of persons is
replaced by the administration of things . . ." (*Anti-Dühring*,
1878). The last phrase is, of course, a reproduction of the famous
Saint-Simonian idea. And the beginning of the passage reminds
one of Proudhonian anarchism. While the entire passage implies that an authoritarian political system—a dominant, coercive state—is in itself a proof of the existence of a class society,
not a few modern political movements, which call themselves
Marxist, derive an exactly opposite conclusion; namely, that the
"taking possession of the means of production" and their operation from then on by the appointed state officials is the essence
of socialism.

It should be no surprise that Marx and Engels enthusiastically
greeted the Paris Commune of 1871. "The Commune," Marx
wrote, "at the very beginning had to acknowledge that the working class, coming into power, could not rule with the old state
machinery . . . that it had to secure itself against its own deputies
and employees, proclaiming that all of them, without exception,
were dispensable at any time." Nor is this all: "The Paris Commune had, of course, to serve as the source for all the large industrial centres of France. As soon as Paris, and other centres,
were brought into communal administration, the old *centralized*
authority had to be replaced in the provinces by *self-managing*
producers" (emphasis added). Decentralization does not mean
particularism: "The unity of the nation was not to be broken,
but, on the contrary, to be organized by the communal organization. It was to become a reality by the destruction of the state
power which claimed to be the embodiment of that unity but
which wanted to be independent of, and superior to, the nation
itself" (*Civil War in France*, 1871). As for the worker-producer,
Engels explained ten years later: "the worker is free only when
he becomes the owner of his own means of production . . . ,"
where ownership is to be interpreted in terms of social, not state
or collective, ownership.

It follows that Marxian socialism means destruction of the
authoritarian state, communal decentralization, and producers'
self-management. This is very different from the way in which
many people, both sympathizers and adversaries, interpret Marxism today. It does not deny the fact that Marx and Engels
were also centralistically oriented and that they thought, or implied, that individual freedom in self-governing socialism can

be achieved by centralistic means, primarily by central administrative planning which would eliminate market, money, and commodity relations. No doubt historical experience makes clear that Marxian means and ends were not fully consistent. No doubt, too, if Marx and Engels had lived to see later developments, they would have changed means, not ends. When faced with the choice, many of their vulgar followers did the opposite.

In 1864, representatives of English and French trade unions (the latter were still illegal and existed under the guise of friendly societies), together with exiles from various countries, established in London the International Working Men's Association, later to be known as the First International. Marx wrote the *Founding Manifesto*. The *Manifesto* surveys economic and social developments since the revolutionary year of 1848 and, among other facts, records that in England and Wales three thousand persons received annually an income larger than the aggregate income of all agricultural workers. For our purpose, more important is Marx's evaluation of cooperative work. The *Manifesto* points out that, though cooperative work is important in principle and useful in practice, it will never be able to stop the expansion of monopolies nor alleviate the burden of misery. In order to liberate the working masses, cooperative labor must be developed on a national scale, which requires national means of finance. But the owners of land and capital will use their political privileges to prevent this from happening. The same idea is elaborated somewhat a year later in Marx's instruction to the delegates of the General Council to the Geneva Congress of the International. The merit of the cooperative movement is seen in the fact that it indicates the possibility of replacing the existing system in which labor is subject to capital by a system of association of free and equal producers. But the latter can be achieved only after producers have assumed state power.

The issue of producers' cooperatives was discussed at the Geneva (1866), Lausanne (1867), and Brussels (1868) congresses of the First International. The first of these congresses declared its support for the promotion of producers' cooperation, but stressed the inadequacy of voluntary cooperation as the basis of the social system. The second called on unions to support cooperatives by investing in them and by offering moral support. The third congress pronounced in favor of cooperative ownership in manufacturing, aided by gratuitous credit through mutual banks —an influence of Proudhon—and communal ownership of land cultivated by agricultural cooperatives. Cooperatives were also discussed at the Copenhagen congress of the Second International (1910). Yet the resolution talked only of consumers' cooperatives, and no mention was made of producers' and agricultural cooperatives. Lenin suggested an amendment declaring that the socializing and democratizing role of cooperatives will become effective only after the expropriation of capitalists, but the amendment was rejected by a large majority.

At this point, it may be useful to evaluate the role of cooperatives in socialist development. The first French and first Owenite producers' cooperatives were conceived as an instrument of social transformation. And so, to a large extent, were those two hundred—mostly unsuccessful—cooperative mills, mines, shops, and factories organized by the Knights of Labor in the 1870s and 1880s in the United States. Yet, producers' cooperatives, in a capitalist environment, turned out to be a failure. Except in agriculture, they either degenerated into capitalist partnerships or joint stock companies or simply disintegrated. Cooperatives encountered insurmountable difficulties in obtaining the necessary credit —hence so many attempts to set up various kinds of mutual banks—and, due to egalitarian distribution of income, could not attract the best managerial services. If in spite of both handicaps they survived in the competition, the founding members tended to treat the newcomers as hired labor, which, of course, was the beginning of the end. As for consumers' cooperation, there was nothing particularly socialist about it. By the 1850s in Britain it lost its connection with the Owenite new society. When the better paid skilled workers could afford to invest in cooperative societies, they were primarily interested in direct benefits: unadulterated goods, fair prices, dividends on purchases, safe investment— a list of goals that would be subscribed to by any good bourgeois. To make things even worse, occasionally cooperatives were used to prevent any socialist development. Germany is a case in point. Here the conservative promoter of cooperatives, Victor Huber, treated them as an alliance between the traditional order and the workers against the claims of the bourgeoisie, while the well-known liberal cooperative organizer Hermann Schulze-Delitzsch expected them to strengthen free enterprise by educating working class entrepreneurs.

One of the characteristics of the last years of the First International was a continuing struggle between Marxists, who favored political action and centralization of the organization, and anarchists, who opposed both. At the Hague congress (1872), which happened to be the last, anarchists and federalists were greatly outvoted. The defeated minority then decided to reconstitute the International (the attempts failed) on the basis of complete decentralization and to keep separate meetings in the future (which they did). At the Geneva (1873) and Brussels (1874) meetings, the Belgian labor leader César de Paepe (1842–1890) was the principal speaker in favor of workers' self-management. Workers' groups, he held, ought to produce under the supervision of local communes. The commune would own the land and main capital assets. Every worker would participate in political decision-making by giving delegates imperative instructions. Communes would be allied into a confederation.[15] One recognizes here the influence of Proudhon, whose ideas had been absorbed into the anarchist teachings of the time.

Anarchists can be divided into individualists and collectivists or anarcho-communists. The former were few—among them Max Stirner in Germany and Benjamin Tucker in the United States —and had nothing to do with socialism. The latter were numerous—Mikhail Bakunin, Prince Kropotkin, Élisée Reclus, Jean Grave, Émil Pouget—and advocated some sort of utopian libertarian socialism. They demanded the abolition of private property and would replace the coercive state by a free federation organized from below. In the 1890s anarcho-collectivists reemerged as revolutionary syndicalists, who organized a working class movement of considerable importance.

Syndicalism developed in France from a rival trade union movement started in the late 1880s as an opposition to the Fédération Nationale des Syndicats, which fell under the influence of the Guedist Parti Ouvrier. The movement aspired to establish local trade union federations, called *bourses du travail*, which would serve as labor exchanges under trade union control and as trades councils engaging in propagandist, organizational, and educational activities. In 1892, the Federation of Bourses was set up. Three years later Fernand Pelloutier (1867–1901) became its secretary, and he laid the foundation for the movement which attracted all those who, like himself, disillusioned with the fights of the contending socialist factions, stood for a revolutionary working class activity independent of political parties. Syndicalists wanted to place the management of industry into the hands of trade unions. Trade unions were to be federated locally into labor bourses which would establish a monopoly of labor, presently take over the ownership of industries, and run them under local self-governing communes. Syndicalists repudiated parliamentary action, relied on a "conscious minority" instead of thoroughly organized big unions or parties, and hoped to achieve their aim by general strike. These four characteristics of the movement explain at once why syndicalists came to be detested by employers and by orthodox unionists; why, by disorganizing it, their action inflicted damage on the working class movement;[16] and why they failed to realize the goal of workers' management. The industrial militancy of the French syndicalist unions reached its peak in 1902–1906; it provoked strong action by the government and a great consolidation of employers' organizations, and the unions were forced to retreat. After World War I, their ideas were basically modified. In this process, a significant role was played by the fact that, as a result of the war, unions multiplied their membership and developed into large, bureaucratic structures. An important legacy of syndicalism was well summarized by Hubert Lagardelle, leader of Le Mouvement Socialiste group which rallied to the side of syndicalists against the parliamentary socialists: "Syndicalism has always laid down as a principle that bourgeois institutions will be eliminated only in proportion as they are replaced by working class institutions."[17]

Apart from France, syndicalism struck roots in Italy and Spain and spread to the United States, where it became known under the name of *industrial unionism*. The organization responsible for it was the Industrial Workers of the World, created in 1905 through a fusion of the mining and lumbering groups of the Far West, and the Leonite and other groups of the Midwest and the eastern states. The IWW was against the orthodox unions and the reformist socialists and agreed that the basis of working class policy ought to be a revolutionary class struggle for a complete overthrow of capitalism and the seizure of political power by organized workers. On other important questions, the IWW was split in several factions, ranging from anarchists, out and out opposed to political action, to the followers of De Leon, who advocated political action carried out by a revolutionary party working in alliance with revolutionary unions.

Daniel De Leon (1852–1914) was a lecturer on international law at Columbia University and considered himself a Marxist. Soon after joining the Socialist Labor Party in 1890, he became its leader. De Leon saw clearly the need for a strong union and for political organization. He and his supporters thus overcame two basic weaknesses of syndicalism. But continuing factional fights prevented the establishment of an efficient organization. The IWW was to a large extent based on the ill-paid immigrant workers and failed to strike firm roots in the American working class. Revolutionary unionism was more a result of lawlessness in the newly opened mining and lumbering areas in the Far West —where a bitter industrial warfare raged—than an expression of the lasting forces of American society. As such, it was gradually driven back and replaced by orthodox unionism. In the meantime, it provoked even more violent reaction than syndicalism in France. A number of states enacted laws which made the propagation of syndicalist doctrines a criminal offense. This frame of mind was also reflected in the judicial murder of two immigrant workers, Sacco and Vanzetti, in Massachusetts in the 1920s. After World War I the IWW was weakened even further when many members left the organization to join the newly founded Communist Party.

Syndicalism and industrial unionism spread to Australia, Canada, Mexico, Ireland, and some other countries. Industrial unionism was pioneered in Britain by James Connolly (1870–1916), an Irish labor leader, who was later executed by the English for his part in the rising of Easter 1915 in Dublin. After a campaign to spread the ideas of Daniel De Leon, Connolly in 1903 split the existing Social Democratic Federation to form a new Socialist Labor Party named after its American equivalent. The influence of these ideas was soon reflected in the famous manifesto of Welsh miners, *The Miners' Next Step* (1912),[18] which proclaimed the goal of "the mines to the miners" in opposition to the official union policy of nationalization. The state, argued the Welsh miners, would be no less tyrannical than private employers and would be a good deal more powerful. What was required was a militant industrial policy of pressing for ever-increasing wages and improved conditions until mines became unprofitable for the owners. Then they would be taken over and organized under the workers' control. If other workers pursued a similar policy, the capitalist system would become unworkable and the road would be cleared for social revolution.

Britain also produced an autochthonous movement of her own, *guild socialism*. This somewhat strange name was due to a historical accident. In 1906, A. J. Penty, a Christian socialist architect who hated capitalist industrialism, wrote a book called *The Res-*

tauration of the Gild System, in which he advocated a return to medieval handicrafts. Soon afterward, S. G. Hobson turned Penty's ideas into something very different—workers as masters of means of production and guilds as agencies for running the industry—which became the basis of the new movement. The most mature formulation of guild socialist ideas is to be found in the writings of G. D. H. Cole (1889–1959).

Cole cites three fundamental assumptions of the movement: (1) essential social values are human values, and society is a complex of associations held together by the will of their members; (2) it is not sufficient for the government to have only the passive consent of the governed, for the ordinary citizen to have little more than the privilege of choosing his ruler; the citizen should be called upon to rule himself, the society should be self-governing; (3) democracy applies not only to politics but to every form of social action. It is not poverty but slavery and insecurity that are the worst evils of contemporary society. The position of a man in the daily labor determines his position as a citizen. Without industrial democracy, political democracy can be only a pretense. "The essence of the Guild Socialist attitude lies in the belief that society ought to be so organized as to afford the greatest possible opportunity for individual and collective self-expression to all its members and that it involves and implies the extension of positive self-government through all its parts."[19] For this purpose, the omnicompetent state with its omnicompetent parliament is utterly unsuitable. Guildsmen invoked Proudhon, Kropotkin, and William Morris against the view that all political issues can be resolved only through a concentrated political power. No man can truly represent other men. The citizen must choose someone to represent his point of view only in relation to some particular purpose or group of purposes, i.e., in relation to some particular function. This *functional democracy* leads to a pluralist society in which there is no single sovereign and in which there is a distribution of power among functional groups.

Production will be carried out by state-chartered guilds of workers based on trade unions. "A National Guild would be an association of all the workers by hand and by brain concerned in the carrying on of a particular industry or service, and its function would be actually to carry on that industry or service on behalf of the whole community."[20] Apart from the producers' organizations or economic guilds, there will be three additional functional organizations: consumers' organizations or cooperatives and collective utility councils; civic service organizations or civic guilds (professions excluding the ministry) ; and citizens' organizations or cultural and health councils. As against these four functional organizations, there will be one communal organization with two main roles: (a) coordinating functional bodies into a single communal system; (b) coordinating bodies operating over smaller areas with bodies operating over larger areas. All functional bodies are represented on the communal boards and all these representatives taken together represent the commune.

The commune has five tasks to perform: (1) it allocates local resources and, to a certain extent, regulates incomes and prices; (2) it serves as a court of appeal for the conflicts of the functional bodies; (3) it determines the line of demarcation between functional bodies; (4) it decides on matters concerning the town as a whole, such as the building of a new town hall; (5) it operates the coercive machinery. "The national co-ordinating machinery of Guild Society would be essentially unlike the present state, and would have few direct administrative functions. It would be mainly a source of a few fundamental decisions on policy, demarcation between functional bodies . . . and of final adjudication on appeals in cases of disputes. . . . Into the National Commune . . . would enter the representatives of the National Guilds, Agricultural, Industrial and Civic, of the National Councils economic and civic, and of the Regional Communes. . . ."[21]

Functional representation in the political sphere leading to political pluralism and a severe reduction of the traditional state authoritarianism, and self-management in all work organizations—this is the essence of guild socialism. This is also the essence of the self-governing organization of a truly socialist society.

Guildsmen were initially a group of intellectuals, some of them Oxford dons. Only after 1912 did the movement begin to attract workers, and after 1914 it became widely influential. In 1915, the National Guilds League was formed. It exerted great influence on the shop stewards' movement and on several unions. The experience in the shop stewards' movement induced J. M. Paton to formulate the policy of "encroaching control," of progressive invasion of capitalist autocracy.[22] According to this concept, by gradually assuming the controlling functions in industry, workers will deprive the owners of an active or useful participation in the industry from which they draw their incomes. Owners will be reduced to a useless appendage to be swept away with relative ease at the time of final transition. The atrophy of the functions of the possessing class will destroy its moral claims to its rights; "busy rich" will change into "idle rich" and will then be "expropriated." The other policy of transition advocated by guildsmen was the capturing of the state by the working class in order to take industry under public ownership. After that, Parliament would hand over the task of administration to the national guilds (former trade unions) within the terms of a parliamentary charter.

Neither policy really worked. During and after the war, a number of small guilds were created. Of greatest importance was the movement to reorganize the building industry as a national guild in which employers were to become salaried administrators, subject to election by the workers employed—a remarkable resurrection of the Owenite Building Guild of 1834. At first the building guilds were quite successful, which Cole explains as due to the fact that ordinary house-building requires almost no fixed capital and there was a heavy demand for houses. Guilds charged lower prices, rendered services of higher quality, and attracted the best workers. However, in the first postwar depression in 1922–1923, the movement collapsed, and a year later guild socialism as an organized movement was dead in Britain.[23] Immediately after the war, national guild leagues spread to South Africa, Australia, and Japan—where they died out as well.

The revolutions

If the first wave brought into existence individual socialist ideologues and isolated groups, and the second produced organized movements, the third wave brought the first realizations. Broadly speaking, the European revolutions of 1848 mark the time when the working class emancipated itself and asserted itself as a separate social class. It might be supposed that in the revolutions which were to follow the working class would attempt to establish industrial self-management and, perhaps more generally, social self-government. Let us examine this hypothesis in the light of the events which actually took place.[24]

The era of proletarian revolutions began with the *Paris Commune* of 1871. Self-government has two fundamental components: functional and territorial. From the very beginning, the Commune developed both of these components. Politically it developed a fully participatory democracy. In the industrial sphere, the Commune passed a decree by which industry was to be reorganized on a cooperative basis and enterprises run by workers. The positive experience of the Paris Commune, the heroism of its citizens, and the tragic outcome of their fighting inspired many individuals—Marx and Lenin, among others—groups, and entire movements. In particular, eighty years later it exerted great influence, through the writings of Marx, on the development of workers' self-management in Yugoslavia. Though Yugoslav institutional arrangements and social theory reflect many ideas contained in Proudhonism and guild socialism, there is no historical continuity in these ideas; they were not known in Yugoslavia and were rediscovered anew. Marx's evaluation of the Commune was well known, however, and influenced thinking and action in the most direct manner.

Next came the *Russian Revolution* of 1905. It produced soviets, a specifically Russian institution of revolutionary power. Since the soviets played a great role in future revolutionary developments, a brief description of their origin is in order. In January 1905, after a strike, troops killed 1000 workers demonstrating in the streets of Petrograd and wounded 5000 more. This set in motion a wave of strikes throughout the country. In May, 30,000 workers of the textile center Ivanovo-Voznesensk stopped working and elected delegates to an assembly of 151 members. This body assumed not only the conduct of the strike but also the political power, and created its own militia and court. That was the first soviet. Others soon followed, the most famous being the Petrograd Soviet, which acted under the leadership of Trotsky. In October, 2,000,000 workers participated in a general strike. Soviets now existed in fifty-odd cities; workers elected delegates who gathered together in city soviets. The first workers' demands were traditional unionist demands concerning wages and working conditions. But these were soon superseded by more radical demands, such as the eight-hour working day, and became mainly political after the October general strike (the end of autocracy, establishment of a Constituent Assembly, freedom of speech and assembly). The tsar was forced to grant concessions and promised to extend civil liberties and establish a parliament. As soon as the situation was again under control, the soviets were liquidated, and most of the concessions taken back.

As we have just seen, soviets developed out of strike committees with the participation of political parties. Their appearance was completely spontaneous, with no relation to an established theory or political strategy, and yet they look as if they were an outcome of industrial unionism. The functional and territorial-political components of self-government are still undifferentiated in a soviet. But the tendency is for the latter to predominate, and during the general strike, soviets became local executive authorities largely replacing the municipal authorities.

Both the Paris Commune and the Russian Revolution of 1905 were crushed, and workers' self-government did not survive them. However, the destiny of the second Russian revolution, the *Great October Socialist Revolution* of 1917, proved different. The chain of events was started by a strike of female Petrograd textile workers on February 23 (March 8 according to the new calendar). Four days later, a soviet was created as a joint organ of Petrograd workers and soldiers. The number of members—who were delegates of factories and military units—soon reached two thousand. Order No. 1 of the soviet, most of whose members were soldiers, was that all military units should set up committees composed of representatives elected from among lower ranks. A month later, Lenin wrote his famous *April Theses* urging a transformation of the bourgeois-democratic revolution into a socialist one. His battle cry was: Power to the soviets! Land to the peasants! Peace to the people! To which workers soon added: Factories to the workers! In the same month, at a Bolshevik conference, the Ural delegate Sverdlov reported that in his region the workers had taken over some factories and that it was believed that soviets would have to assume the management of the factories if the owners refused to operate them. On May 23, the provisional government issued a decree legalizing factory committees but trying to limit them to consultative bodies. Factory committees, however, soon transcended these limits and, in particular, when there was a danger of a factory's closing down, they would assume the management of production. Such workers' takeovers have since then become typical forms of spontaneous introduction of self-management and have been practiced in many countries; in Latin America, they are known as *las tomas de fábricas*.[25]

The peasant soviets appeared somewhat later, but, by the summer of 1917, there were already four hundred of them in existence. In May, the First Congress of Delegates of Workers' and Peasants' Soviets opened in Petrograd. The congress proclaimed in favor of the confiscation of large estates and workers' control in factories. In the same month, the First Petrograd Conference of

Factory Committees took place. Lenin presented a resolution arguing that workers' control represented the only way to avoid economic disaster.[26] The resolution was carried with a great majority, and the conference elected the Council of Factory Committees. After the conference, Lenin explained his position more precisely by pointing out that workers' control meant control by the soviets and not "the ridiculous passing of the railroads into the hands of railwaymen, the leather factories into the hands of leather workers."

On the night of October 24-25 (old calendar), the uprising in Petrograd brought the Bolsheviks to power. The Second Congress of Soviets, then in session, decided that all power in all places would pass into the hands of soviets of workers', soldiers', and peasants' delegates. The Soviet Republic was born.

Two weeks later, the new government issued the Decree on Workers' Control. Councils for workers' control were to supervise the entire operations of enterprises and their decisions were to be binding for the workers. From this time on, this promising development was to take a very different course.

Factory committees were to be responsible to local councils of workers' control, whose members were to be chosen from factory committees, trade unions, and workers' cooperatives. Local councils were subordinated to an All-Russian Council of Workers' Control. Since the old Central Council of Factory Committees, which resulted from the congresses of factory committees from May to October, was still in existence, the new organization implied a duality of leadership. More than that, the two bodies interpreted workers' control very differently. The Central Council issued a *Manual* explaining that decisions of factory committees were binding on the administration of the firms and that noncompliance might be punished by sequestration. The instructions of the All-Russian Council, on the other hand, reserved management for the owner and barred factory committees from confiscating the enterprise under any circumstances. A bitter controversy ensued. One of the most outspoken critics of the approach of the Central Council was the Bolshevik trade unionist A. Lozovsky, who in his book *Workers' Control* argued that it "abolished the entrepreneur" and made the factory committee "the boss of the given enterprise," and pointed out that such transfer of factories to the workers was "not only not socialism but, on the contrary, a step backwards, a strengthening of the capitalist mode of production, albeit along new lines."

The debate was soon streamlined by practical measures. On December 1, the Supreme Economic Council was created. It abolished the All-Russian Council of Workers' Control and made the control function a component of the overall task of regulating the economy. It coordinated a network of local economic councils (*sovnarkhozy*). Thus one rival body was eliminated.

Bolsheviks were now arguing that there was no need for separate workers' organizations after the conquest of power, as in the time when factory committees exerted workers' control and trade unions organized the struggle against the bourgeoisie. In January 1918, the First All-Russian Congress of Trade Unions decided to transform factory committees into primary trade union organs. This device—killing workers' self-management by unionizing it —was later used in some other countries as well. The decision did not pass unopposed, however. At the Second Congress of the Comintern, many delegates continued to treat factory committees, the organizations of direct producers, as more revolutionary than trade unions, which operated through leadership. Yet the congress approved the amalgamation of the two. In March, the Central Council of Petrograd Factory Committees disappeared through absorption into the *sovnarkhozy* of the northern industrial region.[27] In his *Next Tasks of Soviet Power* Lenin wrote that it was necessary to learn how to harmonize the tumultuous democracy of the working masses with the iron discipline at the workplace, with the absolute submission to the will of one single person—the soviet leader—in the process of work.

In May and June, large sectors of the national economy were nationalized. At the same time, the First Congress of the Councils of the National Economy was held. The congress decided that, in nationalized enterprises, management committees would be composed of workers' representatives elected by trade union members (one-third) and of members appointed by the regional or supreme Council of National Economy (two-thirds).[28]

The ensuing civil war, with its concomitant shortages and sabotage, required—or at least it appeared so—strict centralization and military organization of the entire social life of the country. However, as soon as the civil war was over, the quest for self-management reappeared. In 1920 and 1921, Shliapnikov, Kollontai, and a number of other trade union leaders led a movement called the Workers' Opposition. The Opposition demanded nothing less than full workers' self-management under the control of the trade unions. Workers would elect the managerial organ called the workers' committee. The Party could not recall the candidates nominated by the unions. But it was too late. The Opposition was crushed. The trade unions were soon required to operate primarily as an instrument to persuade workers to fulfill the production tasks. Former factory committees were replaced by production cells, which in 1923 developed into production conferences with consultative functions and the primary task of increasing production. Workers soon became disillusioned, and conferences withered away without ever having been officially abolished.[29] The last remnants of workers' control lingered for some time in the managing triangle of director–Party secretary–chairman of the trade union committee, with the director becoming more and more important. In the late twenties, Stalin removed even these remnants, and in a truly Weberian fashion proclaimed that the essential condition for discipline and efficiency was that the director have absolute and complete control over the enterprise and that he be subject only to the orders from above. *Edinonachalie* (one-man management)—already foreshadowed by Lenin, who asked for an absolute submission to the will of one single person —was adopted as the basic principle of social organization. Significantly enough, after a short while the gap between workers' wages and managerial salaries was widened by several times. Workers' control was dead for the time being.

The Russian Revolution had a strong impact on revolutionary fermentation in other European countries. Soviets sprang up all over Europe. In Austria, Germany, and Norway, national conferences of soviets were held in 1918 and 1919. Several thousand workers' and peasants' councils were organized by various political groups in Poland. Soviets appeared sporadically in other countries, such as England (Leeds, June 1917) and Switzerland (Zurich, January 1919). With a lag of a decade, they spread to Asia, where they were organized by Chinese communists and appeared during the 1930 uprising in Indochina. Workers proved able to extort constitutional and legal reforms and occasionally to assume (temporarily, of course) management of their factories. In a way, the most dramatic event was the *Hungarian Revolution*, which gave birth to the Hungarian Soviet Republic in the spring of 1919. Lenin sent greetings. As early as October 1918, workers' and soldiers' councils, mainly under socialist leadership, began to be formed in Budapest and some other places. In large factories, management passed into the hands of factory workers' soviets.

The soviet government was brought to power in March 1919 by an action of the Budapest Council of Workers' and Soldiers' Deputies. The government nationalized industry and trade and entrusted management to production commissars and factory soviets. The Soviet Republic immediately encountered strong internal and external resistance and worsened the situation by committing grave mistakes in taking a rigid and dogmatic course and allowing arbitrary treatment of people, particularly in villages. The civil war began. Hungary was attacked by the Romanians and Czechs. After 135 days of existence, the Hungarian Soviet Republic was crushed by a combined effort of French, Romanian, and Yugoslav troops and a small army of Hungarian emigrants. In August, Romanian troops entered Budapest, and, with the arrival of Admiral Horthy in November, the white terror began. Instead of toward socialism, Hungary was heading toward fascism.

The situation was hardly less revolutionary in another country defeated in the war, *Germany*. But unlike Hungary, Germany was a much more developed country, with a long tradition of working class movements and a well-organized Social Democratic Party professing Marxism and advocating a revolutionary transformation of society. Yet, when the occasion arrived, the old theory proved wholly inadequate and the main body of the party failed to move. Developments were spontaneous and forms of organization unexpected. The revolutionary movement was triggered by the refusal of the fleet in Kiel to leave the harbor for an attack on the British fleet in November 1918. The authorities of course reacted, and hundred of marines were jailed. The rest of the marines requested that their imprisoned comrades be liberated and captured the naval bases on November 3. The next day, soldiers' councils were formed. A day later, councils of soldiers and workers met and a general strike was proclaimed. A general strike burst out that same day in Hamburg, and on November 6 the council of workers and soldiers assumed power. Developments were similar in Lübeck, Bremen, and other harbors. In Stuttgart and in Munich, on November 7, the dynasty was overthrown. In the latter city, a council of workers and soldiers assumed power and proclaimed the Bavarian Republic under the leadership of Kurt Eisner. In the next two days, the revolution spread to several new provinces. On November 10, a new government was formed in Berlin consisting of two groups of Social Democrats. An assembly of councils of workers and soldiers in Berlin, representing the revolutionary movement of all of Germany, elected an Executive Committee of the councils and gave support to the government.

The revolutionary ferment was strongest in Bavaria. On February 15, 1919, Eisner was forced to resign, and four days later the congress of councils—at the initiative of the majority Social Democrats—decided to dissolve and return power to the Landtag in Munich. Just before the Landtag opened, however, on February 21, Eisner was killed. Tensions were increased immensely. On the night of April 6, the Bavarian Councils Republic (Räterepublik) was proclaimed. It lasted until May 1, when it succumbed to the attacks of troops several times stronger that were sent against it. "The uprooting of the Munich revolutionaries," commented G. D. H. Cole, "and the establishment of military rule which ensued, destroyed Bavarian Socialism and made the city into a stronghold of counterrevolution in its most extreme forms."[30]

In December 1918, the National Congress of Councils in Berlin, dominated by majority socialists, voted to hand over power to the forthcoming Constituent Assembly as soon as possible. The decision was carried out in February 1919, when the Assembly met in Weimar. In the meantime, the Social Democratic government brutally suppressed demonstrations in Berlin and allowed the murder of two socialist leaders, Karl Liebknecht and Rosa Luxemburg. It looked as if the revolution had been brought under control, and that more orthodox parliamentary methods would effect the necessary social changes. In fact, the way was paved for fascism.

Spontaneously formed soviets and works councils (of which more will be said in the next section) in Germany stimulated an extensive controversy about their role and functions. In this connection, Anton Pannekoek (1873–1960), a Dutch astronomer, and Karl Korsch (1886–1961), a German philosopher, may be mentioned as the two most important writers. A third, the philosophically trained Italian labor leader Antonio Gramsci (1891–1937), also contributed some new ideas.

In *Italy* in August 1919, at the Fiat center in Turin, an assembly of workers furiously dissatisfied with the existing *commissione interna*[31] succeeded in forcing it to resign and for the first time elected shop stewards who constituted a factory council.[32] In the same year and in the same city, Gramsci established the weekly *Ordine nuovo*. Searching in the Italian tradition for an institution which could serve as an embryo of future soviets, Gramsci and his group advocated the establishment of workers' councils. Gramsci was one of the first labor leaders to realize clearly that trade unions do not transcend the framework of bourgeois society. It is only workers' councils which create the new consciousness of workers and help to build a new structure of production relations. He also understood the need for a differentiated—functional and political—approach to self-government. In one of the first articles in *Ordine nuovo* (June 21, 1919), the opinion is expressed that the slogan, "All power in the factory to workers' committees," under which workers must begin to elect their representative assemblies, ought to be combined with the slogan, "All state power to workers' and peasants' councils." Naturally enough, such ideas did not appeal to the trade union bureaucracy, and it prevented the spread of workers' committees outside Turin.

In August 1920, a long strike of metal workers in Milan was followed by a lockout. Workers retaliated by occupying factory after factory. Even before that, factories would occasionally be taken over by workers, who would continue to work without management. Now most factories in Milan and Turin were occupied. But the entire action was not prepared, and it soon collapsed under the combined pressure of employers and the government. The government promised reforms, but after negotiations were over and factories were returned to the owners, it gave up the idea of passing a law on workers' control. In the face of the workers' claims for a greater share in the control of industry, the employers became restive; they began to consolidate their organizations, and by the summer of 1919 a number of big industrialists started financing fascists as the force most likely to check the working class movement. In October 1922 Mussolini marched on Rome. A few years later, fascism was firmly established in Italy. Gramsci was caught and sentenced to twenty years in jail.

Spain was the next country to experience revolutionary ferment. For more than a decade after World War I, Spain was passing through a period of extreme political instability in which intervals of almost no government were interchanged with military dictatorships. The days of the old monarchy had clearly gone. But the country did not seem ripe for a democratic bourgeois republic. The republic itself was proclaimed in 1931; a military mutiny followed a year later; in 1933, the government suppressed a broad anarchist movement, and a year later a strong popular movement in Asturias was suppressed by armed forces. In such an atmosphere, leftist parties won an absolute majority in the 1936 elections. That was in February. As early as July, General Franco started the military mutiny in Morocco. The civil war began.

In the early months of the civil war, effective power was exercised mainly by the local workers' committees. Even the army was made up mostly of workers' militia. All over the country, workers took over abandoned factories and peasants deserted estates. Workers elected committees to run the factories, and peasants established communes. The committees were composed mainly of militants of the trade union Confederación Nacional de Trabajo. The CNT was largely under anarchist influence; it kept aloof from party politics and proclaimed as a goal a society organized as a loose federation of free local communes. Its influence was strongest in Catalonia, and it was exactly there that the celebrated Decree on Collectivization and Workers' Control was issued in October 1936. The decree envisaged the collectivization of all enterprises with more than a hundred workers, those that had been abandoned or whose owners joined the rebels, and also those in which three-fifths of the workers desired collectivization. In collectivized enterprises, management would be in the hands of workers, represented by enterprise councils. Private industry would be managed by owners subject to the approval of a workers' control committee. The enterprise councils would elect directors and would include government inspectors whose duty would be to insure compliance with the law. The coordination of the activities of individual enterprise councils and the task of drawing up plans for various industries were to be entrusted to general industrial councils composed of the representatives of the enterprise councils and trade unions as well as technicians appointed by the government. Under conditions of civil war, this scheme had little chance to be tried out as envisaged. Somewhat more than two years later, the Spanish Revolution collapsed. *El comunismo libertario* of the CNT Saragossa Congress of 1936 was replaced by a fascist dictatorship. The lesson to be derived from the Hungarian, German, Italian, and Spanish experiences—and from the events of 1973–1974 in Chile—seems to be that unsuccessful or half-successful revolutions are likely to generate fascist dictatorships.

World War II produced new revolutionary upheavals and, with them, new attempts at workers' self-management. The *Yugoslav Revolution* of 1941–1945/1948 (which will be discussed in greater detail later) produced the first successful implementation of an integral system of workers' self-management. Just as the Russian Revolution influenced developments in other countries and led to numerous imitations of soviets, the Yugoslav Revolution popularized workers' councils, which were set up in a number of countries.

The Yugoslav influence was perhaps most strongly felt in *Algeria,* where, as a result of the War for National Liberation (1954–1962), favorable conditions for social change were created. As before in Russia, Hungary, and Spain, workers and peasants were occupying the abandoned estates and establishments of French colons. Spontaneously established *comités de gestion* in the summer of 1962 were supported by UGTA unions as the basic democratic form to offset the autocratic tendencies of the leadership of the National Liberation Front. First elections were held in September 1962, and by October a decree legalized *comités de gestion* in the vacant agricultural estates. The next year, the celebrated March Decrees established management committees as a keystone of Algerian socialism. The Yugoslav formula was adopted: all full-time workers constituted the general assembly and, in enterprises with more than thirty workers, elected a workers' council. The council elected a management committee. However, many members of the state and party machinery were opposed to self-management. Step by step, the state apparatus was increasing its control over the activities of enterprises. Their funds came to be held and administered by state agencies. Finally, the committees were dissolved, except in agriculture, and the enterprises integrated into *sociétés nationales.*[33] Self-managing enterprises of the Yugoslav type were replaced by public corporations patterned on the French model. Once again self-management degenerated into etatism.

Postwar development followed a similar course in many respects in all of the most industrialized East European countries. All these nations were liberated by the Soviet army. In all of them, various forms of workers' management appeared spontaneously near the end of 1944 or at the beginning of 1945. *Betriebsräte* reappeared in East Germany. Factory committees were legalized in Hungary in February 1945. In the same month, a decree was passed on factory councils in Poland. But by 1948, communist regimes consolidated their power and workers' management soon disappeared in all these countries. It was replaced by a *Gleichschaltung* on the Soviet pattern.

After Stalin's death, a new revolutionary tide passed through these countries (except East Germany). In 1956, for the third time within a generation, *Hungarians* attempted to establish workers' management during an uprising. Spontaneously created workers' councils were legalized in November 1956. According to law, the council, elected by the workers, would manage the enterprise and make the binding decisions on all important matters. Territorial workers' councils would not only coordinate the activities of enterprise councils, but function as organs of political power. That was particularly true of the Budapest workers' council.

The Russian military intervention put an end to this development. Unlike in 1917, when the Hungarian revolutionists were enthusiastically greeted by Lenin as allies, in 1956 they were treated as enemies. This attitude was not accidental, nor was it new. In 1917, both countries were experiencing socialist revolutions. In 1956, the etatist Soviet Union crushed socialist revolution in Hungary—just as in 1848 feudal Russia crushed the Hungarian bourgeois revolution. After the defeat, workers' councils continued to exist, and a previously tested device was used—trade unions were urged to assume the leading role. In 1957, workers' councils lost independence and were replaced by factory councils, which were consultative bodies under the leadership of unions. The chairman of the trade union committee was an *ex officio* chairman of the factory council.

In *Poland,* after the Poznan upheavals, workers' councils of various forms were created at a number of enterprises. In November 1956, a law was passed stipulating that the workers' council, elected by all workers, was to manage the enterprise and approve the nomination and dismissal of the general manager. Yet, as soon as the situation was again under control, the authorities encroached upon the rights of the workers' councils, which found it more and more difficult to operate. The new law of 1958 explicitly stated that the principle of *edinonachalie* and self-management was to be replaced by co-participation. The workers' council, trade union committee, and Party committee together represented the Conference of Self-Management, The conference was entitled to make proposals, but all decisions were taken by the director.

Czechoslovakia lagged by about a decade. But when the time arrived, the Czech attempt looked most promising, for industrial democracy was developing within a mature political democracy. The first elements of self-management appeared in 1966 along with the economic reform. But the development was successfully checked by the existing etatist regime. The Prague Spring brought a fundamental change. After the old Stalinists had lost power, in the first months of 1968, self-management became the main subject of discussion in newspapers, journals, and factories. Preparatory committees for future workers' councils (*podnikove rady pracujicich*) began to be established all over the country. In June, trade unions gave support to this initiative and in fact established two-thirds of all preparatory committees, which soon existed in one-half of industrial establishments. The government announced that the law on socialist enterprise, which was to settle all matters concerning self-management, would be promulgated by the end of the year. Conservatives, of course, were opposed. Representative of their views was a document circulated among Party members and prepared by two members of the Party presidium for its session of the fatal night of August 21. It said that the creation of workers' councils generated "the danger that the anarchist and anticommunist elements will gradually acquire the most important positions in the councils and use them to weaken and destroy the positions of the Party, trade unions, and economic agencies in the production process. Bearing in mind transformations occurring in the structure of management, this fact could have very great consequences."[34] The Russian leaders shared this view, and there is some sinister symbolism in the fact that on the very night when the document was to be discussed at the Party presidium, troops of the Warsaw Pact invaded Czechoslovakia. Preparatory committees and workers' councils continued to exist for some time, occasionally operating illegally. The announced law on the socialist enterprise had, of course, never been passed. Soon the old etatist setup was reestablished.

To summarize, in the first century of socialist revolutions, all but two of them produced attempts to establish self-government. The two exceptions—the Chinese and Cuban revolutions—could probably be explained by the very specific nature of these revolutions.[35] Another Latin American revolution, the Bolivian Revolution of 1952, promptly produced *control obrero* (worker control) in nationalized enterprises. Thus, historically speaking, socialism and self-government appear to be synonymous.

It has been frequently stated that wherever workers' management was attempted, it failed. In a sense this is true. After the frustrated attempts, the country would lapse back into capitalism or etatism. But the inference that therefore workers' management must be regarded as an unrealizable utopia is clearly false. In no historical period have new social institutions been successfully established at one stroke, without bitter fights with vested interests, and without many failures. What is significant in the events we have reviewed is not the failure to achieve the goal, but the recurrent attempts *despite* all failures.

The establishment

The three waves described so far could not fail to exert great influence and to modify that relatively stable and sanctified pattern of social life which is denoted as the *establishment*. The establishment itself began to change, and this is the fourth, surface layer of the historical trend we have set out to investigate.

Various kinds of workers' and works councils—the former are composed of workers only, the latter include employers' representatives as well—are as old as the trade union movement. These councils or committees dealt with complaints, welfare work, and conditions of employment. They were always advisory, the employer reserving the power of making the final decision. But for a long time they occurred only sporadically,[36] and did not represent an institution. Similarly, labor legislation dealing with some forms of workers' participation in the factory organization—almost exclusively confined to welfare matters—can be traced back in several countries (Prussia and Austria, for instance) to the end of the last century.[37] These were also sporadic events, and the extent of workers' participation was insignificant. The first landmark in the history of workers' participation in management is represented by World War I and the Russian Revolution.

During the war, in order to enhance war production, the British, French, and German governments sought—and received—the cooperation of the unions. As a result, various forms of management-worker cooperation developed. The events that occurred in these countries are so significant that they warrant a few more words.

The three years preceding the outbreak of the war represent one of the most disturbed epochs in British industry, writes J. B. Seymour, the historian of Whitley councils. At the commencement of the war, a hundred strikes were in progress.[38] It was in this period that syndicalist influence was the strongest in Britain, and, in 1912, miners and the largest of the four railway unions accepted the demand for the complete control of industry by the workers. It was also in this period that the future shop steward movement was announced (Glasgow engineers' strike, 1912).

Before the war, shop stewards were minor officials appointed by the union from among the men in the workshop to see that the union dues were paid and newcomers organized. They had no power to negotiate grievances nor were they officially recognized by the management. Then came the war, which, as was pointed out by C. G. Renold, who watched the events with the eyes of an employer, "was not felt by work-people to be 'their' war. . . . It was regarded by large sections as a capitalists' war and the restrictions, controls and hardships were resented accordingly."[39] It suffices to add that when, in 1915, trade union leaders voluntarily pledged under the treasury agreement not to sanction strikes during the war, the dissent of the rank and file was certain. The big Clyde engineers' strike early in 1915, when the strike committee disregarded superior union officials and won the strike, set the pattern and initiated what became known as the shop stewards' movement.[40] Shop stewards' committees, composed of representatives of all workers in an establishment, spread over the entire country. Locally, delegates of the establishments in an area made up workers' committees, which became federated into an unofficial nationwide workers' committee movement. This spontaneous development very much resembled the appearance of soviets in Russia, and so it is quite natural that after the February Revolution in Russia, soviets became popular in Britain. The previously mentioned Leeds Conference of June 1917 called for formation of workers' and soldiers' councils.

Syndicalism, guild socialism, the shop stewards' movement, the increasing number of working days lost by strikes despite all restrictions—2 million in 1915, 2.5 million in 1916, 5.5 million in 1917—this alarming situation called for government intervention. In October 1916, a committee (known as the Whitley Committee) was appointed to examine methods for securing permanent improvement in industrial relations. The following year, the Whitley Committee produced its scheme of employer-worker cooperation. For each industry, a National Joint Council and district councils were to be formed to bring together employers' organizations and unions, and, in individual establishments, joint works committees were to provide a recognized means of consultation between the management and the employees. But the scheme as a whole failed to work, except in government depart-

ments: "The employers, as a body, have never favored the scheme.
. . . The trade unionists, frightened by the shop stewards' movement, appear to shrink from giving authority to any rank-and-file
movement and away from the central organizations."[41] Out of
about a hundred works committees formed as a response to Whitley Committee recommendations, only half were still alive by
1929. After the war, the government rejected miners' and railwaymen's demands for nationalization and self-government. The first
postwar recession, which started in 1921, killed the shop stewards'
movement and guild socialism.[42] The situation was again normal-
ized and the capitalist machine could again work, as before. But
not quite; the seed had been sown.

In France during World War I, the socialist minister of war
initiated the establishment of enterprise committees, composed of
workers' representatives, in the factories producing war materials.
The committees disintegrated after the war. Unlike Britain and
France, Germany was defeated in the war, and events there took
another form. Defeat coupled with the tremendous influence of
the Russian Revolution produced a German Revolution (1918).
Workers' and soldiers' councils sprang up all over the country.
Frightened to death, employers were ready to go very far in order
to escape full-scale socialism. And so it happened that Germany
became the first capitalist country to obtain a constitution (July
1919) which included among the "fundamental rights" of citizens the following one: "For the purpose of safeguarding their social and economic interests the wage-earning and salaried employees are entitled to be represented in Workers' Councils for
each establishment, as well as in Regional Workers' Councils organized for each industrial area, and in a Federal Workers'
Council."

In 1920, on the basis of the Constitution, a law was passed making works councils (*Betriebsräte*) compulsory in all establishments with twenty or more employees. The councils were to supervise the implementation of collective agreements, to enter
into agreements on conditions of work and subjects not regulated
by wider agreements, and to watch over hirings and dismis-
als; but they were also to advise the employer on how to improve
efficiency and organization. Constitutions and laws are dead letters,
however, if they are not backed by active social forces. The German working class movement of that time was deeply divided,
both in its trade union and in its parliamentary section. The majority, who held the power, were undetermined, compromising,

and hesitating. The state bureaucracy was hostile. This gave the employers a breathing space. The results of the revolution were gradually undermined—the slump of 1924 playing a not insignificant part—and then liquidated. The process came to an end in May 1933 with the abolition of both trade unions and works councils, an event which marked the advent of fascism.

As to other European countries, it suffices to mention that in the period 1919–1920, for similar reasons, laws on enterprise councils of workers' committees were passed in Austria, Czechoslovakia, and Norway. In Yugoslavia, the law on protection of workers (1922) provided for the election of workers' commissioners (*radnički povjereniči*) from the shop floor, whose task it was to protect workers' interests and cooperate with the employer. The attitude of the employers and trade unions very soon reduced this provision to a mere formality. With a lag of a decade, and after a period of strikes, a similar solution was reached under the Popular Front government in France in 1936; it meant the recognition of shop stewards (*délégués ouvriers*) who enjoyed the right to meet with the management every month. In the United States, a somewhat different type of union-management cooperation concerning production problems arose on one of the railways in the 1920s, when the union wanted to reduce costs in order to secure work for railway shops. Other firms and unions explored similar paths until the 1929 depression, which killed experiments of this kind. A decade later, the steelworkers' union developed quite successful cooperation plans in a number of small steel and steel products firms. The steel workers' scheme survived the war and continued to operate in some thirty firms.[43]

The second landmark in the development of workers' participation in management was provided by World War II. Like World War I, it initiated a cycle, though on a much larger scale. Again governments sought the cooperation of workers in order to enhance war production, and joint production committees were set up in various countries (Britain, the United States, Canada). Again Britain was victorious and Germany defeated, and there was a spontaneous development in the former and legislative measures were taken in the latter. Again British miners expected to win self-government; instead they were granted joint consultation. But there were also several novel features, of which the most important was the large-scale nationalization in some countries and full-scale nationalization in a number of others (East

European and Far East Asian countries). And in all nationalized industries, joint consultation between workers and management was introduced as a matter of course.

In Britain, two national agreements during the war set the pattern for the establishment of joint production committees: the committees were to be advisory and were to provide an outlet for the regular exchange of views between workers and employers on welfare and production matters, subject to the qualification that terms and conditions of employment were to be negotiated by unions on behalf of the workers. In 1947, the National Joint Advisory Council recommended to employers' organizations and unions the setting up of joint consultative machinery where it did not already exist. The recommendation was followed, and soon there were several hundred committees in existence in Britain.

In West Germany, the legislature of the Weimar period was not only revived but also pressed a step further: from joint consultation to co-determination (*Mitbestimmung*). In the two basic industries—coal, and iron and steel—unions achieved parity for workers' representatives in the supervisory board (*Aufsichtsrat*), a body which appoints the board of management. Moreover, one member of the usually three-member management board, the personnel director (*Arbeitsdirector*), must be nominated by the union (the law of 1951). In other industries, workers' representatives are still in the minority, although this minority (one-third) may be larger than it was during the Weimar period. Works councils (*Betriebsräte*), representing both wage and salary earners, must be elected in all establishments employing not less than five permanent employees (the law of 1952). In order to promote cooperation between works council and employer, in establishments with more than a hundred employees, an economic committee (*Wirtschaftsausschuss*) must be formed, each side appointing one-half of the members.

In France, a law passed in 1946 made it compulsory for industrial concerns employing more than fifty workers to establish a works committee (*comité d'entreprise*) representing the manual workers and the technical grades. Every act of major management importance must be subject to agreement by the committee. If there is a disagreement, the case is to go to arbitration. In the same year, in Sweden, unions and the employers' association reached an agreement according to which enterprise councils were to be set up in firms with twenty-five or more employees.

The task of these councils may be broadly described as joint consultation on all important matters. It is of some interest to record that when, in 1923, a royal committee headed by E. Vigforss proposed to form similar joint production committees, both unions and employers opposed the idea, and nothing came of it. After World War II, by 1950, enterprise councils were set up in 2,650 firms employing 600,000 workers.[44] Similar joint consultation committees were introduced in Norway (1945) and Denmark (1947) on the basis of union-employer agreements and in Finland by a special law (1946). In Austria, works councils were set up again by a law of 1948 and obtained the right to participate in management, which was not the case in 1919. In Belgium, enterprise councils (conseils d'entreprise) were created by law in 1948, and in the Netherlands similar councils (ondernemingsraad) were set up in 1950. Various forms of joint consultation were also developed in East European etatist countries.

In a number of other countries, the prewar practice of joint consultation was continued after the war as well, or, where it did not exist, it was introduced for the first time. In 1951, the International Labor Organization registered more than thirty countries having permanent organs of workers' participation in management. The practices vary, but they have an important common feature: apart from a few exceptions, they are confined to joint consultation.

After World War II, the movement for workers' participation in management spread also to non-European countries. Algeria has already been mentioned. As early as its first year of independence (1947), India passed an act prescribing that the appropriate state government may require the employer to constitute a works committee consisting of representatives of employers and workmen and having a consultative function. In 1957 a voluntary scheme of joint management councils was launched, based on the idea that "in a socialist democracy labor is a partner in the common task of development. . . . There should be joint consultation and workers and technicians should, whenever possible, be associated progressively in management."[45] By 1969, about 150 joint management councils and 3,133 works committees were set up. In Bolivia, a decree on joint councils was passed in 1960, and another on worker control (control obrero) was enacted in 1963 after the revolution.

A special type of syndicalism developed in Israel, a country with a mixed economy dominated by the public sector. Here the trade union federation, Histadrut, is the largest industrial concern in the country, accounting for one-fourth of national employment. Histadrut proved—what seemed impossible before—that unions can act simultaneously as bargaining agencies and employers. In 1945, Histadrut established joint production committees composed of workers' and management representatives in its own enterprises, and negotiated an agreement with the private Manufacturers' Association to encourage production committees in private firms. This attempt did not prove successful because of managerial resistance and worker apathy. The effort was renewed in 1956, when the Joint Council Plan was to provide in-plant control over all business except wages and benefits. The idea was to establish co-determination, but what finally emerged was joint consultation. The other special feature of the Israeli economy is the kibbutz. Kibbutzim started as rural communal settlements but later moved into manufacturing as well. They produce about one-third of the agricultural output and slightly less than one-tenth of the industrial output of the country. Kibbutzim vary in size from forty or fifty to as many as one thousand members. They represent the most radical form of self-management in existence today, the aim being a complete identification of the individual with the society. All members participate in decision-making, management functions are rotated among members, and members' needs are provided for by communal institutions on an egalitarian basis. However, kibbutzim employ less than 4 percent of the active population, and this percentage appears stagnant.

Like kibbutzim, Chilean *asentamientos* are agricultural settlements. They were established on the land acquired by the agrarian reform in 1964–1970, and, after a transitional period of several years, developed into self-governing cooperatives with indivisible property. In this country, in the manufacturing sphere, a spontaneous movement developed—disregarded and disliked by the government and the opposition, as well as by the unions—which represents genuine workers' self-management. Since 1968, workers have been occupying enterprises, one after another, which were abandoned by the owners, were bankrupt or about to become bankrupt, or just failed to operate successfully. Workers would assume management, continue production, and, as a rule, avoid bankruptcy and improve business results. By 1972, one hundred of such *empresas de trabajadores* were established, employing about ten thousand workers. In the meantime, the government and the unions reached an agreement to establish a joint consultation machinery with elements of co-determination in the public sector. The military coup of 1973 temporarily blocked these developments.

Chile's neighbor, Peru, also carried out an agrarian reform and established self-governing peasant cooperatives. The new military government, which in 1968 replaced the civilian government by means of a coup, acted in a very unorthodox and unmilitary way. The government stated its social philosophy in roughly the following terms: Western capitalism created unbearable social differences, slowed down economic development, and turned the country into an economic colony. Thus capitalism, however reformed, is unacceptable. Eastern communism has created a totalitarian society in which the political freedom of the working people is destroyed or severely limited, and is therefore equally unacceptable. Fortunately, these are not the only alternatives, as people believed before. The third alternative, self-governing society—*democracia social de participación plena,* as Peruvians call it—is the alternative for which one should opt. Large nationalizations, agricultural cooperatives, and self-management in the sugar industry were the first step. With regard to private industry, the government applied a very original idea: firms are obliged by law to put a certain percentage of profits each year in an indivisible trust fund operated by the employed workers who represent a work community, or *comunidad laboral.* As the share of capital belonging to the *comunidad laboral* increases in the total capital of the firm, the voting rights of workers' representatives in management increase proportionally. This scheme, applied intelligently and efficiently, implies nothing less than the use of the very capitalist mechanisms for the expropriation of capitalists.

It remains, finally, to record the first successful attempt to establish workers' self-management on a national scale. The Yugoslav Revolution was made possible and was reinforced by the National Liberation War of 1941–1945. Since partisan warfare requires a maximum amount of local initiative and resourcefulness, the first organs of local self-government and the first self-managed partisan factories were organized as early as 1941. However, the first five years after the armed phase of the revolution were decisive. A law passed in 1945 provided that workers' commissioners (*radnički povjerenići*), as legal representatives of workers, should establish contact with management, government agencies, and union branches with the task of protecting the social and economic interests of the workers and helping in advancing production. The following year, the major portion of the economy was nationalized, and nationalization was completed in 1948. In the meantime, workers' commissioners ceased to exist, and instead trade union factory branches obtained the legal right to put forward proposals to the management. This was a retreat from control to consultation, a dangerous step backward so reminiscent of the Soviet development in the period 1917–1920. However, in 1949, a new change came about: in a number of factories, consultation between the management—mostly people who took an active part in the revolution themselves—and workers came to be spontaneously introduced. In parallel, the fierce attack of the Cominform, launched in the middle of 1948 and continued over a period of several years, acted as a force helping to check the polarization process. In December 1949, the government and the trade unions jointly issued an instruction on the formation of the workers' councils as advisory bodies. Councils were elected in 215 larger enterprises, but soon other enterprises requested to enjoy the same privilege, and by the middle of 1950 there were already 520 councils in existence. In June 1950, the National Assembly passed the law by which councils were transformed from advisory into managing bodies. The working collective of every enterprise elects a workers' council (*radnički savjet*), which, as long as it enjoys the confidence of the electors, is the supreme policy-making body in the enterprise. The council elects its executive body, the managing board (*upravni odbor*), which is concerned with the day-to-day implementation of the council's policy, the actual execution, and the routine coordination of those activities of the enterprise that are performed by the general manager and the expert administrative and technical staff. This piece of legislation did not immediately abolish the perennial management-worker antithesis, but conditions were created for it to be resolved. By 1950, it had already become abundantly clear that, in general, bureaucratic organization results in inefficiency and undesirable social relations, and thus the introduction of workers' management cleared the ground for the series of institutional changes that were to follow. The subsequent development in other spheres of social life, in turn, strengthened the new organization of industry. Self-government of the producers was extended beyond the immediate workplace by establishing for all representative organs, from local councils up to the Federal Assembly, a second chamber: the Council of Producers. In 1953, the

Constitution was changed to take account of the new social institutions. Workers' management had become a part of the establishment.

The Yugoslav solution should not be regarded as the end of a process, but rather as a promising beginning of the development of a genuinely self-governing society. By now, in Yugoslavia, self-management appears to be reasonably well established at the enterprise level. What remains to be done is to extend it to other levels and, in particular, to develop an equally new political system, appropriate for a self-governing society.

An evaluation

Historically and logically, there are two approaches to workers' participation in management: one negative and containing, the other positive and constructive. The former was developed first and has been based on the following reasoning and behavior. Employers and workers represent two social classes with antagonistic interests. Higher profits imply lower wages and vice versa. Thus, a normal state of affairs is a class war conducted by more or less civilized means. On that basis, trade unions were created as fighting organizations of the working class. In radicalized situations, when class tensions are intensified, the traditional collective bargaining is supplemented by a request for workers' control. "Workers' control" may thus be used as the term describing the negative, containing approach to participation. Its historical origins were analyzed in the section on revolutions. It means an aggressive encroachment of trade union or unofficial groups on management powers in a capitalist or etatist framework. By the strength of their organizations, workers exact concessions from the employers. They do not make positive proposals regarding the conduct of business, because they are not asked to, this being a prerogative of the management; they do not assume any responsibility, because the firm is not their property; they determine what *cannot* be done, limiting thus the arbitrary power of the employers, and they try to maximize their share in the cake. While there is capitalism (or etatism), there cannot be cooperation. Since capitalism cannot be abolished overnight, such an attitude is often instrumental in perpetuating capitalism. A modern advocate of radical workers' control, E. Mandel, states its four main goals: (1) access to financial documents (opening of the books) ; (2) control of the system of remuneration; (3) control of the speed of work; and (4) control of dismissals and refusal to close down works. "We require full control and the right of veto for the workers. But we reject even an atom of responsibility for the capitalist management of the enterprise."[46] According to this view, co-determination and self-management are possible only in socialism.

Although interests of employers and workers are basically opposed, they are not totally conflicting. There are some areas—for example, welfare, safety, and health questions—where interests are not opposed and cooperation is possible. Thus, while bargaining about wage rates and conditions of work will in most cases remain reserved for trade unions, workers on the spot will begin to participate in decisions concerning noncontroversial matters. In this way, negative control will be supplemented by constructive participation. Participation passes through three stages: *joint consultation, co-determination,* and *self-management.* The first stage leaves the capitalist and etatist framework intact, but provides an important psychological attack on the managerial autocracy. The second stage already implies a share in power and represents the beginning of the end. It is important to realize that the first two stages are transitional and consequently highly instable.[47] Stability is achieved in the third stage, which, however, is possible only under socialism. Most of the developed countries, both capitalist and etatist, find themselves in the first stage.

In evaluating the development of workers' participation in management, the following five aspects of the problem seem important.

1. The *motivation* for setting up joint consultative machinery falls into three distinct categories. The revolutionary pressure from below compels employers and the government of the day to relax the managerial authoritarianism. Because it is the result of a strong clash of interests, the outcome of the fight must be legally sanctioned to remain permanent (although legal sanctions often prove to be a fiction). The German case is typical for this situation.

Next, during modern totalitarian war, governments are vitally interested in stepping up production and therefore devise and advocate schemes of joint consultation to bridge the gap between employers and workers. This case is typified by British and American practices. With respect to the latter, the International Labor Office study says: "The general purpose of the Labor-Management Production Committees was to raise the quantity and quality of output for war production by the joint effort of labor and management in each war plant." The extent to which this purpose was achieved is visible from the following evaluation of the same study: "While there seems to be little doubt that the committees made a substantial contribution to plant output, a number of committees did not aid to as great an extent as had been expected. . . ."[48] Some five thousand committees were set up in plants with war contracts. Most of them disappeared with the end of the war.

The third type of motivation is that of individual employers who are not forced by law to adopt joint consultation, but adopt it primarily on economic grounds. This point is illuminated by the following statement of C. G. Renold, himself an employer with successful joint consultation in his firm: "In the first place the point should be made that the whole development had its origin in a very practical need—the need felt by the management for closer contact with its men in the interest of smooth working."[49] This need appears when the concern outgrows one-man management.[50] It becomes urgent in the turbulent conditions of war and industrial unrest. And once the works council is set up, it is likely to continue to exist in the ensuing time of military and industrial peace. War has another effect as well: it increases the self-consciousness of the exploited classes and humanizes the members of higher social strata, thus providing a psychological bridge between them.[51] Then there is also a small number of employers who are interested in joint consultation for its own sake, because they regard it as a humanizing institution. This Owenite type of employer, earlier practically nonexistent, is likely to multiply to the degree that there is a decrease in the adverse social pressure, both of the employers' equals and of the establishment as a whole. The example of individual employers, the recurrent interventions of government, and the constant improvement of the educational standard of the workers gradually create an atmosphere in which joint consultation becomes an indispensable part of the managerial routine. Exactly this seems to be happening in Britain today, as demonstrated by the appearance of yet another type of employer. In the majority of firms visited by the National Institute of Industrial Psychology research team, "joint consultation seemed to be regarded as an up-to-date technique for improving management-worker relationships."[52] Competition is the essence of capitalism; accordingly, there is nothing to stop capitalist firms from competing even in the improvement of relations with workers. This sounds paradoxical, but so are the conditions of full employment under capitalism. Clearly, if pursued consistently, such a competition must eventually lead to the destruction of capitalist relationships, but this will be nothing more than a parallel to Schumpeterian "creative destruction," the destruction of profits by competition initiated to increase profits.

Nationalized industries and nationalized economies represent a separate case, where joint consultation is an indispensable minimum to make these systems work at all, that is, to make them socially acceptable. The only development one can visualize is a constant increase of workers' participation in management, either granted by the governing bureaucracy, or won by workers through revolutionary means.

2. What happens to the *discipline* in an organization in which executive authority is undermined by the granting to everyone of the right and the opportunity to question the validity of the commands from above by reference to his own set of criteria? This is the very question our Weberian-minded generation will ask in connection with the practicability of workers' management schemes. For is it not true that an efficient organization requires obedience, obedience being defined as following "such a course that the content of the command may be taken to have become the basis of action for its own sake"?[53]

In fact, however, the literature on joint consultation and workers' management,[54] including the most detailed studies, shows no awareness of the "problem of discipline." One can do no better than to quote two employers' testimonies: "When I first took the step of introducing joint consultation on a very broad basis into my own works," writes G. D. Walpole, "I was told by most of my fellow employers that I was selling the pass to the enemy, and that the first result would be that works discipline would go to the devil. I have found, on the contrary, after two years' experience, that works discipline has improved almost out of recognition, and that every other legitimate interest of ownership has also been catered for in a measure which four years ago I would not have believed possible: production is up, absenteeism is down; wastage is reduced, and valuable time is saved."[55] C. G. Renold explains the mystery of this phenomenon: "The need to base managerial authority on reason rather than on arbitrary power—as is implied in the whole philosophy of joint consultation—has enhanced that authority."[56]

It is hardly necessary to add that the same applies with even greater force to the system based on the philosophy of self-government. An International Labor Organization mission in Yugoslavia found in 1960 that "while the self-government machinery for labor relations has curtailed the former powers of the supervisory staffs, it would not appear to have impaired their authority. . . . It has undoubtedly strengthened the position of the collective vis-à-vis the management, but it does not appear to have undermined labor discipline."[57] Self-government substitutes understanding for obedience, agreement for the exercise of arbitrary power. By eliminating capitalist or bureaucratic duality and polarization of interests, it reduces tensions and improves coordination.

3. The *success* of joint consultation has been quite limited so far, and the reasons for this will be examined in a moment. McKitteric and Roberts evaluate the success of German works councils of the Weimar period by saying that councils "were useful in protecting the workers' interests, but achieved virtually nothing in the way of genuine participation in management." Of the postwar development, the same authors state: "Where workers councils exist the general experience has been that the employees take a keen interest in their activities. . . ."[58] In Britain, broad masses of workers are still apathetic, but four-fifths of workers' representatives in councils support the institution and show a strong interest in it. It is also significant to note that after experience in joint consultation, 37 percent of chief executives, 48 percent of senior management, and 58 percent of workers' representatives took a more favorable view of the institution than they had originally held, whereas only 9 percent, 5 percent, and 1 percent, respectively, changed to a less favorable view.[59]

4. There also exists the problem of the *fundamental relation between capital and labor*. These two opposing sides are reflected in the very term *joint* consultation. The initiative on the part of the employer to introduce joint consultation in his firm is not infrequently a deliberate attempt to anticipate and check the development of unionism.[60] But even if this is not the aim, joint consultation increases loyalty to the firm, and this loyalty and loyalty to one's class are two different, indeed conflicting, loyalties.[61] Joint consultation produces workers' leaders who are not trade union officials and so are outside the grip of the "machinery." Clearly, unions will not be enthusiastic about partnership proposals and frequently will be opposed to them. On the other hand, if a union or shop stewards seek to participate in joint committees,

employers will fear infringement on their own prerogatives. The hopelessness of the situation lies in the fact that *both* sides are right in their fears. With the employers basically opposed to surrendering their arbitrary power and the unions basically unwilling to assume responsibility for the organization of production—because they gain nothing and lose their independence as well as their grip on the membership's loyalties—the status quo is likely to be prolonged and potential changes prevented. The logic of the situation is such that unions act in virtual collusion with employers against workers, a collusion that becomes overt in more turbulent times.[62] This sheds new light on the events we have surveyed: formidable social forces have been and will be opposing workers' participation in management.

5. The trade union paradox illustrates the *working of bureaucratic structures*. In order to protect themselves in a world of polarized interests, a world whose institutions are against them, workers build strong bureaucratic organizations: unions and parties. Once these organizations are built, they acquire their separate interests different from the interests of those who support the whole structure. There is nothing ethically wrong in this, nor does it happen because the leaders are wicked; the development is perfectly natural and, to a certain extent, inevitable. The way out of the impasse is logically easy. The organization must first be used to eliminate the fundamental cause of polarization of interests—in this case, to eliminate private control of production—and then the bureaucratic principle of organization must be replaced by self-government. However, actual unions and socialist parties are not likely to follow this course straight away of their own accord. Having become a part of the establishment with a clearly defined role in it, they are not prone to leave the life of routine and rush into the uncertainties of a full-scale socialization. Self-government, on the other hand, is an idea so alien to the spirit of bureaucracy that it is clear that it will encounter vigorous resistance.[63]

The situation, however, cannot remain completely unchanged. There is no reason to believe that business cycles have died out. But there is some reason to believe that governments of industrial countries in the second half of our century cannot afford to tolerate heavy unemployment without risking major social upheavals. By curing the slump, the first decisive element of change is introduced into the process: an increasing degree of social control. The welfare state is its symbol. However, uninterrupted full employment has a thoroughly anticapitalist effect: it generates competition in the improvement of management-worker relations. For the employers are vitally interested in avoiding labor turnover, in escaping strikes, and in overcoming the resistance toward the introduction of new processes, while workers feel secure and for this reason are actively conscious of their rights and possibilities.[64] By raising the status of the workers, employers gradually surrender their autocratic power, and thus their social function loses its content. In this way, the second element is introduced into the process: the increasing degree of workers' participation in management. It is unlikely that the process will always develop smoothly. However, in the case of revolution, the trend is even clearer.

In the 150 years that have passed since the first Owenite experiment in New Lanark, the relations between employers and workers have been constantly changing. These relations are reflected in the character of meetings between employers and employees, which, as the British National Institute of Industrial Psychology aptly describes it, "over the last 150 years shows a historical development from deputation and negotiation to consultation"[65]—and, we may add, to direct management in the end. This last phase of development supersedes the two-sided nature of the meetings and unifies the interests of all concerned in the institution of self-government. The past five decades have produced joint consultation on a large scale. The last two of these decades have also seen the first attempts to go beyond mere consultation. German co-determination is a case in point, as is Peruvian full participation. Individual firms have also begun to move toward co-determination or even to a state of genuine workers' self-government.[66] A communitarian movement appeared in several European countries following the example set by the watch-case firm of Boimondau in Valence, southern France.[67] These self-governing communities of work—a term which at first sounded rather strange, but which was later to become a legal, even constitutional, term in Yugoslavia (*radna zajednica*) and Peru (*comunidad laboral*)—went beyond producers' cooperatives by treating the productive property as indivisible social property, by eliminating wage labor, and by aspiring to full development of the human potential of their members. Under the pressure of their membership, trade unions began to change their attitudes. In revised laws or union-management agreements, the scope of joint consultation has invariably been increased. Co-determination is introduced in the social welfare sphere and occasionally beyond it. There is little doubt that the world is moving toward a socialist, self-governing society at an accelerated pace.

NOTES

1. The Blanquist and Marxist approaches to the proletarian revolution are often confused, although they are fundamentally different. A quotation from an 1847 writing of Engels will clarify this difference: "From Blanqui's conception of every revolution as the *coup de main* of a small revolutionary minority, follows of itself the necessity of a dictatorship after it succeeds. The dictatorship, of course, not of the whole revolutionary class, the proletariat, but of the small number of those who carried out the *coup* and who are themselves already in advance organized under the dictatorship of one or a few individuals" ("Program of the Blanquist Commune Refugees," *Werke,* Vol. 18, p. 529).

2. The quotation comes from the Introduction to Marx's *Class Struggles in France, 1848–50* and was written in 1895. In this text, Engels provides important information for the evolution of his friend's and his own thinking. About their expectations concerning the 1848 revolution, he writes: "History showed that neither we nor all those who thought similarly were right. It clearly showed that the state of economic development on the Continent was then by far not ripe for the elimination of capitalist production; it showed that by the economic revolution which after 1848 occurred over the entire Continent . . . and all that on a capitalist basis, which, accordingly, in 1848 had still been capable of expansion." He goes on to say that the conditions for fighting changed essentially. "The rebellion of the old style, street fighting with barricades, which in 1848 was finally decisive everywhere, has grown considerably obsolete." In his opinion, German workers transformed universal suffrage from a means of deceit into an instrument of liberation. And that determined a completely new way of fighting for the proletariat. "And so it happened that bourgeoisie and government came to fear the legal action of the workers' party much more than the illegal one, they fear election success more than success in a rebellion."

3. G. D. H. Cole, *A Short History of the British Working Class Movement, 1789–1947* (London: George Allen & Unwin, 1938), Chap. 6.

4. A. Austin, *The Labor Story: A Popular History of American Labor (1786–1949)* (New York: Coward-McCann, 1969), Chap. 4.

5. S. Vidalenc, *Louis Blanc (1811–1882)* (Paris: Presses Universitaires de France, 1948), p. 37.

6. Ibid., pp. 38–39.

7. G. D. H. Cole, *Socialist Thought* (London: Macmillan, 1953), Vol. I: *The Forerunners, 1789–1850,* pp. 177–78.

8. Quoted from R. L. Pavičević, *Država kao federacija komuna* (Belgrade: IMRP, 1969), p. 96. In describing Proudhon's ideas, the author relied mostly on this excellent study.

9. Proudhon's syndrome—ignorance cum pretentiousness—will be found often in the history of socialist thought, and so deserves an additional evaluation. Discussing Proudhon's economics, Joseph Schumpeter remarked: "And we are interested in his economics only because it affords an excellent example of a type of reasoning that is distressingly frequent in a science without prestige: the type of reasoning that arrives, through complete inability to analyse, that is, to handle the tools of economic theory, at results that are no doubt absurd and fully recognized as such by the author. But the author, instead of inferring from this that there is something wrong with his methods, infers that there must be something wrong with the object of his research, so that his mistakes are, with the utmost confidence, promulgated as results. . . . He was, among other things, unable to produce a workable theory of market value. But he did not infer: 'I am a fool', but: 'Value is mad' (*la valeur est folle*)" (*History of Economic Analysis* [New York: Oxford University Press, 1955], p. 457).

10. Cole, *Socialist Thought*, Vol. I, p. 202.

11. William Morris, *News from Nowhere or An Epoch of Rest, being some chapters from A Utopian Romance* (London: Reeves and Turner, 1891). Cf. also G. D. H. Cole, *Socialist Thought* (London: Macmillan, 1957), Vol. II: *Marxism and Anarchism,* p. 420.

12. G. D. H. Cole, *Socialist Thought* (London: Macmillan, 1967), Vol. III: *The Second International,* pp. 565, 863.

13. Marxist social democratic parties began to be created while Marx was still alive and soon were established in most European countries: 1869 in Germany, 1879 in Spain (by Pablo Iglesias) and Denmark, 1882 in France (Partie Ouvrière by Jules Guedes), 1883–1884 in Britain (Hyndman's Social Democratic Federation), 1883 in Russia (Emancipation of Labor group by Plekhanov and Axelrod), 1887 in Norway, 1888 in Austria and Switzerland, 1889 in Sweden and Holland (Social Democratic League), 1892 in Italy, Poland, Finland, and Bulgaria, 1903 in Serbia, etc. Thereafter they began to be formed in non-European countries.

14. For a more complete analysis, see B. Horvat, *An Essay on Yugoslav Society* (White Plains, N.Y.: International Arts and Sciences Press, 1969), Chap. 9: "Marx and Engels on Socialist Economy."

15. Cole, *Socialist Thought,* Vol. II, pp. 202–4.

16. Accordingly, syndicalism—or anarcho-syndicalism—has become a derogatory word in the working class vocabulary. It is of some interest to note how the opponents of workers' self-management invariably use this term in order to denote—and degrade—those in favor of it, even if the latter have no connection with syndicalism.

17. Quoted by Cole, *Socialist Thought,* Vol. III, p. 347.

18. The document was prepared by the graduates of the Central Labor College, which was founded in 1909 as a breakaway from the Ruskin College by dissident Marxist students and teachers. See K. Coates and T. Topham, eds., *Workers' Control: A Book of Readings and Witnesses for Workers' Control* (London: Panther Books, 1970), p. 5.

19. G. D. H. Cole, *Guild Socialism Re-Stated* (London: L. Parsons, 1920), p. 13.

20. Ibid., p. 46.

21. Ibid., pp. 136–37.

22. N. Carpenter, *Guild Socialism: An Historical and Critical Analysis* (New York: D. Appleton, 1922), p. 205.

23. Evaluating this development a few years later, G. D. H. Cole concluded: "With the coming of the slump, the demand for workers' control, though it remained a feature of the political and industrial programmes into which it had forced its way at an earlier stage, ceased to figure effectively in immediate trade union policy. The unions were fighting, not to make fresh gains, but to hold what they held, and it was of no use to preach to them policies which had no chance of success under the existing economic conditions. Guild Socialism passed under a cloud, not because the National Building Guild collapsed, but because it ceased to have any relevance to the immediate situation which the working classes were compelled to face." At that time, Cole became very pessimistic about the practical implementability of guild socialist ideas: "It is good to be free, I argued, and therefore men ought to be free whether they wish it or not. So far I would still go; but I used to push the doctrine to logical conclusions which now seem to provide no solid basis for practical building of policy. Men must be forced to be free, I used to urge; and I added that they should be forced to use their freedom in the particular ways that appealed to me. The idea of work under an externally imposed discipline was repellent to me in my own crafts of writing and teaching;

and I therefore assumed that it ought to be repellent to everybody, whatever the character of his job and whatever the cast of his own mind might be. I despaired of making most work interesting in itself, in the way in which my own work interests me; and I sought to find a substitute for this inherent interest in the adventitious interest of collectively controlling a naturally uninteresting job. I ignored the fact that most men's daily work is dull, and that, provided it is not positively irksome, they do not even want to find in it the overmastering interest which I find in my own job. They have other fish to fry; but of that I did not take proper account. Self-government—the conscious and continuous exercise of the art of citizenship—seemed to me not merely good in itself—which it is—but the good—which it is not. Accordingly, I constructed, along with other politically-minded persons a politically-minded person's Utopia of which, if it could ever exist, the ordinary man would certainly make hay by refusing to behave in the manner expected of him" (*The Next Ten Years in British Social and Economic Policy* [London: Macmillan, 1930], pp. 158–61; more easily accessible in Coates and Topham, op. cit., pp. 275–76).

24. Useful information about contemporary revolutions is to be found in R. Bonchio, ed., *Storia della rivoluzioni del XX secolo*, 4 vols. (Rome: Editori riuniti, 1966).

25. As a social phenomenon, the occupation of the factories by the workers is as old as the labor movement. In February 1819, English tobacco workers, after eleven weeks of striking, began to organize production by themselves. A century and a half later, in 1964, a general strike took place in Argentina; three million workers occupied four thousand enterprises and began to organize production (E. Mandel, ed., *Contrôle ouvrier, conseils ouvriers, autogestion* [Paris: Maspero, 1970], pp. 7–8). In a Colombian study, it was found that *las tomas de fábricas* are undertaken for three main reasons: because of the indebtedness of the enterprise, which stops paying out wages, because of the danger of the enterprise's being closed down, and after prolonged strikes. The largest Colombian enterprise taken over employed two hundred and fifty workers. The enterprises were operated by the workers themselves or by their unions (Centro Colombiano de Investigaciones Marxistas, *Las tomas de fábricas* [Bogotá, 1967], pp. 21, 60–61 et passim). In Chile, the enterprises taken over by the workers formed a national association called Empresas y Brigadas de Trabajadores, which had about one hundred members in 1972.

26. It is of some interest to note the testimony of G. Gurvitch, a well-known sociologist who emigrated to France, who took part in forming factory committees in Petrograd. Gurvitch says that Lenin at that time took the position that planning and social revolution were impossible if they were not based on the direct participation of the workers, on

workers' self-management. This position also went into the second program of the Bolshevik Party, which, however, was destroyed after it was printed. Through the combined efforts of Trotsky and Stalin, says Gurvitch, Lenin was persuaded that workers' management was detrimental to the efficiency of production. It was not possible to check this information. Gurvitch also claims that the first soviets were organized by Proudhonists among the social revolutionaries and the left wing of the social democrats (S. Duvignaud, "Georges Gurvitch: a Sociological Theory of Self-Management," *Autogestion*, No. 1, 1966, 5–6).

27. Paul H. Avrich, "The Bolshevik Revolution and the Workers' Control in Russian Industry," *Slavic Review*, 1963, 62.

28. A. Pankratova, "Comités d'usines en Russie à l'époque de la révolution (1917–1918)," written in 1923 in Russian and translated in *Autogestion*, No. 4, 1967, 3–63.

29. J. Klikovac, "Učestvovanje radnika u upravljanju poduzećem" [The Participation of Workers in Managing the Enterprise], in J. Djordjevic et al., eds., *Teorija i praksa samoupravljanja u Jugoslaviji*, (Belgrade: Radnička štampa, 1972), pp. 209–26.

30. G. D. H. Cole, *Socialist Thought* (London: Macmillan, 1958), Vol. IV: *Communism and Social Democracy*, p. 150.

31. The first internal commission *(commisione interna)* was established in 1906 in the automobile factory Italia in Turin on the basis of a collective agreement between the management and the metalworkers' union. Its task was to resolve the conflicts emerging from collective agreements. During World War I, the Italian government recommended internal commissions as instruments of cooperation, and they were set up in a number of enterprises. See B. Pribičević, ed., *Industrijska demokratija* (Belgrade: Institut za istraživanje radničkog pokreta, 1967), p. 186.

32. G. Maione, "Expérience d'autogestion en Italie (1919–1956)," *Autogestion*, No. 9-10, 1969, 89–120.

33. Cf. Ian Clegg, *Workers' Management in Algeria* (New York: Monthly Review Press, 1971).

34. M. Bárta, "Les conseils ouvriers en tant que movement social," *Autogestion*, No. 9-10, 1969, 30.

35. In China, soviets had been organized sporadically since 1927. But they differed radically from the Russian revolutionary soviets. Their nature is well described by Mao Tse-tung: "In certain places councils of deputies were convened, but they are considered only as provisional organs whose main function is to elect executive committees; after the

elections all power is concentrated in the hands of committees and there is no more talk about the councils of deputies. One cannot say that no council of workers', peasants' and soldiers' deputies, worth its name, is in existence; one can find them, but very few. This is explained by an insufficiency of propaganda and of educational work concerning this political system" (quoted by Mandel, op. cit., p. 296). In December 1927, an uprising established the Canton Commune. In her historical monograph on the Chinese Revolution, E. Calloti Pischel comments: "the participation of the people in the democratic elections of the red government was quite limited, and according to certain sources it was purely imaginary" *(Storia della rivoluzioni del XX secolo,* Vol. IV, *La rivoluzione cinese).*

36. The oldest works council still in existence in Britain is that of the Bourneville works of the cocoa and chocolate manufacturing firm Cadbury Brothers, Ltd. In this firm, works committees were established at the beginning of the century. The aim of the management was defined as the rapprochement of the employer and worker *(A Works Council in Being. An Account of the Scheme in Operation at Bourneville Works* [Publication Department, Bourneville Works, 1921]).

37. For the sake of completeness, an interesting German attempt ought to be mentioned. The Industrial Commission of the revolutionary National Assembly, which met in Frankfurt in 1848, put forward a resolution asking that factory committees, consisting of employers' and workers' representatives, issue work rules subject to the approval of district factory councils elected by the factory committees in the district. The resolution was never enacted because the revolution collapsed shortly afterward (C. W. Guillebaud, *The Works Council* [Cambridge University Press, 1921], p. 1).

38. J. B. Seymour, *The Whitley Councils Scheme* (London: P. S. King, 1932), p. 9.

39. C. G. Renold, *Joint Consultation over Thirty Years* (London: George Allen & Unwin, 1950), p. 16.

40. Characteristic of the mood of workers was the following published statement of Clyde workers: "We hold the view that the trade union officials are the servants, not the masters, of the rank and file, and that they require some pressure at times to move them in the path the rank and file desire them to tread" (H. Wolfe, *Labor Supply and Regulation* [Oxford: Clarendon Press, 1923], p. 151). D. Kirkwood, one of the leading members of the Clyde Workers' Committee, told the visiting prime minister Lloyd George at a meeting in December 1915 that they had organized the strike "in defiance of you, in defiance of the Government . . . and in defiance of the Trade Union

officials" (B. Pribičević, "Demand for Workers' Control in the Railway, Mining and Engineering Industries 1910–1922," doctoral thesis, Nuffield College, Oxford, 1957, p. 568; shortened version published as *The Shop-Stewards' Movement and Workers' Control, 1910–1922* [Oxford: Blackwell, 1959]).

Comparable to the British shop stewards' movement was the German works councils movement after 1918. And comparable to the statements of Clyde strikers was the following published statement of the striking metalworkers in Düsseldorf in 1924: "In a great number of towns the Trade Unions have adhered to the general strike proclaimed by the Works Councils. Where this has not yet taken place, the workers must force them to join the movement. The leaders of the unions who refuse must be ejected from their offices" (Guillebaud, op. cit., p. 70).

41. Seymour, op. cit., p. 191.

42. Disillusioned by the failure to establish workers' self-management, shop stewards passed through an interesting transformation and from ardent supporters turned into fierce opponents. In the Foreword to Pribičević's book cited above, G. D. H. Cole gives the following evaluation of the two movements, which were leading advocates of workers' control during and just after World War I: "The Guild Socialists' weakness was that they never faced the fundamental problem of power and of large-scale organization and planning, whereas the weakness of those who led the shop stewards' movement was that, though during the war they were occupied largely with day-to-day workshop problems, no sooner was the fighting over than they became exclusively preoccupied with the central problem of class power and forgot all about control at the works and workshop level and indeed even denied that such control had anything to recommend it, thus forfeiting the human basis of their appeal. They thus became centralist and totalitarian democrats, and lost sight of the essential purpose of the movement for workers' control in its relation to ordinary men and women."

43. C. A. Myers, *Industrial Relations in Sweden* (Cambridge, Mass.: MIT Press, 1951), p. 55.

44. Ibid., pp. 56–58.

45. Quoted in K. C. Alexander, *Participative Management* (New Delhi: Shri Ram Centre, 1972). Two other studies dealing with Indian experience and released by the same publisher are: N. R. Sheth, *The Joint Management Council*, 1972, and Ž. Tanic, *Workers' Participation in Management: Ideal and Reality in India*, 1969.

46. E. Mandel, "Contrôle ouvrier," *La Gauche* (Brussels), 50, 1970, p. 50.

47. That the co-determination is an unstable arrangement should be obvious. But joint consultation also implies an inherent contradiction which generates forces of change. W. E. S. McCarthy describes well this contradiction: "the notion of joint consultation involves a paradox. . . . It presumes that there are some areas of management activity . . . which are fit and proper subjects of joint determination by collective bargaining; on the other hand there are other areas . . . which must remain the *exclusive* prerogative of management, although they may be discussed with workers' representatives. Yet it is also assumed that the main advantage of holding such discussions is that in matters of this kind the interests of the two sides converge rather than conflict. . . . Thus we come to the paradox, . . . we reach a position in which it is suggested that agreements are only possible when the two sides are basically opposed; when they are really united, there cannot be any question of an agreement" (*The Role of Shop Stewards in British Industrial Relations,* Royal Commission on Trade Unions and Employers' Associations, Research Paper 1 [London: HMSO, 1966], pp. 35–36).

48. International Labor Office, *Labor-Management Co-operation in United States War Production,* Studies and Reports No. 6 (Montreal: International Labor Office, 1948), pp. 197, 257.

49. Renold, op. cit., p. 100.

50. "In many instances the idea took shape in the minds of individual employers or managers faced with rapidly expanding personnel, and was originally intended as no more than a substitute, of sorts, for that direct personal contact which is so easily lost when the pay-roll lengthens and the ratio of skilled and semi-skilled workers increases." This is the testimony of G. S. Walpole, also an employer (*Management and Men* [London: Jonathan Cape, 1945], p. 39).

51. The research team of the National Institute of Industrial Psychology records: "A number of younger executives told us that their favorable attitude to joint consultation had been acquired through experience in the services during the war" (*Joint Consultation in British Industry* [London: Staples Press, 1952], p. 69).

52. Ibid., p. 59. This situation is also well reflected in the contemporary management literature. K. Robertson describes the participative management as "the discipline whereby an organization learns how to tap something of the latent potential of its members. It involves entirely new skills of behaviour. . . . It is . . . the gradual, stressful, risk-taking process of experience by which management matures from its outmoded role of directing, controlling and governing to its new role of enabling, encouraging, assisting and reinforcing achievement

by others" ("Managing People and Jobs," *Personnel Management*, September 1969, 24).

53. M. Weber, *The Theory of Social and Economic Organization* (London: W. Hodge, 1947), p. 300.

54. For joint consultation, see W. H. Scott, *Industrial Leadership and Joint Consultation* (Liverpool: University Press of Liverpool, 1952); E. Jaques, *The Changing Culture of a Factory* (New York: Dryden Press, 1952); International Labor Office and National Institute of Industrial Psychology studies already quoted. For workers' management, see P. Kovač and D. Miljević, *Samoupravljanje proizvodjača u privredi* [The Self-Management of Producers in the Economy] (Belgrade: Savremena administracija, 1958); J. Vanek, *The Economics of Workers' Management: A Yugoslav Case Study* (London: George Allen & Unwin, 1972).

55. Walpole, op. cit., p. 166.

56. Renold, op. cit., p. 119.

57. International Labor Office, *Workers' Management in Yugoslavia* (Geneva: International Labor Office, 1962), p. 203.

58. T. E. M. McKitterick and R. D. V. Roberts, *Workers and Management,* Fabian Research Series No. 160 (London: Fabian Society, 1953), pp. 9, 20.

59. National Institute for Industrial Psychology, op. cit., pp. 64, 65.

60. Describing the conditions in the United States, the International Labor Office study states: "A considerable number of prewar plans for joint committees in factories had been developed primarily by management in order to interest workers in the successful operation of factories and in many instances had been aimed at undercutting the development of unionism" (op. cit., p. 185).

61. The resulting deep psychological conflict of workers is well described in the study by E. Jaques: "it seemed as though the only time the members of the Council could hold their heads high was if there was a management-worker fight on; if there was no fight, they felt guilty as if they were not doing what was expected of them" (op. cit., p. 122). " . . . the desirability of employment with the firm has led workers to look to the management rather than to the trade unions for security of employment, and has aroused in the workers' leaders an acute conflict over loyalties divided between the firm and the trades unions" (ibid., p. 179).

62. Historical illustrations are not difficult to come by. Take the German works councils of the Weimar period, of which Guillebaud says:

"To the German masses the workers' councils stood for the democratization of the industrial system and the attainment, in the economic sphere, of the same rights of self-government and self-determination as they thought they had achieved by the Revolution of 1918 in the political sphere. . . . When it came to the practical working out of the basic and, to the individual workers, the most important part of the structure—the Works Councils, they found that the bulk of the political leaders of labor were in league with the employers to prevent any too wide extension of powers to these Councils" (op. cit., pp. 212–13). Unions were apprehensive of losing leadership (ibid., p. 41), and hence were anxious to insure that works councils did not become really effective; they and their political allies, the majority socialists, "were backed up to the utmost by the employers, who were at least as much concerned to fetter the Works Councils and to confine them within the organization of the Unions. Of the latter the employers were not afraid . . ." (ibid., p. 11).

63. An empirical illustration is provided by two authoritative pronouncements of British unions and party views. The following statement of Mr. Gunter in the parliamentary debate on joint consultation in 1950 is evaluated by the National Institute of Industrial Psychology as a "very well expressed Trade Union view" (op. cit., p. 82): "There has been an amazing revival of the old syndicalist idea of direct workers' control in certain sections of labor. In my opinion it is impossible to envisage any great development in the sphere of joint consultation if we imagine that this old, wooly idea of workers' control can operate. In the last resort management must be allowed to manage and to make decisions, and must accept the responsibility. What we seek is that their decisions and policy shall be translated to the workers so that they may understand their objectives, and thereby help to ensure that co-operation which can result in much better and higher production. I cannot leave the trade union side without expressing my belief that the majority of trade unionists do not desire to see the establishment of workers' control, as it is sometimes called" (ibid., p. 58). The Labor Party's 1957 policy document on nationalized industries, in the chapter on workers' participation, asks whether there should be direct representation and answers the question negatively: "The syndicalist view of industry run by workers, either through their trade unions or through elected boards was objected to by the Labor Movement many years ago" (ibid., p. 61). Note the reference to "syndicalism" in both instances. The situation at the other side of the ocean is described by James Matles, the secretary of the United Electrical, Radio, and Machine Workers of America, in an interview of 1965 as follows: "The key problem facing the rank and file workers in the shop and trade union movement today is the destruction of the shop steward system. The shop steward has been destroyed, undermined or

neutralized through the combined efforts of employers and top union leadership" (Coates and Topham, op. cit., p. 408).

64. Cf. H. A. Clegg: "To-day industrial discipline is a different matter in all industries from the pre-war period of heavy unemployment. This is often said to be one of the greatest difficulties of British industry to-day. At the same time, full employment has done more to make industry more democratic and to raise the status of the worker than any legislation or any machinery for joint consultation could do" (*Industrial Democracy and Nationalization* [Oxford: Blackwell, 1950], p. 78). This is a very lucid statement, but the concluding antithesis is spurious, the causation is different from the one implied: the democratization of the industrial organization produced joint consultation, not the other way round. Once generally applied, joint consultation becomes a social institution and cannot be abolished without social upheavals. But neither can it be petrified in its present form with the attention of workers channeled toward welfare matters, while management reserves the right to make the crucial managerial decisions. Very soon workers will begin to insist that this "toilet democracy" be replaced by "proper democracy." C. A. Myers unintentionally describes something of the kind happening in Sweden when he says: "But unless the committees begin to tackle real problems . . . the 'stagnation' may turn into disgust and revulsion. 'Toilet democracy' as one person described the current concern for better washrooms, lighting, etc., may suffice for a time, but it is hardly the 'industrial democracy' that the labor movement said it was seeking" (op. cit., p. 71).

65. Op. cit., p. 29.

66. Glacier Metal Company is an interesting English example. Its works council constitution reads: "The functions of the Council shall be: . . . to carry the responsibility of deciding the principles and policies which shall govern the Management of the Factory in the light of the opinions of producers and managers, in the light of the interest of consumers, shareholders and the nation at large, and in the light of total Company Policy" (Jaques, op. cit., p. 153). In seeking to achieve this aim—that the management surrender arbitrary executive power and the workers develop responsible and effective collective decision-making instead—both management and workers had to overcome enormous difficulties resulting from their learned attitudes and from the totally uncongenial institutional framework in which they were to work.

67. Cf. C. H. Bishop, *All Things Common* (New York: Harper & Brothers, 1950).

2. Report to the County of Lanark [1820]

ROBERT OWEN

Report to the County of Lanark, of a Plan for relieving Public Distress and Removing Discontent, by giving permanent, productive Employment to the Poor and Working Classes, under Arrangements which will essentially improve their Character, and ameliorate their Condition, diminish the Expenses of Production and Consumption, and create Markets co-extensive with Production. By Robert Owen. May Ist, 1820.

Part III

Details of the Plan

First, the number of persons who can be associated to give the greatest advantages to themselves and to the community. . . .

. . . Viewing it with reference to an improved spade cultivation, and to all the purposes of society, your Reporter ventures to recommend the formation of such arrangements as will unite about

From the book *A New View of Society and Other Writings* by Robert Owen. Introduction by G. D. H. Cole. Everyman's Library Edition. Published by E. P. Dutton & Co., Inc., and used with their permission. Pp. 245, 264–65, 266–67, 267–68, 269–74, 280, 284–85, 286–87, 288–89, 291–92, 296–98.

300 men, women, and children, in their natural proportions, as the *minimum*, and about 2,000 as the *maximum*, for the future associations of the cultivators of the soil, who will be employed also in such additional occupations as may be advantageously annexed to it.

In coming to this conclusion your Reporter never lost sight of that only sure guide to the political economist, the principle *that it is the interest of all men, whatever may be their present artificial station in society, that there should be the largest amount of intrinsically valuable produce created, at the least expense of labour, and in a way the most advantageous to the producers and society....*

It is with reference to this principle that the minimum and maximum above stated (viz., 300 and 2,000) have been fixed upon, as will be more particularly developed under the subsequent heads.

Within this range more advantages can be given to the individuals and to society than by the association of any greater or lesser number.

But from 800 to 1,200 will be found the most desirable number to form into agricultural villages; and unless some very strong local causes interfere, the permanent arrangements should be adapted to the complete accommodation of that amount of population only.

Villages of this extent, in the neighbourhood of others of a similar description, at due distances, will be found capable of combining within themselves all the advantages that city and country residences now afford, without any of the numerous inconveniences and evils which necessarily attach to both those modes of society....

Second, *the extent of land to be cultivated by such association.* This will depend upon the quality of the soil and other local considerations....

Sufficient land, therefore, will be allotted to these cultivators to enable them to raise an abundant supply of food and the necessaries of life for themselves, and as much additional agricultural produce as the public demands may require from such a portion of the population.

Under a well-devised arrangement for the working classes they will all procure for themselves the necessaries and comforts of life in so short a time, and so easily and pleasantly, that the occupation will be experienced to be little more than a recreation, sufficient to keep them in the best health and spirits for rational enjoyment of life.

The surplus produce from the soil will be required only for the higher classes, those who live without manual labour, and those whose nice manual operations will not permit them at any time to be employed in agriculture and gardening.

Of the latter, very few, if any, will be necessary, as mechanism may be made to supersede such operations, which are almost always injurious to health. . . .

Third, *the arrangement for feeding, lodging, and clothing the population, and for training and educating the children.*

It being always most convenient for the workman to reside near to his employment, the site for the dwellings of the cultivators will be chosen as near to the centre of the land as water, proper levels, dry situation, etc., etc., may admit; and as courts, alleys, lanes, and streets may be unnecessary inconveniences, are injurious to health, and destructive to almost all the natural comforts of human life, they will be excluded, and a disposition of the buildings free from these objections and greatly more economical will be adopted.

As it will afterwards appear that the food for the whole population can be provided better and cheaper under one general arrangement of cooking, and that the children can be better trained and educated together under the eye of their parents than under any other circumstances, a large square, or rather parallelogram, will be found to combine the greatest advantages in its form for the domestic arrangements of the association. . . .

The four sides of this figure may be adapted to contain all the private apartments or sleeping and sitting rooms for the adult part of the population; general sleeping apartments for the children while under tuition; store-rooms or warehouses in which to deposit various products; an inn or house for the accommodation of strangers; an infirmary; etc., etc.

In a line across the centre of the parallelogram, leaving free space for air and light and easy communication, might be erected the church, or places for worship; the schools; kitchen and apartments for eating; all in the most convenient situation for the whole population, and under the best possible public superintendence, without trouble, expense, or inconvenience to any party. . . .

This principle of individual interest, opposed as it is perpetually to the public good, is considered, by the most celebrated political economists, to be the corner-stone to the social system, and without which society could not subsist.

Yet when they shall know themselves, and discover the wonderful effects which combination and union can produce, they will acknowledge that the present arrangement of society is the most anti-social, impolitic, and irrational that can be devised; that under its influence all the superior and valuable qualities of human nature are repressed from infancy, and that the most unnatural means are used to bring out the most injurious propensities; in short, that the utmost pains are taken to make that which by nature is the most delightful compound for producing excellence and happiness, absurd, imbecile, and wretched. . . .

Under the present system there is the most minute division of mental power and manual labour in the individuals of the working classes; private interests are placed perpetually at variance with the public good; and in every nation men are purposely trained from infancy to suppose that their well-being is incompatible with the progress and prosperity of other nations. Such are the means by which old society seeks to obtain the desired objects of life. The details now to be submitted have been devised upon principles which will lead to an opposite practice; to the combination of extensive mental and manual powers in the individuals of the working classes; to a complete identity of private and public interest; and to the training of nations to comprehend that their power and happiness cannot attain their full and natural development but through an equal increase of the power and happiness of all other states. These, therefore, are the real points at variance between that which *is* and that which *ought to be.* . . .

Proceeding on these principles, your Reporter recommends arrangements by which the children shall be trained together as though they were literally all of one family. . . .

It may be stated, without fear of contradiction from any party who is master of the subject, that the whole success of these arrangements will depend upon the manner in which the infants and children shall be trained and educated in these schools. Men are, and ever will be, what they are and shall be made in infancy and childhood. The apparent exceptions to this law are the effects of the same causes, combined with subsequent impressions, arising from the new circumstances in which the individuals showing these exceptions have been placed. . . .

Fourth, *the formation and superintendence of these establishments.* . . .

These new farming and general working arrangements may be formed by one or any number of landed proprietors or large capitalists; by established companies having large funds to expend for benevolent and public objects; by parishes and counties, to relieve themselves from paupers and poor-rates; and by associations of the middle and working classes of farmers, mechanics, and tradesmen, to relieve themselves from the evils of the present system. . . .

When one establishment shall have been formed, there will be no great difficulty in providing superintendents for many other establishments. All the children will be trained to be equal to the care of any of the departments, more particularly as there will be no counteraction between those who direct and those who perform the various operations. . . .

The peculiar mode of governing these establishments will depend on the parties who form them.

Those founded by landowners and capitalists, public companies, parishes, or counties will be under the direction of the individuals whom these powers may appoint to superintend them, and will, of course, be subject to the rules and regulations laid down by their founders.

Those formed by the middle and working classes, upon a complete reciprocity of interests, should be governed by themselves, upon principles that will *prevent* divisions, opposition of interest, jealousies, or any of the common and vulgar passions which a contention for power is certain to generate. Their affairs should be conducted by a committee, composed of all the members of the association between certain ages—for instance, of those between thirty-five and forty-five, or between forty and fifty. Perhaps the former will unite more of the activity of youth with the experience of age than the latter; but it is of little moment which period of life may be fixed upon. In a short time the ease with which these associations will proceed in all their operations will be such as to render the business of governing a mere recreation; and as the parties who govern will in a few years again become the governed, they must always be conscious that at a future period they will experience the good or evil effects of the measures of their administration.

By this equitable and natural arrangement all the numberless evils of elections and electioneering will be avoided. . . .

Fifth, *the disposal of the surplus produce, and the connexion which will subsist between the several establishments.*

Under the proposed system the facilities of production, the absence of all the counteracting circumstances which so abundantly exist in common society, with the saving of time and waste in all the domestic arrangements, will secure, other circumstances being equal, *a much larger amount of wealth at a greatly reduced expenditure*. The next question is, in what manner is this produce to be disposed of? . . .

As the easy, regular, healthy, rational employment of the individuals forming these societies will create a very large surplus of their own products, beyond what they will have any desire to consume, each may be freely permitted to receive from the general store of the community whatever they may require. This, in practice, will prove to be the greatest economy, and will at once remove all those preconceived insurmountable difficulties that now haunt the minds of those who have been trained in common society, and who necessarily view all things through the distorted medium of their own little circle of local prejudices.

3. Organization of Work [1840]

LOUIS BLANC

Yes, no doubt a renovated society would call for a new power; but is the existence of power so independent of the existence of the society that you can transform the former without touching the latter? When you have found the means of inaugurating the principle of association and of organizing work according to the rules of reason, justice, and humanity, how do you hope to realize your doctrines? Power is organized force. Power rests on interests that are blind, but stubborn in their blindness; on passions hostile to all that is new. Power has chambers that will menace you with their laws, tribunals that will reach you with their arrests, soldiers who will strike you with their bayonets. Seize power, then, if you do not wish it to crush you. Take it as an instrument, on pain of encountering it as an obstacle.

There is more: the emancipation of the proletariat is too complicated a work; it is linked with too many reforms, it disturbs too many habits, it overthrows too many prejudices, it opposes, not in reality but in appearance, too many interests for it not to be folly to believe that it could be accomplished by a series of partial efforts and isolated attempts. It is necessary to apply all the power of the state, and this is surely not too much for such a

Reprinted from *Organisation du travail* (Paris: Prévot, 1840), pp. 95–97, 108–17, 119, 124–25. Translated by Helen Kramer.

labor. What the proletarians lack for their liberation are the instruments of work: it is up to the government to provide them with these.

No, without political reform no social reform is possible, for if the second is the *goal*, the first is the *means*.

But is it necessary to conclude from this that discussion of social questions is useless, even dangerous, and that one must begin by conquering power, waiting until afterward to see what to do? It would be worth as much to say: let us begin by starting en route; we shall see afterward where we ought to go.

This error is, however, rather common today. . . . The necessity of resolving social questions is not denied; the fact that political reform must be accomplished in order to arrive at a social reform is even recognized; but it is believed that the discussion of these grave difficulties should be postponed to the morrow of the political revolution. Such is not our opinion.

The revolutions that do not fail are those whose goals are precise and have been defined in advance. . . .

How work could be organized

The government would be considered the supreme regulator of production and invested with great power to accomplish its task.

This task consists of using even the weapon of competition in order to make competition disappear.

The government would raise a loan whose yield would be appropriated for the creation of *social workshops* in the most important branches of the national industry.

Since this creation would require an outlay of considerable funds, the number of original workshops would be rigorously circumscribed; but by virtue of their very organization . . . they would be endowed with an immense power of expansion.

Because the government would be considered the unique founder of *social workshops,* it would draw up the by-laws. This drafting, debated and voted on by the national representation, would have the force and power of law.

All workers who offer guarantees of morality would be called on to work in the *social workshops,* to the extent of the capital originally collected for the purchase of the instruments of work.

Since the false and antisocial education given to the current generation leads it to seek emulation and stimulation only when motivated by an increase of remuneration, the difference in wages would be graduated according to the hierarchy of functions; an entirely new education would have to change ideas and customs on this point. It goes without saying that the wage would have to be fully sufficient for the livelihood of the worker.

For the first year after the establishment of the social workshops, the government would regulate the hierarchy of functions. After the first year, there would no longer be any. As the workers would have had time to appraise each other, and as all would be equally interested . . . in the success of the association, hierarchy would be transformed into the elective principle.

Each year calculation would be made of the net profit, which would be divided into three parts: one would be distributed equally among the members of the association; another would be allocated: (1) to the support of the old, sick, and infirm, and (2) to the alleviation of crises that weigh on other industries, all the industries being owed aid and assistance; finally, the third would be devoted to furnishing instruments of work to those who would like to join the association, so that it could expand indefinitely. . . .

The capitalists would be called on in the association and would receive interest on the capital paid in by them, this interest being guaranteed to them by the budget, but they would not share in the profits except in the capacity of workers.

Once the social workshop had been set up, the end result would be understood. In all principal industries . . . there would be a social workshop competing with private industry. Would the struggle be very long? No, because the social workshop would have the advantage over all individual workshops that results from the economies of life in common and a mode of organization in which all the workers without exception are interested in producing quickly and well. Would the struggle be destructive? No, because the government would always be in a position to moderate the effects, while preventing the products coming out of its workshops from falling to too low a level. . . .

. . . Between the industrial war that a large capitalist declares today against a small capitalist and that which the government would declare in our system against the individual, there is no comparison possible. The former necessarily perpetuates fraud, violence, and all the evils that iniquity carries on its flanks; the latter would be conducted without brutality, without shocks, and in a way solely to attain its end, the successive and peaceful absorption of individual workshops by the social workshops. Thus, instead of being—as are the large capitalists today—the master and tyrant of the market, the government would be its regulator. It would make use of the weapon of competition, not in order violently to overthrow private industry . . . but to lead it imperceptibly to combination. Soon, indeed, in every sphere of industry in which a social workshop was established, people would flock to this workshop because of the advantages it would offer to those associated, the workers and capitalists. At the end of a certain time, one would see occur—without usurpation, without injustice, without irreparable disasters, and to the benefit of the principle of association—the phenomenon that today occurs so deplorably, and by dint of tyranny, to the benefit of individual egoism. A very rich industrialist today can, in striking a great blow against his rivals, leave them dead on the spot and monopolize an entire branch of industry; in our system, the state will make itself the master of industry little by little, and instead of monopoly, we would have, as the result of the success achieved, the defeat of competition—association. . . .

. . . Note, in effect, that since after the first year each workshop would be self-sufficient, the role of the government would be limited to supervising the maintenance of the relations of all the centers of production of the same type and preventing the violation of the principles of common regulation. Today there is no public service that does not represent a hundred times more complication. . . .

From the solidarity of all the workers in the same workshop, we have arrived at the solidarity of the workshops in the same industry. To complete the system, it would be necessary to establish the solidarity of different industries. For that we have deducted from the share of the profits realized by each industry a sum by means of which the state would be able to come to the aid of any industry that has been brought to suffering by unforeseen and extraordinary circumstances. Moreover, in the system that we propose, crises would be considerably more rare. From whence do they arise today in large part? From the truly atrocious combat to which all the interests yield themselves, combat which cannot create victors without creating the vanquished, and which, like all combats, harnesses the slaves to the chariot of the triumphant. . . .

What should credit be? A means of furnishing the instruments of work to the worker. Today . . . credit is something entirely different. The banks lend only to the rich. If they wished to lend to the poor, they could not do so without running to ruin. The banks established from the individual point of view could never be other than they are, an admirably conceived procedure for making the rich richer and the powerful more powerful. Always monopoly under the appearances of liberty, always tyranny under the guises of progress! The proposed organization would cut short so many iniquities. This share of profits, specially and invariably devoted to the expansion of the social workshop by the recruitment of workers—that is credit. Now do you need banks? Suppress them.

4. Selected Writings [1840–1865]

PIERRE JOSEPH PROUDHON

Economics, Justice and Equality

Since the law of nature as well as of Justice is equality, and since the aims of both are identical, economists and statesmen no longer have to decide whether economics should be sacrificed to Justice, or Justice to economics. They have to discover how best to exploit the physical, intellectual and economic forces that human intelligence is perpetually discovering in order to restore the social equilibrium, which is momentarily upset by the contingencies of climate, population growth, education, illness and all like accidents of force majeure.

One man, for example, is bigger and stronger than another. One is successful in agriculture, another in industry or shipping. One is able to take in a vast complex of events and ideas at a glance. Another is unequaled in a more limited sphere. In all these cases certain compensations must be made for an equalizing process to be operated that would give rise to stimulating competition and friendly rivalry. The way that man is constituted and the way that industry is divided provides unlimited sources for

Reprinted from Stewart Edwards, ed., *Selected Writings of Pierre Joseph Proudhon* (London and Basingstoke: Macmillan, 1970), pp. 51–52, 56–61, 88–92, 96–100, 102–103, by permission of the publisher.

checking manifestations of superiority and for constantly creating new means of maintaining equality between the unknown forces of nature and society.

This then is the radical and forever insurmountable difference which separates Christian and Malthusian economics, which are both materialistic and mystical, from revolutionary economics.

The first, which bases its judgment on the phenomena of chance and anomaly, does not hesitate to declare that men are by nature unequal. Then, without bothering to compare the kinds of work men do or to examine the results of their labors, their education and the effects of the separation of employment—and taking good care not to look too closely at each man's share of the collective product, nor to compare what he receives with what he contributes—they conclude that this so-called inequality justifies the privileges of exploitation and property-owning.

The Revolution, on the other hand, starts with the assumption that equality is the law of nature and that men are naturally equal. If it turns out in practice that some are less equal, it is because they have not wanted, or have not known how, to make full use of their possibilities. The Revolution considers that the hypothesis that men are unequal is an unfounded insult which is daily disproved by the progress of science and industry. It devotes all its energy to trying to redress the balance, tipped by prejudice, by means of legislation and greater and greater equality of services and wages. This is why it declares that all men have equal rights and are equal before the law. On the one hand it wants all industries, professions, functions, arts, sciences and trades to be considered as equally noble and worthy of merit. On the other it wants all parties in any litigation and competition to be treated equally, except when there is a difference in value between products and services, and so that equal Justice for all may become increasingly widespread in society, it wants all citizens to enjoy equal opportunities for development and action.

De la justice dans la révolution et dans l'église (1858)

Mutualism

Political economy is not the science of society, but it contains the elements of this science just as chaos before creation contained the elements of the universe; in order to arrive at the definitive organization which seems to be the destiny of our species on earth all we have to do is to arrange all our contradictions in the form of a general equation.

But what form will this equation take?

We are already beginning to glimpse it. It must be based on a law of exchange, a theory of Mutuality, a system of guarantees that resolves the old forms of our civil and commercially based societies and satisfies all the conditions of efficiency, progress and justice pointed out by the critics. It will be a society that is not based on convention, but on reality; a society that converts the division of labor into a scientific instrument; a society that stops men from being the slaves of machines and foresees the crisis that these will cause. It will make competition profitable and transform monopoly into a guarantee of security for all. Through the energy of its principle, instead of asking the capitalist for credit and the State for protection, it will make both capital and the State subordinate to labor. Through the genuine nature of exchange it will create true solidarity between peoples. It will, without prohibiting individual initiative or domestic thrift, always restore to the community the wealth that has been privately appropriated. It will be a society that will, through the movement of the outlay and the return of capital, insure the political and industrial equality of its citizens, and through a vast system of public education bring about equality in functions and aptitudes through constantly raising their level. Through justice, prosperity and virtue it will bring a renewal of human consciousness and insure harmony and equilibrium between the generations. In short it will be a society which, since it is based on both an organized structure and on the possibility of change, will be more than provisional; it will guarantee everything while pledging nothing. . . .

The theory of mutuality, or mutuum, that is to say exchange in kind, of which the simplest form is the loan for consumption, where the collective body is concerned, is the synthesis of the notions of private property and collective ownership. This synthesis is as old as its constituent parts since it merely means that society is returning, through a maze of inventions and systems, to its primitive practices as a result of a six-thousand-year-long meditation on the fundamental proposition that $A = A$.

Système des contradictions économiques (1846)

In opposition to this idea of [authoritarian] government is that of the defenders of individual liberty. According to them, society must be thought of not as a hierarchical system of functions and faculties, but as a system of free forces balancing each other; a system in which all individuals are guaranteed the same rights provided they perform the same duties, one in which they will receive the same benefits in return for the same services rendered. This system is thus essentially egalitarian and liberal and precludes all notion of fortune, rank or class. Now this is how these anti-authoritarians or liberals conclude their argument.

They maintain that since human nature is the most elevated expression not to say the embodiment of universal Justice, man as citizen derives his rights from the dignity of his nature. Similarly, he will later gain well-being directly from his personal labor and the good use he makes of his faculties, as well as respect from the free exercise of his talents and virtues. They say therefore that the State is simply the product of the freely consented union formed by equal, independent subjects, all of whom alike are lawmakers. Thus the State represents only group interests, and any debate between Power and the citizen is really only a debate between citizens. Accordingly, the only prerogative in society is liberty, the only supreme force, Law. Authority and charity, they say, have served their time. What we want instead is justice.

From these premises, they conclude in favor of an organization based on the widest possible application of the mutualistic principle. Its law, they say, is service for service, product for product, loan for loan, insurance for insurance, credit for credit, security for security, guarantee for guarantee. It is the ancient law of retaliation, an eye for an eye, a tooth for a tooth, a life for a life, as it were turned upside down and transferred from criminal law and the vile practices of the vendetta to economic law, to the tasks of labor and to the good offices of free fraternity. On it depend all the mutualist institutions: mutual insurance, mutual credit, mutual aid, mutual education; reciprocal guarantees of openings, exchanges and labor for good quality and fairly priced goods, etc. This is what the principle of mutualism claims to use, with the aid of certain institutions, as the foundation of the State, the law of the State, and I will even go as far as to say as a kind of religion of the State, which will be just as easy as it is advantageous. It demands no police force, no repression or restrictions, and can never be a cause of disappointment or ruin for anyone.

In this system the laborer is no longer a serf of the State, swamped by the ocean of the community. He is a free man, truly his own master, who acts on his own initiative and is personally responsible. He knows that he will obtain just and sufficient payment for his products and services, and that his fellow citizens will give him absolute loyalty and complete guarantees for all the consumer goods he might need. The State or government is no longer sovereign. Authority is no longer the antithesis of liberty, and State, government, power, authority, etc., are only expressions that designate liberty in a different way. They are general formulae borrowed from outmoded speech which in certain cases signify the sum, the union, the identity and the solidarity of individual interests.

De la capacité politique des classes ouvrières (1865)

Anarchy

Although I am a strong supporter of order, I am in the fullest sense of the term, an anarchist.

In any given society, the authority man has over man is in inverse ratio to the intellectual level of development reached by that society. The probable duration of that authority may be calculated according to the more or less widespread desire for true government, that is, government based on science. Just as the right of force and the right of artfulness are limited by the ever-increasing bounds of justice, and will finally be eclipsed by equality, so the sovereignty of will is giving way to the sovereignty of reason, and must finally vanish within a form of scientific socialism. Property and royalty have been decaying since the world began. Just as man seeks justice in equality, society seeks order in anarchy.

Anarchy, that is the absence of a ruler or a sovereign. This is the form of government we are moving closer to every day. Because of the deep-rooted habit of taking one man as representing order and of taking his will as law, people regard us as the very summit of disorder and the embodiment of chaos. . . . We all share this prejudice. Every one of us wants a leader or leaders. The most advanced among us are those who want the greatest possible number of sovereigns. Their most ardent wish is for the royal power to be enshrined in the National Guard. Doubtless some person who is jealous of the citizens' militia will soon say, "Every man is king." But my reply to this will be, "No man is king. We are all, whether we like it or not, partners." All questions of domestic policy must be settled in the light of Departmental statistics. All questions of foreign policy are a matter of international statistics. The science of government belongs by right to one of the branches of the Academy of Science, whose permanent secretary must necessarily become Prime Minister. Since citizens may lay a memorandum before the Academy, all citizens are lawmakers. But since no person's opinion carries any weight unless it is supported by facts, no one person's will can override reason, and therefore no one is king. . . .

What then are the people if they are not sovereign and if they are not the source of legislative power? The people are the guardians of the law. The people constitute the executive power. Any citizen may affirm that such and such a thing is true or just, but his conviction binds no one other than himself. If the truth which he is proclaiming is to become law, then it must be generally recognized as such. But what is recognizing a law? It is verifying a mathematical or metaphysical calculation. It is repeating an experiment, observing a phenomenon or taking note of a fact. Only the whole nation has a right to say "Mandons et ordonnons."

Qu'est-ce que la propriété? (1840)

For authority and politics I substituted the notion of ECO-NOMICS—a positive, synthetic idea which, as I see it, is alone capable of leading to a rational, practical conception of social order. Moreover, in this I was simply taking up Saint-Simon's thesis, which has been so strangely distorted by his disciples. This thesis consists of saying, in the light of history and of the incompatibility of the notions of authority and progress, that society is in the process of completing the governmental cycle for the last time; that the public reason has become convinced that politics is powerless to improve the lot of the masses; that the notions of power and authority are being replaced in people's minds, as in the course of history, by the notions of labor and exchange; and that the end result is the substitution of economic organizations for political machinery, etc., etc.

Philosophie du progrès (1853)

I have already mentioned ANARCHY, or the government of

each man by himself—or as the English say, self-government—as being one example of the liberal regime. Since the expression "anarchical government" is a contradiction in terms, the system itself seems to be impossible and the idea absurd. However, it is only language that needs to be criticized. The notion of anarchy in politics is just as rational and positive as any other. It means that once industrial functions have taken over from political functions, then business transactions and exchange alone produce the social order. In these conditions each man could call himself his own master, which is the very opposite of constitutional monarchy.

By the word [anarchy] I wanted to indicate the extreme limit of political progress. Anarchy is, if I may be permitted to put it this way, a form of government or constitution in which public and private consciousness, formed through the development of science and law, is alone sufficient to maintain order and guarantee all liberties. In it, as a consequence, the institutions of the police, preventive and repressive methods, officialdom, taxation, etc., are reduced to a minimum. In it, more especially, the forms of monarchy and intensive centralization disappear, to be replaced by federal institutions and a pattern of life based on the commune. When politics and home life have become one and the same thing, when economic problems have been solved in such a way that individual and collective interests are identical, then—all constraint having disappeared—it is evident that we will be in a state of total liberty or anarchy. Society's laws will operate by themselves through universal spontaneity, and they will not have to be ordered or controlled.

Letter to Mr. X *** (August 20, 1864)

Social Contract

What is the *Social Contract?* Is it an agreement between citizen and government? No, for this would still be to remain trapped within the same idea. The social contract is an agreement between man and man, from which what we call society must emerge. Here the notion of *commutative justice,* established by the primitive fact of exchange and defined by Roman law, is replaced by that of *distributive.* Translate the legal terms *contract* and *commutative justice* into the language of affairs, and you have COMMERCE. That is, in its most elevated sense, the action by which men, declaring themselves to be essentially producers, renounce all claims to governing each other.

Commutative justice, ruled by contract, or in other words, *rule by economics and industry,* these are all different synonyms expressing the idea whose advent must abolish the old systems of *distributive justice, rule by laws,* or to be more concrete, the feudal, governmental or military regime. The future of mankind lies in this change. . . .

The contract or commutative agreement is characterized by the fact that it increases man's liberty and well-being. The setting up of any authority, on the other hand, necessarily decreases it. This is evident if one reflects that a contract is an act by which two or more individuals agree to organize among themselves, within certain limits and for a given time, the industrial force which we call exchange. Consequently they undertake mutual obligations and make reciprocal guarantees for a certain number of services, products, benefits, duties and so on which they are in a position to obtain and render, knowing themselves to be in all other respects totally independent, both in what they consume and what they produce.

Between the contracting parties there is necessarily a real and personal interest involved. The word *contract* implies that a man negotiates with the intention of securing his liberty and his income at the same time, without there being any possibility of compensation. Between governing and governed, on the contrary —whatever the system of representatives or delegation of the governmental power—some part of the citizen's liberty and fortune is necessarily alienated. . . .

A contract is therefore essentially bilateral. It imposes no obligations on the contracting parties other than those resulting from their personal promise of reciprocal service. It is subject to no outside authority. It is the only law that binds the parties. It expects to be fulfilled at their instigation alone.

If such is "contract" in its widest sense and as it is applied from day to day, how can we describe the Social Contract which is supposed to unite all the members of a State in a common interest?

The Social Contract is the supreme act by which each citizen pledges to society his love, his intelligence, his labor, his services, his products and his goods in exchange for the affection, ideas, works, products, services and goods of his fellow citizens. What each man may claim is always determined by what he contributes; as he makes his contributions, so will he receive his compensation.

Thus the social contract must include the whole body of citizens, their interests and relations. If even one man were excluded from the contract, if even one problem which the citizens, who are intelligent, industrious and sensitive, were called upon to deal with were omitted, the contract would be more or less partial and exclusive. It could not be called social. . . .

Furthermore, the social contract being discussed here is in no way similar to the contract with society. By the latter . . . the contracting party alienates some of his liberty and submits to a solidarity of a burdensome and often hazardous kind in the somewhat dubiously grounded hope of gain. The social contract is of the nature of the commutative contract. Not only does it leave the contracting party free, but it also increases his freedom. Not only does it leave him all his possessions, but it also actually increases his property. It makes no stipulations with regard to his labor; it is concerned only with exchange. None of these things is true of the contract with society; in fact, they are all completely contrary to it . . . .

We have already explained that we would substitute industrial organization for government.

Instead of laws we would have contracts. No laws would be passed, either by majority vote or unanimously. Each citizen, each commune or corporation, would make its own laws.

Instead of political power we would have economic forces.

Instead of the old class divisions between citizen, noble and commoner, bourgeoisie and proletariat, we would have categories and classes relating to various functions: agriculture, industry, commerce and so on.

Instead of public forces we would have collective forces.

Instead of standing armies we would have industrial companies.

Instead of a police force, we would have a collective interest.

Instead of political centralization we would have economic centralization.

What need have we of government when a state of harmony has been reached? Surely the National Bank with all its branches provides us with centralization and unity? Surely the agreements made between farm laborers for the compensation, liquidation and redemption of agrarian estates create unity? Do not the workers' companies formed for the development of the large industries also create unity in a different way? And is not also the constitution of value, the contract of contracts as we have called it, the highest and most indestructible form of unity?

If I have to convince you by providing examples of precedents within your own experience: has not the system of weights and measures, the greatest monument to the Convention, formed for the last fifty years the cornerstone of economic unity, which through the progress of ideas is destined to replace political unity?

Therefore ask no further questions as to what we would have instead of government, nor what will become of society when there are no longer governments. I warrant that in future it will be easier to conceive of society without a government than it will be to conceive of society with one.

Idée générale de la révolution au XIX siècle (1851)

Federalism

All political conditions and all forms of government, including federalism, may be reduced to the following formula: *the balancing of authority by liberty,* and vice versa. It is as a consequence of this that the categories *monarchy, aristocracy, democracy, etc.,* used since Aristotle by so many writers to classify government, to distinguish between forms of states and to make distinctions between nations, can all, except for federalism, be shown to be hypothetical constructions based on mere experience, which are barely able to satisfy the demands of reason and justice. . . .

Two different forms of government may be deduced *a priori* from these two fundamental notions [authority and liberty], according to which one is given preference, namely *Government based on Authority* and *Government based on Liberty.*

Futhermore, since society is composed of individuals, and since the relation of the individual to the group may be thought of in four different ways so far as politics is concerned, there are as a result four forms of governments, two for each system.

1. Government based on authority

A. The government of all men by one man, that is, MONARCHY or PATRIARCHY.

a. Government of all men by all men, that is PANARCHY or COMMUNISM.

The essential feature of this system, in both its forms, is that there is no division of power.

2. Government based on liberty

B. The government of all men by each man, that is DE-MOCRACY.

b. The government of each man by himself, that is ANARCHY or SELF-GOVERNMENT.

The essential feature of this system, in both its forms, is the division of power.

Du principe féderatif (1863)

5. Freeland [1890]

THEODOR HERTZKA

Model statute

1. Membership in every association is free to everyone, whether or not he is simultaneously a member of other associations; everyone also may leave any association at any time.

2. Every member has the right to a share of the association's net proceeds corresponding to his work performance.

3. The work performance will be calculated for every member in relation to the hours of work expended; however, for older members, a bonus of x percent is granted for every year which they belong to the association longer than later associates. Likewise, for skilled labor a bonus will be agreed upon by means of a free contract.

4. The work performance of the manager or directors will be set equal to a certain number of daily expended work hours by means of a free contract entered into with each individual.

5. The association's proceeds will first be calculated at the end of each year of operation and distributed after deduction of capital repayments and taxes to be paid to the Freeland Common-

Reprinted from *Freiland: Ein sociales Zukunftsbild* (Leipzig: Duncker & Humblot, 1890), pp. 149–53, 159, 211–12, 218, 220–21, 388, 399–400, by permission of the publisher. Translated by Helen Kramer.

wealth. In the meantime, the members receive cash advances in the amount of x percent of the previous year's net proceeds for each expended or calculated hour of work.

6. In the case of the disbanding or liquidating of the association, the members are responsible in equal parts for contracted loans, the security for which is assigned also to new members in proportion to the amounts already paid out. The disassociation of a member does not nullify his responsibility for loans already contracted. This liability for the debts of the association corresponds to the claim of the responsible member to the available means in the case of dissolution or liquidation.

7. The highest administrative authority of the association is the General Assembly, in which each member enjoys an equal right to vote and eligibility as long as his work performance is not less than half of the average achieved by all other members. The General Assembly makes its decisions by simple majority; a three-fourths majority is necessary for amendment of the Statute and for disbandment and liquidation of the association.

8. The General Assembly exercises its rights either directly as such or through its elected officials, who are responsible to it for their conduct.

9. The management of the cooperative business is assigned to a directorate of x members who are elected for x years by the General Assembly but whose mandate is nevertheless recallable at any time. The lower officials of the management will be appointed by the director; the determination of the salary of these officials— measured in hours of work—is made at the suggestion of the director by the General Assembly.

10. The General Assembly annually elects one of the x members of the existing supervisory board to control the accounts as well as the conduct of the management and periodically to render a report.

It is immediately striking that, in this Statute, only in the case of dissolution of the association (clause 6) is there any discussion of what apparently should be viewed as the main point, namely, the "property" of the association and the claims of the members to this property. The basis of the matter is that a *property* of the association, in the generally used sense of the term, does not exist at all. The members, to be sure, possess the right to use the available capital; however, since they share this right with every suitable new entrant at all times and should be bound to the association through nothing other than interest in the proceeds of their labor, property interests in the association may not be given at all as long as the same people are in the firm. And, in fact, an object —however useful—which anyone can use is not property. There are no owners, only users of the association's capital. And should a contradiction perhaps be seen in the stipulation that the loaned productive capital must be repaid by the association, it must not be overlooked that this capital repayment—with the exception of the cited case of liquidation—will be carried out by the members and in their capacity as users of the means of production. When the capital repayments have been deducted from the proceeds, these are divided among the members according to work performance; hence, payment is made to every member according to his work performance. . . .

One sees that productive capitals, as a consequence of this simply and certainly functioning arrangement, are strictly taken to be as ownerless as the land; they belong to everyone and hence properly to no one. The community of producers gives them over and uses them exactly according to the amount of the work performance of each individual, and payment for goods consumed is made by the community of all consumers, once more each exactly according to the amount of his consumption. . . .

Of course, in Freeland, as everywhere in the world, there is better and poorer land, but since more workers stream to the better land than to the less good, and since, according to a well-known economic law, the greater application of labor to equal plots of land entails relatively diminishing returns, in general no higher net return falls to the share of the individual worker or the individual hour of work on the best land than on the poorest land worked.

The constitution

The fundamental law runs:

1. Every inhabitant of Freeland has the same inalienable right to the common land and to the means of production provided by the collectivity.

2. Women, children, the aged, and those unfit for work have the right to sufficient maintenance fairly corresponding to the amount of the general abundance.

3. No one can be hindered in the exercise of his free individual will, as long as he does not touch the sphere of rights of another.

4. Public affairs will be conducted according to the resolution of all adult inhabitants (over twenty years old) of Freeland without regard to sex, and collectively having the same electoral and suffrage rights in all affairs concerning the Commonwealth.

5. The decision-making as well as the executive authority is divided according to industries in such a way that the collectivity of voters elects for the principal public industries special representatives who render their decisions separately and control the conduct of the existing managerial bodies of the industries in question.

The essence of the public law of Freeland is laid down in these five points; everything further is but the obvious result or the close derivative of the same. The principles on which associations are built—the right of workers to the profits, distribution of the latter according to work performance and free agreement with higher valued labor—are thus demonstrated to issue naturally and necessarily from the first and third basic laws. Since everyone has access to the common means of work, no one can be obliged to renounce the proceeds of his own work, and no one can be forced to place his greater capabilities at the disposal of others; these greater capabilities must find a corresponding value by means of free agreement insofar as they are needed for the carrying out of production. . . .

Imagine a European or American state in which the experienced representatives of each branch of interests can make, carry out, and control the laws of the sphere closely interesting them: manufacturers for manufacturing, farmers for agricultural production, railroadmen for transport, etc. Since in an exploitative society the struggle for existence is directed to mutual oppression and dispossession, the consequences of such an "order" must be terrible for it, and in those cases known under the collective concept of political corruption, where individual special interests succeed in foisting their will upon the community, the shamelessness of exploitation in fact also exceeds all limits.

It is otherwise in Freeland; there are no special interests opposing the common interest or not completely harmonized with it. Producers, for example, who hit upon the idea of increasing their profits by imposing customs duties upon imports must be idiots; for it will serve them nothing to force consumers to pay more for their products, since the inflow of labor will reduce their profit again to its average level. On the contrary, it would damage them to have made the production of all other producers more difficult, for thereby even that average level of profit, above which they can never raise their own, will be forced down. And this holds for all our spheres of interest. Since all of these are accessible to each, and no one has the right and power to claim for himself alone a growing share anywhere, we are in the fortunate position of entrusting decision-making on all questions of interest to those most closely involved and therefore most experienced. Thereby, however, not only are legislation and administration expertly formed in the highest degree, but that vehement bias that is the characteristic trait of the party machine disappears from public life. . . .

We *prohibit* interest on capital as little as we "prohibit" the profit of the employer or land rent. These three types of income do not exist in this country merely for the reason that no one is in the distressed condition of having to pay them. . . .

You see, exactly the same holds for interest on capital as for entrepreneurial profit and land rent: the attained capability of the association lifts from workers the necessity under which everywhere they cede part of the proceeds of their production to third persons. Interest disappears quite by itself, like profit and rent, on the decisive ground alone that the freely associated worker will be his own capitalist as well as his own employer and landowner. Or if one so wishes: *interest, profit,* and *rent* remain, they lose only their special characteristic detached from wages; they blend with the latter in single and indivisible work remuneration.

6.   The Future of the Labor Exchanges [1901]

FERNAND PELLOUTIER

Here is how the report tabled in the name of the Labor Exchange of Nîmes . . . resolved the question posed. What are the attributes of the Labor Exchanges? asked the report. They are, first, to know at every moment with exactitude, and for each profession, the number of unemployed workers and, at the same time, the multiple causes of the disturbances introduced each day into the conditions of work and working life; then, to borrow from statistics . . ."the cost of living of each individual, compared to the wages granted, the number of professions, number of workers included in each, number of products manufactured, extracted, or harvested, and, in turn, the total of products necessary for the feeding and maintenance of the population in the entire region within the radius of the Labor Exchange."

Let us now suppose, continued the report, that the Exchanges have suitably fulfilled this role, and that social and corporative action has brought about a social transformation—what will the Exchange do? And the report replies: "Each profession is organized in a trade union; each trade union names a council that we could call a professional council of labor; these trade unions in turn are federated by profession nationally and internationally.

Reprinted from *Histoire des bourses du travail* (Paris: Alfred Costes, 1946), pp. 250–55, 262–64. Translated by Helen Kramer.

"Property is no longer individual: the land, mines, factories, workshops, means of transport, houses, etc., have become social property. Social property—let us understand well—and not exclusive and inalienable property of the workers who improve it, unless one wishes to see there arise among the corporations the conflicts that arose among the capitalists, and society again become the victim of competition—competition of corporate collectives instead of capitalist individuals! . . .

"Society needs so much wheat, so much clothing; the farmers and tailors receive from society—whether in money, as long as the latter exists, or in exchange value—the means of consumption of or use of the products produced by other workers. These are the bases on which work should be organized in order for society to be truly egalitarian. . . .

"The Exchanges, knowing the quantity of products that must be manufactured, inform the professional councils of labor of each corporation, which employ all the members of the profession in the manufacture of the necessary products. . . . Through their statistics, the Exchanges know the surplus or deficit production of their surrounding areas; they then determine the exchange of products between territories endowed by nature for special production. . . .

"Since tools will be improved more and more, science will be making new conquests each day, the workers will have a large direct interest in aiding and intensifying the march of progress, and society will be able to improve the natural wealth and forces that our capitalist society was obliged to abandon, the social wealth will increase considerably; consumption too will increase, for no one will any longer be obliged to deprive himself of food, clothing, and furniture, or of luxury and art, those two essential factors of taste and intelligence! . . ."

In its turn, the Federal Committee of Labor Exchanges, in a report on the same question, stated:

". . . The social revolution should then have the objective of suppressing exchange *value*, the capital it engenders, the institutions it creates. We derive from this principle the conception that the revolutionary task should be to liberate men not only of all authority but of every institution that does not essentially have as its aim the development of production. Consequently, we could imagine the future society only as 'the voluntary and free association of producers.' But what is the role of these associations? . . .

"Each of them has care of a branch of production. . . . All must

inquire first of all into the needs of consumption, then into the
resources available to satisfy them. How much granite must be
quarried, flour milled, entertainments organized for a given population each day? These quantities known, how much granite and
flour can be obtained on the spot? How many entertainments organized? How many workers and artists are necessary? How much
of materials or producers must be requested of neighboring associations? How should the task be divided? How should public
warehouses be established? How should scientific discoveries be
used once they are known? . . .

"Knowing, first of all, the relation of production to consumption, the workers' associations use the materials produced or extracted by their members. Knowing, likewise the quantity of the
products they lack and the quantity of which they have a surplus,
they request elsewhere either the associates whom they need or
the special products that nature has denied their soil. . . .

"The consequence of this new state, of this suppression of useless social bodies, of this simplification of the necessary machinery, is that man produces better, more, and faster; that he can, as
a result, devote long hours to his intellectual development, thus
accelerate the progress of mechanization, relieve himself more
and more of onerous manual labor, and order his existence in a
way more conformable to the instinctive aspirations for studious
repose."

One now knows the origin of the Labor Exchanges, the way in
which they are constituted, the services created by them and those
they contemplate creating—in a word, the role that they aim to
play in the present economic and political organization. Is it surprising after that to learn "that they do not consider themselves to
be only an instrument of struggle against capital," or modest employment bureaus, but that they aim at a higher role in the formation of the future social state? Assuredly, one should not be
more optimistic than is reasonable, and we admit that, among the
majority of workers, economic instruction—the only certain
guide for the workers' associations—has been hardly sketched out.
But have they not found the key to the organic system of societies
in the intellectual communion that the Exchanges alone could facilitate for them, and do they thus require anything except time
to be able to substitute for the influence of capital in the administration of human interests the unique justifiable sovereignty—
that of labor? Enumerate the results obtained by workers' groups
in the field of education; consult the program of the courses insti-

tuted by the trade unions and Labor Exchanges, a program from which nothing is omitted that makes moral life full, dignified, and satisfying; see which authors are represented in workers' libraries; admire the syndical and cooperative organization which expands each day and embraces new categories of producers, this inclusion of all the proletarian forces in a close network of trade unions, cooperative societies, and resistance leagues, this constantly growing intervention in diverse social manifestations, this examination of methods of production and of redistribution of wealth—and say whether this organization, this program, this described tendency toward the beautiful and the good, such an aspiration toward the perfect blossoming of the individual, does not justify all the pride felt by the Labor Exchanges.

If it is correct that the future belongs to the "free association of producers"—anticipated by Bakunin, announced by all the manifestations of this century, and proclaimed even by the most qualified defenders of the present political regime—it will no doubt lie in these Labor Exchanges or in similar organizations, but organizations open to all who think and act, so that men will meet together to seek in common the means of disciplining natural forces and making them serve human well-being.

7. Haywoodism and Industrialism [April 13, 1913]

DANIEL DE LEON

The "political State" is that social structure which marks the epoch since which society was ruptured into classes, and class-rule began. This fact determines the foundation of the political State. The foundation of the political State is not, as it was with previous society, man; the foundation of the political State is property. The governmental structure, that is the reflex of such a socio-economic foundation, must needs match the socio-economic status on which it is reared. The immediate consequence, the consequence of importance to the subject in hand, is that the constituencies of the political State are territorial. . . . The essence of the fact is graphically condensed in the Socialist dictum concerning bourgeois society: "Property rules man, not man property." . . .

The political State was the step that ethnic-sociologic law compelled society to take. It was within the shell of the political State that the tool, or machinery, of production was to be perfected; production itself organized; co-operative labor brought about; and, thanks to the abundance thus rendered potential, lift from the shoulders of man the primal curse of the brute's arduous toil for bare physical existence. This to accomplish being the ethnic-

Reprinted from *Industrial Unionism, Selected Editorials* (New York: New York Labor News Company, 1944), pp. 71–79, by permission of the publisher.

sociologic mission of the political State, the arrival of the human race at that stage—the stage that our generation has reached—when abundance for all is possible without arduous physical toil for any, is the trumpet-blast announcement that the shell of the political State is no longer needed, and should be broken through and cast off.

At this stage of social evolution arises Industrialism, or, the Industrial Union, as the next logical link in the evolutionary chain; hence, it is the vital aspect of Socialism. It is the aspect of Socialism which drills, by educating, the "army of occupation" that, by supplanting the political State, is to re-establish the government of the race's original days of Liberty, Equality, and Fraternity—the government that rests upon man, and of man over property. In other words, it is the aspect of Socialism that attends the recasting of Modern Society into the constituencies of Future Society, in keeping with the altered, improved, and perfected, in short, revolutionized economic possibilities. In still other words, Industrialism is the aspect of Socialism which gathers and organizes the new constituencies in the mold of Industry, in order to supplant the property-and-class-rule-dictated mold of territory, and thereby overthrow the property-and-class-rule-dictated governmental structure of the political State.

In addressing itself to its historic task, the Industrial Union connects intimately, as all evolutionary processes must, with the present from which it evolves. America being the highest developed class-rule State, under the highest expression of class-rule, to wit, untrammeled capitalism, it is here in America that—gathering the experience, left in rough outline by previous efforts in the same direction, and its steps lighted by the Marxian triple teachings of demanding the overthrow of the political State, of simultaneously warning against "parliamentary idiocy," and of pointing to the necessity of joint political and economic action, with the economic organization of the proletariat as the basis for the political revolt—it is here in America that Industrialism first arose, first promulgated its program, and first formulated its structure. This it did with epoch-making precision at the first national convention of the Industrial Workers of the World, in Chicago, 1905.

Needless to say, it was the political State, hence, a political Government that the Revolutionary Fathers established in America. Nevertheless, the State and Government which they established was, and, as a matter of course, has increasingly developed into the nearest point of transition from the political State and Government to the Industrial or Socialist Republic, with the Government appertaining thereto. The fact transpires from two historic documents that are of prime import in Social Science—the Constitution, and Washington's Farewell Address.

The Constitution that the Revolutionary fathers set up is the first in recorded history to legalize revolution—a marked innovation in the spirit and traditions of the political State—an innovation that meant nothing less than the contemplation, and rendering at least theoretically possible, of institutional change without the hitherto inevitable accompaniment of violence and stoppage of industry. The Constitution accomplished the feat of legalizing revolution by means of its amendments clause, thereby providing for the overthrow of the institution which itself had reared, and thereby also providing for the method—political action—thereby raising the revolutionary propaganda above the murky and murky-thoughts-promoting level of conspiracy, and thereby enabling the revolutionary propaganda to preach and teach, and clear the way for revolution in the open.

Washington's Farewell Address rings the note of warning against the seductions, and against those who would promote the seductions, of State Autonomy. Let not, said he—I quote the substance, and from memory—let not your pride lie in being citizens of Pennsylvania, as against South Carolina, or citizens of Virginia as against Massachusetts; let your pride lie in being citizens of the Nation. The Nation is greater than any one State; it is something vastly greater than the mere sum of all the individual States put together.

The Constitution and Washington's Farewell Address are but convergencies with the sociologic evolution which begets the Industrial Union.

Connecting with the Constitution, Industrialism plants itself flat-footed upon the field of political action—a field upon which every member of the proletariat, even if not equipped with the ballot, can exert his or her activity as an agent of civilized revolutionary propaganda. Accordingly, Industrialism projects what Marx designated as the only bona fide political party of the Working Class. . . .

As the broad mission of Industrialism—the re-construction of the Nation—dictates to the Industrial Union that it gather all the population engaged in useful occupations into *one Union,* a Union co-extensive with the Nation's confines, so does the specific mission of Industrialism—the reconstruction of the governmental constituencies—dictate to the Industrial Union that it organize the Nation's usefully occupied population into Industries. . . .

What the several States are to the present Nation, the several Industries are to the Industrial, the Socialist, or Co-operative Republic—with the difference that, whereas the boundary lines of the States are arbitrarily geographic, the boundary lines of the Industries are dictated by the output.

Aiming at the abolition of class-rule, Industrialism bends its efforts to the overthrow of the political State.

Aiming at the overthrow of the political State, Industrialism brings together, in the integrally organized industrial forces of the proletariat, both the requisite Might wherewith to make good the Right, and also the new constituencies through the representatives of which to seize the reins of government, and administer production.

Aiming at bringing together the integrally organized industrial forces of the land, Industrialism proclaims the necessity of proletarian unity upon the political field as the only field upon which the revolution can be openly preached.

What, then, is Haywoodism?

The circumstance that Industrialism carries in its fold the requisite Might to enforce its Right, prompts the temperamentally unstrung to doctrines of pure and simple physical force.

The circumstance that Industrialism is uncompromisingly opposed to the autonomous Craft organization, and promulgates the program of *one* Union embracing the whole population of useful occupations, starts with the shallow, the notion that the ideal in Unionism is promiscuity of occupations.

The circumstance that Industrialism lays down the principle that the prime mission of a bona fide political party of Socialism is to promote the economic organization of the proletariat, without which class-conscious and goal-conscious organization the day of victory by a political party of Socialism would be the day of its defeat—that circumstance induces minds constructed on the popgun, one-idea principle to discard and jeer at political action as a waste of time and effort.

The circumstance that Industrialism proudly issues through its Preamble the call for Working Class expropriation of the machinery of production, prompts unbalanced minds to acts of "individual expropriation."

The circumstance that Industrialism implies the smash-up of

class-rule, together with its political State and other institutional appendages of Despotism and Exploitation, fans in undisciplined and heated brains the flames of Revenge.

The collective manifestation of these errors, half-truths, and confusions of thought, hooped together with lurid declamation, is Haywoodism. Unresponsive to the warnings of Experience which denies creative power to physical force, Haywoodism attaches to physical force creative powers, and, by pushing physical force agitation to the fore, places the cart before the horse of Revolution. . . .

Unresponsive to the sociologic tenet that, important though the vote is, it is not the only, or most important factor in political action, the leading purpose of which is to preach the revolution upon the only field on which it can be preached to a purpose, hence that investiture with the suffrage is a non-essential for political action—unresponsive to all that, Haywoodism persistently asks: "What sense is there in political action when 75 per cent of the working people are not voters?"

Unresponsive to the sharp distinction between individual and collective, private and public, single and mass action, Haywoodism advocates by preachment and example acts of petty and private mischief, such as "sabotage," theft, and even worse.

Unresponsive to the loftily constructive demand of the Age, Haywoodism raises Destruction to the dignity of a goal.

The world being one city; the human race one; and the human mind working, within narrow limits of variation, within the same channel; it is impossible to fail to detect in the partly written, partly unwritten, program of Haywoodism the theoretic note and practical conduct of the officially adopted program of Bakounin's Revolutionary International Brothers—a mob whose staff, "having the devil in their bowels," confused the "revolutionary idea" with "destruction," and had no conception of revolutionary agitation, education and organization other than—to use Bakounin's official expression—"the unchaining of what we have been taught to call the bad passions."

From the camp of Haywoodism the definition has come of Industrialism as Socialism with its working clothes on. Taking the terms "Industrialism," "Socialism," and "working clothes" in their proper sense, the definition fits—and, therefore, it hints at the definition of Haywoodism itself as "Industrialism with its shirt off."

8. Industrial Unionism and Constructive Socialism [1908]

JAMES CONNOLLY

"There is not a Socialist in the world today who can indicate with any degree of clearness how we can bring about the co-operative commonwealth except along the lines suggested by industrial organization of the workers.

"Political institutions are not adapted to the administration of industry. Only industrial organizations are adapted to the administration of a co-operative commonwealth that we are working for. Only the industrial form of organization offers us even a theoretical constructive Socialist programme. There is no constructive Socialism except in the industrial field."

The above extracts from the speech of Delegate Stirton, editor of the *Wage Slave,* of Hancock, Michigan, so well embody my ideas upon this matter that I have thought well to take them as a text for an article in explanation of the structural form of Socialist society. In a previous chapter I have analysed the weakness of the craft or trade union form of organization alike as a weapon of defence against the capitalist class in everyday conflict on the economic field, and as a generator of class consciousness on the polit-

Reprinted from Ken Coates and Tony Topham, eds., *Workers' Control: A Book of Readings and Witnesses for Workers' Control* (London: Panther Books, 1970), pp. 10–14, by permission of Granada Publishing. Originally published as "The Axe to the Root, and Old Wine in New Bottles," in *Socialism Made Easy* (1908).

ical field, and pointed out the greater effectiveness for both purposes of an industrial form of organization.

Organizing constructively

In the present article I desire to show how they who are engaged in building up industrial organizations for the practical purposes of today are at the same time preparing the framework of the society of the future. It is the realization of that fact that indeed marks the emergence of Socialism as a revolutionary force from the critical to the positive stage. Time was when Socialists, if asked how society would be organized under Socialism, replied invariably, and airily, that such things would be left to the future to decide. The fact was that they had not considered the matter, but the development of the Trust and Organized Capital in general, making imperative the Industrial Organizations of Labour on similar lines, has provided us with an answer at once more complete to ourselves and more satisfying to our questioners.

Now to analyse briefly the logical consequences of the position embodied in the above quotation.

"Political institutions are not adapted to the administration of industry."

Here is a statement that no Socialist with a clear knowledge of the essentials of his doctrine can dispute. The political institutions of today are simply the coercive forces of capitalist society; they have grown up out of, and are based upon, territorial divisions of power in the hands of the ruling class in past ages, and were carried over into capitalist society to suit the needs of the capitalist class when that class overthrew the domination of its predecessors.

The old order and the new

The delegation of the function of government into the hands of representatives elected from certain districts, States, or territories, represents no real natural division suited to the requirements of modern society, but is a survival from a time when territorial influences were more potent in the world than industrial influences, and for that reason is totally unsuited to the needs of the new social order, which must be based upon industry.

The Socialist thinker, when he paints the structural form of the new social order, does not imagine an industrial system directed or ruled by a body of men or women elected from an indiscriminate mass of residents within given districts, said residents working at a heterogeneous collection of trades and industries. To give the ruling, controlling, and directing of industry into the hands of such a body would be too utterly foolish.

What the Socialist does realize is that under a social democratic form of society the administration of affairs will be in the hands of representatives of the various industries of the nation; that the workers in the shops and factories will organize themselves into unions, each union comprising all the workers at a given industry; that said union will democratically control the workshop life of its own industry, electing all foremen, etc., and regulating the routine of labour in that industry in subordination to the needs of society in general, to the needs of its allied trades, and to the departments of industry to which it belongs; that representatives elected from these various departments of industry will meet and form the industrial administration or national government of the country.

Begin in the workshop

In short, social democracy, as its name implies, is the application to industry, or to the social life of the nation, of the fundamental principles of democracy. Such application will necessarily have to begin in the workshop, and proceed logically and consecutively upward through all the grades of industrial organization until it reaches the culminating point of national executive power and direction. In other words, social democracy must proceed from the bottom upward, whereas capitalist political society is organized from above downward.

Social democracy will be administered by a committee of experts elected from the industries and professions of the land; capitalist society is governed by representatives elected from districts, and is based upon territorial division.

The local and national governing, or rather administrative, bodies of Socialism will approach every question with impartial minds, armed with the fullest expert knowledge born of experience; the governing bodies of capitalist society have to call in an expensive professional expert to instruct them on every technical question, and know that the impartiality of said expert varies with, and depends upon, the size of his fee.

No "servile state"

It will be seen that this conception of Socialism destroys at one blow all the fears of a bureaucratic State, ruling and ordering the lives of every individual from above, and thus gives assurance that the social order of the future will be an extension of the freedom of the individual, and not the suppression of it. In short, it blends the fullest democratic control with the most absolute expert supervision, something unthinkable of any society built upon the political State.

To focus the idea properly in your mind you have but to realize how industry today transcends all limitations of territory and leaps across rivers, mountains, and continents; then you can understand how impossible it would be to apply to such far-reaching intricate enterprises the principle of democratic control by the workers through the medium of political territorial divisions.

Under Socialism, States, territories, or provinces will exist only as geographical expressions, and have no existence as sources of governmental power, though they may be seats of administrative bodies.

Now, having grasped the idea that the administrative force of the Socialist republic of the future will function through unions industrially organized, that the principle of democratic control will operate through the workers correctly organized in such industrial unions, and that the political territorial State of capitalist society will have no place or function under Socialism, you will at once grasp the full truth embodied in the words of this member of the Socialist Party whom I have just quoted, that "only the industrial form of organization offers us even a theoretical constructive Socialist programme."

The political state and its uses

To some minds constructive Socialism is embodied in the work of our representatives on the various public bodies to which they have been elected. The various measures against the evils of capitalist property brought forward by, or as a result of, the agitation of Socialist representatives on legislative bodies are figured as being of the nature of constructive Socialism.

As we have shown, the political State of capitalism has no place under Socialism; therefore, measures which aim to place industries in the hands of, or under the control of, such a political State are in no sense steps towards that ideal; they are but useful measures to restrict the greed of capitalism and to familiarize the workers with the conception of common ownership. This latter is, indeed, their chief function.

But the enrolment of the workers in unions patterned closely after the structure of modern industries, and following the organic lines of industrial development, is par excellence the swiftest, safest, and most peaceful form of constructive work the Socialist can engage in. It prepares within the framework of capitalist society the working forms of the Socialist republic, and thus, while increasing the resisting power of the worker against present encroachments of the capitalist class, it familiarizes him with the idea that the union he is helping to build up is destined to supplant that class in the control of the industry in which he is employed.

The unions can build freedom

The power of this idea to transform the dry detail work of trade union organization into the constructive work of revolutionary Socialism, and thus to make of the unimaginative trade unionist a potent factor in the launching of a new system of society, cannot be over-estimated. It invests the sordid details of the daily incidents of the class struggle with a new and beautiful meaning, and presents them in their true light as skirmishes between the two opposing armies of light and darkness.

In the light of this principle of industrial unionism every fresh shop or factory organized under its banner is a fort wrenched from the control of the capitalist class and manned with the soldiers of the Revolution to be held by them for the workers.

On the day that the political and economic forces of Labour finally break with capitalist society and proclaim the Workers' Republic, these shops and factories so manned by industrial unionists will be taken charge of by the workers there employed, and force and effectiveness be thus given to that proclamation. Then and thus the new society will spring into existence, ready equipped to perform all the useful functions of its predecessor.

9.   The Miners' Next Step [1912]

REFORM COMMITTEE OF
THE SOUTH WALES MINERS

Collective bargaining old and new

So long as the system of working for wages endures, collective bargaining remains essential. From the men's side we cannot permit individual bargains to be made. Such individual bargains have a tendency to debase wages and conditions. On the employer's side there is no great desire for change in this matter. As will be seen by recent speeches by Mr. D. A. Thomas and Lord Merthyr, they realize its value, in its present form, to them. They have no time to bother with individuals, but prefer to purchase their labour power in bulk, on an agreed schedule. On the men's side, however, it is being realized that collective bargaining can be made so wide-reaching and all-embracing that it includes the whole of the working class. In this form the employers and the old school of labour leaders have no love for it. The employers, because they realize its dangers to their profits. The labour leaders, because it will degrade their power and influence by necessitating a much more stringent and effective democratic control than at present obtains. Let us, in order to clearly realize this, examine at close quarters the labour leader and his functions.

Reprinted from Ken Coates and Tony Topham, eds., *Workers' Control: A Book of Readings and Witnesses for Workers' Control* (London: Panther Books, 1970), pp. 14–24, by permission of Granada Publishing.

Are leaders good and necessary?

This is not a double question, since if leaders are necessary, they are perforce good. Let us then examine the leader, and see if he is necessary. A leader implies at the outset some men who are being led; and the term is used to describe a man who, in a representative capacity, has acquired combined administrative and legislative power. As such, he sees no need for any high level of intelligence in the rank and file, except to applaud his actions. Indeed such intelligence from his point of view, by breeding criticism and opposition, is an obstacle and causes confusion. His motto is "Men, be loyal to your leaders." His logical basis: Plenary powers. His social and economic prestige is dependent upon his being respected by "the public" and the employers. These are the three principles which form the platform upon which the leader stands. He presents, in common with other institutions, a good and a bad aspect.

The good side of leadership

1. Leadership tends to efficiency

One decided man who knows his own mind is stronger than a hesitating crowd. It takes time for a number of people to agree upon a given policy. One man soon makes up his mind.

2. He takes all responsibility

As a responsible leader, he knows that his advice is almost equivalent to a command, and this ensures that his advice will have been carefully and gravely considered before being tendered.

3. He stands for order and system

All too frequently, "What is everybody's business is nobody's business," and if no one stands in a position to ensure order and system, many things are omitted which will cause the men's interest to suffer.

4. He affords a standard of goodness and ability

In the sphere of public usefulness there is a great field of emulation. The good wishes of the masses can only be obtained by new aspirants for office showing a higher status of ability than the existing leaders. This tends to his continued efficiency or elimination.

5. His faithfulness and honesty are guarded

Hero worship has great attractions for the hero, and a leader has great inducements on this side, apart from pecuniary considerations, to remain faithful and honest.

The bad side of leadership

1. Leadership implies power

Leadership implies power held by the leader. Without power the leader is inept. The possession of power inevitably leads to corruption. All leaders become corrupt, in spite of their own good intentions. No man was ever good enough, brave enough, or strong enough, to have such power at his disposal, as real leadership implies.

2. Consider what it means

This power of initiative, this sense of responsibility, the self-respect which comes from expressed manhood, is taken from the men, and consolidated in the leader. The sum of their initiative, their responsibility, their self-respect becomes his.

3. The order and system

The order and system he maintains is based upon the suppression of the men, from being independent thinkers into being "the men" or "the mob." Every argument which could be advanced to justify leadership on this score would apply equally well to the Czar of all the Russians and his policy of repression. In order to be effective, the leader must keep the men in order, or he forfeits the respect of the employers and "the public," and thus becomes ineffective as a leader.

4. He corrupts the aspirants to public usefulness

He is compelled, in order to maintain his power, to see to it that only those who are willing to act as his drill sergeants or coercive agents shall enjoy his patronage. In a word, he is compelled to become an autocrat and a foe to democracy.

5. He prevents solidarity

Sheep cannot be said to have solidarity. In obedience to a shepherd, they will go up or down, backwards or forwards as they are driven by him and his dogs. But they have no solidarity, for that means unity and loyalty. Unity and loyalty not to an individual, or the policy of an individual, but to an interest and a policy which is understood and worked for by all.

6. Finally he prevents the legislative power of the workers

An industrial vote will affect the lives and happiness of workmen far more than a political vote. The power to vote whether there shall or shall not be a strike, or upon an industrial policy to be pursued by his union, will affect far more important issues to the workman's life than the political vote can ever touch. Hence it should be more sought after, and its privileges jealously guarded. Think of the tremendous power going to waste because of leadership, of the inevitable stop-block he becomes on progress, because quite naturally leaders examine every new proposal, and ask first how it will affect their position and power. It prevents large and comprehensive policies being initiated and carried out, which depend upon the understanding and watchfulness of the great majority. National strikes and policies can only be carried out when the bulk of the people see their necessity, and themselves prepare and arrange them.

Workmen the "bosses," "leaders" the servants

Is it possible to devise such an organization as will bring the above from the realm of the ideal to the realm of practicability? Those responsible for this pamphlet, men who, residing in all parts of South Wales, have given their time and thought to this problem, answer confidently in the affirmative. In these chapters they present their scheme, believing it to be not only possible, but the only practicable form of organization for us to achieve. It is divided into four parts, each of which depends upon the other. They are, the Preamble, which summarizes the needs and indicates the requirements of such an organization. The Programme, which states the objective—immediate and ultimate. The Constitution, which gives the framework in which the real worker's organization shall move, and the policy which illustrates the spirit and tactics of that organization. A careful reading of this chapter will place our scheme squarely and simply before you. Bear in mind when reading and discussing it, the faults and failures of the old form of organization, the abortiveness of all up to the present suggested improvements; and endeavour to realize, as we have done, that a complete alteration in the structure and policy of the organization is imperative.

Preamble

1. A united industrial organization, which, recognizing the war of interest between workers and employers, is constructed on fighting lines, allowing for a rapid and simultaneous stoppage of wheels throughout the mining industry.

2. A constitution giving free and rapid control by the rank and file acting in such a way that conditions will be unified throughout the coalfield; so that pressure at one point would automatically affect all others and thus readily command united action and resistance.

3. A programme of a wide and evolutionary working-class character, admitting and encouraging sympathetic action with other sections of the workers.

4. A policy which will compel the prompt and persistent use of the utmost ounce of strength, to ensure that the conditions of the workmen shall always be as good as it is possible for them to be under the then existing circumstances.

We have endeavoured to suggest methods whereby such an organization might be formed. Appended will be found our draft proposals. We simply ask that they may receive your earnest consideration, even if you think they do not entirely fit the present situation. We feel sure that they contain suggestions that will help in the solution of some of our most pressing problems. . . .

Programme

Ultimate objective

One organization to cover the whole of the Coal, Ore, Slate, Stone, Clay, Salt, mining or quarrying industry of Great Britain, with one Central Executive.

That as a step to the attainment of that ideal, strenuous efforts be made to weld all National, County, or District Federations, at present comprising the Miners' Federation of Great Britain, into one compact organization with one Central Executive, whose province it shall be to negotiate agreements and other matters requiring common action. That a cardinal principle of that organization be: that every man working in or about the mine, no matter what his craft or occupation—provisions having been made for representation on the Executive—be required to both join and observe its decisions.

Programme—political

That the organization shall engage in political action, both local and national, on the basis of complete independence of, and hostility to, all capitalist parties, with an avowed policy of wresting whatever advantage it can for the working class.

In the event of any representative of the organization losing his seat, he shall be entitled to, and receive, the full protection of the organization against victimization.

General

Alliances to be formed, and trades organizations fostered, with a view to steps being taken to amalgamate all workers into one National and International union, to work for the taking over of all industries by the workmen themselves.

The Programme is very comprehensive, because it deals with immediate objects, as well as ultimate aims. We must have our desired end in view all the time, in order to test new proposals and policies, to see whether they tend in that direction or not. For example, the working class, if it is to fight effectually, must be an army, not a mob. It must be classified, regimented and brigaded, along the lines indicated by the Product. Thus, all miners, etc., have this in common, they delve in the earth to produce the minerals, ores, gems, salt, stone, etc., which form the basis of raw material for all other industries. Similarly the railwaymen, dockers, seamen, carters, etc., form the transport industry. Therefore, before an organized and self-disciplined working class can achieve its emancipation, it must coalesce on these lines. . . . No statement of principles, however wide, embracing no programme, however widely desired and shrewdly planned; no constitution, however admirable in its structure, can be of any avail, unless the whole is quickened and animated by that which will give it the breath of life—a militant, aggressive policy. For this reason our examination of the policy must be minute and searching. The main principles are as follows:

Decentralization for negotiating

The Lodges, it will be seen, take all effective control of affairs, as long as there is any utility in local negotiation. With such a policy, Lodges become responsible and self-reliant units, with every stimulus to work out their own local salvation in their own way.

Centralization for fighting

It will be noticed that all questions are ensured a rapid settlement. So soon as the Lodge finds itself at the end of its resources, the whole fighting strength of the organization is turned on. We thus reverse the present order of things, where in the main, we centralize our negotiations and sectionalize our fighting.

The use of the irritation strike

Pending the publication of a pamphlet, which will deal in a comprehensive and orderly way with different methods and ways of striking, the following brief explanation must suffice. The Irritation Strike depends for its successful adoption on the men holding clearly the point of view that their interests and the employers' are necessarily hostile. Further that the employer is vulnerable only in one place, his profits! Therefore if the men wish to bring effective pressure to bear, they must use methods which tend to reduce profits. One way of doing this is to decrease production, while continuing at work. Quite a number of instances where this method has been successfully adopted in South Wales could be adduced. The following will serve as an example:

At a certain colliery some years ago, the management desired to introduce the use of screens for checking small coal. The men who were paid through and through for coal getting, e.g., large and small coal in gross, objected, as they saw in this the thin end of the wedge of a move to reduce their earnings. The management persisted, and the men, instead of coming out on strike, reduced their output by half. Instead of sending four trams of coal from a stall, two only were filled and so on. The management thus saw its output cut in half, while its running expenses remained the same. A few days' experience of a profitable industry turned into a losing one ended in the men winning hands down. Plenty of other instances will occur to the reader, who will readily see that production cannot be maintained at a high pressure without the willing co-operation of the workmen; so soon as they withdraw this willingness and show their discontent in a practical fashion, the wheels begin to creak. And only when the employer pours out the oil of his loving kindness by removing the grievance does the machinery begin to work smoothly again. This method is useless for the establishment of general principles over the whole industry, but can be used, like the policeman's club, to bring individual employers to reason.

Joint action by lodges

The tendency of large meetings is always towards purity of tone and breadth of outlook. The reactionary cuts a poor figure under such circumstances, however successful he may be when surrounded in his own circle by a special clique.

Unifying the men by unifying demands

It is intolerable that we should ask men to strike and suffer, if nothing is coming to them when they have helped to win the battle. We have seen many fights in this coalfield, in which all sections of underground workmen were engaged, but only to benefit one section, i.e., on a haulier's or collier's question. We must economize our strength, and see to it that every man who takes part in a fight receives something, either in improved conditions or wages as his share of the victory.

The elimination of the employer

This can only be obtained gradually and in one way. We cannot get rid of employers and slave-driving in the mining industry until all other industries have organized for, and progressed towards, the same objective. Their rate of progress conditions ours, all we can do is to set an example and the pace.

Nationalization of mines

Does not lead in this direction, but simply makes a national trust, with all the force of the Government behind it, whose one concern will be to see that the industry is run in such a way as to pay the interest on the bonds with which the Coalowners are paid out, and to extract as much more profit as possible, in order to relieve the taxation of other landlords and capitalists.

Our only concern is to see to it that those who create the value receive it. And if by the force of a more perfect organization and more militant policy, we reduce profits, we shall at the same time tend to eliminate the shareholders who own the coalfield. As they feel the increasing pressure we shall be bringing on their profits, they will loudly cry for nationalization. We shall and must strenuously oppose this in our own interests, and in the interests of our objective.

Industrial democracy the objective

Today the shareholders own and rule the coalfields. They own and rule them mainly through paid officials. The men who work in the mine are surely as competent to elect these as shareholders who may never have seen a colliery. To have a vote in determining who shall be your foreman, manager, inspector, etc., is to have a vote in determining the conditions which shall rule your working life. On that vote will depend in a large measure your safety of life and limb, your freedom from oppression by petty bosses, and would give you an intelligent interest in and control over your conditions of work. To vote for a man to represent you in Parliament, to make rules for, and assist in appointing officials to rule you, is a different proposition altogether.

Our objective begins to take shape before your eyes. Every industry thoroughly organized, in the first place, to fight, to gain control of, and then to administer that industry. The co-ordination of all industries on a Central Production Board, which, with a statistical department to ascertain the needs of the people, will issue its demands on the different departments of industry, leaving to the men themselves to determine under what conditions and how the work should be done. This would mean real democracy in real life, making for real manhood and womanhood. Any other form of democracy is a delusion and a snare.

Every fight for and victory won by the men will inevitably assist them in arriving at a clearer conception of the responsibilities and duties before them. It will also assist them to see that so long as shareholders are permitted to continue their ownership, or the State administers on behalf of the shareholders, slavery and oppression are bound to be the rule in industry. And with this realization, the agelong oppression of labour will draw to its end. The weary sigh of the over-driven slave, pitilessly exploited and regarded as an animated tool or beast of burden; the medieval serf fast bound to the soil, and life-long prisoner on his lord's domain, subject to all the caprices of his lord's lust or anger; the modern wage-slave, with nothing but his labour to sell selling that, with his manhood as a wrapper, in the world's market-place for a mess of pottage: these three phases of slavery, each in their turn inevitable and unavoidable, will have exhausted the possibilities of slavery, and mankind shall at last have leisure and inclination to really live as men, and not as the beasts which perish.

10. Guild Socialism Re-stated

[1920]

G. D. H. COLE

The demand for freedom

Guildsmen assume that the essential social values are human values, and that Society is to be regarded as a complex of associations held together by the wills of their members, whose well-being is its purpose. They assume further that it is not enough that the forms of government should have the passive or "implied" consent of the governed, but that the Society will be in health only if it is in the full sense democratic and self-governing, which implies not only that all the citizens should have a "right" to influence its policy if they so desire, but that the greatest possible opportunity should be afforded for every citizen actually to exercise this right. In other words, the Guild Socialist conception of democracy, which it assumes to be good, involves an active and not merely a passive citizenship on the part of the members. Moreover, and this is perhaps the most vital and significant assumption of all, it regards this democratic principle as applying, not only or mainly to some special sphere of social action known as "politics," but to any and every form of social action, and, in

Reprinted from *Guild Socialism Re-stated* (London: Leonard Parsons, 1920), pp. 12–15, 32–40, 46–50, 69–70, 118–29, 132–34, 136–37, by permission of Dame Margaret Cole.

especial, to industrial and economic fully as much as to political affairs.

In calling these the fundamental assumptions of Guild Socialism, I do not mean to imply that they are altogether beyond the province of argument. They can indeed be sustained by arguments of obvious force; for it seems clear enough that only a community which is self-governing in this complete sense, over the whole length and breadth of its activities, can hope to call out what is best in its members, or to give them that maximum opportunity for personal and social self-expression which is requisite to real freedom. But such arguments as this, by which the assumptions stated above may be sustained and reinforced, really depend for their appeal upon the same considerations, and are, in the last resort, different ways of stating the same fundamental position. The essence of the Guild Socialist attitude lies in the belief that Society ought to be so organised as to afford the greatest possible opportunity for individual and collective self-expression to all its members, and that this involves and implies the extension of positive self-government through all its parts.

No one can reasonably maintain that Society is organised on such a principle to-day. We do, indeed, possess in theory a very large measure of democracy; but there are at least three sufficient reasons which make this theoretical democracy largely inoperative in practice. In the first place, even the theory of democracy to-day is still largely of the "consciousness of consent" type. It assigns to the ordinary citizen little more than a privilege—which is in practice mainly illusory—of choosing his rulers, and does not call upon him, or assign to him the opportunity, himself to rule. Present-day practice has, indeed, pushed the theory of representative government to the length of substituting almost completely, even in theory, the representative for the represented. This is the essential meaning of the doctrine of the "sovereignty of Parliament." Secondly, such democracy as is recognised is conceived in a narrowly "political" sense, as applying to a quite peculiar sphere known as politics, and not in a broader and more comprehensive sense, as applying to all the acts which men do in association or conjunction. The result is that theoretical "democrats" totally ignore the effects of undemocratic organisation and convention in non-political spheres of social action, not only upon the lives which men lead in those spheres, but also in preventing and annihilating in practice the theoretical democracy of modern politics. They ignore the fact that vast inequalities of wealth and status, resulting in vast inequalities of education, power and control of environment, are necessarily fatal to any real democracy, whether in politics or in any other sphere. Thirdly, the theory of representative government is distorted not only by the substitution of the representative for the represented, but also as a consequence of the extended activity of political government falsifying the operation of the representative method. As long as the purposes of political government are comparatively few and limited, and the vast mass of social activities is either not regulated, or regulated by other means, such as the Mediaeval Gilds, it is perhaps possible for a body of men to choose one to represent them in relation to all the purposes with which a representative political body has to deal.[1] But, as the purposes covered by political government expand, and more and more of social life is brought under political regulation, the representation which may once, within its limitations, have been real, turns into misrepresentation, and the person elected for an indefinitely large number of disparate purposes ceases to have any real representative relation to those who elect him. . . .

The basis of democracy

The omnicompetent State, with its omnicompetent Parliament, is thus utterly unsuitable to any really democratic community, and must be destroyed or painlessly extinguished as it has destroyed or extinguished its rivals in the sphere of communal organisation. Whatever the structure of the new Society may be, the Guildsman is sure that it will have no place for the survival of the *factotum* State of to-day.

The essentials of democratic representation, positively stated, are, first, that the represented shall have free choice of, constant contact with, and considerable control over, his representative.[2] The second is that he should be called upon, not to choose someone to represent him as a man or as a citizen in all the aspects of citizenship, but only to choose someone to represent his point of view in relation to some particular purpose or group of purposes,

---

1. Thus government in Great Britain for some time after 1689 was a fairly adequate representation of the aristocracy, whom alone it set out to represent.

2. I am not suggesting that the representative should be reduced to the status of a delegate. . . .

in other words, some particular *function*. All true and democratic representation is therefore *functional* representation. . . .

Man should have as many distinct, and separately exercised, votes, as he has distinct social purposes or interests. But the democratic principle applies, not only to the whole body of citizens in a community in relation to each set of purposes which they have in common, but also and equally to each group of citizens who act in co-operation for the performance of any social function or who possess a common social interest. There are indeed two distinct kinds of bond which may link together in association members of the same community, and each of these bonds may exist either between all or between some of the members. The first bond is that of common vocation, the performance in common of some form of social service, whether of an economic character or not; the second bond is that of common interest, the receiving, using or consuming of such services. In the working-class world to-day, Trade Unionism is the outstanding example of the former type, and Co-operation of the latter.

In a democratic community, it is essential that the principle of self-government should apply to the affairs of every one of the associations arising out of either of these forms of common purpose. It is, from this point of view, immaterial whether a particular association includes all, or only some, of the whole body of citizens, provided that it adequately represents those who possess the common purpose which it exists to fulfil. Thus, the form of representative government or administration required for each particular service or interest will be that which most adequately represents the persons concerned in it.

But, it will be said, surely to a great extent everything is everybody's concern. It is certainly not the exclusive concern of the coal miners, or of the workers in any other particular industry, how their service is conducted; for everybody, including every other industry, is concerned as a consumer of coal. Nor is it by any means the exclusive concern of the teachers what the educational system is, or how it is administered; for the whole people is concerned in education as the greatest civic service. On the other hand, the coal industry clearly concerns the miner, and education concerns the teacher, in a way different from that in which they concern the rest of the people; for, whereas for the latter coal is only one among a number of commodities, and education one among several civic services, to the miner or the teacher his own calling is the most important single concern in social life.

This distinction really brings us to the heart of our problem, and to the great practical difference between Guild Socialism and other schools of Socialist opinion. For the Guildsman maintains that in a right apprehension of this distinction, and in the framing of social arrangements which recognise and make full provision for it, lies the key to the whole question at issue. It is absurd to deny the common interest which all the members of the community have, as consumers and users, in the vital industries, or as sharers of a common culture and code in such a service as education; but it is no less futile to deny the special, and even more intense, concern which the miners have in the organisation of their industry, or the teachers in the conduct of the educational system.

Nevertheless, there are schools of Socialist, or quasi-Socialist thought, which take their stand upon each of these impossible denials. The Collectivist, or State Socialist, who regards the State as representing the consumer, and the purely "Co-operative" idealist, who sees in Co-operation a far better consumers' champion, are alike in refusing to recognise the claim of the producer, or service renderer, to self-government in his calling. The pure "Syndicalist," or the pure "Industrial Unionist," on the other hand, denies, or at least used to deny, the need of any special representation of the consumers' standpoint, and presses for an organisation of Society based wholly on production or the rendering of service.

It has been the work of Guild Socialism to hold the balance between these two schools of thought, not by splitting the difference, but by pointing out that the solution lies in a clear distinction of function and sphere of activity. The phrase "control of industry"[3] is in fact loosely used to include the claims of both producers and consumers; but it has, in the two uses, really to a great extent different meanings, and, still more, different associations. When the "Syndicalist" or the Guild Socialist speaks of the need for control by the producers, or when a Trade Union itself demands control, the reference is mainly to the internal conditions of the industry, to the way in which the factory or place of work is managed, the administrators appointed, the conditions determined, and, above all, to the amount of freedom *at his work*

---

3. For the rest of this chapter I shall speak only in terms of industry, and not of services such as education, not because I think that one phraseology or treatment will cover both, but because I am reserving the "civic services" for separate discussion. . . .

which the worker by hand or brain enjoys. When, on the other hand, a State Socialist or a Co-operator speaks of the need for "consumers' control," he is thinking mainly of the quantity and quality of the goods supplied, of the excellence of the distribution, of the price of sale—in short, of a set of considerations which, while they are intimately bound up with those which chiefly concern the producer, are still in essence distinct, and have to do far less with the internal conduct of the industry than with its external relations. . . .

The Guild Socialist endeavours to hold the scales fairly, and to decide, as far as the matter can be decided except in practice, what are the fair claims on each side.

In doing this, the Guildsman has not to face any problem of arbitrating between divergent interests. In a democratic Society, the whole body of consumers and the whole body of producers are practically the same people, only ranged in the two cases in different formations. . . .

The Guild Socialist contends, then, that the internal management and control of each industry or service must be placed, as a trust on behalf of the community, in the hands of the workers engaged in it; but he holds no less strongly that full provision must be made for the representation and safeguarding of the consumers' point of view in relation to each service. Similarly, he contends that general questions of industrial administration extending to all industries should, where they mainly concern the whole body of producers, be entrusted to an organisation representing all the producers; but he holds equally that the general point of view of all types of consumers must be fully represented and safeguarded in relation to industry as a whole. . . . Let us ask ourselves whether, if all industry passed under the management of a "State," however democratic, or of a Co-operative Movement, however enlightened, the workers engaged in its various branches would have the sense of being free and self-governing in relation to their work. It is true that they would be voters in the democratic State, or members of the Co-operative Society, and would therefore, in a sense, be ultimately part-controllers in some degree of their conditions; but would they regard this as freedom, when, although their concern in the internal arrangements of their industry was far closer than that of others, they had at most only the same voice with others in determining them? Obviously, the answer is that they neither would, nor could be expected to, take any such view; for, by the time their share in determining conditions had gone its roundabout course through the consumers' organisation, it would have ceased to be recognisable as even the most indirect sort of freedom. . . .

A guild in being

The element of identity between the Mediaeval Gilds and the National Guilds proposed by the Guild Socialists to-day is far more of spirit than of organisation. A National Guild would be an association of all the workers by hand and brain concerned in the carrying on of a particular industry or service, and its function would be actually to carry on that industry or service on behalf of the whole community. Thus, the Railway Guild would include all the workers of every type—from general managers and technicians to porters and engine cleaners—required for the conduct of the railways as a public service. This association would be entrusted by the community with the duty and responsibility of administering the railways efficiently for the public benefit, and would be left itself to make the internal arrangements for the running of trains and to choose its own officers, administrators, and methods of organisation.

I do not pretend to know or prophesy exactly how many Guilds there would be, or what would be the lines of demarcation between them. For example, railways and road transport might be organised by separate Guilds, or by a single Guild with internal subdivisions. So might engineering and shipbuilding, and a host of other closely-related industries. This is a matter, not of principle, but of convenience; for there is no reason why the various Guilds should be of anything like uniform size. The general basis of the proposed Guild organisation is clear enough: it is industrial, and each National Guild will represent a distinct and coherent service or group of services.

It must not, however, be imagined that Guildsmen are advocating a highly centralised system, in which the whole of each industry will be placed under a rigid central control. The degree of centralisation will largely depend on the character of the service. Thus, the railway industry obviously demands a much higher degree of centralisation than the building industry, which serves mainly a local market. But, apart from this, Guildsmen are keen advocates of the greatest possible extension of local initiative and of autonomy for the small group, in which they see the best chance of keeping the whole organisation keen, fresh and adaptable, and of avoiding the tendency to rigidity and conservatism in the wrong things, so characteristic of large-scale organisation, and especially of trusts and combines under capitalism to-day. The National Guilds would be, indeed, for the most part co-ordinating rather than directly controlling bodies, and would be concerned more with the adjustment of supply and demand than with the direct control or management of their several industries. . . .

The factory, or place of work, will be the natural unit of Guild life. It will be, to a great extent, internally self-governing, and it will be the unit and basis of the wider local and national government of the Guild. The freedom of the particular factory as a unit is of fundamental importance, because the object of the whole Guild system is to call out the spirit of free service by establishing really democratic conditions in industry. This democracy, if it is to be real, must come home to, and be exercisable directly by, every individual member of the Guild. He must feel that he is enjoying real self-government and freedom *at his work;* or he will not work well and under the impulse of the communal spirit. Moreover, the essential basis of the Guild being associative service, the spirit of association must be given free play in the sphere in which it is best able to find expression. This is manifestly the factory, in which men have the habit and tradition of working together. The factory is the natural and fundamental unit of industrial democracy. This involves, not only that the factory must be free, as far as possible, to manage its own affairs, but also that the democratic unit of the factory must be made the basis of the larger democracy of the Guild, and that the larger organs of Guild administration and government must be based largely on the principle of factory[4] representation. I have spoken of the Guilds as examples of "industrial democracy" and "democratic association," and we must understand clearly wherein this Guild democracy consists, and especially how it bears on the relations between the different classes of workers included in a single Guild. For since a Guild includes *all* the workers by hand and brain engaged in a common service, it is clear that there will be among its members very wide divergences of function, of technical skill, and of admin-

---

4. It should be understood throughout that, when I speak thus of the "factory," I mean to include under it also the mine, the shipyard, the dock, the station, and every corresponding place which is a natural centre of production or service. Every industry has some more or less close equivalent for the factory.

istrative authority. Neither the Guild as a whole nor the Guild factory can determine all issues by the expedient of the mass vote, nor can Guild democracy mean that, on all questions, each member is to count as one and none as more than one. A mass vote on a matter of technique understood only by a few experts would be a manifest absurdity, and, even if the element of technique is left out of account, a factory administered by constant mass votes would be neither efficient nor at all a pleasant place to work in. . . .

Guild system in industry

The Industrial Guilds Congress, successor to the Trades Union Congress of to-day, would represent directly every Guild concerned with industry or economic service. It too would have its local and regional counterparts in local and regional Guild Councils, successors to the Trades Councils and Federations of Trades Councils which now exist. And again, in order that the tendency to a centralising point of view may be avoided, these local Councils, or at least the regional Councils representative of them, should be directly represented in the Industrial Guilds Congress. The local point of view will require to be strongly put, and, since the bulk of inter-Guild exchange will be likely to take place locally, these Local Guild Councils will clearly be bodies of very great economic importance. . . .

The structure of the commune

We have so far passed in review four distinct forms of organisation, each of which has subdivisions of its own. First we reviewed the *producers'* organisation of the economic Guilds; then, the *consumers'* organisation of the Co-operative Movement and the Collective Utility Councils; then the *civic service* of the Civic Guilds; and lastly, the *civic,* or *citizen organisation* of the Cultural and Health Councils. . . .

This leads us directly to a further consideration of the position of "the State"; for orthodox social theorists usually claim for "the State" the supreme task of expressing the spirit of the community, and the positive power of co-ordinating and directing the activities of all the various parts of the social structure. First, we criticised the structure of the State from the point of view of functional democracy, showing that its undifferentiated representative theory unfitted it to be the expression of a democratic spirit which ought to find utterance in every separate aspect of social activity. By this criticism we destroyed the idea of State "omnicompetence." Secondly, in dealing with Collectivist theories in the economic sphere, we destroyed the idea that the State represents the consumer, and so excluded it from functional participation in the control of industry or service. Inferentially, this criticism applied also to the civic services in relation to which we showed that representation must equally have a functional basis. We have thus, besides destroying the notion of State "omnicompetence," definitely excluded it from a place in the control of economic and civic services alike. We have not, however, as yet overthrown the notion of State Sovereignty in a form in which it has been re-stated with the definite purpose of meeting these objections.[5]

This revised theory rejects State omnicompetence and agrees, at least in general terms, to the exclusion of the State from the normal working of all social functions; but it retains in the background a State "whose function is Sovereignty," that is, which has no other task than that of co-ordinating the activities of the various functional bodies in Society. Now, it is, of course, perfectly clear that the functional democracy which we have been expounding requires and must have a clearly recognised co-ordinating agency, and there would be no objection to calling this agency "the State," if the name did not immediately suggest two entirely misleading ideas. The first is that this new body will be historically continuous with the present political machinery of Society; the second is that it will, to a great extent, reproduce its structure, especially in being based on direct, non-functional election. The co-ordinating body which is required cannot be, in any real sense, historically continuous with the present State, and it must not reproduce in any important respect the structure of the present State. . . .

The new co-ordinating body will not be continuous with the present political machinery of Society for two good and sufficient reasons. The first, clearly laid down in modern Marxist teaching, and most clearly of all by Lenin,[6] is that the present political

---

5. For instance, in a series of articles in the *New Age* a few years ago.

6. See his book, *The State and Revolution.*

machine is definitely an organ of class domination, not merely because it has been perverted by the power of capitalists, but because it is based on coercion, and is primarily an instrument of coercion. Its essential idea is that of an externally imposed "order," and its transformation into a form expressive of self-government and freedom is impossible. . . .

In the second place, this machine, where it has adapted itself to so-called "political democracy," is based essentially on the false idea of representative government which assumes that one man can represent another, not *ad hoc,* in relation to a particular purpose or group of purposes, but absolutely. This false notion of representation we have already rejected in favour of the functional idea.

But it may be argued that the defence of the State, in its new form, meets this argument; for the new "function of the State" is simply co-ordination, and nothing else. This contention, however, will not hold water; for the co-ordination of functions is not, and cannot be, itself a function. Either co-ordination includes the functions which it co-ordinates, in which case the whole of social organisation comes again under the domination of the State, and the whole principle of functional democracy is destroyed; or it excludes them, and in this case it clearly cannot co-ordinate. In other words, the State "representative" either controls the economic and civic spheres or he does not: if he does, the representatives in these spheres lose their self-government; if he does not, he cannot regulate their mutual relationships. . . .

We can, then, safely assume that not only will the present political machine lose its economic and civic functions to new bodies, but that the task of co-ordinating these functions will also pass out of its hands. It will thus, at the least, "wither away" to a very considerable extent, and I have no hesitation in saying that, in my belief, it will disappear altogether, either after a frontal attack, or by atrophy following upon dispossession of its vital powers. . . .

We have, then, to seek a new form of co-ordinating body which will not be inconsistent with the functional democracy on which our whole system is based. This can be nothing other than a bringing together of the various functional bodies whose separate working we have already described. Co-ordination is inevitably coercive unless it is self-co-ordination, and it must therefore be accomplished by the common action of the various bodies which require co-ordination.

This problem of co-ordination has two separate aspects. It is first a problem of co-ordinating the functional bodies of the various types into a single communal system, and it is secondly a problem of co-ordinating bodies operating over a smaller with bodies operating over a larger area. Both these problems have to be solved in the structure of the co-ordinating, or as I shall henceforward call it, the *communal,* organisation of Guild Socialist Society.

In order, for the first discussion, to reduce the problem to as simple elements as possible, let us take it in the form in which it presents itself in a single town—say Norwich. In Norwich there will be at least the following bodies possessing important social functions:

(a) A number of Industrial Guilds organising and managing various industries and economic services united in a Guild Council of delegates or representatives drawn from these Guilds; (b) a Co-operative Council; (c) a Collective Utilities Council; (d) a number of Guilds organising and managing various civic services —Civil Guilds; (e) a Cultural Council; and (f) a Health Council.

All these, not necessarily in the same proportions, have clearly a right to be represented on the communal body, which I shall call hereafter simply the *Commune.* . . .

The bodies so far mentioned, however, do not necessarily complete the composition of the Commune. In any instance, there might be special organisations to which it would be desirable, on account of their importance in the town, to give representation. Again, what is far more important, the town as a whole cannot be treated as an undifferentiated unit. In electing their representatives to serve on the four Councils mentioned above,[7] the citizens, if the town were of any size, would almost certainly vote by Wards and each member of a Council would sit there as a Ward representative in relation to his particular function. It is of the first importance, if this representation is to be a reality, that the Ward should exist, not merely as a polling district for various elections, but also as an active centre for the expression of local opinion, which requires, for its successful eliciting, to be made articulate within the smallest natural areas of common feeling. Indeed, in the sphere both of consumers and of civic organisation, the Ward in the town and the village in the country form the nat-

7. I. e., Councils as distinct from Guilds, which would have their own varying electoral methods.

ural equivalents for the workshop in the sphere of industry or the school in the sphere of education.

The Wards, then, in our case of Norwich, must have a real existence, and the Ward representatives must report back regularly to, and receive instructions and advice from, Ward Meetings of all the dwellers in the Ward who choose to attend. The Ward Meeting would also exercise, within the limits to be discussed hereafter, the right of recalling from any Council the Ward representative. It would also, especially in the larger towns, have assigned to it certain administrative functions which are best carried out over a very small area, and would execute these either in full Ward Meeting, or by the appointment of *ad hoc* and usually temporary committees or officers. Where, in a larger centre, the functions of the Wards expanded, standing Ward Committees might be developed, and it might be desirable that these Ward Committees should have direct representation in respect of their functions, on the Town Commune.[8] In such cases, these representatives would form a third group distinct both from the Guild and from the Council representatives.

Having laid down the essential structure of the Norwich Commune, let us try to see more explicitly what work it would have to do. What we say under this head will apply, with small changes, to the other types of Commune hereafter described. Clearly, it would be, in the main, not an administrative but a co-ordinating body. The various services would be managed by their Guilds and their policy would be determined by the co-operative working of the Guilds and the appropriate citizen Councils. Five essential tasks would remain for the Commune itself. First, it would have to agree upon the allocation of the local resources among the various services calling for expenditure—that is, it would have essential *financial* functions, and would be, indeed, the financial pivot of the whole Guild system in the area. Secondly, it would be the court of appeal in all cases of differences between functional bodies of different types. Thus, if the Co-operative Society could not agree on some point of policy with the Guilds operating in the sphere of "domestic" production and distribution, the Commune would have to hear the case and give its judgement. Thirdly, it would determine the lines of demarcation between the various functional bodies, where any question con-

8. I assume that the election of the various Council representatives would be by ballot of the Wards, but that these Ward Committee representatives would be chosen either by the Ward Committee, or, better, from the Ward Committee by the Ward Meeting. Uniformity, however, is not necessary.

cerning them arose.[9] Fourthly, it would itself take the initiative in any matter concerning the town as a whole and not in any functional capacity, such as a proposed extension of town boundaries or a proposal to build a new town hall. The original suggestion, in such cases, would probably come from one of the functional bodies or from a Ward; but they would be matters for the Town Commune itself to decide. Fifthly, so far as coercive machinery, such as a police force, remained, it should be controlled, not by any single functional body, but by all jointly—that is, by the Commune. This, as we shall see, applies also in the realm of law. The Commune could decide to hand over, and would, wherever possible, be wise to hand over actual administrative functions falling within its sphere to the Wards, in order to preserve the most direct form of popular control. Thus, I should like to see the Wards appoint and control the police—a reversion to the days of the town or village constable. . . .

Each region would be a complex of town and country, and the Regional Commune would have to be based on a full recognition of this fact. It would, of course, have to provide in the first place for the direct representation of the various functional bodies within the Region. The form of this representation is clear enough on the Guild side; for the Guilds, industrial, agricultural, or civic, would have their own regional administrations, and from these the Guild representatives would be drawn. But we have so far said nothing of regional organisation of consumers or of citizens, which is clearly required to correspond to the regional Guilds and to express the consumers' or the civic point of view in relation to the regional services.

Clearly, then, there must be regional Cooperative Societies or Unions, regional Collective Utilities Councils, and regional Cultural Councils and Health Councils. These, I believe, would be best constituted of representatives from the various local functional Councils of the Towns and Townships within the Region. This, it is true, involves indirect election, to which many professing democrats take objection; but I have no faith at all in the virtues of direct election except when it can be combined with a constant touch of the body of voters with their representative. Thus, direct election is good in the village or the Ward, because

---

9. I do not mean, of course, that if two Industrial Guilds fell out, the Commune would settle the matter. It would go to the Guild Council. But if the Guild Council failed to settle it, even such a difference might go to the Commune.

all the electors can meet with, question, and instruct their representative face to face; but it is a farce in the case of Parliament, where the constituency is too large for the elected person to preserve any real contact with those who elected him. The real safeguard for the voter is to preserve the fullest form of democracy, including the right of recall, in the small units within which real contact is possible, and to rely on this contact and power of recall for the carrying out of the popular will in the larger bodies. These larger bodies can themselves best be composed of delegates from the bodies working within the smaller areas, always provided that these delegates themselves preserve constant contact with the smaller bodies which choose them, and are subject to the right of these bodies to recall them at any time....

According to our current terminology, all the foregoing Communes would be regarded as organs of Local Government. At present, however, we draw a sharp and almost absolute distinction between Local and Central Government. In the decentralised Guild Society of which we are speaking, no such sharp distinction would exist; for by far the greatest part of the work of the community would be carried on and administered locally or regionally, and the central work would be divided, according to the function, among a considerable number of distinct organisations. There would therefore be neither need nor opportunity for a centre round which a vast aggregation of bureaucratic and coercive machinery could grow up. The national co-ordinating machinery of Guild Society would be essentially unlike the present State, and would have few direct administrative functions. It would be mainly a source of a few fundamental decisions on policy, demarcation between functional bodies, and similar issues, and of final adjudications on appeals in cases of dispute; but it would not possess any vast machinery of its own, save that, as long as military and naval force continued to be employed, it would have to exercise directly the control of such force, as it would indirectly and in the last resort of the law. Foreign relations, so far as they did not deal exclusively with matters falling within the sphere either of the economic or of the civic bodies, would fall to its lot; but the victory of democracy in other communities would tend to reduce these non-functional external activities to a minimum. The existence, which we have already assumed, of national functional organisations, based on the local and regional bodies, in all the various spheres of social action, would functionalise national equally with local and regional activities.

11. Two Years' Working of the Building Guilds in England [1922]

C. S. JOSLYN

The following is a brief summary of an investigation undertaken by the writer during the winter and spring of 1921–1922 into the work of the Building Guilds of Great Britain. Only a few aspects of the many-sided development of the Guilds can here be treated.

Extent of operations

Some idea of the magnitude of the Guild operations to date may be gathered from the following facts. The National Building Guild, Ltd., probably represents the largest single building concern in England to-day. Its organization is reported to comprise over 140 local Guild committees, only about half of which, however, are active. It employs 6,000 operatives, a number constituting between one and two per cent of the total Building Trade Union membership. Its contracts on hand total approximately £2,500,000, of which the London Guild has about £650,000, and its plant and equipment in London alone is valued at something over £20,000. Finally, it has to its credit about 1,200

Reprinted from Niles Carpenter, *Guild Socialism: An Historical and Critical Analysis* (New York: D. Appleton, 1922), Appendix I, pp. 329–35, by permission of Prentice-Hall, Inc.

houses constructed for Local Authorities throughout the United Kingdom, at an estimated cost of £1,000,000.

Structure of the guilds

The fundamental unit of Building organization is the local Guild committee. This is ordinarily composed of one or two, but not more than two, representatives from each local Trade Union connected with the Building Industry. In addition to this, one elected representative from any "approved group" of building trades workers, whether administrative, technical, or operative, may sit upon the committee. The London Guild, owing to the wide extent of the metropolitan area, has evolved a supplemental type of Guild organization known as the Area Committee, composed of one or two representatives from each local committee in a designated area or district. In other cases, as at Walthamstow, where the work in hand is centered mainly in a single locality, the Area Committee may take direct representation from the local Trade Unions. These and other anomalies in the Guild structure are now being overhauled.

An extra-constitutional development in the local Building Guild organization is the Works Committee, set up in connection with each contract of any considerable size, and usually composed of one representative from each craft at work on the job and elected by the workers on the site. At Walthamstow and Greenwich the Works Committees on the two housing schemes are represented on the Area Committees through cooption. The status of the Works Committee is still a cause for much spirited dispute among the Guildsmen, but it is certain to play an important part in the Guild organization of the future and before long its functions will probably be more clearly defined in the Constitution.

The Regional Council, of which there are nominally ten in Great Britain, is formed of not less than ten Guild Committees, and is based upon the regional areas of the National Federation of Building Trades Operatives. In London the Council is composed of eleven members representing the unions affiliated to the N.F.B.T.O., nine members representing the Area Committees in different parts of London, one representative of an approved group of architects and surveyors, one from the Electrical Trades Union, and one from the National Union of Clerks.

The National Board, the governing body of the National

Building Guild, is composed of one representative from each Regional Council, nominated and elected by the Guild Committees in that region. The Trade Unions, as such, are not represented on the National Board, but it is expected that arrangements will soon be made for such representation, inasmuch as the Building Guild, to use the words of Mr. S. G. Hobson, is "throughout its structure a Trade Union body." Indeed, this is the outstanding feature of the organization and functioning of the Guilds.

Administrators and technicians

At the head of each Guild Committee, and elected by its members, are a chairman and secretary, who may or may not be members of the Committee, but must be members in good standing of their own Trade Unions. Supervising the work of each craft on a job is a departmental foreman, appointed by the Guild Committee upon the recommendation of the Managing Committee of the Trade Union concerned. The general foreman, who has charge of all the work on a given contract, is appointed by the Guild Committee, subject to the approval of the Regional Board, from candidates submitted to the Committee by the various Trade Unions. No foreman, it should be remarked, is appointed by the men working on a given contract, a fact which may account in some measure for the considerable vogue which the Works Committees have so far achieved among the rank and file. The decision to recall is in the hands of the appointing committees.

The Regional Council or Board appoints its own officers, selecting them from applications sent in by suitable candidates. These are: the Regional Secretary, whose work, to use the words of Mr. Malcolm Sparkes, is "to open up new business for the Guild, to conduct its general administration, and to organize its publicity"; the Accountant, who has charge of the cost and other accounting; and, in London, the Building Organizer, who issues estimates and conducts the building operations.

In addition to this, each Regional Council is supposed to possess a full complement of technicians, including architects, surveyors, engineers, etc., although in practice this ideal is seldom realized. The surveyor is usually paid on a salary or commission basis (three-fourths percent), while the architects receive the customary fees prevailing in private industry. The salaries of the heads of departments, e.g., the Regional Secretary and the Accountant, are from 25 to 50 percent above those of general foremen, which, in turn, are about twice the standard rate for operatives. Departmental foremen receive 3d. per hour above the standard rate.

Distribution of function

A prominent characteristic, and a troublesome one, of the Guild distribution of control, is that of local autonomy. The local Guild Committee is responsible in all cases for the carrying out of contracts, appoints its own foremen, and controls its own bank account, drawing and signing checks for wages, materials, and all other purposes. It cannot, however, pledge the credit of the Regional Council without the Council's consent, nor can that body in turn pledge the credit of the National Board—which, under the recent amalgamation, is the legal entity for the purpose of signing contracts, arranging credit, organizing finance, and in general assuming the legal liabilities involved in the business— without the Board's consent. Subject to these limitations, the Regional Councils have full power to enter into and carry out all contracts, exercising general supervision over the work of the Guild Committees for this purpose, and also have general charge of supplies, finance, continuous pay, etc.

No one holding a managerial position can have a vote on the Regional Council. The departmental heads do, however, attend the meetings of the Board in an advisory capacity, and are likely to have their way if they can carry conviction among the members by a reasoned statement of their views. No formal referendum is ever taken among the rank and file on questions of policy or technique, but in London there has developed an unofficial organization known as the Area Conference. This is a monthly meeting of delegates from all the Area Committees, at which the management is fully represented, and its purpose is to bring the rank and file into close touch with administrative problems of the Guild. Many questions are referred from the Regional Board to the Area Conference for discussion and settlement.

The distribution of function as between the Works Committee and the Guild Committee is still an unsettled question. There is a strong pressure of opinion among the rank and file for extending the functions of the Works Committees to include even that of actual management, and it is undeniable that some resentment has been caused by the manner of appointment of foremen and administrators, who are not subject to direct control by the rank and file. To the writer, wherever he has carried his investigation, this has seemed in the highest degree providential. It is pretty generally the opinion among the Guild management that control by Works Committees is not conducive to the greatest efficiency, and their counsel in this matter is likely to prevail.

Continuous pay[1]

The standard rate established by the Wages and Conditions Council of the Building Industry constitutes the basic rate of pay for all operatives in the service of the Guild. In addition to this the workers receive: (1) pay for time lost through accidents at approximately the standard rate, including the amount payable under the Workmen's Compensation Act; (2) pay for time lost through holidays or bad weather at the full standard rate; and (3) pay for time lost through sickness, at 50 percent of the standard rate, for terms varying from four weeks to six weeks per man per year, according to the length of service. This modified scale of sick pay was adopted in January, 1922.

The cost of continuous pay for the London Guilds for the year ending March 31, 1922, works out at something like 3½ percent of the total wages bill.

Building costs

Only the single instance of the Walthamstow Guild can here be cited. Tenders from seven different competitors for the erection of the 400 houses were received by the Walthamstow Urban District Council. The accepted estimate of the London Guild works out at more than £14,000 below the lowest estimate submitted by the private contractors. Figures in the writer's possession show an *average* saving over *average* basic price on houses so far completed, as follows: on Type 119, of about £38 per house; on Type 183, of about £10 per house; and on Type 171, of about £12 per house. Similar figures for Greenwich show an approximate saving, over the estimates, of £73 per house on Type B. 3. S., and of £33 per house on Type B. 4. N.[2]

Guild workmanship

The workmanship of the Guilds is almost universally admitted to be superior to that of the general run of private contractors. Not least in significance is the testimony of the employers themselves, who from time to time have submitted evidence purporting to show that the efficiency of labor on Guild contracts, as regards costs, is over twice that on private builders' work. Experts are virtually unanimous in the opinion that the workmanship of the Guildsmen, as regards quality, is markedly superior to the workers on private contracts. From personal observation the writer can state that, although the efficiency of Guild labor did not strike him as anything remarkable, at least when compared with American standards, it certainly excelled the average of the private contractors and came very near to equaling, in external appearance at least, even the best organized of private building concerns.

NOTES

1. "Maintenance"–*N.C.*

2. *Author's note.* It might be well to point out the significance of these facts. The Building Guilds have been able pretty consistently to underbid "private" contractors, and then have saved money *on their own estimates.* This means that their costs have been low enough to permit them to cut under the average prices for building work, and to make additional savings on those reduced rates. The total economics represented by this double saving must be very considerable. This circumstance is the more remarkable in view of the fact that the Guilds had at least two types of expense which the average "private" builder did not encounter. First, they made heavy outlays for "continuous pay," amounting, as shown above, to $3\frac{1}{2}$ percent of their total wages bill, and, second, as new enterprises, operating on slender financial resources, they must have had to make heavy provision for offices, "plant," and the inevitable losses involved in new undertakings. Furthermore, as the succeeding section shows, there is general agreement that the *quality* of the Guilds' work has been superior to that of ordinary "private" contracting. This means that economy has not been achieved at the expense of workmanship and material; on the contrary, the Guilds have been more liberal with both than their rivals.

The conclusion seems inevitable that—at least in this industry, and at this stage of development—the Building Guilds have secured such a large measure of personal efficiency, organizing ability, and all-around *esprit de corps,* as to enable them to do better work than the average "private" builder at very much less cost–*N.C.*

12. Roads to Freedom [1918]

BERTRAND RUSSELL

From the point of view of liberty, what system would be the best? In what direction should we wish the forces of progress to move?

From this point of view, neglecting for the moment all other considerations, I have no doubt that the best system would be one not far removed from that advocated by Kropotkin, but rendered more practicable by the adoption of the main principles of Guild Socialism. Since every point can be disputed, I will set down without argument the kind of organization of work that would seem best.

Education should be compulsory up to the age of sixteen, or perhaps longer; after that, it should be continued or not at the option of the pupil, but remain free (for those who desire it) up to at least the age of twenty-one. When education is finished, no one should be *compelled* to work, and those who choose not to work should receive a bare livelihood, and be left completely free; but probably it would be desirable that there should be a strong public opinion in favour of work, so that only comparatively few should choose idleness. One great advantage of making idleness economically possible is that it would afford a powerful

Reprinted from *Roads to Freedom* (London: George Allen & Unwin, 1918), pp. 192–210, by permission of the publisher.

motive for making work not disagreeable; and no community where most work is disagreeable can be said to have found a solution of economic problems. I think it reasonable to assume that few would choose idleness, in view of the fact that even now at least nine out of ten of those who have (say) £100 a year from investments prefer to increase their income by paid work.

Coming now to that great majority who will not choose idleness, I think we may assume that, with the help of science, and by the elimination of the vast amount of unproductive work involved in internal and international competition, the whole community could be kept in comfort by means of four hours' work a day. It is already being urged by experienced employers that their employees can actually produce as much in a six hours' day as they can when they work eight hours. In a world where there is a much higher level of technical instruction than there is now, the same tendency will be accentuated. People will be taught not only, as at present, one trade, or one small portion of a trade, but several trades, so that they can vary their occupation according to the seasons and the fluctuations of demand. Every industry will be self-governing as regards all internal affairs, and even separate factories will decide for themselves all questions that only concern those who work in them. There will be no capitalist management, as at present, but management by elected representatives, as in politics. Relations between different groups of producers will be settled by the Guild Congress, matters concerning the community as the inhabitants of a certain area will continue to be decided by Parliament, while all disputes between Parliament and the Guild Congress will be decided by a body composed of representatives of both in equal numbers.

Payment will not be made, as at present, only for work actually required and performed, but for willingness to work. This system is already adopted in much of the better paid work: a man occupies a certain position, and retains it even at times when there happens to be very little to do. The dread of unemployment and loss of livelihood will no longer haunt men like a nightmare. Whether all who are willing to work will be paid equally, or whether exceptional skill will still command exceptional pay, is a matter which may be left to each Guild to decide for itself. An opera-singer who received no more pay than a scene-shifter might choose to be a scene-shifter until the system was changed: if so, higher pay would probably be found necessary. But if it were freely voted by the Guild, it could hardly constitute a grievance.

Whatever might be done towards making work agreeable, it is to be presumed that some trades would always remain unpleasant. Men could be attracted into these by higher pay or shorter hours, instead of being driven into them by destitution. The community would then have a strong economic motive for finding ways of diminishing the disagreeableness of these exceptional trades. . . .

Government and Law will still exist in our community, but both will be reduced to a minimum. There will still be acts which will be forbidden—for example, murder. But very nearly the whole of that part of the criminal law which deals with property will have become obsolete, and many of the motives which now produce murders will be no longer operative. Those who nevertheless still do commit crimes will not be blamed or regarded as wicked: they will be regarded as unfortunate, and kept in some kind of mental hospital until it is thought that they are no longer a danger. By education and freedom and the abolition of private capital, the number of crimes can be made exceedingly small. By the method of individual curative treatment it will generally be possible to secure that a man's first offence shall also be his last, except in the case of lunatics and the feeble-minded, for whom of course a more prolonged but not less kindly detention may be necessary.

Government may be regarded as consisting of two parts: the one, the decisions of the community or its recognized organs; the other, the enforcing of those decisions upon all who resist them. The first part is not objected to by Anarchists. The second part, in an ordinary civilized State, may remain entirely in the background: those who have resisted a new law while it was being debated will, as a rule, submit to it when it is passed, because resistance is generally useless in a settled and orderly community. But the possibility of governmental force remains, and indeed is the very reason for the submission which makes force unnecessary. . . .

The practice of government by majorities, which Anarchists criticise, is in fact open to most of the objections which they urge against it. Still more objectionable is the power of the executive in matters vitally affecting the happiness of all, such as peace and war. But neither can be dispensed with suddenly. There are, however, two methods of diminishing the harm done by them. (1) Government by majorities can be made less oppressive by devolution, by placing the decision of questions primarily affecting only a section of the community in the hands of that section, rather than of a Central Chamber. In this way, men are no longer forced to submit to decisions made in a hurry by people mostly ignorant of the matter in hand and not personally interested. Autonomy for internal affairs should be given, not only to areas but to all groups, such as industries or Churches, which have important common interests not shared by the rest of the community. (2) The great powers vested in the executive of a modern State are chiefly due to the frequent need of rapid decisions, especially as regards foreign affairs. If the danger of war were practically eliminated, more cumbrous but less autocratic methods would be possible, and the Legislature might recover many of the powers which the executive has usurped. By these two methods, the intensity of the interference with liberty involved in government can be gradually diminished. . . .

The process of leading men's thought and imagination away from the use of force will be greatly accelerated by the abolition of the capitalist system, provided it is not succeeded by a form of State Socialism in which officials have enormous power. At present, the capitalist has more control over the lives of others than any man ought to have; his friends have authority in the State; his economic power is the pattern for political power. In a world where all men and women enjoy economic freedom, there will not be the same habit of command nor, consequently, the same love of despotism; a gentler type of character than that now prevalent will gradually grow up. Men are formed by their circumstances, not born ready-made. The bad effect of the present economic system on character, and the immensely better effect to be expected from communal ownership, are among the strongest reasons for advocating the change. . . .

Our discussion has led us to the belief that the communal ownership of land and capital, which constitutes the characteristic doctrine of Socialism and Anarchist Communism, is a necessary step towards the removal of the evils from which the world suffers at present and the creation of such a society as any humane man must wish to see realized. But though a necessary step, Socialism alone is by no means sufficient. There are various forms of Socialism: the form in which the State is the employer and all who work receive wages from it involves dangers of tyranny and interference with progress which would make it, if possible, even worse than the present *régime*. On the other hand, Anarchism, which avoids the dangers of State Socialism, has dangers and difficulties of its own, which make it probable that, within any reasonable period of time, it could not last long even if it were established. Nevertheless it remains an ideal to which we should wish to approach as nearly as possible, and which, in some distant age, we hope may be reached completely. Syndicalism shares many of the defects of Anarchism, and, like it, would prove unstable, since the need of a central government would make itself felt almost at once.

The system we have advocated is a form of Guild Socialism, leaning more, perhaps, towards Anarchism than the official Guildsman would approve. It is in the matters that politicians usually ignore—science and art, human relations, and the joy of life—that Anarchism is strongest, and it is chiefly for the sake of these things that we included such more or less Anarchist proposals as the "vagabond's wage." It is by its effects outside economics and politics, at least as much as by effects inside them, that a social system should be judged. And if Socialism ever comes, it is only likely to prove beneficent if non-economic goods are valued and consciously pursued.

The world that we must seek is a world in which the creative spirit is alive, in which life is an adventure full of joy and hope, based rather upon the impulse to construct than upon the desire to retain what we possess or to seize what is possessed by others. It must be a world in which affection has free play, in which love is purged of the instinct for domination, in which cruelty and envy have been dispelled by happiness and the unfettered development of all the instincts that build up life and fill it with mental delights. Such a world is possible; it waits only for men to wish to create it.

Meantime the world in which we exist has other aims. But it will pass away, burnt up in the fire of its own hot passions; and from its ashes will spring a new and younger world, full of fresh hope, with the light of morning in its eyes.

13. Decree on the Requisition of Closed Factories [1871]

The Paris Commune, considering that a large number of factories have been abandoned by their directors, who have fled in order to escape from their duties as citizens without caring about the workers' interests,

considering that, as a consequence of this cowardly flight, numerous industries important for communal life have been interrupted, and that the existence of the workers is at stake,

decrees:

that the syndical labor societies are convened to appoint a committee of inquiry that will have the task of:

1. establishing statistics of abandoned factories as well as a precise inventory of the state in which they are found and the condition of the instruments of work they contain;

2. making a report presenting the practical conditions for activating these factories immediately, not by the deserters who have abandoned them, but by the cooperative association of the workers employed in these factories;

3. elaborating a plan for the formation of these cooperative workers' societies;

4. instituting an arbitration tribunal which will determine at

Reprinted from Ernest Mandel, ed., *Contrôle ouvrier, conseils ouvriers, autogestion: anthologie* (Paris: François Maspero, 1970), pp. 60–61, by permission of René Coeckelberghs Partisanförlag. Translated by Helen Kramer.

the time of the entrepreneurs' return the conditions of definitive cession of the factories to the workers' societies and the compensation to be paid to the entrepreneurs by the societies.

This committee of inquiry shall present its report to the Committee for Labor and Commerce and the latter shall submit to the Commune as quickly as possible a draft law that shall render justice to the Commune's interests as well as to those of the workers.

Paris, April 16, 1871

14. The Civil War in France
[1871]

KARL MARX

On the dawn of the eighteenth of March, Paris arose to the thunderburst of "Vive la Commune!" What is the Commune, that sphinx so tantalizing to the bourgeois mind!

"The proletarians of Paris," said the Central Committee in its manifesto of the eighteenth of March, "amidst the failures and treasons of the ruling classes, have understood that the hour has struck for them to save the situation by taking into their own hands the direction of public affairs.

". . . They have understood that it is their imperious duty and their absolute right to render themselves masters of their own destinies, by seizing upon the government power." But the working class cannot simply lay hold of the ready-made state machinery and wield it for its own purposes.

The centralized state power, with its ubiquitous organs of standing army, police, bureaucracy, clergy, and judicature—organs wrought after the plan of a systematic and hierarchic division of labor—originates from the days of absolute monarchy, serving nascent middle-class society as a mighty weapon in its struggles against feudalism. Still, its development remained

Reprinted from Lewis S. Feuer, ed., *Marx and Engels: Basic Writings on Politics and Philosophy* (Garden City, N.Y.: Anchor Books, Doubleday, 1959), pp. 362–75, by permission of the publisher.

clogged by all manner of medieval rubbish, seignorial rights, local privileges, municipal and guild monopolies and provincial constitutions. The gigantic broom of the French Revolution of the eighteenth century swept away all these relics of bygone times, thus clearing simultaneously the social soil of its last hindrances to the superstructure of the modern state edifice raised under the First Empire, itself the offspring of the coalition wars of old semi-feudal Europe against modern France. During the subsequent regimes the government, placed under parliamentary control—that is, under the direct control of the propertied classes —became not only a hotbed of huge national debts and crushing taxes; with its irresistible allurements of place, pelf, and patronage, it not only became the bone of contention between the rival factions and adventurers of the ruling classes, but its political character changed simultaneously with the economic changes of society. At the same pace at which the progress of modern industry developed, widened, intensified the class antagonism between capital and labor, the state power assumed more and more the character of the national power of capital over labor, of a public force organized for social enslavement, of an engine of class despotism. After every revolution marking a progressive phase in the class struggle the purely repressive character of the state power stands out in bolder and bolder relief. The Revolution of 1830, resulting in the transfer of government from the landlords to the capitalists, transferred it from the more remote to the more direct antagonists of the working men.   The bourgeois republicans, who, in the name of the revolution of February, took the state power, used it for the June massacres, in order to convince the working class that "social" republic meant the republic ensuring their social subjection, and in order to convince the royalist bulk of the bourgeois and landlord class that they might safely leave the cares and emoluments of government to the bourgeois "republicans." However, after their one heroic exploit of June, the bourgeois republicans had, from the front, to fall back to the rear of the "party of order"—a combination formed by all the rival fractions and factions of the appropriating class in their now openly declared antagonism to the producing classes. The proper form of their joint-stock government was the *parliamentary republic,* with Louis Bonaparte for its president. Theirs was a regime of avowed class terrorism and deliberate insult toward the "vile multitude." If the parliamentary republic, as M. Thiers said, "divided them [the different fractions of the ruling class] least," it opened an abyss between that class and the whole body of society outside their spare ranks. The restraints by which their own divisions had, under former regimes, still checked the state power were removed by their union, and in view of the threatening upheaval of the proletariat, they now used that state power mercilessly and ostentatiously as the national war engine of capital against labor. In their uninterrupted crusade against the producing masses they were, however, bound not only to invest the executive with continually increased powers of repression, but at the same time to divest their own parliamentary stronghold—the National Assembly—one by one, of all its own means of defense against the executive. The executive, in the person of Louis Bonaparte, turned them out. The natural offspring of the "party of order" republic was the Second Empire.

The empire, with the *coup d'état* for its certificate of birth, universal suffrage for its sanction, and the sword for its scepter, professed to rest upon the peasantry, the large mass of producers not directly involved in the struggle of capital and labor. It professed to save the working class by breaking down Parliamentarism and, with it, the undisguised subservience of government to the propertied classes. It professed to unite all classes by reviving for all the chimera of national glory. In reality it was the only form of government possible at a time when the bourgeoisie had already lost, and the working class had not yet acquired, the faculty of ruling the nation. It was acclaimed throughout the world as the savior of society. Under its sway bourgeois society, freed from political cares, attained a development unexpected even by itself. Its industry and commerce expanded to colossal dimensions, financial swindling celebrated cosmopolitan orgies, the misery of the masses was set off by a shameless display of gorgeous, meretricious, and debased luxury. The state power, apparently soaring high above society, was at the same time itself the greatest scandal of that society and the very hotbed of all its corruptions. Its own rottenness and the rottenness of the society it had saved were laid bare by the bayonet of Prussia, herself eagerly bent upon transferring the supreme seat of that regime from Paris to Berlin. Imperialism is, at the same time, the most prostitute and the ultimate form of the state power which nascent middle-class society had commenced to elaborate as a means of its own emancipation from feudalism and which full-grown bourgeois society had finally transformed into a means for the enslavement of labor by capital.

The direct antithesis to the empire was the Commune. The cry of "social republic," with which the revolution of February was ushered in by the Paris proletariat, did but express a vague aspiration after a republic that was not only to supersede the monarchical form of class rule, but class rule itself. The Commune was the positive form of that republic.

Paris, the central seat of the old government power and, at the same time, the social stronghold of the French working class, had risen in arms against the attempt of Thiers and the rurals to restore and perpetuate that old government power bequeathed to them by the empire. Paris could resist only because, in consequence of the siege, it had got rid of the army and replaced it by a National Guard, the bulk of which consisted of workingmen. This fact was now to be transformed into an institution. The first decree of the Commune, therefore, was the suppression of the standing army and the substitution for it of the armed people.

The Commune was formed of the municipal councilors, chosen by universal suffrage in the various wards of the town, responsible and revocable at short terms. The majority of its members were naturally workingmen, or acknowledged representatives of the working class. The Commune was to be a working, not a parliamentary, body, executive and legislative at the same time. Instead of continuing to be the agent of the central government the police was at once stripped of its political attributes and turned into the responsible and at all times revocable agent of the Commune. So were the officials of all other branches of the Administration. From the members of the Commune downwards the public service had to be done at *workmen's wages.* The vested interests and the representation allowances of the high dignitaries of state disappeared along with the high dignitaries themselves. Public functions ceased to be the private property of the tools of the central government. Not only municipal administration, but the whole initiative hitherto exercised by the state was put into the hands of the Commune.

Having once got rid of the standing army and the police, the physical force elements of the old government, the Commune was anxious to break the spiritual force of the repression, the "parson power," by the disestablishment and disendowment of all churches as proprietary bodies. The priests were sent back to the recesses of private life, there to feed upon the alms of the faithful in imitation of their predecessors, the Apostles. The whole of the educational institutions were opened to the people gratuitously, and at the same time cleared of all interference of church and state. Thus not only was education made accessible to all, but science itself freed from the fetters which class prejudice and governmental force had imposed upon it.

The judicial functionaries were to be divested of that sham independence which had but served to mask their abject subservience to all succeeding governments to which, in turn, they had taken, and broken, the oaths of allegiance. Like the rest of public servants, magistrates and judges were to be elective, responsible, and revocable.

The Paris Commune was, of course, to serve as a model to all the great industrial centers of France. The communal regime once established in Paris and the secondary centers, the old centralized government would in the provinces, too, have to give way to the self-government of the producers. In a rough sketch of national organization which the Commune had no time to develop, it states clearly that the commune was to be the political form of even the smallest country hamlet, and that in the rural districts the standing army was to be replaced by a national militia, with an extremely short term of service. The rural communes of every district were to administer their common affairs by an assembly of delegates in the central town, and these district assemblies were again to send deputies to the national delegation in Paris, each delegate to be at any time revocable and bound by the *mandat impératif* [formal instructions] of his constituents. The few but important functions which still would remain for a central government were not to be suppressed, as has been intentionally misstated, but were to be discharged by communal, and therefore strictly responsible, agents. The unity of the nation was not to be broken, but, on the contrary, to be organized by the communal constitution, and to become a reality by the destruction of the state power which claimed to be the embodiment of that unity independent of, and superior to, the nation itself, from which it was but a parasitic excrescence. While the merely repressive organs of the old government power were to be amputated, its legitimate functions were to be wrested from an authority usurping pre-eminence over society itself and restored to the responsible agents of society. Instead of deciding once in three or six years which member of the ruling class was to misrepresent the people in Parliament, universal suffrage was to serve the people, constituted in communes, as individual suffrage serves every other employer in the search for the workmen and managers for his business. And it is well known that companies, like individuals, in matters of real business generally know how to put the right man in the right place, and if they for once make a mistake to redress it promptly. On the other hand, nothing could be more foreign to the spirit of the Commune than to supersede universal suffrage by hierarchic investiture.

It is generally the fate of completely new historical creations to be mistaken for the counterpart of older and even defunct forms of social life, to which they may bear a certain likeness. Thus, this new Commune, which breaks the modern state power, has been mistaken for a reproduction of the medieval communes, which first preceded, and afterwards became the substratum of, that very state power. The communal constitution has been mistaken for an attempt to break up into a federation of small states, as dreamed of by Montesquieu and the Girondins, that unity of great nations which, if originally brought about by political force, has now become a powerful coefficient of social production. The antagonism of the Commune against the state power has been mistaken for an exaggerated form of the ancient struggle against overcentralization. Peculiar historical circumstances may have prevented the classical development, as in France, of the bourgeois form of government, and may have allowed, as in England, the completion of the great central state organs by corrupt vestries, jobbing councilors, and ferocious poor-law guardians in the towns, and virtually hereditary magistrates in the counties. The communal constitution would have restored to the social body all the forces hitherto absorbed by the state parasite feeding upon, and clogging the free movement of, society. By this one act it would have initiated the regeneration of France. The provincial French middle class saw in the Commune an attempt to restore the sway their order had held over the country under Louis Philippe, and which, under Louis Napoleon, was supplanted by the pretended rule of the country over the towns. In reality the communal constitution brought the rural producers under the intellectual lead of the central towns of their districts, and these secured to them, in the workingmen, the natural trustees of their interests. The very existence of the Commune involved, as a matter of course, local municipal liberty, but no longer as a check upon the now superseded state power. It could only enter into the head of a Bismarck, who, when not engaged in his intrigues of blood and iron, always likes to resume his old trade, so befitting his mental caliber, of contributor to *Kladeradatsch* [the Berlin *Punch*]; it could only enter into such a head to ascribe to the Paris Commune aspirations after that caricature of the old French municipal organization of 1791 the Prussian municipal constitution which degrades the town governments to mere secondary wheels in the police machinery of the Prussian state. The Commune made that catchword of bourgeois revolutions, "cheap government," a reality by destroying the two greatest sources of expenditure—the standing army and state functionarism. Its very existence presupposed the non-existence of monarchy, which, in Europe at least, is the normal encumbrance and indispensable cloak of class rule. It supplied the republic with the basis of really democratic institutions. But neither cheap government nor the "true republic" was its ultimate aim; they were its mere concomitants.

The multiplicity of interpretations to which the Commune has been subjected and the multiplicity of interests which have construed it in their favor show that it was a thoroughly expansive political form, while all previous forms of government had been emphatically repressive. Its true secret was this. It was essentially a working-class government, the product of the struggle of the producing against the appropriating class, the political form at last discovered under which to work out the economic emancipation of labor.

Except on this last condition, the communal constitution would have been an impossibility and a delusion. The political rule of the producer cannot coexist with the perpetuation of his social slavery. The Commune was therefore to serve as a lever for uprooting the economic foundations upon which rests the existence of classes, and therefore of class rule. With labor emancipated, every man becomes a workingman and productive labor ceases to be a class attribute.

It is a strange fact. In spite of all the tall talk and all the immense literature, for the last sixty years, about emancipation of labor, no sooner do the workingmen anywhere take the subject into their own hands with a will then uprises at once all the apologetic phraseology of the mouthpieces of present society with its two poles of capital and wage slavery (the landlord now is but the sleeping partner of the capitalist), as if capitalist society was still in its purest state of virgin innocence, with its antagonisms still undeveloped, with its delusions still unexploded, with its prostitute realities not yet laid bare. The Commune, they exclaim, intends to abolish property, the basis of all civilization!

Yes, gentlemen, the Commune intended to abolish that class property which makes the labor of the many the wealth of the few. It aimed at the expropriation of the expropriators. It wanted to make individual property a truth by transforming the means of production, land and capital, now chiefly the means of enslaving and exploiting labor, into mere instruments of free and associated labor. But this is communism, "impossible" communism! Why, those members of the ruling classes who are intelligent enough to perceive the impossibility of continuing the present system—and they are many—have become the obtrusive and full-mouthed apostles of co-operative production. If co-operative production is not to remain a sham and a snare; if it is to supersede the capitalist system; if united co-operative societies are to regulate national production upon a common plan, thus taking it under their own control and putting an end to the constant anarchy and periodical convulsions which are the fatality of capitalist production, what else, gentlemen, would it be but communism, "possible" communism?

The working class did not expect miracles from the Commune. They have no ready-made utopias to introduce *par décret du peuple* [by decree of the people]. They know that in order to work out their own emancipation, and along with it that higher form to which present society is irresistibly tending by its own economic agencies, they will have to pass through long struggles, through a series of historic processes, transforming circumstances and men. They have no ideals to realize but to set free the elements of the new society with which old collapsing bourgeois society itself is pregnant. In the full consciousness of their historic mission, and with the heroic resolve to act up to it, the working class can afford to smile at the coarse invective of the gentlemen's gentlemen with the pen and inkhorn, and at the didactic patronage of well-wishing bourgeois doctrinaires, pouring forth their ignorant platitudes and sectarian crotchets in the oracular tone of scientific infallibility.

When the Paris Commune took the management of the revolution in its own hands; when plain workingmen for the first time dared to infringe upon the government privilege of their "natural superiors," and under circumstances of unexampled difficulty performed their work modestly, conscientiously, and efficiently —performed it at salaries the highest of which barely amounted to one-fifth of what, according to high scientific authority [Professor Huxley], is the minimum required for a secretary to a certain metropolitan school board—the old world writhed in convulsions of rage at the sight of the red flag, the symbol of the republic of labor, floating over the Hôtel de Ville.

And yet this was the first revolution in which the working class was openly acknowledged as the only class capable of social initiative, even by the great bulk of the Paris middle class—shopkeepers, tradesmen, merchants—the wealthy capitalists alone excepted. The Commune had saved them by a sagacious settlement of that ever recurring cause of dispute among the middle classes themselves—the debtor and creditor accounts. The same portion of the middle class, after they had assisted in putting down the workingmen's insurrection of June 1848, had been at once unceremoniously sacrificed to their creditors by the then Constituent Assembly. But this was not their only motive for now rallying round the working class. They felt that there was but one alternative—the Commune, or the empire—under whatever name it might reappear. The empire had ruined them economically by the havoc it made of public wealth, by the wholesale financial swindling it fostered, by the props it lent to the artificially accelerated centralization of capital, and the concomitant expropriation of their own ranks. It had suppressed them politically, it had shocked them morally by its orgies, it had insulted their Voltairianism by handing over the education of their children to the *frères Ignorantins,* it had revolted their national feeling as Frenchmen by precipitating them headlong into a war which left only one equivalent for the ruins it made—the disappearance of the empire. In fact, after the exodus from Paris of the high Bonapartist and capitalist *bohème* the true middle-class party of order came out in the shape of the "union républicaine," enrolling themselves under the colors of the Commune and defending it against the willful misconstruction of Thiers. Whether the gratitude of this great body of the middle class will stand the present severe trial, time must show.

The Commune was perfectly right in telling the peasants that "its victory was their only hope." Of all the lies hatched at Versailles and re-echoed by the glorious European penny-a-line, one of the most tremendous was that the rurals represented the French peasantry. Think only of the love of the French peasant for the men to whom, after 1815, he had to pay the milliard of indemnity. In the eyes of the French peasant the very existence of a great landed proprietor is in itself an encroachment on his conquests of 1789. The bourgeois, in 1848, had burdened his plot of land with the additional tax of forty-five cents on the franc, but then he did so in the name of the revolution, while now he fomented a civil war against the revolution, to shift onto the peasant's shoulders the chief load of the five billions of indemnity to be paid to the Prussian. The Commune, on the other hand, in one of its first proclamations declared that the true originators of the war would be made to pay its cost. The Commune would have delivered the peasant of the blood tax—would have given him a cheap government—transformed his present bloodsuckers, the notary, advocate, executor, and other judicial vampires, into salaried communal agents, elected by, and responsible to, himself. It would have freed him of the tyranny of the *garde champêtre,* the gendarme, and the prefect; would have put enlightenment by the schoolmaster in the place of stultification by the priest. And the French peasant is above all, a man of reckoning. He would find it extremely reasonable that the pay of the priest, instead of being extorted by the taxgatherer, should depend only upon the spontaneous action of the parishioners' religious instincts. Such were the great immediate boons which the rule of the Commune —and that rule alone—held out to the French peasantry. It is, therefore, quite superfluous here to expatiate upon the more complicated but vital problems which the Commune alone was able, and at the same time compelled, to solve in favor of the peasant, viz., the hypothecary debt, lying like an incubus upon his parcel of soil, the *prolétariat foncier* [the rural proletariat], daily growing upon it, and his expropriation from it enforced, at a more and more rapid rate, by the very development of modern agriculture and the competition of capitalist farming.

The French peasant had elected Louis Bonaparte president of the republic; but the party of order created the empire. What the French peasant really wants he commenced to show in 1849 and 1850, by opposing his *maire* to the government's prefect, his schoolmaster to the government's priest, and himself to the government's gendarme. All the laws made by the party of order in January and February 1850 were avowed measures of repression against the peasant. The peasant was a Bonapartist, because the Great Revolution, with all its benefits to him, was, in his eyes, personified in Napoleon. This delusion, rapidly breaking down under the Second Empire (and in its very nature hostile to the rurals), this prejudice of the past, how could it have withstood the appeal of the Commune to the living interests and urgent wants of the peasantry?

The rurals—this was, in fact, their chief apprehension—knew that three months' free communication of communal Paris with the provinces would bring about a general rising of the peasants, and hence their anxiety to establish a police blockade around Paris, so as to stop the spread of the rinderpest.

If the Commune was thus the true representative of all the healthy elements of French society, and therefore the truly national government, it was, at the same time, as a workingmen's government, as the bold champion of the emancipation of labor, emphatically international. Within sight of the Prussian Army, that had annexed to Germany two French provinces, the Commune annexed to France the working people all over the world.

The Second Empire had been the jubilee of cosmopolitan blacklegism, the rakes of all countries rushing in at its call for a share in its orgies and in the plunder of the French people. Even at this moment the right hand of Thiers is Ganesco, the foul Wallachian, and his left hand is Markovsky, the Russian spy. The Commune admitted all foreigners to the honor of dying for an immortal cause. Between the foreign war lost by their treason and the civil war fomented by their conspiracy with the foreign invader, the bourgeoisie had found the time to display their patriotism by organizing police hunts upon the Germans in France. The Commune made a German workingman its Minister of Labor. Thiers, the bourgeoisie, the Second Empire, had continually deluded Poland by loud professions of sympathy, while in reality betraying her to, and doing the dirty work of, Russia. The Commune honored the heroic sons of Poland by placing them at the head of the defenders of Paris. And, to broadly mark the new era of history it was conscious of initiating, under the eyes of the conquering Prussians on the one side and of the Bonapartist army, led by Bonapartist generals, on the other, the Commune pulled down that colossal symbol of martial glory, the Vendôme Column.

The great social measure of the Commune was its own working existence. Its special measures could but betoken the tendency of a government of the people by the people. Such were the abolition of the night work of journeymen bakers; the prohibition, under penalty, of the employers' practice to reduce wages by levying upon their workpeople fines under manifold pretext—a process in which the employer combines in his own person the parts of legislator, judge, and executor, and filches the money to boot. Another measure of this class was the surrender, to associations of workmen, under reserve of compensation, of all closed workshops and factories, no matter whether the respective capitalists had absconded or preferred to strike work.

The financial measures of the Commune, remarkable for their sagacity and moderation, could be only such as were compatible with the state of a besieged town. Considering the colossal robberies committed upon the city of Paris by the great financial companies and contractors, under the protection of Haussmann, the Commune would have had an incomparably better title to confiscate their property than Louis Napoleon had against the Orleans family. The Hohenzollern and the English oligarchs, who both have derived a good deal of their estates from church plunder, were, of course, greatly shocked at the Commune clearing but eight thousand francs out of secularization.

While the Versailles government, as soon as it had recovered some spirit and strength, used the most violent means against the Commune; while it put down the free expression of opinion all over France, even to the forbidding of meetings of delegates from the large towns; while it subjected Versailles and the rest of France to an espionage far surpassing that of the Second Empire; while it burned by its gendarme inquisitors all papers printed at Paris, and sifted all correspondence from and to Paris; while in the National Assembly the most timid attempts to put in a word for Paris were howled down in a manner unknown even to the *Chambre introuvable* of 1816; with the savage warfare of Versailles outside, and its attempts at corruption and conspiracy inside Paris, would the Commune not have shamefully betrayed its trust by affecting to keep up all the decencies and appearances of liberalism, as in a time of profound peace? Had the government of the Commune been akin to that of M. Thiers, there would have been no more occasion to suppress party of order papers at Paris than there was to suppress communal papers at Versailles.

15. The State and Revolution [1917]

V. I. LENIN

The special measures adopted by the Commune and emphasized by Marx, are particularly noteworthy: the abolition of all representative allowances, and of all special salaries in the case of officials; and the lowering of the payment of *all* servants of the State to the level of the *workmen's wages*. Here is shown, more clearly than anywhere else, the *break*—from a bourgeois democracy to a proletarian democracy; from the democracy of the oppressors to the democracy of the oppressed; from the domination of a "special force" for the suppression of a given class to the suppression of the oppressors by the whole force of the majority of the nation—the proletariat and the peasants. And it is precisely on this most obvious point, perhaps the most important so far as the problem of the State is concerned, that the teachings of Marx have been forgotten. It is entirely neglected in all the innumerable popular commentaries. It is not "proper" to speak about it as if it were a piece of old-fashioned *"naiveté"*; just as the Christians, having attained the position of a State religion, "forget" the *"naiveté"* of primitive Christianity, with its revolutionary democratic spirit.

From pp. 183–87 and 244–45 in *The Essential Left: Marx, Engels, Lenin* (Barnes & Noble Book Division). By permission of Harper & Row, Publishers, Inc., and George Allen & Unwin.

The lowering of the pay of the highest State officials seems simply a naive, primitive demand of Democracy. One of the "founders" of the newest Opportunism, the former Social-Democrat, E. Bernstein, has more than once exercised his talents in the repetition of the vulgar capitalist jeers at "primitive" Democracy. Like all opportunists, like the present followers of Kautsky, he quite failed to understand that, first of all, the transition from Capitalism to Socialism is impossible without "return," in a measure, to "primitive" Democracy. How can we otherwise pass on to the discharge of all the functions of Government by the majority of the population and by every individual of the population? And, secondly, he forgets that "primitive Democracy" on the basis of Capitalism and capitalist culture is not the same primitive Democracy as in pre-historic or pre-capitalist times. Capitalist culture has created industry on a large scale in the shape of factories, railways, posts, telephones and so forth; and *on this basis* the great majority of functions of "the old State" have become enormously simplified and reduced, in practice, to very simple operations such as registration, filing and checking. Hence they will be quite within the reach of every literate person, and it will be possible to perform them for the usual "working man's wage." This circumstance ought and will strip them of all their former glamour as "Government" and, therefore, privileged service.

The control of all officials, without exception, by the unreserved application of the principle of election and, *at any time,* re-call; and the approximation of their salaries to the "ordinary pay of the workers"—these are simple and "self-evident" democratic measures, which harmonize completely the interests of the workers and the majority of peasants; and, at the same time, serve as a bridge, leading from Capitalism to Socialism. These measures refer to the State, that is, to the purely political reconstruction of society; but, of course, they only acquire their full meaning and importance when accompanied by the "expropriation of the expropriators" or at least by the preliminary steps towards it, that is, by the passage from capitalist private ownership of the means of production to social ownership. . . .

"In a Socialist society [Kautsky writes] there can exist, side by side, the most varied forms of industrial undertakings—bureaucratic [??], trade unionist, co-operative, individual." "There are, for instance, such enterprises as cannot do without a bureaucratic [??] organization: such are the railways. Here democratic organization might take the following form: The workers elect delegates, who form something in the nature of a parliament, and this parliament determines the conditions of work, and superintends the management of the bureaucratic apparatus. Other enterprises might be handed over to the workers' unions, which again could be organized on a co-operative basis."

This view is erroneous, and represents a step backward by comparison with the deductions of Marx and Engels in the seventies from the example of the Commune.

So far as this assumed necessity of "bureaucratic" organization is concerned, there is no difference whatever between railways and any other form of big industry, any factory, great commercial undertaking or extensive capitalist farm. The conduct of all such enterprises requires the strictest discipline, the nicest accuracy in the apportionment of the work, under peril of damage to mechanism or product, or even the confusion and stoppage of the whole business. In all such enterprises the workers will, of course, "choose delegates who will form something in the nature of a parliament."

But herein lies the crux: this "something in the nature of a parliament" will not be a parliament in the middle-class sense. Kautsky's ideas do not go beyond the boundaries of middle-class parliamentarism. This "something in the nature of a parliament" will not merely "determine the conditions of work, and superintend the management of the bureaucratic apparatus," as imagined by Kautsky. In a Socialist society, this "something in the nature of a parliament," consisting of workers' delegates, will determine the conditions of work, and superintend the management of the "apparatus"—but this apparatus will not be "bureaucratic." The workers, having conquered political power, will break up the old bureaucratic apparatus, they will shatter it from its foundations up, until not one stone is left standing upon another; and the new machine which they will fashion to take its place will be formed out of these same workers and employees themselves. To guard against their transformation into bureaucrats, measures will be taken at once, which have been analyzed in detail by Marx and Engels: (1) Not only will they be elected, but they will be subject to recall at any time. (2) They will receive payment no higher than that of ordinary workers. (3) There will be an immediate preparation for a state of things when *all* shall fulfill the functions of control and superintendence, so that *all* shall become "bureaucrats" for a time, and no one should therefore have the opportunity of becoming "bureaucrats" at all.

16. Works Committees in Russia in the Period of Revolution [1917-1918]

ANNA PANKRATOVA

The factory constitution and the law of April 23, 1917

Let us now see the manifestations of worker creation in the domain of the establishment of the "factory constitution."

The most precious and audacious "constitution" in its formulation of problems and its spirit is the one elaborated by the conference of factory committees of the war industry of the city of Petrograd in April 1917, even before the promulgation of the law of April 23. Paragraphs 5–7 of this statute of the factory committees, very much in advance of the powers sanctioned by the law, are the most interesting.

"All the ordinances concerning the internal procedure fixed by the law [such as regulation of working time, wages, hiring and firing, holidays, etc.] issue from the factory committee with notification to the director of the factory or of the section."

"All administrative personnel [higher cadres, heads of sections or of workshops, technicians] are engaged with the consent of the factory committee, which must announce the appointment at the

Reprinted from *Autogestion*, December 1967, 12–14, 36–41, 46–48, 52–63, by permission of the publisher. Translated by Helen Kramer.

general meeting of the whole factory or through the intermediary of the workshop committees."

"The factory committee has the right to reject administration personnel who cannot guarantee normal relations with the workers."

"The factory committee constitutes the body which controls the activity of the management in the administrative, economic, and technical domains. In order to carry out this preliminary control, the factory committee sends one of its members to represent it, alongside the management, in the economic and technical committees as well as in the different sections of the factory; in addition, all the management's official documents, budgets of production and expenditures, as well as all the documents of inputs and outputs must be presented to the representative of the factory committee to keep it informed."

Thus, from April 1917, from this "constitution" of the Petrograd workers, particularly the metallurgists, the idea of workers' control and the coordination of industry was born by anticipation. At that time, no "factory constitution" had gone as far.

The attempts made in Moscow and the provinces to create a "constitution" were more modest, although all exceeded the limits fixed by the law of April 23.

The "explanatory note" of the Moscow work section belonging to the soviet of workers' deputies accompanies the point by point analysis of the law of April 23; it explains how this law should be understood and applied and gives rather detailed indications concerning the instructions that were at the base of the "rules" elaborated in the most important Moscow enterprises.

"The Workers' Committee shall constitute the body for the defense of the workers' economic, professional, and cultural interests," states the note; "when the professional organizations are weak, it is incumbent upon the workers' committees to assume from the beginning the direction of the economic struggle, the conduct of strikes."

Further on, the factory committee is charged with participating in the elaboration of rules of internal order and hiring conditions, observation of sanitary regulations, control of factory canteens, investigation of measures to be taken against the crisis in food products, regulation of conflicts with the help of conciliation boards, etc. "The workers' committee shall be a powerful support of the professional organization and of the soviet of workers' deputies." . . .

The struggle for workers' control

... The conference of March 13, 1917, unifying for the first time the factory committees of the largest enterprises working for the artillery, which had fallen into the hands of the workers as a consequence of the flight of the management, declared that the workers did not consent to assume the responsibility of technical, administrative, and economic organization of production insofar as the complete socialization of the entire statist and private economy had not been realized. . . .

The workers substituted for guard posts the control judged indispensable by the internal regulations. From that time on, the contradictions of capitalist relations were revealed to them with a pitiless clarity. The movement from passive control to active control was dictated by the same logic of preservation. The intervention of the workers' committees in hiring and firing was the first step toward the active interference of the workers in the production process. This is why the capitalists offered such resistance. Later the passage toward higher forms of technical and financial control became inevitable.

This placed before the proletariat a new problem: the seizure of power, the establishment of new relations of production, the economic and political dictatorship of the proletariat.

Workers' control, becoming a heavy hammer in the hands of the workers, crushed the autocracy of capital in the country and the factory. This action put an end to the historic role of the bourgeoisie. . . .

In order to combat the lockout in [the textile] industry, on June 16 and 17 a conference was convened of the factory committees of the 164 textile enterprises of the central industrial region partially or entirely subjected to the destructive action of the "Likinsk policy."

"The proletariat of the textile industry has understood very well the plan of the employers who take recourse to sabotage and the lockout in order to deliver a blow to the essential interests of the working class," declared the conference, which called for blow by blow response by unanimous resistance.

This "plan" was effectively understood by the whole working class. The proletariat found itself confronting a dilemma: "to submit to the reduction of production or risk being fired while intervening actively in production and taking into its hands the control and normalization of work in the enterprise."

Thus the question was posed to the first conference of the workers' committees by the worker delegate of the Putilov factory, where forty thousand workers were laboring under the constant threat of the closing of the enterprise for lack of fuel. Thus it was presented before the entire Russian proletariat. . . .

In spite of the attempts of some Mensheviks to reduce everything to a few words about "the democratic control of the state," the resolution adopted by the conference in accord with the report of Comrade Zinoviev insisted on workers' control in a clear and decisive fashion. "It is not by following the bureaucratic way, that is, by creating an institution of capitalist dominance, it is not by protecting the privileges of the capitalists and their omnipotence in production that one can save oneself from catastrophe. The way of salvation lies only in the establishment of real workers' control."

Further on, the resolution contains the entire program concerning this control, which was the ultimate cause of a cruel war against capital that had passed over to the defensive.

The principal points of this program can be summarized as follows:

1. Workers' control shall develop under conditions of the complete normalization of production and distribution.

2. Workers' control shall extend to all financial and banking operations.

3. The greatest part of the privileges and revenues of the large capitalist economy shall pass into the workers' hands.

4. The exchange of agricultural objects and machines for the products of the land to the workers through the intermediary of cooperatives shall be organized.

5. The obligation to work shall be implemented and the workers' militia shall be created.

6. The labor force shall be directed toward production of edible oil, production of raw materials, and transport, and toward the manufacture of products for economic reconstruction.

7. Power shall be taken by the soviets. . . .

The struggle for the socialist factory

. . . The First All-Russian Conference of Factory Committees, meeting from October 17 to October 22, on the eve of the revolutionary offensive and the seizure of power by the proletariat, undertook [to unite the dispersed manifestations of the factory committees in their struggle for Soviet power] . . . .

The decision on workers' control had to impose itself naturally from the combat position taken by the All-Russian Conference.

"1) After having overthrown absolutism on the political level, [explains the resolution] the working class also wants to make its democratic aspirations triumph on the economic level. The idea of workers' control, arising in the full economic ruin that the criminal policy of the dominant class has created, is the expression of these aspirations.

"2) The organization of workers' control is a healthy manifestation of the spirit of proletarian initiative in the domain of production, as is the activity of the Party in the domain of politics, that of the trade unions in the domain of wages, that of cooperatives in the domain of consumption, and that of clubs in the domain of instruction.

"3) The workers, more than the employers, are interested in the regular and uninterrupted work of the enterprises. In this respect, the introduction of workers' control guarantees the interests of all of contemporary society, of all the people, much more than the sole autocratic judgment of the employers, who are guided by considerations of material or political profit.

"Only workers' control of the capitalist enterprise, taking into account its objectives and social importance, will create conditions favorable to the installation of our strong workers' self-management and to the development of productive labor." . . .

From workers' control to workers' management

. . . The practice of workers' control before October sometimes even yielded negative results. The natural concern of the factory committees to help the worker escape from poverty and unemployment obliged them to act as a sort of "machinery" charged with procuring by any means raw materials, fuels, and other materials indispensable to production. The management of factories sometimes tended to use the factory committees by confiding to them the responsibility of the enterprise, imperceptibly making the workers' organizations its agents and assistants. If the employers abandoned their enterprises and the factory committees became the masters by the force of circumstances, the latter often adopted the "employer" point of view and, forgetting the general economic utility, defended their own factory, even if other factories were more important for the state and better equipped.

Competition and the tendency to wrest away the scarce resources that assured the enterprise's life put the factory committees in a situation of mutual economic struggle, thus transforming the factories into semianarchic "autonomous federations." The anarchists, profiting by these tendencies, demanded that the management of enterprises pass into the hands of the factory committees.

"The production control committees not only should be verifiers [enjoying no more than the right to examine enterprise accounts] but should, at the present time, prepare the transfer of production to the hands of the workers"; this is what the anarchists proposed in their resolution at the session of the First All-Russian Congress of Factory Committees on October 20.

These tendencies manifested themselves in the practice of workers' control from the first days following the October Revolution, the more easily and with more success as the capitalists' resistance increased. But the proletariat relied on workers' power and through the revolutionary organs subdued the recalcitrant entrepreneurs. The working class accepted the use of all means, from compulsory arbitration to the arrest of employers and the sequestration of enterprises, to break the resistance of the capitalists. . . .

The first steps in this direction were made by the central committee of the factory committees, which decreed on February 6, 1918, the instructions and the practical manual on control. All the essential points of these instructions enlarge the control cadres and surpass by far those established by the decree:

"Worker control of industry, as an integral part of all economic life, shall not be understood in the narrow sense of a simple review but, on the contrary, in the broad sense of interference in internal management: capital, the enterprise's property, raw materials and manufactured products, regular fulfillment of orders, consumption of energy and manpower, participation in the organization of production on rational bases, etc. Control shall be considered precisely as a transitional stage toward the organization of all economic life of the country on socialist foundations, as the first indispensable step in this direction, made by the base parallel to the work at the summit in the central organs of the national economy."

This broad interpretation of workers' control precedes the instructions given by the Central Soviet of Factory Committees. The decree defines the functioning of workers' control in the spirit of the proposed instruction while confiding its application to the factory committees and to their associations: the district committees are already no longer simple observers of employer activities, they are ceasing to be "machinery" in the search for fuels and raw materials that help the capitalists to keep their enterprises going. According to the sense of the powers with which they are invested, they are the effective guides of all the enterprise's affairs. The factory committees can check the initiatives of the employers and management and require that no measure, no matter how important, be taken without their agreement. They manage the manufactured products, raw materials, fuel, and manpower; they establish the plan of work, together with the technicians, examine the orders with the management and decide on their execution, demobilize the enterprises and manpower, control the financial operations, and also supervise the observance of work interests with respect to the internal order, the raising of wages, technical and sanitary conditions, and cultural education.

The organizational outline elaborated by the Central Soviet of Factory Committees with respect to the practical application of workers' control can be roughly summarized in this way: the factory committee designates five committees—organization of production, demobilization, raw materials supply, fuel supply, and organization of work. These basic committees can create any necessary subcommittees. The factory committees unite in district soviets of workers' control which, in turn, join in urban, provincial, and regional soviets of the national economy working under the leadership of the Central Soviet of Factory Committees. The soviets of the national economy are divided into sectors according to branches of industry. Where soviets of the national economy do not exist, all the practical work for directing the application of control is carried out by the Central Soviet of Factory Committees, divided in turn into corresponding committees and production sections. . . .

Workers' control is in fact applied in the following way: when the factories need raw materials, fuel, money, etc., the Supreme Soviet of the National Economy, represented by the corresponding section of production, demands of the control committees formed in the factories justifying statements, subsequently verified on the spot. This measure is necessary because the employers often abuse the confidence of these committees and profit by their lack of experience in technical and administrative questions. Too often the factory committees and the control committees interpret too liberally or too arbitrarily the decrees and instructions on workers' control. Problems arise then on this ground not only with the management of factories but also with the Soviet of the National Economy.

No problems concerning the life of the enterprise can be resolved without the organs of workers' control. The conflicts, the struggle of the employers, and the liquidation and management of abandoned enterprises during the Revolution caused precious time to be lost. . . .

The further deepening of the economic revolution requires organization of production on socialist bases. But a more efficient form of organization than the factory committee and a broader method than workers' control were required. The management of the new factory had to be linked to the principle of a unique economic plan prepared in terms of the general socialist perspectives of the young proletarian state. For that, national organs for normalization and management of production had to be set up. The factory committees lacked the experience and technical knowledge to assimilate the complicated work of control of production. The modern development of the latter is linked by so many threads to the external world, to other enterprises, to the situation on the market, to the state of transportation, to the labor market, etc., that the factory committees, as well as their all-Russian union, could not grasp all these links; they lacked the prerogatives of state power. Financial control was particularly difficult to achieve. In order for it to be fully accomplished, all the enormous power of financial capital, as well as the legal order it had established, had to be broken. Establishment of compulsory trade unionism, the grouping of isolated branches of production into trusts, the nationalization of banks, the creation of a new fiscal system, all those immense economic tasks of the period of transition to socialism required the creation of a universal center normalizing the entire national economy on a statewide scale. The proletariat understood this necessity and, freeing from their mandate the factory committees, which no longer corresponded to the new economic exigencies, delegated their powers to newly created organs, the soviets of the national economy. . . .

One after another, the enterprises became the property of the proletarian state. By about June 1, 1918, more than five hundred enterprises, among them the most important, were already nationalized. Up to the First Congress of Soviets of the National Economy in May–June 1918, all the fundamental branches of industry as well as private commerce were subjected to nationalization. . . .

The resolution of the Congress defined the functions, rights, and duties of workers' control as follows: "Workers' control not only extends to the inventory of raw materials, to production, finance, etc., but also establishes selling prices and verifies whether the enterprise works in conformity with the plans elaborated by the soviets of the national economy. In cases in which activity does not conform to the defined tasks, the organs of workers' control immediately communicate all the shortcomings and variances to the regional or provincial soviet of the national economy without waiting for the decision of the administrative council. The soviet of the national economy shall, on its part, urgently undertake all the measures necessary to eliminate the noted shortcomings. Workers' control concerns not only the employer or the head of the enterprise, but also the workers, for whom it fixes the efficiency of work, norms of production, and work discipline. Workers' control thus conceived makes industrial activity known to the workers and contributes to the gradual and systematic carrying out of nationalization by the regional soviets, until the measures taken by the Supreme Soviet of the National Economy have been implemented."

But in addition to the regulation on workers' control and the creation of control committees—slightly modified in comparison with the preceding instructions—the Congress of the Soviets of the National Economy adopted the "Regulation on the Management of Nationalized Enterprises."

Paragraph 2 of this regulation states: "A works management committee is formed in every plant, factory, mine, etc., that has become the property of the Republic. Two-thirds of the members of this committee are designated by the regional soviet of the Supreme Soviet of the National Economy (if the enterprise is directly subjected to central direction); in addition, the Soviet of the National Economy has the right to permit the regional or national trade union to propose half of its candidates.

"A third of the members of the management committee are

elected by the unionized workers of the enterprise. The factory management committee shall include a third of specialists from among the technical and commercial employees."

Thus, on the one hand, such a system of organization of management allowed the work of normalizing production according to a single plan to be advanced to a considerable degree; but, in addition, it stamped a proletarian character on management by linking to it the working masses, who could directly designate their representatives to the factory management committees.

17. Tasks of the Trade Unions: Theses of the Workers' Opposition for the Tenth Party Session [January 1921]

A. SHLIAPNIKOV ET AL.

General principles

1. The role and tasks of the trade unions in the transition period, in which we now find ourselves, will be determined precisely and clearly in the Resolution of the All-Russian Trade Union Congress. The First All-Russian Trade Union Congress in January 1918 defined the task of the trade unions as follows: "The focus of the trade unions' activity at the present moment must lie in the organizational-economic sector. As class organizations of the proletariat, built according to the production principle, the trade unions must carry out their main work through the organization of production and the restoration of the disrupted productive forces of the country."

The Second Congress in February 1919 established that "in the course of the mutual practical work of the Soviet government in strengthening and organizing the national economy, the trade unions passed from control of production to its organization, in which they actively participated both in the management of individual enterprises and in the overall economic life of the country."

Reprinted from *Naše teme* (Zagreb), December 1971, 2223–29, 2230–31. Translated by Helen Kramer.

The conclusion of the Resolution states: "The trade unions, which directly participate in all areas of Soviet labor and from which state organs are formed, must therefore train their organizations and the broad working masses not only for management of production, but also for participation in the entire state apparatus, and must prepare them to interest themselves in Soviet work."

The Third Congress, held in April 1920, confirmed—in truth, formally—the most important conclusions of both preceding congresses, but limited itself to giving a series of instructions and recommendations with respect to the manner in which the trade unions should participate in the organization of the national economy in areas outlined by the resolutions of the First and Second congresses. The practical tasks of the trade unions were set forth with particular clarity and distinctness in the Program of the Russian Communist Party (RKP), which was adopted at the Eighth Congress in March 1919.

In the Program of the RKP, we find the following in the section "In the Economic Sector" under point 5: "The organizational apparatus of socialized industry must first of all rest on the trade union."

Since the trade unions, according to the laws of the Soviet Republic and the practice which has developed, participate in practically all local and central managerial organs of industry, it must follow that the complete direction of the entire national economy as a unified economic whole is concentrated in their hands.

2. The transition from military tasks to economic construction and from militaristic work methods to democratic methods provoked a crisis in the trade unions that is observed in the failure of the content of their daily work to agree with the tasks elaborated in the Resolution of the congress and placed in the Party Program. The practice of the Party centers and state organs in the last two years has systematically limited the area of activity of the trade unions and practically removed the influence of the unions in the Soviet state. The role of the trade unions in organizing and managing production is reduced in reality to the role of an information bureau or bureau for recommendations, while state officials have assumed the managerial positions; there is no agreement between the state organs and the trade unions, and the Party organizations are burdened by conflicts. A clear illustration of the position of the trade unions is offered by the report on the situation of the trade union press. The unions have neither print-

ing presses nor paper. The journal of the large unions appears with many months' delay. The state printing establishment receives the unions' printing orders reluctantly and does not care that they are given lowest priority.

3. This narrowing of the role and importance of the trade unions occurs at a time when the experience of the last three years of the proletarian revolution shows that the union consistently carries out the communist line and further has behind it a circle of unbiased working masses, and when it is clear to everyone that the realization of the Program of the RKP in our country, in which the population consists mainly of small commodity producers, requires a strong, authoritative organization of the working masses which is accessible to broad circles of the proletariat. The narrowing of the importance and the real role of the trade union organizations in Soviet Russia is a manifestation of the bourgeois class enemy of the proletariat and must be immediately ended.

The next tasks and activity of the unions

4. The real breathing spell offered to the workers' republic for the first time in the bloody armed struggle against internal and foreign counterrevolution and against world imperialism makes it possible to concentrate all the forces and resources of the country first of all on struggling against economic disruption and on increasing as much as possible the productive forces of our republic. The experience of four revolutionary years and three and a half years of Soviet construction and struggle taught us that the tasks posed could be solved to the extent to which the broadest strata of the working masses participated. We must take into consideration this experience and organize our work so that it will now be focused toward the direct participation of the working masses in managing the economy of our country.

5. We shall be able to overcome disruption and renew and increase the productive forces of our country only if the existing system and practical methods of the organization and management of the national economy of the republic are changed from the foundation up. The system and methods of construction that rest on heavy bureaucratic machinery exclude every creative initiative, every independent activity of the producers who are organized in trade unions. That system of economic policy which is

conducted by officials and dubious experts in a bureaucratic way, independently of the organized producers, led to conflict in managing the economy and constantly provokes conflicts between the work committee and the enterprise management, between the unions and the economic organs. The conditions created by that system hardly allow enthusiasm for productive work to appear among the broad working masses, and prevent them from becoming active and systematic collaborators in overcoming economic disturbances. Such a system must be decisively rejected.

6. This effort . . . to carry out in an indirect way the programmatic conclusions of the Party congress on the role and tasks of the trade unions in the Soviet state testifies to the lack of confidence in the powers of the working class. The conscious, progressive elements of the working class, whom the communists organize, must try with all their might to overcome that lack of confidence and bureaucratic inertness which prevail in the Party itself. The necessity of abolishing the present system is dictated by the fact that the trade unions educated and ideologically prepared huge masses of the proletariat to see the effective defense of the class interests of the producers at the present moment to lie in the overcoming of economic disturbances and the renewing and raising of the Republic's productive forces; the very existence of the working class of our country depends on the successful completion of this task. The bureaucratic method connected with the present economic construction, however, prevents the attainment of as great productive successes as are possible and introduces disagreement, lack of confidence, and demoralization into the ranks of the workers. . . .

8. The occupational and industrial associations of workers are organizations of collective economic experience, built according to the principles of workers' democracy, election, and responsibility of all organs from the bottom to the top. In the period of their existence, the workers' councils have acquired sufficient experience and obtained people with managerial, technical, and economic capabilities. Worker-managers administer whole branches of our war, machinery, metal, and other industries. A collegium or even individual worker-managers lead several hundred complicated industrial enterprises. As representatives of the workers' unions in the economic organs, they are not responsible to the organizations that delegated them, and are not obliged to account to them, they cannot be suddenly recalled, and they are responsible only to the economic organ.

Transferring the administration of production to the unions will eliminate this harmful phenomenon.

9. The abandonment of the present type of bureaucratic administration of the economy, which does not take into account the initiative of the working masses, must be carried out in an organized way and must begin with the strengthening of the lowest cells of the workers' unions, from the workers' committees in the factories on up, with the goal of preparing them for direct administration of the economy. Thus the transition of the unions from their present position as passive supporters of the national economic organs to active, conscious, independent, and creative participants in the administration of the entire economy of the country would be guaranteed. To hasten that transition, the following measures must be undertaken:

a) A limitation with respect to the characteristics of production must be carried out among individual workers' unions.

b) The strengthening of the unions in terms of officials and technical and other material resources must begin without delay so that they can be prepared for new tasks.

c) Officials of the workers' unions and workers' committees must be elected with regard to their capacity to carry out the tasks confronting the unions. This election must be initiated from below and under the control of the unions.

d) Where the participation of the unions in organizing and administering the economy is concerned, all the prevailing principles of parity between the Supreme Council of the National Economy and the All-Russian Council of Trade Unions must be broadened to increase the rights and privileges of the workers' organizations.

e) No one may be entrusted with a job in managing the economy without the unions' knowledge.

f) No candidate proposed by the unions may be rejected; the highest national council and its organs must unconditionally accept all candidates.

g) All officials whom the unions have appointed or proposed are to be responsible to those unions and subject to recall by them at any time.

h) The unions entrusted by the All-Russian Central Council of Trade Unions with the organization of direct administration of all industrial branches must carry out that right regardless of whether other unions agree.

10. The whole attention and total activity of the unions must be

directed toward factories and workshops, enterprises and government offices, and must be concentrated on the development of the activity and consciousness of producers in their own process and, based on the success of that process, on the development of the consciousness of liberated producers, and on the organization of work so that the worker, instead of being a dead appendage of the economic machine, will become a conscious creator of communism, building communism on the foundation of the appropriate and economical division of labor. . . .

11. The forms of organizing and administering the economy and the system of relations among the various economic sectors should in their final form enable the administration of the national economy as a unified, economic whole to be concentrated in the hands of the unions.

12. This concentration of administration of the Republic's unified economy shall be achieved by introducing an order in which all the administrative organs of the national economy . . . are elected from among the representatives of the organized producers. In this way, a unified will is achieved, which is necessary for organizing the national economy, and, in addition, the broad working strata are given the real possibility of influencing, by their own initiatives, the organization and development of our economy.

13. The All-Russian Congress of Producers, comprised of union members, shall organize the administration of the entire national economy; it shall also elect the central organ of administration of the entire national economy.

a) The all-Russian congresses of the unions of individual industries shall elect the organs for administering economic sectors of production and product groups.

b) The corresponding local union congresses shall appoint the administrative organs of the regions, provinces, districts, etc. Thus a connection is established between centralization of production and local initiative. . . .

14. Medium-size enterprises with similar production shall be united in groups (alliances, joint committees) for the sake of optimal use of technical equipment and materials. Similar enterprises located in the same city or place shall be united under a common leadership created in a general form by the union. The management of united enterprises that are spatially separated from each other shall be appointed by congresses of the workers' committees of the corresponding enterprises convoked by the union.

Organizing workers' committees
for managing enterprises

15. All workers and employees of all enterprises and services of the Republic who are trade union members must systematically and actively participate in the administration of the national economy with the goal of organizing work and production as quickly as possible according to socialist principles.

16. All workers and employees, regardless of position and title, who are employed in individual economic units such as factories and mines, in all enterprises, government offices, and services, in trade, in the post office, as well as in all branches of agriculture, directly dispose of the values entrusted to them; this, as well as suitable income, is guaranteed to all workers of the Republic.

17. As participants in the organization and management of enterprises, workers and employees employed in factories, workshops, and government offices, in trade, the postal service, and the signal service, and in other places in economic units that comprise enterprises, elect an organ for the management of the enterprise, the workers' committee.

18. The workers' committee is the basic organizational cell of the trade union of the related industry and is created under the leadership and control of the related union.

19. Management of the concerned work or enterprise is among the tasks of the workers' committee, and includes:

a) Management of the productive activity of all workers and employees of the concerned economic unit;

b) concern for all the producers' needs.

The committee members shall divide up their tasks in managing the enterprise according to the rules and instructions of the union in such a way that, in addition to their collective responsibility, which is borne first of all by the chairman, the personal responsibility of each individually is precisely established.

20. The workers employed in the concerned enterprise elaborate and approve the entire activity, work program, and internal order of the enterprise, in the framework of the allocated tasks and prevailing legal regulations and under the responsible leadership of the workers' committee of the trade union. . . .

22. All the measures already cited shall be carried out first of all in socialized enterprises. They shall be carried out from time to time in private enterprises only with the union's permission.

Wherever measures are of a collective nature and concern entire enterprises, they should be carried out in every enterprise in accordance with work achievement. Measures which have a purely personal significance for individual workers should be carried out in the form of stimulation, which should begin with the workers with greatest achievements.

> *Signed by A. Shliapnikov and other members of the Central Committee of the All-Russian Union of Metalworkers, various directors and chairmen of industrial units, representatives of the miners', textile workers', and agricultural workers' unions, and a member of the Party Control Committee of the Central Committee of the RKP*

18. The Workers' Opposition in Russia [1921]

ALEKSANDRA KOLLONTAI

The roots of the controversy

Before examining the cause of the ever growing split between the "Workers' Opposition" and the official viewpoint of our leading organs, it is necessary to draw attention to two facts:

1) The Workers' Opposition emerged from the womb of the industrial proletariat in Soviet Russia and is a consequence not only of the intolerable living and working conditions of seven million industrial workers, but also of the vacillations, the inconsistency, and the serious deviations of our Soviet policy from the class principles that are clearly expressed in the communist program.

2) The Opposition does not have its origin in any particular organization, nor is it the product of any personal dispute or controversy; on the contrary, it extends throughout all of Russia, where it has met with clamorous accord. . . .

The two differing points of view, as they have been expressed by the leaders of our Party and the representatives of the members of working class organizations, were brought out into the

Reprinted from Aleksandra Kollontai, *L'opposizione operaia in Russia* (Milan: Edit. Azione Comune, 1962), pp. 19-25, 28-29, 31-32, 35-36, 42-46, 53-54, 58-59, 70-72. Translated by Michel Vale.

light for the first time at the Ninth Congress of our Party, when it discussed the problem of "collective or individual management of industry." . . .

The fact of the matter is that, although both sides vehemently denied that a question of principle was at stake, this controversy was the manifestation of two historically irreconcilable points of view. "Individual management" is a product of the individualist viewpoint of the bourgeois class. "Individual management" amounts basically to the unrestrained, isolated, and arbitrary exercise of will by one person bound in no way with the collectivity.

This idea is reflected in every domain of human activity, from the function of head of state to that of general manager of a factory. It is the ultimate wisdom of bourgeois thought. The bourgeoisie has no faith in the power of a collective body and hence finds it useful to reduce the masses to an obedient flock and lead them wherever its unrestrained will desires. . . .

Long before the Workers' Opposition appeared with its theses, and before it indicated the basis on which, in its opinion, the proletarian dictatorship should evolve during industrial reconstruction, the Party leaders were already in strong disagreement in their estimation of the role that should be played by the working class organizations in the reconstruction of industry on communist foundations. The Central Committee of the Party split into two groups. Comrade Lenin was opposed to Trotsky, while Bukharin took a middle position. At the Eighth Congress of Soviets and immediately thereafter, it became clear that there existed within the Party itself a cohesive group held together above all by the fundamental positions of its members concerning the trade unions. This group, the "Workers' Opposition," did not have any major theoreticians, but despite the resolute resistance of the most popular Party leaders, it continued to grow in strength and spread steadily throughout all of proletarian Russia. . . .

The crisis in the party

. . . What was the cause of this "cautious prudence" (particularly evident in the lack of confidence of the central Party organs in the abilities of the labor unions in matters concerning industry) , a prudence that has recently spread throughout all our organs? What, really, is the cause of this? If we undertake a close scrutiny of the reasons behind the controversy within our Party, it is apparent that the Party is going through a crisis that has three basic causes.

The first of these is the difficult situation in which our Party is constrained to operate and act. The Russian Communist Party must construct communism and make its program a reality: (a) in a situation in which the economic structure is completely destroyed and the economy in total collapse; (b) against the ruthless pressures of the imperialist states and the White Guards—which show no signs of abating; (c) in a situation in which the Russian working class is forced to go about the task of constructing communism and creating new forms of communist economy in an economically backward country, with a population in which the peasantry comprise a majority, where the fundamental economic prerequisites for socialization of production and distribution are lacking, and where capitalism has proved itself incapable of completing its full cycle of development (from the unrestrained competition of the first stages of capitalism to its mature form, planning of production by capitalist associations, i.e., the trusts).

It is to be expected that all these factors should obstruct the practical implementation of our program (especially its essential part, the reconstruction of industry on new foundations) and give rise to diverse tendencies and lack of homogeneity in our economic policies. . . .

From the standpoint of the economy as a whole, however, the matter is quite different. Production, organized production, is the essence of communism. To exclude the workers from the organization of industry, to deprive their industrial organizations of the opportunity to develop their abilities in the creation of new forms of production in industry through the trade unions, to deny this expression of the class organization of the proletariat, while placing full confidence in the "competence" of specialists trained and educated to manage production under a totally different system of production, means to depart from the mainstream of scientific Marxist thought. . . .

As military questions recede into the background and economic questions emerge to the fore, and the more acute our urgent needs become, the greater becomes the influence of this group, which is not only inherently alien to communism but also totally incapable of developing the correct tendencies in introducing new forms of organization of labor, new incentives for increasing production, and *new outlets for production and distribution*. All these technicians, experienced men, and business experts —who have only now emerged to the surface in Soviet life and are bringing their influence to bear on our economic life—are making strenuous efforts to establish ties with the leaders of our Party by means of the soviets. . . .

As long as the working class felt itself to be the sole creator of communism—during the first phase of the Revolution—there was perfect unanimity in the Party. During the days immediately following the October Revolution, it would have been impossible for anyone to entertain the thought that "superiors" were in some way different from "inferiors." Because, quite simply, in those days the advanced workers were actively involved in making our communist program a reality, point by point. The peasants who obtained land did not insist on being an integral part of the whole, citizens of the Soviet Republic with full rights. The intellectuals, the specialists, the businessmen, the entire petty bourgeoisie, and the pseudospecialists who are today making their way, one step at a time, up the Soviet ladder of success, passing themselves off as "experts," kept their distance at that time, waiting warily and thus giving full liberty to the advanced working masses to develop their creative capacities.

Now, however, the exact opposite is the case. The worker at every instant feels, sees, and understands that the specialists—and, even worse, the illiterate nonexperts who pass themselves off as specialists—step over the worker and invade administrative posts within our industrial and economic institutions. And the Party, instead of checking this tendency of individuals who are totally alien to the working class and communism, encourages it and attempts to seek a way out of the economic chaos not in the workers but precisely in these individuals. The workers perceive this, and, despite the unanimity and unity in the Party, a split arises. . . .

The base of the protest

. . . The more our industrial establishments and the trade unions are deprived of their best elements by the Party, which sends them to the front or to Soviet institutions, the weaker become the links between the proletarian base and the leading bodies of the Party. The gap widens, until now the division is beginning to show in the base of the Party itself. The workers, through their Workers' Opposition, ask themselves: "Who are we? Are we really the bedrock of the dictatorship of the proletariat, or are we only an obedient flock serving as a support to those who, after having severed all their ties with the masses, carry through their personal policies, constructing industry with no regard whatsoever for our views and creative capacities, protected by the secure name of the Party?" . . .

The role of the trade unions

. . . To find an incentive for labor—this is the major task of the working class at the threshold of communism. In any case, no one outside of the working class, in its organized form, is capable of resolving this great problem. . . .

The Workers' Opposition has confidence in the creative capacities of its own class, the working class. The rest of its program is based on this faith.

But at just this point the Workers' Opposition begins to deviate from the line followed by the Party leaders. The essence of the theses endorsed by our Party leaders amounts to no more than mistrust of the working class (not in the political arena but in the question of creative economic abilities). The leaders do not believe that the hand of the worker, technically uneducated, is capable of carving out the economic forms from which a harmonious system of communist production will develop over the years.

For all—including Lenin, Trotsky, Zinoviev, and Bukharin—production seems to be a "delicate" thing which cannot be driven forward without the assistance of the leaders. First, we have to "educate" the workers, "instruct them," and only when they have become adults will we dispense with all the coaching from the Supreme Council of the National Economy and permit the trade unions to assume control over production. Indeed, it is significant that all the theses endorsed by the leaders of the Party converge on one point: we will not yet give control of production to the trade unions; for the present, it is better to wait. There are doubtless differences of opinion among Trotsky, Lenin, Zinoviev, and Bukharin as regards the particular areas in which management of industry should not yet be given to the workers, but all concur on one point: that at this present juncture, production must be managed *from above,* through a bureaucratic system inherited from the past. . . .

To sum up: what is the Workers' Opposition aiming at?

1) The formation of an organization by and for the workers themselves—the producers—to administer the nation's economy.

2) So that the trade unions, instead of continuing to perform their function of passive collaboration with economic institutions, may participate actively and have the opportunity to manifest their creative capacities, the Workers' Opposition proposes a series of preliminary measures for the gradual and systematic attainment of this objective.

3) The transferral of the administrative functions in industry into the hands of the trade union will not be possible until the All-Russian Central Executive Committee decides that the trade unions are sufficiently prepared and capable of carrying out this task.

4) All those nominated for economic and administrative posts must have the prior approval of the trade unions. None of the candidates nominated by the trade unions may be recalled by the Party. All responsible officials nominated by the trade unions shall be accountable to the trade unions and may be recalled by them alone.

5) To carry out all these proposals, it is necessary to reinforce the rank and file of the trade unions and prepare the factory committees and section committees for the management of industry.

6) By concentrating the entire administration of the public economy in a single body (thereby eliminating the dualism between the Supreme Council for the National Economy and the All-Russian Executive Committee of the trade unions) , a unified will should be created to facilitate the plan and to give life to the system of communist production. . . .

Bureaucracy or autonomous action of the masses?

. . . In an effort to institute democracy in the Party and to eliminate the bureaucracy, the Workers' Opposition proposes three basic principles:

1) A return to the elective principle in all areas and the elimination of the bureaucracy, so that all responsible officials are accountable to the masses for their behavior.

2) A broadening of the scope for public debate within the Party, whether on problems of a general or a particular nature; greater consideration for the opinions of the rank and file (wide discussion of all problems by the rank and file, and final decision by the leaders; admission of any member to the meetings of the executive organs of the Party, except in cases where problems requiring special secrecy are to be discussed) ; institution of freedom of opinion and expression (granting the right not only to criticize freely in the course of discussions but also to use funds for the publication of written documents proposed by the various factions within the Party) .

3) The creation of a Party that is truly proletarian, placing restrictions on those presently occupying posts in the Party and in Soviet institutions.

This last demand is particularly essential inasmuch as it is the task of the Party not only to construct communism but also to set the stage for preparing the masses for a long period of struggle against world capitalism, which may assume new and unexpected forms. . . .

This is the line pursued by the Workers' Opposition, and this is its historical task. And whatever methods of derision are adopted by the leaders of our Party to repulse the Opposition, we affirm that it is the only existing vital force against which they are constrained to struggle and to which they must devote their attention.

19. On the Occupation of Factories and Works [1923]

PIOTR ARCHINOV

We established in Part I that the foundation of the revolution lies in its positive and creative aspect, that the most important and urgent task consists in organizing the entire economy of the country—industry and agriculture first of all—on the basis of principles of equality and general self-management of the workers, and that the new mode of production must be unitarian production covering all the fundamental activities of work in its entirety, in order to avoid falling back into bourgeois contradictions.

It goes without saying that the accomplishment of this fundamental task must be preceded by the revolutionary combats of the workers against Capital. It is not possible to pass to the construction of a new economy and new social relations while the power of the state, protecting the servile order of things, remains unbroken, and while the workers do not hold in their hands the workshops and factories.

The economy, the system of production, and its operation constitute the base on which the life and well-being of the dominant classes rest. It is because of this that the latter resort to all means of armed struggle of which the state disposes in order to remove from themselves the mortal danger of social revolution.

Reprinted from "Les problèmes constructifs de la révolution sociale," *Autogestion*, No. 18-19 (January–April 1972), 207–212, by permission of the publisher. (Originally published in *Anarkhicheskii vestnik*, Berlin, 1923.) Translated by Helen Kramer.

Consequently, the occupation of workshops and factories by the workers will take place simultaneously with an armed confrontation against the power of the state. In this sense, the first steps of the peasants and workers appear as the most critical moment of the revolution.

The workers must necessarily break with their long submission and their humility in order to pass to the direct offensive. This is not easy: all the hesitant forces inclined to moderation, calm, and compromises included in the working class will stand in the way. These elements will present numerous arguments to show that, "given the circumstances," the social revolution can only be doomed to defeat, and will more or less check its evolution.

Let us briefly refute here this antirevolutionary argument, since it everywhere and on all occasions fetters the revolutionary action of the workers.

Its classical considerations and conclusions are the following: the workers, in their entirety, are not ready to manage production themselves—they do not have the necessary knowledge nor sufficient experience; there are not enough raw materials in the factories and workshops, thus the takeover of industry by the workers will be a failure; the neighboring countries are not yet ready for the social revolution, hence, if it begins in a single country, it will inevitably be defeated; the country does not have an abundance of products, and, given such a lack, a rule regulating the distribution of material goods must be instituted in the revolution; order and restriction are necessary. Consequently, the social revolution, in its modern libertarian aspect, is not possible.

These arguments and many others are invariably advanced each time the workers aspire to a decisive movement to take over industry.

It is not difficult to see in these arguments, in the first place, the moderation inherent more in the individual than in the broad masses, and, in the second place, the conscious playing on this moderation by the dominant classes, which attempt to reinforce it by theoretical and scientific considerations and in this way utilize it to their profit.

Nevertheless, the revolutionary experience of the workers decisively surmounts this moderation, as well as all the calculations that rest on it in order to counteract the revolutionary tendencies of the workers.

At first, the social revolution as an act of struggle and of construction of a new world does not tolerate the shadow of moderation: it calls only for action and audacity. Its success depends not only on the capacity of the workers to organize themselves, but also on their spirit of decision and audacity.

On the same level, the experience of the mass revolutionary actions of our epoch of collective work categorically refutes all the assertions about the unpreparedness of the workers radically to transform social life. The latter argument was one of those most employed in connection with the Russian workers. However, these considerations are confirmed as devoid of all foundation: the workers and peasants of Russia showed themselves entirely ready and capable of resolving the fundamental problems of the social revolution. . . .

However, the overthrow of the power of the state and the takeover of industry by the workers does not yet guarantee the success of the revolution; errors are still possible, errors that could reduce to nothing the conquests of the workers. The Russian Revolution is a striking example of this. Instead of passing immediately to the organization of production on the basis of self-management, after the overthrow of power and the takeover of industry, the workers allowed a new power to establish itself which, once well installed, concentrated in its hands the entire economy of the country and eliminated the forms of independent management of production.

20. Resolution of the Workers of Budapest on the Formation of Workers' Councils

[January 15, 1918]

The Budapest workers proclaim that Socialist Party policy which corresponds to the present times, adapts to the development of events, and uses without hesitation and fear all possible means of class struggle, can lead or begin to lead if the workers take it into their hands and constantly and directly exercise control over its course. In the interest of the goals that the proletarian movement can achieve today, the workers consider it essential to relieve the Party leadership of its political and historical responsibility in the explained way and thereby enable more decisive and far-reaching policy to be instituted. For the sake of the practical realization of the above, a Workers' Council of Budapest is formed immediately, in which all factories and professional organizations shall be represented on the basis of a democratic statute which shall be adopted. The council shall be supplemented by delegates of workers' councils that will be formed in the country. The Workers' Council of Budapest shall be responsible for all the activity of the Party leadership, which at all times shall act in accordance with the policy of the workers' council.

Reprinted from Andrija Krešić and Trivo Indjić, eds., *Diktatura proletarijata i radnička samouprava* (Belgrade: Sedma Sila, 1967), pp. 133–34, by permission of the editors. Translated by Helen Kramer.

21. Statute of the Workers' Council of Budapest

[November 5, 1918]

The Party leadership, trade union council, and Party activists have worked out the following statute for the Workers' Council of Budapest:

1) With the aim of suitable representation of its class interests, the organized workers of Hungary, not touching the highest forums of organized socialist workers—the organization of Party activists, the Party leadership, the Party plenum, and the resolutions of congresses that are in force—organize workers' councils.

2) Workers' Councils are founded in cities or at the headquarters of Party organizations. Their central forum is the Party leadership and the executive committee of the Party plenum.

3) The task of workers' councils is to take a position on all more important questions that touch the interests of the working class and to serve as a guidepost to workers.

4) The workers' councils are convened by the central Party leadership in Budapest, and by the local Party leadership in the countryside. The council is also convened if a third of its members so demand in writing.

5) Persons are elected to the workers' council who have been

Reprinted from Andrija Krešić and Trivo Indjić, eds., *Dikatura proletarijata i radnića samouprava* (Belgrade: Sedma Sila, 1967), pp. 134–36, by permission of the editors. Translated by Helen Kramer.

members of political and professional associations for at least a year and have subscribed to the Party press for at least a year.

6) The Workers' Council of Budapest and Environs is founded on the basis of the following principles, which should be taken into account in accordance with local conditions when councils are founded in the countryside:

a) Permanent members are the trade union council, the executive committee of the Party plenum, and the Party leadership.

b) Delegated members are:

General consumers' cooperative	2 members
Territorial women's committee	2 members
National committees	2 members each
The executive board of the capital	2 members
Organizational committee of working youth	2 members
Territorial and independent centers of free trade unions belonging to the trade union federation	1 member each
District Party organizations of Budapest	1 member each
Party organization of Kispest	2 members
Party organization of Csépel	2 members
Party organization of Erzsébetfalva	2 members
Delegates of the Party organization of Újpest	2 members

c) Elected members: territorial and independent local free trade unions elect 1 member for each 500 of its own members on the basis of the number of members in 1917.

The workers' council in addition can elect 1 delegate for each additional 500 members.

Organizations with less than 250 members are not taken into account, while any number of members above 250 is considered as 500.

At least two-thirds of the elected delegates should be chosen from among workers employed in the workshops of the enterprise that falls under the organization concerned. Delegates elected by enterprises can be only persons who truly work in the enterprise concerned.

7) After acceptance of the statute, the members of the workers' council should be elected without delay; elections are held every year.

8) Under point (b), item (6), the leaderships of the organizations concerned choose the delegates for the workers' council. Delegates noted under point (c) on free organization are divided in proportion to the size of the enterprises which are members of

it in such a way that, if possible, the largest enterprises and those that work with organized workers in individual professions are represented in the workers' council. The workers of the enterprise concerned elect the delegates of the enterprise. The enterprise's agent signs the identification card of the elected delegate. The delegate supplied with identification reports to the Party secretariat.

Total number of members of the workers' council	Number of delegates
Party leadership	16
Trade union council	16
Executive committee of the Party plenum	5
Cooperative	2
Women's committee	2
German committee	2
Slovak committee	2
Serbian committee	2
Romanian committee	2
Executive committee of the Party organization of the capital	2
Territorial committee of working youth	2
Delegates of district and Party organizations	21
Party organization of Kispest	2
Party organization of Csépel	2
Party organization of Erzsébetfalva	2
Party organization of Újpest	2
Leadership of territorial free organizations	44
Total delegated members	126
Elected delegates on the basis of statistics of 1917	239
Total number of members of the workers' council	365

9) Members of the workers' council are elected at the meeting of the commissioned territorial and independent local free organizations, at the joint conference of the Party commissioners of the Party organizations of the capital, and at the conference of the Party commissioners of Csépel, Újpest, Kispest, and Erzsébetfalva.

10) The list of names of the elected members is submitted without delay to the Party secretariat.

11) The central executive board of the workers' council consists of the delegates of the Party leadership, the trade union council, the executive committee of the Party plenum, the Party

organizations, national committees, and the leaderships of the territorial free organizations.

12) The workers' council is formed at a plenary session and, after founding, a joint meeting is called as needed.

13) All resolutions of the Workers' Council of Budapest and Environs are immediately transmitted to the workers' councils formed in the countryside.

We are publishing this statute so that its basic principles may serve as guidelines in the founding of workers' councils in the countryside.

22. Decree of the Revolutionary Executive Soviet on the Socialization of Mines and Industrial and Transport Enterprises [1919]

1. The Soviet Republic considers it its task to take over the means of production and deliver them to the ownership of the workers, to organize and strengthen production.

The Soviet Republic takes into common ownership all mines and industrial and transport enterprises that exceed the limits of small industry and with one blow puts them under the management of the entire proletariat and puts all enterprises under the supervision of the workers employed in them.

All industrial and transport enterprises and mines which employed more than twenty workers on March 22, 1919, fall under state management and workers' control.

2. Enterprises taken into social ownership are managed by commissioners of production, who are appointed by the National Commissariat for the Economy of the Soviet Republic. The National Commissariat for the Economy can subordinate several enterprises to one commissioner of production. The commissioner of production is the representative of the entire proletariat in that enterprise at whose head he is placed.

3. In indicated enterprises, the workers elect a supervisory

Reprinted from Andrija Krešić and Trivo Indjić, eds., *Diktatura proletarijata i radnička samouprava* (Belgrade: Sedma Sila, 1967), pp. 138–39, by permission of the editors. Translated by Helen Kramer.

workers' soviet. If the number of workers does not exceed one hundred, a supervisory workers' soviet of three members is elected; if it exceeds one hundred, five members are elected; and if it exceeds five hundred, a maximum of seven members is elected.

Every worker older then eighteen years of age can elect and be elected. If at least one-fourth of the workers demand it, elections are held by secret vote. Employees are also considered workers.

4. The task of the supervisory workers' soviet is to establish proletarian work discipline, protection of the property of the working people, and control of production.

5. The Soviet Republic concerns itself, with the aid of controllers sent from time to time, with the expert and economically highest control in the enterprises under social ownership.

6. If a dispute occurs between the supervisory workers' soviet and the commissioner of production, the workers' soviet does not have the power to act arbitrarily, but can complain to the National Commissariat for the Economy, which urgently considers the complaint and makes a decision on it. A decision is obligatory. Until the decision is made, the orders of the commissioner of production should be followed.

7. This decree goes into effect on the day of its proclamation. Budapest, March 26, 1919. Revolutionary Executive Soviet.

23. Legal Decree of the Presidium on Workers' Councils [1956]

The practical realization of socialist democracy can be insured only if the management of factories, mines, and enterprises (hereafter referred to as industrial enterprises) which are the property of the entire people is carried out by a workers' council elected by the workers of the enterprises concerned. The Presidium of the People's Republic of Hungary has passed the following legal decree in connection with the election, authority, and activity of workers' councils:

1. A workers' council shall be elected in every industrial enterprise, mine, and state agricultural farm, including producing industrial enterprises of individual state institutions (state railroads, postal service, etc.).

2. Workers' councils shall not be elected by boards, institutions, and organizations that do not carry out productive activity, such as railroads and postal communications, public bus transportation, trolley and air transport.

3. The regulations of this paragraph do not relate to handicraft cooperatives, home work cooperatives, or agricultural and other cooperatives whose work is governed by chosen organs—the parliament, management, etc.

Reprinted from Andrija Krešić and Trivo Indjić, eds., *Diktatura proletarijata i radnička samouprava* (Belgrade: Sedma Sila, 1967), pp. 140–41, by permission of the editors. Translated by Helen Kramer.

Election of workers' councils

...4.2 Representation of all strata of the enterprise's workers in the workers' council should be insured. Two-thirds of the members of the workers' council should be elected from the ranks of all workers who directly work in production (factory workers, supervisors, technicians, engineers) . . . .

6.2. A member of the workers' council may be recalled before the expiration of the mandate of one year. Two-thirds of the votes of the workers who elected it are necessary for the recall of the workers' council.

Authority of the workers' council

The workers' council makes decisions on the most important questions of the enterprise. It leads the entire activity of the enterprise. In this framework, it:

1) looks after payment of wages and other payments to workers;

2) insures the continuity of production and the most economical business operation of the enterprise;

3) insures the carrying out of obligations to the state;

4) looks after the carrying out of enterprise obligations prescribed in a collective agreement worked out in cooperation with the trade unions and accepted by the workers; supports the director in insuring work discipline;

5) establishes the enterprise's plans and number of workers;

6) determines the organizational scheme of the enterprise, as well as the activity of individual workers' managerial organs in the enterprise;

7) within the framework of legal regulations, determines the minimum and maximum wage of workers and employees, approves the incomes of workers and employees, and establishes the forms of wages in the enterprise as well as the fields of their application;

8) decides on that part of the whole profit, the percentage of which will be determined later by legal regulations, that remains to the enterprise after it settles its obligations to the state; in this respect, it establishes the proportion and amount of the sums that will be spent out of the profit of the enterprise for productive, social, and cultural investments and repairs, as well as those that will be paid to workers in the form of surplus profit or

used for various purposes; a fund shall be created of the available sum;

9) submits a proposal to the government for permission for the enterprise to carry out import and export transactions directly;

10) directs the financial business of the enterprise:

    a) within the framework of existing laws, disposes of the fixed and working capital of the enterprise;

    b) permits the taking of loans;

    c) approves the enterprise's balance sheet.

11) The workers' council has the right to transfer any right granted to it to the presidency or the director, with an obligatory report.

> *President of the Presidium of the People's Republic of Hungary, István Dobi*
>
> *Secretary of the Presidium of the People's Republic of Hungary, István Kristei*
>
> *(Radio Kossuth, Budapest, November 21, 1956)*

24. On Socialization [1919]

KARL KORSCH

Those forms of socialization that pose the danger of a *consumer capitalism* are socialization through nationalization, through communalization, and through merger of production plants with consumer cooperatives. In contrast, the danger of *producer capitalism* arises in attempts at socialization along the lines of the producer cooperative movement and modern trade unionism ("the mines to the miners," "the railroads to the rail-waymen," etc.). The goal of socialization in the spirit of socialism is, however, neither consumer capitalism nor producer capitalism, but true common ownership for the totality of producers and consumers. . . .

The compromise of conflicts of interests between producers and consumers

The most important result of the foregoing presentation is the following: neither the takeover of the means of production from the private sphere of authority by the public organs of the

Reprinted from *Schriften zur Sozialisierung* (Frankfurt am Main: Europäische Verlagsanstalt, 1969), pp. 25, 32–38, 53–54, by permission of the publisher. Translated by Helen Kramer.

community (nationalization, communalization, etc.) nor the transfer of the means of production from the possession of the private owners to the common possession of collective production associations (producer cooperative–trade union socialization) represents *in itself* a replacement of capitalist particular property [*Sondereigentum*] by true socialist common property. Rather, besides these two measures, an inner transformation of the property concept, a complete subordination of every particular property to the point of view of the common interest of the community, is still required. The idea pushed to the foreground by Bernstein that stresses the lasting importance of all those measures designed to weaken the generally pernicious workings of the private capitalist economic mode even within the existing capitalist society (so-called social policy) here comes into its own. These measures, as we now see, still remain necessary at the *completion* of socialization, when capitalist private property is completely done away with and replaced by a cooperative particular property, whether this is the particular property of officials of the collectivity of consumers or the particular property of a producer cooperative. It also remains necessary, with respect to this particular property, to see to a just distribution of the production proceeds in the interests of all segments of society and generally "to place production and economic life under the control of the collectivity [*Allgemeinheit*]." Only in this way will the development of social production relations lead from the "private property" of an individual person through the "particular property" of an individual part of society to the "common property" of the whole society.

The socialization of means of production as "industrial autonomy"

Thus the socialization of the means of production consists of mutually different, complementary transformations of the private capitalist mode of production to bring about true common property: the transfer of the means of production from the power sphere of individual private owners to the power sphere of some sort of social functionaries, and the legal restriction of the competency of the present directors of social production in the interest of the community.

The simultaneous carrying out of both these transformations

gives rise neither to what one today usually understands to be nationalization (communalization, etc.) and what is in reality a mere state capitalism, nor to what one today calls producer cooperative–trade unionist socialization, which is in reality only a producer capitalism. Rather, through these transformations, a new and more complete form of the socialization of the means of production is created, which will be designated in what follows as "industrial autonomy."

The realization of industrial autonomy

The socialization of an industry in the form of industrial autonomy will turn out differently according to the requirements of the individual case. It is possible to carry out the socialization of an *individual* plant in the form of institutionalization . . . for which the classic example of success, even under a capitalist social order, is the Carl Zeiss Foundation in Jena, already in existence for decades. The possibility that entire industries that are not—and perhaps never will be—ripe for centralistic "nationalization" can be immediately socialized by means of industrial autonomy and thus transformed into the common property of society has greater significance for the present situation. Autonomy exists in such a socialized industry in various forms: 1. The trade union embracing all the plants of the industry concerned possesses autonomy in relation to state central administration, limited only by the necessary regard for the interests of consumers. 2. The individual plant possesses limited autonomy in relation to the trade union embracing the plants and in part centrally deciding on their administration. 3. Within the administration of the trade union (1), as well as of the individual plant (2), the various strata of the other production participants (the employees and workers in the narrower sense) possess a limited autonomous sphere of rights, a right to regulate the matters particularly concerning them, independently of the top business management (works management).

The way in which the interest of the totality of *consumers* is taken into consideration in relation to these "autonomous" industries will vary according to the requirements of the individual case. The general economic *goal* here is cooperation of the consumer organizations (state, community, consumer cooperatives, and specially founded local administrative unions) in public *de-*

termination of needs obligatory for the autonomous trade unions and individual plants, which replaces exchange economy production for the market with a pure production for needs. As long as such a pure needs economy remains infeasible today, the present exchange economy among individual persons will be replaced at first by an exchange economy of the various industries among themselves. In this situation, the individual industries will produce not solely for *needs*, but partially still for the *market* (here one thinks particularly of the export trade). A case could also arise here in which one plant would achieve disproportionately high profits, while another would be unable even once to earn the necessary proceeds for the scanty wages of its workers. Insofar as one and the same unionized industry is concerned with various plants, the deficit of one plant must naturally be offset by the extra profit of another; technically, entirely defective plants will be shut down by the trade union. Apart from this, each autonomous plant and likewise each autonomous trade union must set the prices of its products high enough so that the total proceeds of the plant (of plants included as a body in the trade union) insure a lasting adequate maintenance to all working participants in production. Overpricing of the totality of consumer goods by the particular groups of producers which constitute the individual autonomous works or the autonomous trade union will be avoided by legally guaranteed cooperation of the consumer organizations in price setting. Further participation of consumers in the management of production, limiting the autonomy of producer groups, grows out of the . . . principle of the division of the total proceeds of each plant (of each industry) into two parts, only one of which is available for the working participants in production, while the other, for example, in the form of *taxation,* will be drawn for the common aims of the consumer collectivity. . . . After the absolute quantity of consumption necessary for total consumer needs is determined, the covering of the consumption will be divided among the individual industries (the individual plants) according to the principle that each industry (each plant) must deliver more of its product, the greater is the total value (land and labor value) of the *means of production* used for production in relation to the *number* of workers employed. Only the part of the product of an industry (plant) then remaining is available for the particular aims of the producer community concerned (for example, formation of reserves, plant improvement and expansion, payment of the workers, pensions, etc.) . Thus, even as early as this stage of communal economic development, when a pure needs economy still does not exist, the autonomy of producers also finds its limits in the consideration of the general consumption requirements to be satisfied by the total production of society. However, the consumer organizations (state, community, consumer cooperatives, etc.) again look after the maintenance of these limits, for which objective a joint right of determination in the management of the autonomous industries will be granted. . . .

Industrial autonomy better than "nationalization"

The inexperienced usually conceive of "socialization" as simple *nationalization*. The majority of objections commonly raised against "socialization" rest on this equating of socialization and nationalization. Thus, the objection is raised that socialization of the means of production is generally feasible without danger of inefficiency only for a narrowly limited sphere of branches of production, for plants that have become "ripe" for centralized management; as for all other branches of production, their gradual ripening must first be awaited. In addition, many branches of production do not develop at all in the direction of a gradual ripening for centralization, but in precisely the opposite direction; these could therefore never be "socialized" without inefficiency, without a reduction of productivity. Further, the objection is raised that every "socialization" leads generally to bureaucratization, to schematization, and, with that, to the deadening of private initiative and to torpidity.

The objections have merit as demurrals against a centralistic "nationalization" of production branches that are not suited for it. They are not significant, however, against socialization itself, against the replacement of capitalist private property by socialist common property to be generally begun immediately. For as we have seen, this socialist common property is in no way synonymous with state property. Nationalization was to us only *one* of the forms of socialization, and all forms of socialization would be recognized by us generally as true, socialist "socialization" only when in their later forms they lead beyond to that regulation of social production relations which we have designated as the form of *industrial autonomy*.

All the objections usually raised against centralized "nationalization" become factually without foundation in relation to this socialization in the form of industrial autonomy. A bureaucratic schematization and rigidity is excluded, and private initiative will not be killed, but where possible still heightened, since the possibilities for the exercise of such initiative through autonomy will be extended to a circle of enterprise participants who, under capitalist private economy, have no opportunity to exercise initiative. And a danger of inefficiency could arise, at the most, from the fact that, as a consequence of the exclusion of private owners from production, *private selfishness* will cease to provide a stimulus to achieve the most economic production possible. However, . . . an exclusion of private selfishness from the motives of production is in no way connected with the mere socialization of the *means of production*; rather, through socialization of the means of production in the first phase of the collective economy, private selfishness can be made serviceable as the motive for the most economic and productive output possible and even increased volume of production. . . .

When "socialization" is demanded today, there no longer stands behind this word merely the demand for the delivery of the means of production into the possession of the community or of "control from above." Rather, alongside this control from above, in whichever form it is carried out, must go an equally effective "control from below," in which everywhere the mass of workers (hand and brain) will participate in the management of the plant or in the control of this management.

Thus, the demand for "socialization" today contains *two* mutually complementary demands, which both aim at restricting the hitherto existing "free economy" (which was "free" only for the capitalist private owners, the possessors of the means of production, but which was a particularly oppressive unfreedom for the overwhelming majority of the propertyless!) : in place of the regulation of goods production by the free option of a more or less large number of capitalist entrepreneurs, there shall gradually emerge the planned management of production and distribution by society. That is the first. In addition, however, in every industry, and, within certain limits, even in every individual plant, the undivided sway of the capitalist employer class should be done away with even today, before the complete carrying out of control from above. The masters of the plant, up to now responsible only to themselves and perhaps to their creditors, shall become the first servants of their plant, who will be accountable for their plant management to the collectivity of all workers and employees collaborating in the plant. To be sure, the immediate, general realization of such a "control from the bottom" will not bring about a real, valid socialization of economic life, a "socialist" social order, since for this the drawing up and carrying out of an overall economic plan is indispensable. However, through the immediate introduction of this control from below, all of production will be changed from the private concern of individual production profiteers into the common concern of the production participants themselves, and thereby the "wage slave" of the old system will with one blow be turned into the co-determining "working citizen" of the social constitutional state.

The only way, however, in which *both* these demands presently contained in the call for socialization—control from above (through the collectivity) and control from below (through the direct participants)—can be realized side by side with certainty and speed is the "council system" so often mentioned and so little understood today. Only through this, and only under the assumption that it will also be really constituted in conformity with the principles determined by its double task, can a situation be achieved in which the control from below and the control from above will not come into conflict with each other and then become played off against each other by the enterprise system, which shuns every control, but rather harmoniously unite for the overcoming and successive replacement of the common opponent and for the organized construction of a regulated collective economy.

25. Proclamation of the German-Austrian Social Democracy [1919]

Socialization of industry

1. Every industry in which goods production is concentrated in a *few large plants* will be *socialized*. Thus, for example, metal and coal mining, the iron and steel industry, etc., will be socialized.

Each socialized industry will be managed by a managerial board completely independent of the government. The management board will be composed as follows: one-third of the members will be representatives of the state, who will be elected by the National Assembly, but not from its midst. A second third will consist of representatives of the workers, employees, and officials employed in the industry; they will be elected by the trade union and employee organizations. The last third will be representatives of the consumers. On the management boards of industries that produce raw materials, representatives of the entrepreneurs and workers of those industries that process these raw materials will be convened as trustees of the consumers. On the management boards of those industries that produce consumer

Reprinted from Karl Korsch, *Schriften zur Sozialisierung* (Frankfurt am Main: Europäische Verlagsanstalt, 1969), pp. 45–48, by permission of the publisher. Translated by Helen Kramer.

goods, the representatives of the consumers will be elected by the consumer associations.

The *management* of the socialized industries is the duty of the management board composed in this way; *no* influence in the management belongs to the government. Particularly incumbent upon the management board are the appointment of the leading officials, price setting, the conclusion of collective work contracts with the trade unions of the workers and employees, and the division of profits.

The *profits* of each socialized industry will be applied in the following way: one-third will fall to the state treasury. One-third will be distributed among the *workers, employees,* and *officials* of the industry as profit shares. The last third will be applied when needed, to *expansion* or to the technical improvement of the plant; if this is not necessary, the last third will be applied to *lowering* the product prices.

The management of the individual plant will be looked after by technical officials and commercial employees with the legally regulated cooperation of workers' committees which will be elected by the workers, employees, and officials of the plant. Every bureaucratization of the management is to be avoided. The principle that a third of every increase of revenues will be applied to raising the income of the officials, employees, and workers guarantees intensive work in the plant and careful handling of the means of work. A special profit share can be granted to the officials.

2. The right will be granted to the community by law to expropriate plants that serve local needs (gas and electricity works, tramways, vehicle enterprises, bread factories, dairies, brickworks, and such).

Likewise, the self-governing bodies of the district and region will compulsorily expropriate plants that serve the requirements of their administrative district (for example, local railways, long-distance power stations, breweries, mills, and such).

The principles governing the management of socialized plants also have appropriate application in these cases. A similar expropriation right can be conceded to consumer associations, producer cooperatives, and agricultural cooperatives under legally determined conditions.

3. Those industries that are not yet ripe for socialization will be organized into *industrial combines.* Each industrial combine comprises all the enterprises of its industry. The industrial com-

bines replace the existing cartels, centrals, and military combines.

Each industrial combine will be managed by a managerial board. The managerial board will be composed in the following way: one-fourth of the members will be representatives of the state, who will be elected by the National Assembly, but not from its midst; one-fourth, representatives of the entrepreneurs of the industry concerned; a third fourth, representatives of the workers, employees, and officials of the industry; the last fourth, representatives of the consumers.

The industrial combine shall promote the technical development of the industry and lower production costs through establishment of drafting offices, laboratories, and materials testing institutes, through the standardization of the goods to be produced, and through the allocation of the production of individual types of goods to individual plants. The industrial combine can concentrate the purchase of raw materials and the sale of goods in its central office, thereby suspending the *competition* among the individual entrepreneurs and saving society the costs of the competitive struggle. The industrial combine regulates the amount of production, adapts it to need, and thereby prevents severe crises. The industrial combine sets the prices of goods; it must set them so that the profit of the entrepreneur equals a suitable wage for the work performed by him. Finally, the industrial combine concludes the collective labor contracts with the trade unions of the workers and employees; the contracts concluded by it are binding on all the enterprises in the industry. The costs of the industrial combine's activity are borne by the industry entrepreneurs.

In the framework of the regulations issued by the industrial combine, the management of the individual plant is left to the entrepreneurs. However, cooperation in the management of the plant will be insured by law to the workers' committees.

One of the most important tasks of the industrial combine consists of concentrating production in the technically most advanced plants. The industrial combine has the authority to order that technically defective plants be shut down and their share of production be transferred to the technically more improved plants. The owners of the closed plants will be compensated at the expense of those enterprises to which their production share has been allocated. If, in this way, the production is finally concentrated in a few technically improved plants, the industry will be socialized. The organization of the industry into an industrial combine is thus a transititional stage leading to its socialization.

26. The Council System in Germany [1921]

RICHARD MÜLLER

1. The origin of the idea of councils

. . . What developed in Russia and England we also find
in Germany. Although the causes of this phenomenon are the
same, the forms that result nevertheless differ outwardly. When
the new organization of proletarian struggle—the workers' council—was formed in Germany in November 1918, it was designated as an imitation of "Bolshevik methods." However, this new
organization of struggle was not first formed as a product of the
November events, but had already been created earlier, during
the war, before the November collapse was at hand. It resulted
from the economic effects of the war, from the suppression of
every free movement of the working class through the administration of the state of siege and the complete refusal of the trade unions and the political parties to act. The trade unions were hindered in their functioning because of the state of siege and were,
in addition, made servile to the war policy by the trade union bureaucracy. The political party of the working class was split.
While one part supported the regime's war policy without reser-

Reprinted from "Die Ideen und Entwicklung des Sozialismus," in *Die Befreiung der
Menschheit: Freiheitsideen in Verganggenheit und Gegenwart* (Berlin: Deutsches
Verlaghaus Bong. u. Co., 1921), pp. 168-76. Translated by Helen Kramer.

vation, the other was too weak to offer resistance. The politically mature and revolutionary-minded part of the working class sought a new form of proletarian class struggle; sought, therefore, a new organization of struggle. These strivings manifested themselves first in the factories and also found firm forms there.

When, in July 1916, fifty-five thousand Berlin workers suddenly went on strike not in order to improve their economic position but on *political* grounds, bourgeois society, the leaders of social democracy, and the trade unions could not at all grasp this unheard of fact. It simply turned upside down all the previous experiences of the workers' movement. Where did the causes lie? Who prepared and led this strike? Bourgeois society, as well as the leaders of the trade unions, cared little about the first question. They did not see, or did not wish to see, what revolutionary tendencies the war and the brutal suppression of the working class must release. Hence, they sought by all means to lay hold of the leaders of this movement. They seized them in the large factories, in the Ludwig Loewe Company, the Schwarzkopff works, and elsewhere. They were workers who had joined together in "factory committees" which operated like the factory committees of large Petersburg concerns in 1905, though they had no knowledge of the latter's activity. The political struggle in July 1916 could not have been carried out with the help of the parties and trade unions. The leaders of the latter organizations were opponents of such a struggle; after the struggle, they also helped to deliver the leaders of this political strike to the military authorities. These "factory committees"—the designation is not entirely appropriate —can be considered the forerunners of the present-day revolutionary workers' councils in Germany. The idea of councils, born out of circumstances, struck its first roots in Germany at that time. What was manifested in July 1916 developed further and took effect in the great political general strike in April 1917, in which three hundred thousand workers participated, and further in the great political general strike in January and February 1918, in which over five hundred thousand workers took part. These struggles were not supported or led by the existing party and trade union organizations. Here the beginnings of a third organization—of *workers' councils*—appeared. The large plants were the supporters of the movement. The leading persons in the movement, who were well organized by trade unions and politically and, indeed, occupied many offices in the organizations, nevertheless had to pass on to create new organizations of proletarian struggle. In all these struggles, the designation "workers' councils" or "council system" or "council organization" was never applied.

After the great general strike of January and February 1918, the preparations for the violent overthrow of the old regime were made. I do not wish to imply, however, that the November revolution was "created." The objective causes of this revolution lie in the military, political, and economic collapse of Germany. As early as the beginning of 1918, the moment of this collapse could be foreseen. At that time, it was vital to concentrate the revolutionary energy stored up in the working class and to prevent it from dissipating in individual actions; to contain it and, in a given situation, to set out in closed ranks to overthrow the old regime. In these preparations, it appeared further that the great concern was to find the place where the revolutionary energies of the working class could best be concentrated. In all these preparations, what organization should be created after the decisive struggle, after the downfall of the old regime, was never mentioned. The idea of having workers' councils immediately elected everywhere was never discussed. One troubled oneself little over what should happen after the struggle. It was vital first of all to prepare and successfully carry out the struggle. When the November collapse came, the workers' councils grew out of the revolutionary relationships, even where this overthrow was never thought of before.

This brief presentation of the development shows us that the idea of councils is not a specifically Russian phenomenon but that it has grown out of the development of economic and political relationships as a new form of organization of the proletarian class struggle. The life struggle of the working class did not advance the idea of class community and a feeling of common belonging in the existing organizations; that occurred where the masses stood under the same pressure. The effectiveness of the workers' organizations was limited by external force and internal contradictions. These organizations did not happen to include a large part of the working class. The situation was otherwise in the big factories created through the capitalist form of production. Here the proletariat, regardless of its religious and political conviction, found itself together in a common destiny. Here lay the roots of the new organizational form, of the council idea. . . .

2. Democracy or the council system

In the council system, the workers' councils will bring together the representatives of the working people. Exploiters of others' labor are excluded from the right to vote. In this way, the economic antithesis which lies at the basis of the parliamentary system of formal democracy is done away with. The workers' councils move in close relationship with their electors and are under their constant control. They will not be elected for a definite term but may be recalled at any time. Out of this grows a strong feeling of responsibility in the workers' councils. The influence of the voter on legislation and administration will be far stronger than is the case in the formal democracy of the parliamentary system. In the council system, legislation and administration are united in the hands of the workers' councils, and thus all bureaucracy must disappear by itself. The council system will accordingly be the basis of a new social order. The council system will operate politically and economically. In the transition period, politically it will be the sovereign organization of the proletariat; its organs must take over the political administration. Economically, it will become the organization of production.

In its political application, the council system becomes, then, the organization of revolutionary struggle of the proletariat. It unites the proletariat in a unitary mode of struggle to holding down its opposition. This situation is not and must not be lasting. As soon as socialist democracy, the abolition of private property in the means of production, is attained, the dictatorship of the proletariat ceases. Thereby the state also withers away and a socialist community takes its place. Karl Marx wrote of this transition period: "Between the capitalist and the communist society lies the period of the revolutionary transformation of the former into the latter. To this there also corresponds a political transition period, in which the state can be nothing other than the *revolutionary dictatorship of the proletariat.*"

The council system includes the working people in individual trades. True democracy is thereby more nearly attained, for only a small minority is excluded and thus the dictatorship of the proletariat is the expression of the will of the overwhelming majority of the people. It brings the means of production into the possession of the entire society; it introduces the first phase of communist society. . . .

3. Socialization and the system of councils

By socialization we understand the delivery of the means of production into the ownership of society. Socialization is not yet socialism and is by no means communism. The tearing away of economic power from capitalist society, which is possible only through political struggle, is called socialization. Socialization is impossible as long as the democratic state exists. All socialization measures of the democratic state authority maintain the capitalist mode of production, which has only pseudodemocratic draperies. In the most favorable case, the state itself enters next to the owner of the means of production as the exploiter of labor and both divide the surplus value created by labor. "Plant democracy" will be promised to the worker, and he may seemingly put in a word; in reality, the exploitation rights of the entrepreneurs will be more firmly ordained, their profit insured.

The council system in its political form of application must lead the struggle in order to achieve socialization and the overthrow of capitalism. Socialization also stipulates, however, the continuing of production on the foundations created by capitalism. These foundations may not be disturbed; therefore, the organized socialist needs-satisfying economy must immediately take the place of anarchical capitalist production. But this is not to say that overall uniform socialization must begin on a certain day. There are large, extensive spheres of production that must be immediately socialized, while other, less important ones can at first remain undisturbed. Socialization cannot be left to the workers in the plant; it can happen only through the common action of all workers and consumers, and the cooperation of scholars is likewise necessary. The organization of these forces in the council system rests on economic participation. Two organizations, that of workers and that of consumers, are united in the council system. Both organizations are distinct; in both, science must assert its influence. . . .

Production will be carried out through the organizations of works councils. The workers and employees elect from their midst the works councils, which control production. The control organs for the sphere of production, having as their highest level a national economic council, will be elected from the works councils. The organization of consumption is united with the organization of production in the national economic council.

Management of the plant lies in the hands of the works council. It will be appointed by the district group council, which is composed of representatives of the production branches of the economic sphere. Scholars cooperate actively in plant managements, as well as in the control organs of production (district group council, national group council, national economic council).

The planned organization of production requires the building of an economic council organization. Through it the self-management of all professions, branches of industry, crafts, trade, and transportation should be guaranteed. The basis of this organization is the workplaces, the smallest socially productive units of economic life. The *trusted persons* of the working people will be elected from the plants. This council organization includes all working forces of the people. *It is built up organizationally into a central organization comprising the entire popular and economic life.*

The German Republic forms an economic unit which will be centrally administered. It will be divided into economic districts in which productive activities will be included in *district organizations.* Total production is organized according to industrial, trade, and transportation branches and independent professions.

The organizational structure has the following groups:

1. agriculture, horticulture, animal husbandry, forestry and fishing
2. mining, metallurgy and salt works, peat cutting
3. stone and earth industries, building trades
4. metals industry
5. chemical industry
6. textiles and clothing industry
7. paper industry and printing trades
8. leather and shoe industry
9. wood and wood products industry
10. necessities and luxuries trade
11. banking, insurance, and trade
12. transportation and communications
13. officials and workers in state and communal works
14. free professions

Within each of the above-cited groups, the organization of work is built from the works councils on up to a *national group organization.* In each independent plant, a works council will be

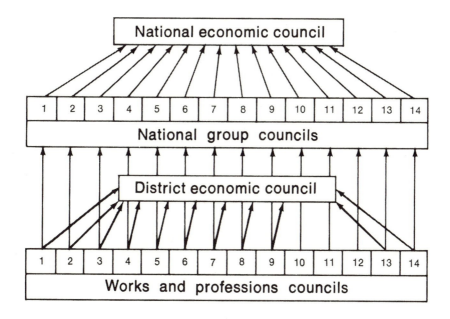

elected, with the groups of employees and workers taken into consideration. *The works council, together with the works management, superintends and regulates all affairs of the enterprise.*

When an enterprise consists of several plants or independent divisions, a works council will be elected for each plant. These works councils combine in a *joint works council,* which elects from its midst the supervisory council alongside the management of the overall enterprise.

When there are independent small and medium-sized plants with similar production, individual plants are combined geographically in local or regional councils. The works councils of large plants of the *same* type of production can also be included in them through the *district group council.*

Independent small manufacturers and other occupational groups that cannot be included in the factories elect a joint works council (vocational council) in counties and large towns by districts.

The works councils, local councils, regional councils, or joint works councils of each group within an economic district unite in a district group council and elect an executive committee. The district group council oversees and regulates the production in the district according to stipulations determined by the *national group council.* Within the district, the district group council is the highest authority for deciding all questions arising from the production relations of *its own* group.

The district group council of each group elects from its midst the delegates to the *district economic council.* The latter decides questions of jurisdiction among the existing groups in the district; in addition, production and economic questions that can be regulated *only within the district* are subject to the decision-making of the district economic council.

The district group council of each group elects from its midst delegates to a *national group council,* which is composed of representatives of the same group of *all districts.*

The national group council is the central authority of the group. It must regulate, according to the overall economic plan of the national economic council, the kind and volume of production, the planning and allocation of raw materials, and the sale of the product, as well as all questions concerning the group. It can form special committees, which can be supplemented by experts, to settle all questions in its competence.

The national group councils of the enumerated industrial, craft, and trade branches elect from their midst representatives of the *national economic council.*

The representation of the national group councils in the national economic council is regulated according to the total number employed in the individual groups.

The national economic council is composed in equal parts of representatives of the enumerated fourteen economic groups and of representatives of the consumers' organization. The national economic council is led by the deputies of the central council.

27. What Happened at Leeds
[1917]

Report Published by the Council of Workers' and Soldiers' Delegates

The Fourth Resolution passed at the Leeds Convention, Workers' and Soldiers' Councils:

"The Conference calls upon the constituent bodies at once to establish in every town, urban and rural district, Councils of Workmen's and Soldiers' delegates for initiating and co-ordinating working-class activity in support of the policy set out in the foregoing resolution, and to work strenuously for a peace made by the peoples of the various countries, and for the complete political and economic emancipation of international labour. Such Councils shall also watch diligently for and resist every encroachment upon industrial and civil liberty; shall give special attention to the position of women employed in industry and generally support the work of the trade unions; shall take active steps to stop the exploitation of food and all other necessaries of life, and shall concern themselves with questions affecting the pensions of wounded and disabled soldiers and the maintenance grants to the dependents of men serving with the Army and

Reprinted from Ken Coates and Tony Topham, eds., *Workers' Control: A Book of Readings and Witnesses for Workers' Control* (London: Panther Books, 1970), pp. 116–17, by permission of Granada Publishing.

Navy; and the making of adequate provision for the training of disabled soldiers and for suitable and remunerative work for the men on their return to civilian life. And, further, that the conveners of this Conference be appointed as a Provisional Committee, whose duty shall be to assist the formation of local Workmen's and Soldiers' Councils, and generally to give effect to the policy determined by this Conference."

Moved by W. C. Anderson, M.P.; seconded by Robert Williams.

W. C. Anderson, M.P., moving the resolution before the Convention, said:

"I gather from the Press reports that this Fourth Resolution is regarded as the ugly duckling among the resolutions, and therefore I claim for it on that ground your special solicitude and support. (Hear, hear!) I saw a paragraph the other day in that dear old mid-Victorian journal the *Morning Post* (laughter) which states that the Fourth Resolution is the one that really matters, being more than mere rhetoric. 'This resolution is clearly,' it says, 'a violation of the law, as inciting to the subversion of Army discipline and military authorities.' (Hear, hear!) 'Those who move such a resolution and those who act on it are liable to severe penalties.' (Laughter.) 'It is therefore unthinkable that the Government will wittingly permit such action.' Well, I move the resolution without any apology of any kind, and if they want criminals (the speaker made a sweep of his arm towards the packed hall), there is a pretty haul of them in this hall. (Cheers.) But I wish to say emphatically that the resolution was not intended to be subversive of military responsibilities. What we do say is that soldiers and workmen alike are men and have the rights of men, and we ask the newspapers to howl until they are black in the face if they so desire. (Cheers.) If we are going to have justice for the soldiers, for the wives and the widows and the children of the soldiers, and if we are going to have industrial freedom for the workmen, the workman and the soldier must join hands. (Cheers.) Ah, they say, this is revolution. If a revolution be the conquest of political power by a hitherto disinherited class, if revolution be that we are not going to put up in the future with what we have put up with in the past, we are not going to have the shams and the poverty of the past, then the sooner we have revolution in this country the better. (Cheers.) . . . We are going to try first of all to bring into closer and more organic touch the democracy of Britain with the democracy of Russia and with the democracy of every other country. . . ."

28. Selected Writings from *L'ordine nuovo* [1919–1920]

ANTONIO GRAMSCI

Workers' Democracy

There is one problem of urgent concern today facing every socialist with a vital sense of the historical responsibility resting on the shoulders of the working class and on the Party, which represents the critical and active consciousness of the mission of that class.

How may the immense social forces unleashed by the war be harnessed? How may they be disciplined and given a political form that would have the potential to develop by a continuous process of organic growth until the first rudiments of the socialist state, the embodiment of the dictatorship of the proletariat, begin to emerge? How may the present be welded to the future, satisfying the needs of the one while at the same time working effectively to create and anticipate the other?

This article is intended as a stimulus to thought and action; it is an invitation to the best and most conscious workers to reflect on the problem, each within the range of his own abilities and activity, and to work toward its solution by focusing the attention of their comrades and organizations on its terms. Concrete, con-

Reprinted from *Opere di Antonio Gramsci*, Vol. 9: *L'ordine nuovo* (Turin: Giulio Einaudi, 1955), pp. 10–13, 36–39, 45–47, 123–27, 132–35, by permission of Istituto Gramsci. Translated by Michel Vale.

structive action can only emerge from a joint and cooperative effort of clarification, persuasion, and mutual education.

The socialist state already exists potentially within the social institutions characteristic of the exploited working class. To link these institutions together, to coordinate them and subordinate them in a highly centralized hierarchy of jurisdictions and powers, while respecting their necessary areas of autonomy and interconnections, means to begin at once to create a true and genuine workers' democracy in effective opposition to the bourgeois state and prepared at any time to replace it in all its essential functions of administration and control of the national patrimony. . . .

Only many years, even decades, of work will enable the Socialist Party and the trade unions to absorb the entire working class. They will not immediately become identical with the proletarian state. Indeed, in the communist republics they have continued to exist independently of the state, as a driving force (the Party) or as institutions of supervision and partial implementation (the unions). The Party must continue to be the organ of communist education, the guardian of the faith, the repository of doctrine, and the supreme power that harmonizes and leads the organized and disciplined forces of the working class and peasantry toward their goal. Precisely because it must rigorously carry out this task, the Party cannot throw open its door to an invasion of new members unused to the exercise of responsibility and discipline.

But the social life of the working class is rich in institutions and takes on multiple forms of activity. These institutions and this activity must be developed, organized in a complex manner, and united in a broad and flexible system which can absorb and discipline the entire working class.

The shop with its internal committees, socialist circles, and the peasant communities are the centers of proletarian life, and we must work directly within them.

The internal committees are organs of workers' democracy which must be freed from the limitations imposed upon them by management and infused with new life and energy. Today, the internal committees limit the power of the capitalist in the factories and perform the functions of arbitration and discipline. Tomorrow, developed and enriched, they must be the organs of proletarian power that will replace the capitalist in all his useful functions of management and administration.

The workers should proceed forthwith to the election of broad assemblies of delegates, chosen from among the best and most conscious comrades, under the slogan "All power in the shop to the shop committees," together with a second, "All state power to the workers' and peasants' councils."

A vast field for concrete revolutionary propaganda would open up before communists, organized in the Party and the ward circles. The circles, in accord with the urban sections, should make an assessment of the workers' forces in their zone and become the seat of the ward council of the shop delegates, the vital nerve center of all the proletarian energies of the ward. The electoral systems could be varied according to the size of the shops, but the target should be one elected delegate for every fifteen workers, broken down by category (as is done in English factories). In this way, by a series of electoral stages, the final committee of factory delegates should include representatives of the entire labor process (workers, clerical staff, technicians). The ward committee should also strive to include delegates from the other categories of workers living in that ward as well: servants, cabdrivers, streetcar conductors, railroad workers, street cleaners, salesclerks, etc.

The ward committee should be the expression of the *entire working class* living in the ward, a legitimate and authoritative body capable of generating respect for a system of discipline invested with voluntarily delegated power and of ordering an immediate and total work stoppage throughout the entire ward.

The ward committees would be linked up in citywide committees, controlled and disciplined by the Socialist Party and the trade union federations.

Such a system of workers' democracy (coordinated with their equivalent peasant organizations) would provide a permanent form and discipline to the masses. It would be a magnificent school for political and administrative experience and would include all of the masses down to the last man; within it the masses would learn tenacity and perseverance and would become accustomed to regarding themselves as an army in the field that requires a strong cohesiveness if it is not to be destroyed and reduced to slavery.

Each factory would constitute one or more regiments of this army, with its commanders, its liaison officers, its officers' corps, and its general staff, each with powers delegated by free election, not imposed in an authoritarian manner. Meetings held in the shops and ceaseless propaganda and persuasion by the most conscious workers should bring about a radical transformation of the workers' psychology, improve the preparedness of the masses to

exercise power and their ability to do so, and inculcate an awareness of the rights and duties of both comrade and worker, an
awareness that is both concrete and effective because it is derived
directly from living historical experience.

Antonio Gramsci and Palmiro Togliatti, June 21, 1919

Trade Unions and Councils

Trade unionism has shown itself to be no more than another form of capitalist society, not a potential supersession of it.
It organizes the workers not as producers but as wage earners,
that is, as products of the capitalist system of private property, as
sellers of the commodity of labor. Trade unionism unites the
workers on the basis of the tool they use in their labor or the material they must transform; in other words, it unites them on the
basis of the forms imposed upon them by the capitalist system,
the system of economic individualism. Using one tool or processing one material rather than another cultivates different skills
and different attitudes toward labor and earnings. The worker
becomes fixed in his skill and attitude and comes to conceive of
them not as a factor in or aspect of production but as a mere
means to earn money.

The trade union, or the industrial union, unites the worker
with his comrades in the same trade or same industry, with those
who use the same tool or transform the same material; in so
doing, it reinforces this psychology, making the possibility of the
worker's ever conceiving of himself as a "producer" increasingly
more remote. The worker is led to consider himself a "commodity" on a national or international market, whose price and value
are determined by competition.

The worker will be able to see himself as a producer only if he
sees himself as an inseparable part of the entire system of labor
subsumed in the manufactured object, only if he lives the unity
of the industrial process, which requires the collaboration of
skilled and unskilled worker, of the office employee, the engineer,
and the technical manager alike. . . . Moving from this primary
element, seen as a unity, as the creator of a specific product, the
worker rises to an understanding of an ever broader unity until
his thought embraces the nation, which in its entirety is a gigan-

tic system of production, characterized by its exports, by the sum of the wealth it exchanges against an equivalent sum of wealth flowing from every part of the world, from the numerous other gigantic systems of production of which the world is constituted. When his thought has accomplished this movement, the operator has become a producer: he has acquired the consciousness of his function within the entire productive process from the factory to the nation, and to the world. Then the worker perceives his class and becomes a communist because he sees that private property is not a function of productivity; then he becomes a revolutionary because he perceives the capitalist, the private owner, as a dead spot, an obstacle that must be eliminated. He then understands the "state," that complex organization of society, as a concrete form of society; he sees that it is only a particular form of the gigantic system of production that reflects—with all the new and higher relations, interlockings, and functions demanded by its immanent grandeur—the life of the factory. He sees that the state represents the totality of the finely balanced and hierarchically ordered conditions necessary for his industry, his factory, and his person as producer to live and grow.

November 8, 1919

The dictatorship of the proletariat can only be embodied in a type of organization that is specific to the activity of producers, not wage earners, the slaves of capital. The factory council is the basic unit of such an organization. All branches of labor are represented in the factory council in proportion to the contribution each craft (trade) and each branch of labor makes to the manufacture of the object the factory produces for the society at large; it is therefore a class institution and a social institution. Its raison d'être rests in labor, in industrial production—that is, in a permanent fact—and no longer in wages, in class division, i.e., in a fact that is transitory and which for that very reason we wish to supersede.

Hence, the council makes the unity of the working class a reality, gives the masses a cohesiveness and a form that reproduce the cohesiveness and form assumed by the masses in the general organization of society.

The factory council is the model for the proletarian state. All the problems inherent in the organization of the proletarian state are to be found in the organization of the council. In both, the concept of citizen gives way to the concept of comrade: collaboration in useful and high-quality production develops solidarity and multiplies the bonds of affection and fraternity. Everyone is indispensable, everyone has a function and a position. Even the most ignorant and backward of workers, even the most vain and "polite" of engineers will ultimately be persuaded of this truth in the experience of the factory organization: all will eventually acquire a communist consciousness capable of grasping the great advance a communist economy represents over a capitalist economy. The council is the body best suited to see to the mutual process of education and the development of the new social spirit gestating in the proletariat's vibrant and rich experience of the community of labor. In the trade union, workers' solidarity developed through their struggle against capitalism in suffering and in sacrifice, while in the council it is a positive and permanent phenomenon. It is inherent in the most magnificent aspect of industrial production, contained in the exhilarating consciousness of being an organic whole, a homogeneous and compact system, which by the provision of useful labor and by the disinterested production of wealth affirms its sovereignty and its power and freedom to make history. . . .

The factory council is also based on the trades. In every department, the workers are separated into teams, and each team is a labor unit (a trade unit); the council is made up of the representatives whom the workers elect by departmental team (craft). But whereas a trade union is based on the individual, the council is based on the organic and concrete unity of the trade as it is forged by the discipline of the industrial process. The team (trade) senses its distinctness within the homogeneous body of the class, but at the same time it feels itself an integral unit in the system of discipline and order that makes possible the development of production by functioning with exactitude and precision. In its economic and political interests, a trade is in perfect union with the class as a whole; insofar as it represents a separate technical interest and the development of a particular instrument used in the labor process, it is distinct from it. In the same way, all industries constitute an integral and homogeneous whole as regards their aim of perfecting the production, distribution, and accumulation of social wealth. But each industry has distinct interests where the technical organization of its specific activity is concerned.

The existence of the councils gives the workers direct responsibility over production, induces them to improve their work, and institutes a conscious and voluntary discipline; it creates the psychology of a producer, of the maker of history. The workers will carry this new consciousness into the unions, and now, rather than restricting its activity to the class struggle alone, the union will devote itself to the fundamental work of imposing a new structure on economic life and the technology of labor, and to working out the form of economic life and occupational technique proper to communist society. In this sense, the unions, made up of the best and most conscious workers, will realize the highest moment of the class struggle and the dictatorship of the proletariat: they will create the objective conditions in which classes can no longer exist or reemerge. . . .

Organization by factory will bring together the class (the entire class) into a homogeneous and cohesive unity that can adapt to the industrial process of production and dominate it by placing it under control once and for all. Factory organization, therefore, is the embodiment of the dictatorship of the proletariat, the communist state that destroys class domination in the political superstructures and their general interworkings.

Trade unions and industrial unions are the solid backbone of the great body of the proletariat. They elaborate and accumulate individual and local experience, bringing about on a national scale the equalization of the conditions of labor and production on which communist equality is concretely based. But if it is to be possible to impress this positive class and communist direction on the unions, the workers must apply the full force of their will and conviction to the consolidation and propagation of the councils and to the organic unification of the working class. On this homogeneous and solid foundation, all the higher structures of communist dictatorship and communist economy will flourish and develop.

October 11, 1919

The emergence of industrial legality was a major victory for the working class, but it is not the ultimate and definitive victory. Industrial legality has improved the material living conditions of the working class, but it is no more than a compromise which had to be made and which must be supported until the balance of power tips in favor of the working class. If the officials of the trade union organization consider industrial legality a necessary, though not permanent, compromise; if they devote the means at their disposal toward improving the balance of forces in favor of the working class; if they make all the necessary moral and material preparation to enable the working class, at the appropriate moment, to launch a successful offensive against capital and subject it to its law, then the union is an instrument serving the revolution, and union discipline, even when it is used to make the workers respect industrial legality, is a revolutionary discipline.

The relations that should prevail between a trade union and a factory council must be considered in the light of our appraisal of the nature and value of industrial legality.

The council is the negation of industrial legality. It tends to abolish it at every instant, drives the working class unwaveringly onward toward the conquest of industrial power, and aims at placing the source of that power in the hands of the working class. The union represents legality and must undertake to see that this legality is respected by its members. The trade union is responsible to the industrialists, but only to the extent that it is responsible to its own members: it guarantees a steady job and income to workers and their families—that is, it guarantees workers enough to eat and a roof over their heads. Through its revolutionary spontaneity, the council is at the verge of unleashing class war at any moment. The trade union, because of its bureaucratic form, tends to prevent class war from ever erupting. The relationships between these two institutions should be such that they tend to create a situation in which a capricious impulse on the part of the council will not mean a step backward, a routing, for the working class; that is, a situation in which the council accepts and assimilates the discipline of the trade union, while the revolutionary character of the council, in turn, exercises influence on the trade union, dissolving, as it were, its bureaucratism.

The council strives at every moment to pass beyond the bounds of industrial legality. The council is the exploited, tyrannized masses, compelled to perform servile labor; hence, it tends to universalize any rebellion, to give a revolutionary value and scope to each of its acts of power. The trade union, as an organization jointly and severally committed to legality, tends to universalize and perpetuate this legality. The relations between trade union and council should be such that they create conditions in which the constraints of legality are transcended and the proletarian offensive launched at the most opportune moment for the working class, when it has at least the minimum of preparation necessary for a durable victory.

The links between trade union and council can be established on only one basis: the majority or a substantial part of the voting members of the council must be organized in the union. Any attempt to join the two institutions in a hierarchical dependence can only lead to the destruction of both.

If the conception of the council as a mere instrument of the trade union struggle is allowed to prevail, with the trade union exercising discipline and direct control over the council, the council will be rendered powerless as a force in revolutionary expansion, as a form contributing to the real development of the revolutionary proletariat, a form that tends spontaneously to create new modes of discipline, new modes of production and labor—in a word, communist society. The emergence of the councils is a result of the position that the working class has won for itself in industrial production; it is a manifestation of the historical necessity of the working class. Hence, any attempt to subordinate the council hierarchically to the trade union will sooner or later precipitate a clash between the two institutions. The council derives its power from its intimacy, its unity, with the consciousness of the working masses, who are striving toward an autonomous act of emancipation and a free hand in the creation of history: the entire masses participate in the life of the council and feel that they count for something in its activity. But only a very restricted number of the masses participate in the life of the trade union, and their real strength derives from this fact. But this fact also contains a weakness that cannot be put to test without grave risks.

If, on the other hand, the trade union were to rest directly on the councils—not to dominate them but to become a higher form of them—then the inherent tendency of the councils to pass beyond industrial legality at every moment, and at any moment unleash the revolutionary act of class war, would be reflected in the trade union. The latter would forfeit its ability to make commitments and would lose its capacity to act as a disciplinary and regulative force on the impulsiveness of the working class.

If its members establish revolutionary discipline within the union, a discipline which the masses recognize as a necessity for the victory of the proletarian revolution and not as an enslavement to capital, this discipline will unquestionably be accepted and assimilated by the council as its own. If the trade union becomes an organization for revolutionary preparation and appears as such to the masses in its ongoing practice, in the men who compose it, and in its propaganda, then its centralized and absolute character will be viewed by the masses as a major revolutionary force, as one more condition—and a very important one—for the success of the struggle to which they are wholly committed. . . .

Communists strive to make the revolutionary act as conscious and responsible as possible; they therefore want the choice (to the extent that it is a choice) of the moment to unleash the workers' offensive to remain in the hands of the most conscious and responsible segment of the working class; that is, of those workers who are organized in the Socialist Party and actively participate in the life of the organization. For this reason, communists cannot wish to see the trade union lose its discipline and systematic centralization.

June 12, 1920

The Factory Council

The proletarian revolution is not the arbitrary act of an organization or set of organizations proclaiming themselves to be revolutionary. It is a long and drawn out historical process brought to its fruition by the emergence and development of specific forces of production (which are summed up in the expression "proletariat") in a specific historical context (to which we refer by the expressions "private property," "capitalist mode of production," "factory system," "organization of society in a democratic proletarian state") . . . .

The true process of the proletarian revolution cannot be identified with the development and actions of revolutionary organizations of a voluntary and contractual nature such as the political party and the trade union; these are organizations born on the terrain of bourgeois democracy and political freedom as the affirmation and further development of political freedom. These organizations, to the extent that they embody a doctrine that interprets the revolutionary process and predicts its development (within certain limits of historical probability) and are recognized by the masses as a reflection of their interests and their embryonic system of government, are at present—and are becoming increasingly so—the direct and responsible agents of the successive acts of liberation that will be undertaken by the entire working class in the course of the revolutionary process. But even so, these organizations are not the embodiment of that process; they do not supersede the bourgeois state, nor do they—nor can they —embrace all the multiple pulsating foci of revolutionary forces that capitalism unleashes as it moves implacably forward as a machine of exploitation and oppression. . . .

Revolutionary organizations (the political party, the trade union) are born on the terrain of political freedom, the soil of bourgeois democracy, as the affirmation and development of freedom and democracy in general, where relationships of citizen to citizen subsist. The revolutionary process takes place on the terrain of production, in the factory, where the relations are those of oppressor to oppressed, exploiter to exploited, where freedom does not exist for the worker, where democracy does not exist. The revolutionary process takes place where the worker is nothing and wants to become all, where the power of the proprietor is unlimited, and where this power is life and death over the worker, the worker's wife, and his children. . . .

When do we say that the historical process of the workers' revolution has burst forth into the light of day as a controllable and documentable force?

We say this when the entire working class has become revolutionary, no longer in the sense that it categorically refuses to participate in the bourgeois institutions of government and thus represents an opposition within the structures of bourgeois democracy, but in the sense that the entire working class, as it exists in the factory, initiates a series of events that must necessarily result in the founding of a workers' state—that is, in the transformation of human society into a form altogether different from anything that had previously existed, into a universal form that embraces the entire Workers' International and hence the whole of humanity. Furthermore, we say that the present period is revolutionary because we observe that the working class in every country is struggling with all its energies (but also with all the mistakes, gropings, and impediments peculiar to an oppressed class that has no historical experience and must do everything for the first time) to give birth to proletariat institutions of a new type, institutions with a representative basis within an industrial framework. We say that the present period is revolutionary because the working class is trying with all its energy and with all its will to found its own state. That is the reason we say that the birth of the workers' factory councils represents a major historical event, heralding a new era in the history of mankind; with this event the revolutionary process has burst forth into the light of day and has entered into a phase that is controllable and documentable. . . .

In the factory, the working class becomes a determinate "instrument of production" within a determinate organic system. The participation of every worker in this system is governed by "chance"; that is, by chance as far as his will is concerned, but by no means as regards his role as a source of labor, since in the labor process and in production his position is both necessary and specifically defined. It is only for this reason that he is hired, only for this reason that he is able to earn his bread. He is a cog in the mechanical division of labor, in the working class constituted into an instrument of production. If the worker acquires a clear consciousness of his "determinate necessity" and makes it the basis of a representative state system (that is, not voluntary or contractual, through a membership card, but absolute and organic, as a part of a reality that must be acknowledged if one wants to be assured of food, clothes, housing, industrial production) ; if the worker, if the working class, does this, it accomplishes something of momentous impact: it initiates a new era of history, the era of workers' states that are destined to coalesce to form the communist society, a world organized on the basis of and with the sturdiness of a large engineering works, a Communist International in which every people, every part of mankind, has its place, defined by the performance of a particular form of production and no longer by the fact that it is organized as a state with particular borders.

In building this representative system, the working class is actually completing the expropriation of the first machine of all, the most important instrument of production—the working class itself. In so doing, the working class rediscovers itself, acquiring a consciousness of its organic unity and counterposing itself as a whole to capitalism. The working class thus proclaims that industrial power and its source must be returned to the factory; it places the factory in a new light, from the workers' point of view, as a form in which the working class constitutes itself into a concrete body, as the prime element of a new state, the workers' state, and as the basis for a new representative system, the council system. The workers' state, since it is born out of a specific set of production relations, already creates thereby the conditions for its own development and ultimate withering away as a state, and for its organic integration into the world system of the Communist International.

In the council of a large engineering works today, every work team (constituted by trade) is organically linked, from the proletarian point of view, with the other teams of a section, and every aspect of industrial production merges with all other aspects, throwing the productive process into relief; thus, throughout the world, English coal joins with Russian petroleum, Siberian wheat with Sicilian sulfur, Vercellian rice with wood from Styria, to form a single, organic whole subject to an international administration that governs the riches of the world in the name of all of humanity. In this sense, the workers' factory council is the primary element of a historical process that must ultimately lead to the Communist International, no longer as a political organization of the revolutionary proletariat but as a reorganization of the world economy and of the whole of the human community on a national and international scale. Every real revolutionary action has a value and is real in the historical sense to the extent that it participates in this process and is understood as an act toward the liberation of this process from the bourgeois superstructures that restrict and obstruct it.

The relations that should exist between the political party and the factory council, and between the trade union and the factory council, are already implicit in what we have said. The party and the trade union must not set themselves above this institution, in which the historical process of revolution takes a controllable historical form, as its mentors or as ready-made superstructures; they must become the conscious agents of its liberation from the restrictive forces inherent in the bourgeois state, they must set themselves the task of organizing the general external (political) conditions in which the process of revolution can be expedited to the greatest possible degree and the liberated productive forces achieve their greatest expansion.

June 5, 1920

29. Report of the Graphic Arts Trade Union of Barcelona

[1936]

A. MARTÍNEZ, G. SUÁREZ, B. CASTILLO, D. A. DE SANTILLÁN

Fundamental aspirations of libertarian communism

The National Confederation of Labor, in the following points, establishes its fundamental aspirations as conditions for proletarian emancipation and human solidarity.

1. Socialization of the social wealth—land, raw materials, tools and machines, means of transportation, health and educational institutions—so that no person can live from the work of others nor profit from particular privileges at the expense of the community.

2. Suppression of all political power that makes the law for all and imposes it by coercive means.

3. Reorganization of economic and social life on the basis of work, taken in its broad meaning of manual, administrative, and technical work.

4. Guarantee of the means of life to those—children, the aged, and the ill—who cannot contribute at present or can no longer contribute to the process of production.

Reprinted from *Autogestion*, No. 18–19 (January–April 1972), 104–109, by permission of the publisher. Translated by Helen Kramer.

5. Suppression of all ecclesiastic establishment, instrument of spiritual oppression, but respect nevertheless of the religious, philosophic, social, and political beliefs of each individual.

6. Abolition of national frontiers, demasking the lie of nationalism, favoring the understanding, solidarity, and mutual aid of all peoples and all races.

7. Reconstruction of the family by free love, in freedom from all religious, political, or economic constraint.

A society of free producers and consumers

All the known social forms—of religious origin or political establishment—rest on the recognition of classes and privileges, imposing on a part of the population that is obliged to sell its labor as a commodity, the task of sustaining the idleness and enjoyment of the other part.

The National Confederation of Labor wishes to organize the social community on the basis of work for all and the just distribution of production among the members of society.

Socially useful and socially recognized work alone can guarantee the consumption of the fruits of human effort.

While in the known economic systems production has been separated from consumption, from the satisfaction of human needs, as a consequence of the primacy that the privileges and monopolies have arrogated to themselves, in the new community work has a sole mission and sole raison d'être: the satisfaction of material needs as well as those of the cultural order of man.

For the structuring of these forms of life, in which work will be the common foundation and the unavoidable basis of enjoyment for all, the National Confederation of Labor takes as the point of departure the productive cell, the place of work, independent of the religious faith, political belief, spiritual orientation, and residence of its members.

While in an organization of the political type the order to which the population is subjected rests on place of residence, religious creed, and political choice, in a society of free producers and consumers, the place of work and its connections by professional affinities shall replace the structures resulting from the statist institution and order—parliaments, city halls, etc.

While the possibility of multiple social agreements based on

personal affinities, common interests, proximity, and particular
tastes is not disregarded, their social regulation is not considered
necessary. But, in contrast, economic regulation, which affects
each one and obeys an indisputable need, is necessary. It is for
this reason that what interests the National Confederation of
Labor in the first place is the regulation of the economic life of
the regime to come.

In order to arrive at this state of things—which is the supreme
aspiration of those disinherited from the social wealth—it is necessary to proceed in two parallel and interdependent directions:

a) the insurrectional preparation—that is to say, preparation
of the violent struggle against the reigning privileges and monopolies—by means of the general strike; the occupation of the factories, the land, and the means of transport and communication;
the refusal to produce for capitalism and to obey the state; the
defense of conquered positions by all means, and aid to regions
where the forces of labor have not yet succeeded;

b) the economic preparation to substitute for financial direction of productive life in the interest of privileged minorities, the
direction of the producers and distributors themselves in the interest of the whole laboring collective.

Plan of economic reorganization

The direction and control of production in the hands of the producers themselves

The place of work. The first productive cell, the first
expression of the socialized economy, is at the place of work:
factory, farm, mine, vessel, school, etc.

All the manual, administrative, and technical personnel of each
place of work form by delegation of its sections a committee of
the factory, farm, mine, etc.

These committees, recallable at any moment, organize work at
the place of their jurisdiction and are responsible for their functions and management to the personnel that appoint them. The
places of work enter into reciprocal relations by affinities of function on the local level and create sections or trade unions. These
sections or trade unions of a particular industry constitute a federation or council of the industrial branch.

Federations or councils of industrial branches

Thus, from below on up, from the place of work to the industrial level, embracing by industry the whole of activities that tend to the satisfaction of a human need, are formed as many branch federations or councils as there are industrial functions in each locality. . . .

Local liaison

The industrial federations or councils are associated in a local federation of industrial branches (or local council of the economy) in which the particular interests of various guilds are balanced, production and distribution are coordinated, common regulation is established, the exceptions permitted to this regulation on the local level are studied, and statistical and demographic data are centralized.

National liaison

Two lines of permanent liaison run from the place of work to the association of all the country's productive forces:

a) the geographic line reaches from the trade union, federation, or industrial branch council to the local federation of industrial councils, whence it rises to the regional economic federation or council and from there to the national economic council;

b) the other, professional line leads from the place of work to the trade union or section, from this to the industrial branch or federation of the locality, then to the regional federation of the industry in question, and from the latter to the national body.

In a statist structure, each inhabitant of a country is registered in the records of the civil service, the military archives, or the bureau of taxation; in the new economy inhabitants will also be registered—not as citizens, future soldiers, or taxpayers, but as producers and consumers.

The natural and spontaneous play of these forces of production excludes parasitic entities, whose function yields no benefit to useful work. Thus courts, jailers, police, professional armies, state functionaries, the financial apparatus, rentiers, speculators, and clergy disappear. . . .

Mechanism of public opinion

As counterweight to the economic organism of the new social community, public opinion is fully manifested and can be expressed:

1) at the place of work, then in the section or trade union, in the industrial branch council, in the federation or local center of the economy, and thence further (it is understood that in the general assemblies of the industrial section or federation or branch council, those who are engaged in the productive process and those who, owing to illness, invalidity, or age have ceased to be in it, will have an equal deliberative voice) ;

2) in the social liaisons created by common attachments, interests, proximity, etc.; the public assemblies, press, etc., will be employed in making known the initiatives taken and in obtaining for those concerned the decisions of the productive structures.

30. Decree on the Collectivization and Control of Industry and Trade in Catalonia

[October 24, 1936]

Introduction

The criminal military uprising of July 19 caused an extraordinary disturbance in the country's economy. The General Council must see to it that the severe wounds inflicted on the industry and trade of Catalonia by the treachery of those who tried to impose a government of force on our country are healed. The people's reaction to that uprising was so strong that it evoked a deep socioeconomic transformation whose bases are now being strengthened in Catalonia. The accumulation of wealth in the hands of a small group of people who constantly replace each other had as its consequence the increase of misery among the working class. Since that group, in order to save its privileges, did not hesitate to evoke a criminal war, the victory of the people will be the death of capitalism.

It is necessary, however, to organize production and guide it so that the people are the only beneficiaries, which means that the leading role in the new social order should belong to the worker. The abolition of incomes that do not correspond to work is obligatory.

Reprinted from Andrija Krešić and Trivo Indjić, eds., *Diktatura proletarijata i radnički samouprava* (Belgrade: Sedma Sila, 1967), pp. 152–59, by permission of the editors. Translated by Helen Kramer.

The principle of the economic and social organization of large industry must be collectivized production. . . .

In keeping with the above considerations, and after inspection of the report of the Economic Council, on the proposal of the Minister of the Economy and with the agreement of the Council, it is ruled:

Article 1. In accordance with the basic principles established in this decree, the industrial and trade enterprises of Catalonia are divided into:

a) collectivized enterprises in which the responsibility of management lies with the workers of the enterprise and which will be represented by the works council;

b) private enterprises, in which management is the task of the owner or manager, with the cooperation and financial control of the workers' control board.

I. Collectivized enterprises

Article 2. All industrial and trade enterprises which on June 30, 1936, employed more than one hundred persons, and also those which employed fewer workers but whose employers were proclaimed as rebels or abandoned the enterprise, are compulsorily collectivized.

Enterprises with less than one hundred workers can also be collectivized if not only a majority of the workers but also the owner or owners agree to it.

Enterprises with more than fifty but less than one hundred workers can be collectivized in the same way if three-fourths of the workers agree.

The Economic Council can make decisions as to the collectivization of those industries that, because of their importance for the national economy or other special characteristics, would be best torn away from the influence of private enterprise.

Article 3. Only people's courts can proclaim a person a rebel in order to apply the preceding article. . . .

II. Works councils

Article 10. The collectivized plant is managed by the works council which the workers elect from their ranks at a general assembly. This assembly determines the number of workers that will comprise the works council. It must be between five and fifteen. In forming the works council, different branches of employment must be represented (production, management, technical services, and commercial transactions). Where that is the case, the various trade unions to which the workers belong must be proportionately represented in the works council. The mandate lasts two years. Each year, half of the membership is renewed. Reelection is permitted.

Article 11. The works councils take over the functions and responsibilities of the former management boards (supervisory boards) in corporations, as well as the conducting of business.

For the conducting of business, they are responsible to the workers of their own factory and to the corresponding general council of the industry. . . .

Article 19. The works councils, at the end of their mandate, are obliged to submit accounts of their management to the workers at a general assembly. Furthermore, the works councils are obliged to submit to the general council of the industry a copy of their balance sheets and a semiannual and annual report which shall show details of the enterprise's situation and future plans.

Article 20. The general assembly of workers or the general council of the industry concerned can, in the case of evident incapacity or resistance against the guidelines of the latter, remove the entire works council or a part of it from duty.

If the general council of the concerned industry has ordered a recall, then the general assembly of workers of the factory can complain against this decision to the Minister of Economy, whose decision—after a prior report of the Economic Council—is final.

III. Control boards in private enterprises

Article 21. A workers' control board shall be established compulsorily in industrial or trade enterprises that are not collectivized. All branches of the enterprise (production, management, technical services) must be represented in this body. The workers freely determine the number of board members. Each trade union should be represented in proportion to the number of its members in the plant.

Article 22. The control board has the following tasks:

a) control of the conditions of work, i.e., control of the exact execution of prevailing regulations in relation to wages, working hours, social insurance, hygiene, safety, etc., as well as control over strict work discipline; all communications and announcements of the manager to the personnel are made through the board;

b) control of management in the sense of supervision of revenues and expenditures, both in cash and through the bank, in which the needs of the enterprise should be taken into account; further, control of all other commercial operations;

c) control of production, which consists of close cooperation with the employer with the goal of improving the production process. The workers' control boards shall establish the best possible relations with the technical staff in order to insure the good flow of work.

Article 23. Employers are obliged to submit balance sheets and annual reports to the workers' control boards, which transmit them with their opinion to the authorized general council of the industry.

IV. General councils of industry

Article 24. The general councils of industry are formed in the following way:

—four elected representatives of the works council; the electoral system shall be announced in good time;

—eight representatives of the various trade unions, chosen in proportion to the number of their members; the numerical relation of the trade union representatives shall be determined by a procedure decided upon jointly by the headquarters of the unions;

—four technicians appointed by the Economic Council.

The authorized member of the Economic Council of Catalonia shall preside over the industrial councils.

Article 25. The general councils of industry have the following tasks:

—adopting plans of work of general importance for the respective industry, in relation to which they give directives to the works councils regarding their tasks.

In addition, they are responsible for:

—regulating all of industrial production;

—maintaining uniform prices in order to avoid competition as much as possible;

—investigating the general needs of industry;

—investigating the needs of the consumers of the industry's products;

—examining the possibility of selling on the Iberian Peninsula and abroad;

—controlling the general course of industry and determining the limits of the rhythm of production for each article;

—proposing the decrease and the increase of the number of factories in conformity with the needs of industry and consumption; likewise merging certain factories;

—proposing reforms of certain methods of work, credit, and circulation;

—taking the initiative in changes in tariff rates and trade agreements;

—founding buying and selling centers for machines and raw materials;

—conducting certain business affairs with the industries of other localities of the Peninsula or abroad;

—seeking banking or other discounts;

—collectively founding technical research laboratories;

—collecting statistics on production and consumption;

—substituting raw materials in the country for those of foreign origin.

In addition, the general councils of industry can examine and apply means that they consider necessary and that are important for the better development of the work for which they are responsible.

Article 26. The decisions of the general councils of Industry are legal and obligatory. Neither the works councils nor the private enterprise, under any excuse whatever, however well founded, may neglect their carrying out. They can only complain against them to the Minister of Economy, whose decision—after a prior report of the Economic Council—is final.

31. Law on Workers' Councils
[November 20, 1956]

In order to realize the initiatives of the working class with respect to its direct participation in the management of enterprises, the following is decided:

Article 1. Workers' councils shall be formed in state industrial and construction enterprises, as well as on state farms, if a majority of the workers employed in them so declare.

Article 2. 1. The workers' council, in the name of the collective, manages the enterprise, which represents national property.

2. The workers' council operates on the basis of compulsory legal regulations and tasks that emerge from the national economic plan, aiming at the development of the enterprise, the increase of production, the lowering of the costs of the products and improvement of their quality, and improvement of the conditions of work and life of the collective.

3. The workers' council makes decisions in the framework of the authorization given by the Council of Ministers to the enterprise.

Article 3. The jurisdiction of the work of the workers' council includes particularly:

Reprinted from Andrija Krešić and Trivo Indjić, eds., *Diktatura proletarijata i radnička samouprava* (Belgrade: Sedma Sila, 1967), pp. 157–58, by permission of the editors. Translated by Helen Kramer.

1. giving opinions of the forecasts of the annual indicators of the planning goals;

2. adopting annual plans of the enterprise on the basis of indicators that derive from the national economic plan;

3. adopting the operational plans of the enterprise;

4. determining the enterprise's structure and organization;

5. determining the directions of the enterprise's development;

6. determining basic directives for improving production, particularly for the rationalizations of technological processes, the improvement of the quality and appearance of products, the raising of the productivity of labor, the improvement of the safety conditions and hygiene of work, and the conservation of materials and fuel;

7. judging the economic activity of the enterprise and also confirming the annual balance sheets after the authorized supervisory organ receives them;

8. deciding on the sale of surplus machines and tools, on the basis of the director's opinion;

9. determining, in the framework of the enterprise's authorization and on the basis of a collective agreement, the work norms, pay scales according to job, and standards for awarding premiums;

10. deciding on the use of the part of profit that belongs to the enterprise for objectives connected with the enterprise's economic activity;

11. deciding on the distribution of the enterprise's fund or the part of profit that belongs to the collective;

12. adopting the internal rules of the enterprise. . . .

Article 7. 1. The workers' council is elected from the ranks of the workers, engineers, technicians, economists, and other workers and employees of the enterprise.

2. If possible, two-thirds of the members of the workers' council should be workers.

3. The enterprise's director is an ex officio member of the workers' council. . . .

Article 13. 1. The director of the enterprise and his deputy are appointed and replaced by the authorized state organ after agreement is reached with the workers' council.

2. The workers' council has the right to make proposals with respect to appointing and replacing the director and his deputy.

32. Factory Committees and Workers' Control (Theses of the Second Congress of the Communist International) [1920]

1. The economic struggle of the proletariat for the increase of wages and for the general improvement of the living conditions of the masses constantly accentuates its nature as a dead-end struggle. The economic disorganization that engulfs one country after another in a continually growing proportion demonstrates, even to the most backward workers, that it is not sufficient to struggle for the increase of wages and the reduction of the working day; that, more and more, the capitalist class is losing the capacity to reestablish economic life and to guarantee to workers merely the conditions of existence that were assured them before the war. The continually growing consciousness of the working masses is bringing to birth among them a tendency to create organizations capable of broaching the struggle for the economic renaissance by means of workers' control exercised over industry through production councils. This tendency to create industrial workers' councils, which is attracting the workers of all countries, draws its origin from different and multiple factors (struggle against reactionary bureaucracy, fatigue caused by the defeats sustained by the trade unions, tendencies toward the

Reprinted from Ernest Mandel, ed., *Contrôle ouvrier, conseils ouvriers, autogestion: anthologie* (Paris: François Maspero, 1970), pp. 126–28, by permission of René Coeckelberghs Partisanförlag. Translated by Helen Kramer.

creation of organizations embracing all workers) and is definitively inspired by the effort made to realize control of industry, the special historical task of the industrial workers' council. This is why one errs when one seeks to form only councils of workers committed to the dictatorship of the proletariat. The task of the Communist Party, on the contrary, consists in profiting from the economic disorganization in order to organize the workers and point them toward the necessity to struggle for the dictatorship of the proletariat while extending the idea of the struggle for workers' control, an idea that all now understand.

2. The Communist Party will be able to carry out this task only by consolidating in the consciousness of the masses the firm assurance that the restoration of economic life on the capitalist basis is presently impossible, and that it would, in addition, signify a new subservience to the capitalist class. Economic organization corresponding to the interests of the working masses is possible only if the state is governed by the working class and if the firm hand of the dictatorship of the proletariat is charged with the abolition of capitalism and the establishment of the new socialist organization.

3. The struggle of the factory and works committees against capitalism has as its immediate goal the introduction of workers' councils in all the branches of industry. The workers of each enterprise, independently of their professions, suffer from the sabotage of the capitalists, who judge often enough that the suspension of the activity of this or that industry will be advantageous to them, and hunger forces the workers to accept the most difficult conditions in order that some capitalist may avoid an increase of costs. The struggle against this sort of sabotage unites the majority of workers independently of their political ideas and makes the works and factory committees, elected by all the workers of an enterprise, true organizations of the mass of the proletariat. But the disorganization of the capitalist economy is not only the consequence of the conscious will of the capitalists but also—and much more—the result of the irresistible decadence of their regime. Also, the workers' committees will be forced, in their action against the consequences of this decadence, to exceed the bounds of control of isolated factories and works and will soon find themselves faced by the question of workers' control to be exercised over entire branches of industry and industry as a whole. The attempts of workers to exercise their control not only over the provisioning of factories and works with raw materials but also over

the financial operations of industrial enterprises will, however, provoke measures of force against the working class on the part of the bourgeoisie and the capitalist government, which will transform the workers' struggle for the control of industry into a struggle for the conquest of power by the working class. . . .

5. The industrial workers' councils will not know how to replace the trade unions. They can only organize themselves in the course of action in various branches of industry and create little by little a general apparatus capable of directing the entire struggle. Already at present the trade unions represent centralized organs of combat, although they do not encompass working masses as large as the industrial workers' councils can embrace in their type of organization, which is accessible to all the worker enterprises. The division of all the tasks of the working class between the industrial workers' councils and the trade unions is the result of the historical development of the social revolution. The trade unions organized the working masses with the goal of struggling for the increase of wages and for the reduction of the working day and carried out the struggle on a large scale. The industrial workers' councils are organized to establish worker control of industry and to struggle against economic disorganization; they encompass all the worker enterprises, but the struggle that they undertake can only very slowly assume a general political character. It is only to the extent that the trade unions succeed in surmounting the counterrevolutionary tendencies of their bureaucracy or become the conscious organs of the revolution that communists will have the duty of supporting the industrial workers' councils in their tendencies to become industrial trade union groups.

6. The task of communists reduces to assuring that the trade unions and industrial workers' councils are penetrated with the same spirit of combative revolution, consciousness, and understanding of the best methods of combat—that is to say, with the communist spirit. In order to carry out this task, communists must, in fact, subordinate the trade unions and the workers' committees to the Communist Party and thus create proletarian organs of the masses that will serve as the base of a powerful, centralized proletarian party, encompassing all the proletarian organizations and making them all march on the path that leads to the victory of the working class and to the dictatorship of the proletariat—to communism.

7. While the communists make the trade unions and the industrial councils a powerful weapon for the revolution, these or-

ganizations of the masses prepare themselves for the grand role that will devolve to them with the establishment of the dictatorship of the proletariat. In effect, it will be their duty to become the socialist base of the new organization of economic life. The trade unions, organized as pillars of industry, relying on the industrial workers' councils which will represent the organizations of the factories and works, will teach the working masses their industrial duty, make the most advanced workers enterprise directors, and organize technical control of specialists; together with the representatives of worker power, they will study and execute the plans of socialist economic policy.

33. The Control of Production

[1922]

ALEKSANDER LOZOVSKY

In the present period, the entire struggle of the working class should be concentrated on the control of production. Without control of the enterprises, it is impossible at the present time to resolve any question whatever that is posed to the working class. The problem of unemployment, the problem of the closing of enterprises, etc.—all this is linked to the control of production. Here there can be no compromise, no attempt to find a middle path or to organize a control that would be as acceptable to the employers as to the workers.

It is not a matter of formal financial control. It is not a question of establishing a review committee of the sort that will once or twice a year examine the accounts or the various circulars of the enterprise. That is not control of production, nor even a substitute for control, but simply a caricature of the very idea of workers' control. The object of control of production is to submit the multiple activities of each enterprise—industrial, technical, financial, commercial—to workers' control; in short, the multiple and diverse forms of contemporary productive activity must be submitted to the meticulous control of workers.

Reprinted from Ernest Mandel, ed., *Contrôle ouvrier, conseils ouvriers, autogestion: anthologie* (Paris: François Maspero, 1970), pp. 136–38, 140–41, by permission of René Coeckelberghs Partisanförlag. Translated by Helen Kramer.

250

But does not such a control organized by workers violate the interest of private property? It constitutes the interference of workers in a domain that, for all eternity, has belonged to the employers in a sanctuary closed to workers. Yes, the control of production is actually an interference of workers in the relations of private property. But this interference has become a historical necessity and must be realized in the interest of the preservation of the working class. The terrible waste of productive forces and values that took place during the war and that is observed in equal measure at the present time will cease only when the working class is put in direct contact with production, only when it is not merely an element of the economy but participates in it directly, only when it is not simply a part of the machine but the conscious director of the industrial mechanism. The transformation of the working class from *a class for others* into *a class for itself,* as Marx said, will evidently be made only after the social revolution, after the establishment of the socialist regime. But the very installation of this regime depends on the direction that will be taken in the near future by the working class in its attempt to establish control over production in the capitalist economy.

The idea of control over production was born long ago, well before the war. During the war it acquired citizenship in all countries when the bourgeois states, serving the interests of the bourgeois class, controlled the different branches of the national economy in seeking to preserve and perpetuate the domination of the bourgeoisie as a class. The government subordinated the different elements of the dominant class to its general interests. State control was the dominant economic idea during the entire war period. The end of the war was marked by the cessation of this state control, by the destruction of the command economy and the free play of all capitalist forces. But the free play of capitalist forces now runs counter to the particular interests of the working class. Hence, the idea that took root during the war period, and especially in the course of the Russian Revolution, of establishing a real rather than a fictive workers' control. The idea of control over production has spread so much at the present time that the bourgeois governments themselves are forced to become concerned with the question. When, at the end of 1920, the Italian workers occupied a certain number of factories for several weeks, Giollitti declared himself in favor of workers' control and even submitted to Parliament a corresponding draft of law. . . .

The working class is not inspired by the idea of equal rights and does not hold the point of view of some sort of worker democracy. . . . Workers' control must be established in fact by the workers themselves, and the organization of control committees must take place outside of any sort of authorization. The control committee oversees all that occurs within the enterprise and all the relations of its enterprise with the outside. Thus, at the same time that control over production is established, the working class must also achieve financial control, which is the most difficult task of workers' control. The First Congress of Revolutionary Trade Unions adopted a detailed resolution on the subject of workers' control whose thrust is expressed in the following brief propositions:

1. Workers' control is an indispensable and important school in the work of preparing the working masses for the social revolution.

2. Workers' control must be placed on the agenda in all the capitalist countries as a combat slogan of the trade union movement and must be employed energetically for the divulgence of commercial and financial secrets.

3. Workers' control must be used largely for the transformation of the trade unions into combat organizations of the working class.

4. Workers' control must be used as a means of reconstructing the trade unions by industry and not by occupation, an outdated system harmful to the revolutionary workers' movement.

5. Workers' control is incompatible with the principle of equality proposed by the bourgeoisie, nationalization, etc., and opposes the dictatorship of the proletariat to the dictatorship of the bourgeoisie.

6. In the realization of technical, financial, or mixed control, and also during the occupation of enterprises, it is especially indispensable to attempt to draw the most backward proletarian masses into the discussion of questions linked to this control. At the same time, in the process of realizing this control, it is necessary to make a census of the most active and most capable workers and prepare them for a directing role in the organization of production.

7. For the regular organization of workers' control on the spot, it is absolutely necessary that the trade unions direct the factory committees; they must link and combine the work of the factory committees in the enterprises of the same industry and forestall in that way the inevitable attempts to cultivate the factory localism that can be produced if control is scattered.

8. The trade unions must in the beginning help the control committees, elaborating to this end some special conditions; discuss the question in the daily press; and conduct broad agitation in favor of control in the works and factories, not only when explaining their tasks, but when making reports on the results of this control by enterprise and by groups of enterprises, in factory meetings, local conferences, etc.

34. Constitution of the Weimar Republic [August 1919]

Article 165. Workers and employees are called upon to cooperate on an equal basis in association with employers in the regulation of wages and working conditions as well as in the overall economic development of the forces of production. The mutual organizations and their agreements will be recognized.

To look out for their social and economic interests, workers and employees maintain legal representation in factory workers' councils as well as in district workers' councils according to economic regions and in a national workers' council.

The regional workers' councils and the national workers' council meet with representatives of the employers as well as representatives of the participating popular circles in district economic councils and a national economic council to perform common economic tasks and to cooperate in carrying out the nationalization decrees. The district economic councils and the national economic council are to be composed of representatives of the most important vocational groups according to their national economic and social significance.

Legislative proposals concerning sociopolitical and economic policy of fundamental importance shall be presented by the cabinet to the national economic council for its opinion before intro-

Translated by Helen Kramer.

duction to the Parliament. The national economic council itself has the right to propose such laws to the Parliament, and they are to receive equal treatment with bills of the cabinet or of the Council of State. The council can delegate representatives who can participate in parliamentary discussions on an equal basis with representatives of the regions.

Control and administrative powers in the spheres assigned to them can be transmitted to the workers' councils and economic councils.

35. Basic Law on the Management of State Enterprises and Holding Companies by Work Collectives [June 27, 1950]

I. Basic principles

Article 1. Factories, mines, and communications, and transport, trade, agricultural, forestry, communal, and other state enterprises, as public property, are managed by work collectives in the name of the social community within the framework of the state economic plan and on the basis of rights and responsibilities determined by the laws and other legal regulations.

Work collectives carry out this management through workers' councils and management boards of enterprises and of holding companies, in which several enterprises are merged.

Article 2. The workers' council of the enterprise and of the holding company is elected and dismissed by the work collectives.

In smaller enterprises, the entire work collective is the workers' council.

Article 3. The workers' council is elected for one year.

The workers' council as well as its individual members can be recalled before the expiration of the period for which it was elected.

Article 4. The workers' council, as the representative of the work collective, elects and dismisses the management board and exercises other rights determined by law.

Translated by Helen Kramer.

Article 5. The management board manages the enterprise or holding company and is responsible to the workers' council and authorized state organs for its work, and the management board of the enterprise also is responsible to the management board of the holding company.

In accordance with this responsibility, the management board works on the basis of law and other regulations, the conclusions of its workers' council, and the orders and instructions of the authorized state organs or of the management board of the holding company.

Article 6. The management board is elected for one year.

A maximum of one-third of the members of the management board from the preceding year can be reelected to the management board.

No one can be a member of the management board more than two years in a row.

During their mandate, the members of the management board do not give up their regular responsibilities and work in the enterprise.

Members are not paid for their work on the management board.

Article 7. During his mandate, a member of the management board cannot be dismissed from work, nor can he be transferred without his consent.

Article 8. The enterprise's director administers the enterprise's production and business affairs, and the holding company's director administers the work and business affairs of the holding company.

Until otherwise determined by law, to insure correct, competent administration of the enterprise and holding company, the enterprise director is appointed by the management board of the holding company, or the authorized state organ if the enterprise is not merged, and the director of the holding company is appointed by the authorized state organ.

The workers' council or management board of the enterprise can propose replacement of the director.

Article 9. The director is ex officio a member of the management board.

The enterprise director is responsible to the enterprise's management board, the holding company's management board and director, as well as the authorized state organ for his work, and the director of the holding company is responsible to the management board and the authorized state organ.

36. Constitution of Yugoslavia [April 7, 1963]

Part II. Socioeconomic organization

Article 6. The basis of the socioeconomic system of Yugoslavia is free, associated labor with socially owned means of production and self-management of the working people in production and distribution of the national product in the work organization and social community.

Article 7. Only work and the results of work shall determine a person's material and social position.

No one may directly or indirectly gain material or other advantages by exploiting the work of others.

Article 8. The means of production and other means of socially organized work, as well as mineral and other natural resources, are social property.

The employment of the means of production and other socially owned means and all other rights over these and other means shall be regulated by law in accordance with their nature and purpose.

Article 9. Self-management in the work organization shall include in particular the right and duty of the working people to:

1) manage the work organization directly or through organs of management elected by themselves;

Translated by Helen Kramer.

2) organize production or other activity, attend to the development of the work organization, and determine plans and programs of work and development;

3) decide on commerce in products and services and on other business matters of the work organization;

4) decide on the use of socially owned means and their disposal, and employ them economically so as to gain the greatest return for the work organization and the social community;

5) distribute the work organization's income and provide for the development of the material basis of its work; distribute income among the working people; meet the work organization's obligations to the social community;

6) decide on the admission of working people into the work organization, the cessation of their work, and other labor relations; determine hours of work in the organization in accordance with general working conditions; regulate other matters of common concern; secure internal supervision and render their work public;

7) regulate and promote their working conditions; organize labor safety and recreation; provide conditions for their education and advance their own and the general standard of living;

8) decide on dissociation of a part of the work organization and its establishment as a separate organization and decide on merger and association of the work organization with other work organizations.

In attaining self-government, the working people in the sociopolitical communities shall decide on the course of economic and social development, the distribution of the national product, and other matters of common concern.

Citizens and representatives of organizations concerned and of the social community may participate in the management of a work organization in affairs of special concern to the community.

In order to secure the uniform socioeconomic position of the working people, provision shall be made in law and statute determining the rights of self-management of people who work in the state administration and sociopolitical organizations or associations, in accordance with the nature of the work of these organizations.

The working people shall exercise self-management in the unified socioeconomic system in accordance with the Constitution, laws, and statutes, and shall be held responsible for their work.

Any act violating the right of self-management of the working people is unconstitutional.

Article 10. The working people of an organization, as members of the working community, shall establish mutual work relations and shall be equals in self-management.

The organization of work and management should enable the working people at every level and in every part of the work process that constitutes a whole to decide as directly as possible on matters of work, organization of mutual relations, distribution of income, and other matters affecting their economic position, and assure at the same time the most favorable conditions for the work and business activity of the organization as a whole.

Article 11. The product of socially organized work created in work organizations, as the basis of economic growth and the satisfaction of social needs and the personal and common needs of the working people, shall be allocated according to a uniform system of distribution and on the basis of uniform conditions and standards, assuring economic growth, distribution according to work, and social self-government.

The work organization, after providing the means for renewing the value of resources expended in work, and after allocating a part of the revenue from sale of output for equalization of conditions of work and of earning income, shall apportion the work organization's income into a fund to expand the material base of work and a fund to satisfy the personal and common needs of the working people.

To expand the material base of its work, the work organization shall be assured a part of the created value of the product, proportionate to its share in producing the means of economic growth, and, in noneconomic activities, a part in accordance with the tasks of the work organization and social needs. The work organization shall be entitled to a part of the created value of the product for satisfaction of the personal and common needs of the working people, proportionate to the productivity of labor and depending on the business success of the work organization, and, in noneconomic activities, proportionate to the results of the work done to satisfy social needs.

The funds of the work organization allocated for renewing and expanding the material base of work, as common funds for economic growth, shall be used to expand the material base of the work organization and the social community as a whole. The work organization shall employ these means in accordance with uniform principles of utilization of the means of economic growth determined by federal law and conditions and standards

determined by the regulations coordinating economic development and the attainment of the other basic relations envisaged by
the social plans.

To expand the material base of its work, the organization shall
be assured other social means, apart from those created by its own
work, under equal conditions and in accordance with the uniform principle of the credit system.

Article 12. In accordance with the principle of distribution according to work, each worker shall be entitled to personal income
proportionate to the results of his work and to the work of his
unit and of the work organization as a whole.

37. Program of the League of Communists of Yugoslavia [1958]

The position of producers and the role of the state

The state and production

Social ownership of the means of production makes it possible to exclude not only the private owner but ultimately also the state as an intermediary between the producer and the means of production. The producer becomes the bearer of the social function of managing production and, at the same time, an active participant in the function of distribution of the national product. The state appears less and less in direct production as political authority.

State organs, however, are still an important and essential factor in the carrying out of a number of social functions in relation to the economy and other spheres of society. The role of the state in that area of social relations does not derive from the political power that it has, nor from economic monopoly, but from the fact that the state itself is changing; that is, in this area it is be-

Reprinted from J. Djordjević et al., eds., *Teorija i praksa samoupravljanja u Ju-goslaviji* (Belgrade: Radnička štampa, 1972), pp. 117-22. Translated by Helen Kramer.

coming, and increasingly must become, a system of territorial-political self-governing organizations of the producers-consumers and their socioeconomic community on various levels from the township to the federation. This points simultaneously to the necessity of the commune, as the basic territorial organization of producers-consumers, in the social regulation of production and distribution, as well as to the changing role of the state organization in socialism. Among the functions of a state thus altered is decision-making in matters of common interest for both producers and citizens in general and their territorial communities. With respect to the nature of these functions, although for the most part they still appear as acts of political power, they no longer relate to the direct management of producers—to all those affairs that producers and citizens and their direct organs are in a position to handle—but have in essence a planning control, coordinational, and regulative character.

The direct producer in production and distribution

Such a role of the state is determined primarily by the new position of the producers in the economic organization and outside of it. The new social position of the producers under the conditions of socialist construction and their changed relationship toward production derives from the fact that the producers have been transformed from wage laborers into the direct managers of production and distribution, and from the fact that by this management they daily realize their personal interests—higher earnings, an increased personal and social standard of living. Under market conditions of production, the producers associated in work collectives necessarily are organized as independent economic organizations and realize their social rights and obligations in the management of production, entering into mutual business relations. Since under such conditions the personal interest of the producers depends not only on the result of the individual job but also on the work of the entire collective, on the business of the enterprise and its funds, on the level of economic development of the commune in which they live, on general economic conditions and the state of the market, on the social community as a whole, on its economic policy, etc., that personal interest is at the same time a constant stimulus to personal work and to conscious and active participation of producers in the organs of management, above all in the workers' council, in the commune and the producers' chambers, and, through them, in the overall system of government and social self-government as well.

Proceeding from such an assumption, the League of Communists of Yugoslavia considers that the producer and work collective must enjoy—within the framework of general social interests, expressed by the social plan which guides economic development and by other decisions of social organs—maximum independence in their work and business activity; that is, in production and the disposal of certain funds in the enterprise. This means that producers and work collectives can, within certain planning and legal frameworks, directly and independently manage production; merge, link up, and cooperate with other organizations in accordance with the needs of production; and independently and freely develop their creative initiative in the direction of increasing the productivity of labor and total production. Under conditions of socialist social self-government, working people should be offered the real possibility of deciding on the creation and overall distribution of the national product. Only under such conditions does the working man obtain full insight into necessary material trends and thus emancipate himself—that is, by adjusting his work and social activity to the essential material frameworks of society, he becomes the master of his fate.

Abolishing the wage relation— emancipation of labor

The individual producer and the collective directly influence their own material position. Work becomes emancipated, and work relations lose the character of the wage relation. Such free, creative work at the same time becomes a factor of the material progress of society and the constant advancement of socialist relations among people. Conditions begin to be created for the gradual elimination of the contrast between mental and physical labor. Society as a whole is increasingly constituted as a community of producers, in which all are interested in as rational as possible a management of things and in as productive work from each and all as is possible. The results in that area of material and social relations determine not only the level of material well-being but also the degree of the real freedom of the individual.

When each person works according to his abilities and when the personal income of the individual and the conditions for the development of economic organizations depend on the intensity and quality of their work and success in business, every effort of the individual producer and of the entire work collective toward greater satisfaction of their material needs through more productive labor and better business operation of the enterprise represents, at the same time, effort to the benefit of general social interests and to the faster progress of society. Only if that interest of the direct producers is awakened and transformed into the basic material factor of economic progress can maximum success be realized for the planning and regulatory measures that the community as a whole consciously undertakes to guide economic development, advance production, develop productive forces, and further develop socialist social relations. Socialism cannot subordinate man's personal happiness to some sort of "higher goals," for the highest goal of socialism is man's personal happiness. On the other hand, no one has the right to realize his personal interest at the expense of the common interest of all.

Emphasizing the personal and material interest of the working man as the driving force of his creative activity in the capacity of producer and social being, the League of Communists of Yugoslavia does not consider that this factor automatically solves the problem of social progress and that it exhausts the content of personal life. On the contrary, as a conscious social being under socialist conditions, man will increasingly liberate himself of blind subordination to material processes and will become, to an increasing degree, the master of nature and of his own material position. Hence, ideas, moral factors, spiritual creativity, and even the bearing of material sacrifices to attain certain ideological, moral, and cultural-political goals gain increasing importance in social development. Precisely these factors represent social consciousness and become the spiritual driving force and orientation of practice. . . .

The rights of the individual to work, personal income in keeping with his work and the business operation of the entire collective, participation in the management of the social means of production, security in the case of accident at work, protection in case of illness and provision for his family in case of death, protection in the work relation, and other socioeconomic and political rights that grow and develop on the basis of social ownership and the constant widening and enriching of the economic base of socialist society, become a component part of the personal rights of the working man who produces by use of social means of production.

Internal contradictions in socialism and their overcoming

. . . As a new society, still undeveloped and class structured, socialism in Yugoslavia is developing in conjunction with the existence of an important state role within the framework of a market economy. Distribution is carried out by means of money in conformity with the principle of payment according to work. Under these conditions, contradictions appear, are overcome, and reappear between the collective and individual interests of the producers, the state and social self-government, the commune and higher levels of government, compulsion and freedom, the general policy and a man's personal self-determination, etc.

The essence of socialism lies not in the forced and seeming abolition of these contradictions by means of an omnipotent state. In socialist society, internal contradictions are resolved less by the antagonistic reactions characteristic of a class society and increasingly by the conscious action of the leading social forces and by continual evolution.

Conscious that as long as the state exists there is still a danger that it might obtain independent power and thereby heighten certain contradictions of socialist development and transform them into antagonistic ones, the League of Communists considers that, in the contemporary socialist phase of the development of Yugoslavia, the state will have a positive role insofar as it itself develops into a democratic mechanism through which the interests of the basic socialist factors—the producers, work collective, commune, and society as a community of producers—are expressed and harmonized. The role of the state will be progressive insofar as the contradictions that arise on that basis can be democratically resolved without, on the one hand, checking the independence of the socialist producer and his economic and social initiative, nor, on the other, allowing necessary contradictions to develop into anarchic haphazardness and antagonistic conflicts, which would lead to the destruction of the basis of socialism.

Precisely from such contradictions emerges the necessity of limiting the producers' independence by certain centralized economic institutions and functions of society and the state, and of limiting the power and economic function of the central social and state organs by the independence and self-management of the producers and basic factors of socialist material development.

In realizing the personal and common interests of the producers-consumers in Yugoslavia, in addition to the economic organizations managed by workers' councils, the territorial-political communities also have a special role and place, among which the most basic belongs to the self-governing commune. In such socialist communities, social questions, the economy, and culture become the common political affairs, and politics is transformed into social activity which orients people not toward individual party leadership—as happens under conditions of bourgeois democracy—but toward public affairs, which are theirs; that is, it turns them directly toward social affairs. Thus, the work collectives, along with the workers' councils and the communes, become the basis and starting point for the further construction of the overall political structure of socialism and for the final prevailing of the common interests of free citizens over the elements of haphazardness, anarchy, and bureaucracy. In this sense, such a political system of the socialist state, based and developed on social self-government, replaces the political system of the bourgeois multiparty state and is incomparably more capable than the latter of resolving, by peaceful social evolution and the democratic struggle of opinions, the social contradictions in the process of gradual development in the social base itself. . . .

Administration of things

The development of the most suitable social mechanism for the administration of things under conditions of social ownership of the means of production is expressed above all in the division between management of a technological process and general economic and political management in the enterprise, as well as in the development of production and business cooperation and various forms of vertical association of individual branches of the economy and other social activities.

Vertical linking of the basic institutions of social self-government by the creation of higher forms (chambers of commerce, mergers, various forms of production and business cooperation and communities, higher bureaus of social insurance, etc.) represents a democratic form of uniting those expert, technical, and coordinating functions that a modern society should manage centrally. The social and democratic character of this uniting lies in the fact that it is carried out not mechanically, by administrative measures from outside, but only in the interest of the associated producers and citizens themselves through their voluntary cooperation, without taking away from the institutions and organs of the working people the essential functions of self-government.

The same process also occurs in the fields of education, science, culture, health, social insurance, and social protection, as well as other fields in which various institutions carry out public functions and public services. The functions of management, along with suitably allocated rights and cooperation, are transferred to the representatives of the work collectives and of the social community. These organs are elected and recalled by the citizens who are interested in carrying out the corresponding public services by broad participation and control in the managerial organs. At the same time, the state administrative organs in the fields of education, culture, health, social services, and such increasingly become, in both composition and functions, organs of social self-government.

This process, finally, is expressed in the development of various forms of social control and cooperation of interested citizens with enterprises and institutions. Without changing the status of workers' self-management, self-management of the working people is supplemented in the field of trade and in some other areas by organs of social self-government such as consumers' councils, consumer cooperatives, and the like; and in economic organizations engaged in educational, cultural, and other activities (publishing enterprises, newspaper enterprises, various enterprises in the field of film, etc.), by organs such as councils including representatives of cultural and educational life and the public in general. Such forms of social self-government help to assure that the public functions in which these organizations are engaged are executed in harmony with the needs and interests of socialist society.

The system of social self-government also includes housing, as well as a number of other buildings and services of common interest for individual communities.

All these relations and institutions arise out of the direct needs of the work and business activity of individual enterprises and organizations, as well as the direct, vital needs of citizens in the areas of the family household, consumption, culture, entertainment, social needs, etc. Hence, they must necessarily be very diverse in both organizational forms and methods of work.

The struggle for the constant advancement of all these relations and institutions simultaneously means a struggle for better operation of enterprises and organizations, for better material supplying of the population, for faster technical and cultural development, for the prevention of bureaucracy and conservatism, for faster and more just solution of social problems, etc., and, at the same time, for the constant progress of socialist and democratic relations among people.

38. Theses of Pulacayo: Text Adopted by the Trade Union Federation of Miners of Bolivia* [November 8, 1946]

6. Workers' control of the mines

The TUFMB supports all measures undertaken by the trade unions in the direction of achieving effective workers' control over all aspects of the functioning of the mines. We must reveal the managerial secrets of exploitation, technical accounting, transformation of minerals, etc., in order to establish the direct intervention of the workers as such in the so-called secrets. Since our objective is the occupation of the mines, we must interest ourselves in throwing light on the employer's secrets.

The workers should control the technical direction of exploitation, control the account books, and intervene in the appointment of employees, and they should particularly interest themselves in the publication of the profits received by the large mining companies and the frauds they perpetrate in connection with the payment of taxes to the state and contributions to the Workers' Security and Savings Bank.

To the reformers who speak of the sacred right of the employers, we oppose the slogan *Workers' control over the mines.*

Reprinted from Ernest Mandel, ed., *Contrôle ouvrier, conseils ouvriers, autogestion: anthologie* (Paris: François Maspero, 1970), pp. 343–44, by permission of René Coeckelberghs Partisanförlag. Translated by Helen Kramer.

*The Bolivian miners' trade union adopted the demand for workers' control in its Theses of Pulacayo in November 1946. It was achieved in the aftermath of the revolution of 1953, then slowly perverted, as manifested by the Theses of Colquiri of December 1963. But in the meantime, workers' control had become a reality.

39. Theses of Colquiri: Adopted by the Trade Union Federation of Miners of Bolivia [December 5, 1963]

1. We repeat what was already stated at the congress of Colquiri–San José: the antinational attitude of the present government enters violently into conflict with the orientation of the workers, who are seeking to consolidate the conquests made up to today and to surpass them. Political evolution is moving into a division into two well-defined camps: (a) the government, which is subservient to imperialist and bourgeois interests, and (b) the workers' movement, which is seeking to consolidate national and social liberation by the transformation of Bolivia. Imperialism has imposed its designs on the government of the Nationalist Revolutionary Movement and through it openly exploits the country. We miners see nothing in such designs and we reject them. We are alien to the delivery of the mines, petroleum, and forest areas to financial Capital. We suffer from the fact that all social functions of education and the army have been confided to the hands of the Yankees. The fate of official policy is decided by the ambassador of the United States.

2. The defeat of the official administration, inept and immoral, has brought the mines to a situation of total bankruptcy. When, by our blood, we won the nationalization of the mines, we were sure that they would be put at the disposal of the country and not

Reprinted from Ernest Mandel, ed., *Contrôle ouvrier, conseils ouvriers, autogestion: anthologie* (Paris: François Maspero, 1970), pp. 346–47, by permission of René Coeckelberghs Partisanförlag. Translated by Helen Kramer.

converted into the property of profiteers who proliferate in the shadow of political power. It is the generous offering of the life of the workers that has permitted the nationalization of the mines, but it is elements foreign to our cause . . . who profit from it. Nationalization, in the hands of the present government and gradually as time passes, tends to be converted into a hollow word, for the real employer is none other than the BID.

3. The government seeks to force the miners to work under the menace of terror and to exclude the working class totally from the direction of COMIBOL (Bolivian National Mining Corporation). If the administrative criterion is maintained, the bourgeois characteristics of nationalization will be accentuated. We workers are fighting for an opposing thesis: the creative capacity of the working class (which is expressed solely when it acts collectively organized) , with the will to win and the certainty that its directing role must become the real cement of the new administration of the mines, enabling them to emerge from their present chaos and to increase perceptibly the production figures.

4. This constitutes an elementary duty of the miners to take the mines out of the hands of the present usurpers. We say to the country that we are struggling firmly in order to impose workers' management as the unique means of putting the mines at the service of the national majority. Workers' management signifies that the class, acting collectively, takes into its hands the destiny of our basic industry.

5. Finally, it is this class, mobilized from the base, which will be capable of tearing the mines out of the hands of those who possess the actual usufruct. The future of the mines is the future of the country itself, and one cannot pose the problem as marginal to the future of political power.

Worker unity to reconquer the mines from their usurpers.

Worker administration to save the mines from ruin and to increase production.

40. General Law of Industries— Decree-Law No. 18350 [July 1970]

Title VIII

On industrial community

Article 23. The Industrial Community is a juridical person hereby created in Industrial Companies. It represents the whole of the workers engaged full time therein, and it aims at the administration of the property that may be acquired for the benefit of said workers, in accordance with this legal provision.

Article 24. The assets of the Industrial Community will be progressively constituted by the monthly deduction of 15 percent of the Industrial Company's Net Income, which will be reinvested in the same Company, free from income tax.

If reinvestment in the same Industrial Company is not convenient and the Industrial Community has not reached the ownership of 50 percent of the Company's Capital, the corresponding percentage of the Net Income will be invested—following authorization from the Ministry of Industry and Commerce—in the acquisition of part of the Company's Corporate Capital belonging to other partners or shareholders.

The Industrial Community Assets are increased when the Company reinvests the Net Income corresponding to the Capital owned by the Industrial Community therein.

Article 25. When they reach ownership of 50 percent of the Corporate Capital of the Company, the workers will individually own the shares or participation in said 50 percent under the conditions of Industrial Cooperation established by the Law of Industrial Community, and the Industrial Community shall continue within the Company as per Article 23 of the Decree-Law.

Article 26. By exception, those Industrial Companies of the Public Sector that work in the basic Industry shall contribute to the Industrial Community 15 percent of the Net Income in bonds of the same Company; these lacking, the contribution will be made by shares or participation in Industrial Companies that have approved reinvestment plans, at the Industrial Community's choice and following authorization from the Ministry of Industry and Commerce.

The Companies in other sectors which by concession are exploiting basic industries shall deliver to the Industrial Community 15 percent of their Net Income in shares of, or in participation in, the Industrial Companies mentioned in the previous paragraph, following the authorization therein indicated.

Article 27. The distributable profits obtained by the Industrial Community from premiums and interest on its bonds shall be distributed among the workers who are really and effectively engaged full time for more than one year in the following manner: 50 percent pro rata and 50 percent proportionally to the number of service years.

If a worker shall leave his post, he will be excluded from benefits of the Industrial Community.

Article 28. The Directorate of the Industrial Company shall include at least one representative of the Industrial Community.

In the public Industrial Companies that operate in the basic industry, the Directorate will include two representatives from the Industrial Community.

Article 29. In no case can the Industrial Community transfer to any title the shares or the participation in its Industrial Company, nor can it waive its profits.

41. Experiences of the Agrarian Reform [1964–1970]

RAMÓN DOWNEY

The institution of a system of workers' enterprises, both in the direct working of the land and in the processing and distribution of the output, is the economic and social foundation of the Chilean experiment in agrarian reform over the last six years. Before laying out the guidelines which derive from the application of this system, it would seem appropriate to describe some of its characteristics.

The basic productive unit of this system is the settlement, or the agrarian reform cooperative, each of which comprises one or several of the old expropriated landholdings. Whether this unit is called a settlement or cooperative depends exclusively on whether or not the land has been made the property of the peasants.

Initially, the settlement was conceived of as an organization in which the Agrarian Reform Corporation (CORA) would have a much greater power of intervention in order to help the peasant in his transition from the status of tenant to that of worker, the master of his own destiny. However, from the very beginning, after the land was expropriated, the experiment led to the institu-

Reprinted from Ramón Downey, "Dos criterios importantes para la instauración de un sistema de empresas de trabajadores que fluyen de la experiencia en reforma agraria 1964-1970," in R. Downey, E. Ortega, and M. Zañartu, *La autogestión* (Santiago: Instituto de Estudios Políticos, 1971, pp. 35-44, by permission of the authors. Translated by Michel Vale.

tion of a much freer system, focused on the responsibility and abilities of the peasant. For this reason, the management of both the settlement and the cooperative, as well as their relationships with credit, technical, and commercial organizations, evolved along basically similar lines.

The fundamental features of these workers' enterprises are the following:

In the first place, supreme authority is invested in the peasants' assembly, where all members of the settlement or cooperative have the right to a voice and vote (the sole condition of "membership" is that one be a permanent worker in the settlement or cooperative). Besides deciding the general guidelines for operations, investment, social welfare, etc., this assembly appoints the permanent executive authority—the administrative council—from among its members. This administrative council is composed of five peasants, elected by free and secret ballot, and is encharged with the administration of the enterprise. The directors (members of the council) divide the responsibilities among themselves, each one taking charge of organizing individual specific tasks bearing on production as well as on the sales and manufacturing of products and the financing and stocking of the raw materials necessary for production. Obviously, the peasant enterprises count on the technical aid of CORA and other public organizations, along with any assistance that they contract directly from the private sector to carry out these tasks. But this public or private assistance does not alter the fact that the internal decision-making power within the enterprise lies with the group of workers and its leaders.

These basic units function by buying their materials and selling their products in the market. The main advantage they have over other producers is low-interest, long-term credits for purchasing land, creating an infrastructure, and acquiring working capital. They furthermore obtain low-cost, short-term credits for daily operations.

As mentioned earlier, the basic difference between a settlement and a cooperative is peasant ownership of the land. In the settlement, the land is legally the property of CORA, even though it has been turned over to the peasants for their management and use. In the agrarian reform cooperative, the land becomes definitively the property of the peasants. Whether they receive it in a communal or individual form depends basically on their democratically expressed will. CORA can only modify such a decision when there are outstanding technical reasons that would make one or the other form more appropriate. In fact, under the previous government, this authority was never used, yet more than 95 percent of the land was still allotted in communal form on the decision of the peasant beneficiaries.

The institution of this workers' enterprise system could not remain solely at the level of basic units. Therefore, as the process expanded, the peasants began organizing in area groups, regional federations, and finally in a National Confederation of Settlements. This organization, structured along the lines of a professional association, served in turn as the basis for organizing the peasant economy at local, regional, and national levels. Though this effort was necessarily slow during the years from 1964 to 1970, it resulted in the formation of the economic and trade committees at local and regional levels, in the establishment of fourteen multiactive regional cooperatives which encompass a large part of the country in their activity, and in the establishment of various regional cooperatives or enterprises with specific purposes, such as the export of certain products or the processing and sales of others. All of these agencies are constituted and managed by the peasants. In addition, the association structure allowed authentic representation of the peasants in the councils and management boards of various public or semiprivate organizations linked to their interests.

The point of the above description is not to paint an idyllic picture of the agrarian reform experiment, but to show the main features of the principal achievements that have accrued in the six years since the establishment of the new system. Time does not permit us to go over all its main problems and advantages. Hence we have chosen to introduce two general principles deriving from this experience that, although of great importance for the future, are not usually pointed out in writings and discussions on this process.

The need for a general reference point for the new society

During the development of the agrarian reform, a persistent problem was the inadequacy of many existing structures and institutions for incorporating, servicing, and establishing ties with the new units being formed as a result of the process. One of many such examples is the lack of an educational, professional, and technical training program that would address the specific cultural and training needs of the peasants as they face the emergent social, economic, and technical relations. Another is the lack of a credit system employing special services, sensitive to the peasants' needs, and guided by economic criteria appropriate to the new type of economic structure being created.

The main problems in this respect were to some extent resolved by the Christian Democratic government through special services offered mainly by those institutions responsible for the agrarian reform or other public or semiprivate institutions. But if the process expands into this sector and others, there is no doubt that partial solutions will have to be worked out unless a much more fundamental reorganization takes place in the social, cultural, and political spheres, as well as in the economic sphere. In all these areas, the institution of a system of workers' enterprise will require that actions be guided by new values, that conflicts of interest be resolved by different criteria, that new attitudes be encouraged while many of the old be rejected. All of this should be reflected in a new type of institutional framework cemented together by the central values of the new system. The primary distinctive features of this new framework should be that it establish a mechanism for generating power and for controlling the exercise of that power, that it assure fidelity to the principles and objectives of a workers' society, and that it not restrict itself merely to the transfer of power from some people to others or from individuals to the state.

We should stress that this new institutional framework cannot be limited to a particular sector or to particular areas of different sectors, but must encompass the whole of the social system. Only in that way will it be able to fulfill its expected function—that is, to give coherence, efficiency, and harmony to the new society and the various stages along the way toward it.

Obviously, the institutional framework of the transitional period will be substantially different from the final one, which will develop clear outlines and take on concrete form as experience is gained. But this does not prevent us from beginning immediately to give some specific definition to the most fundamental elements of the ultimate social system and to the transitional institutions leading to it.

This task represents not merely a need but an absolute necessity demanding political action from those who believe in communal socialism, or socialism with genuine participation of workers. First of all, the idealist, humanist, popular, and above all elegant proposals of the present government with respect to the social model it wishes to establish in the long run can only be carried out efficiently to the extent that there exists a long-term social, economic, and political program. At least the basic concepts of this program should be clear and concrete. This is especially important for the youth and the intelligentsia. Second, the magnitude of the structural changes the government is making requires a vigilant attitude and immediate action so that the new institutions and structures are, if not precisely appropriate, at least not too greatly at variance with a social system of effective worker participation. That vigilant attitude and the action it generates are possible only to the extent that there is clarity about the mediating institutional forms we mentioned before.

Advantages offered by a workers' enterprise system for the transitional period within a democracy

Here we would like to emphasize an advantage of the workers' enterprise system which can clearly be gleaned from the experiences of the agrarian reform. This advantage consists in the fact that it permits the minimization, or at least the substantial reduction, of the social and economic costs of a structural change of the scope that is intended in Chile. This advantage is especially evident when those changes are to be instituted within a democratic framework and in a country such as Chile, which is in a relatively advanced stage of political and social development.

In other words, if the long-term project is communal socialism and not state socialism, it is much easier to design a transitional mechanism within a democracy which would avoid serious economic setbacks for the country and unmanageable social tensions.

The Christian Democratic government's agrarian reform is a clear step in that direction. The fact that agricultural production more than doubled its rate of growth and social tensions were maintained at a manageable level (although, to be sure, some quite regrettable personal tragedies occurred), while more than 20 percent of the agricultural productive potential and almost 30 percent of the expropriable landholdings were expropriated, was not an accident: it was made possible by the intelligent use of the inherent characteristics of the system.

The first characteristic of the system which permits the reduction of the economic and social costs of transition is the fact that it allows those capitalist enterprises whose continued functioning is necessary during the transition to mark out a relatively well-defined status for themselves. Before complete transformation of the social and economic system, they will have the opportunity to integrate themselves slowly into the final framework. For example, in the case of the agrarian reform, I am referring to the large landholdings which could not initially be expropriated and the small and medium producers for whom a solution of eventual integration was sought. This characteristic derives from the fact that a workers' enterprise system presupposes not only centralized planning which directs the productive apparatus on the basis of social efficiency, but also an individual economic incentive system that permits the operation of decentralized productive units. It is the existence of these mechanisms of individual incentives (call it market or whatever) which, together with the planning system, is one of the pillars of efficiency in a system of workers' enterprises. This permits the definition of clear guidelines and the opening of prospects toward a final solution as much for the organizations that will be able to maintain their present functions only temporarily as for those which, with the necessary adjustments, will be able to coexist with the system over the long run.

In a situation in which common standards are routinely applied to measure the contribution of each member of society toward the furtherance of sound goals (a plan-guided incentive system) and in which the organizational forms are necessarily multiple and flexible, any well-meaning person or group can find feasible ways to integrate himself or itself. This is true even when these individuals or groups have lost power or economic and social position.

State socialism, on the other hand, focuses its efficiency on the direct and centralized steering of the productive apparatus by planning mechanisms. The nonexistence or irrelevance of a system of economic incentive and its implicit contradiction with other elements of the state apparatus is largely what impedes the working out of even relatively clear solutions, whether transitional or final, for the above-mentioned groups or organizations.

The second characteristic of communal socialism which facilitates the transition toward its definitive establishment within a democratic system is that it demands a profound respect for genuinely democratic social norms. Its claim to social and economic efficiency is based on the capacity, dynamism, and responsibility of the workers in directing the productive tasks at all levels, and not merely on the centralized planning of the productive process in accordance with social criteria. In so doing, communal socialism implicitly opts for a transition in which the fundamental tool for change is majority consent to carry out the desired transformations, rather than simply the imposition of these transformations by the state. State socialism, on the other hand, makes its claim to efficiency on the basis of centralized management by the "political representatives" of the people and on the changes they are able to institute. Hence, it tends to concentrate on implementing these changes, which are usually conceived a priori and subjected to little consultation, criticism, or approval on the part of the workers, while, by the same token, the administration of the productive process is necessarily infected with a high degree of sectarianism and arbitrariness. The inherent necessity of communal socialism to move along profoundly democratic lines creates an environment in which social tensions are reduced and unnecessary economic setbacks are avoided during the transition.

The reduction of economic and social costs, which makes the above two characteristics of a workers' enterprise system possible, is, in my opinion, an essential requirement if the changes of the dimensions envisioned for Chile are to be instituted within a democratic framework.

It might be argued that the example of the agrarian reform is a poor one because its pace was extremely slow and because it was concentrated on a specific sector of the economy without affecting the others in any way whatsoever. However, while recognizing quantitative limitations, we should bear in mind that it involved the introduction of an extraordinarily profound and conflict-laden structural change that normally should have unleashed grave economic and social consequences. That these were avoided or minimized tells us something important about the advantages of communal socialism during transitional phases. In any case, our argument does not rest on this specific experience but on aspects of the basic characteristics of worker-controlled enterprises. It is these characteristics that really make possible a transition less

42. Experiences of the Federation of Workers' Brigades and Enterprises [1972]

VICTOR ARROYO

I would like to speak about the question of participation by relating the experience of those of us who now constitute the so-called Federation of Workers' Brigades and Enterprises. This experience has the virtue of being precisely that—experience—rather than merely a pure product of the imagination. For those who do not know of us, our adventure began four years ago when we took over the factory in which we worked. That was our reaction to the merciless exploitation to which we were subjected in this small enterprise. Although many may find it hard to believe, it is in the small and medium-sized industries that the most flagrant instances of injustice are found.

We have traveled a hazardous road, but we have come out ahead. We have lived through a hard and painful experience. And we believe that hard and painful experience is a far better teacher than any model analysis designed by theoreticians who know workers only by their external characteristics.

To us it is very clear that an alternative form of participation exists in which the essential aspects of the exploitative conditions under which we have suffered so far would be maintained. To

Reprinted from Victor Arroyo, "Desde diversas trincheras se analize el problema de la participación (mesa redonda) ," *Panorama económico,* No. 271 (1972) , 22-23, by permission of the publisher. Translated by Michel Vale.

make it appear more attractive, it might be disguised in novel wrappings: for example, the distribution of company shares to the workers and employees or the participation of the workers in the ownership of the company, without any actual transfer of power into their hands. We are all too well acquainted with this alternative; in our arduous pilgrimage, we have received many such offers.

When we took possession of the factory, we confess we were guided by a purely economic motive. We declared, "The ownership of the enterprise should be in the hands of its workers." A year later, we discovered that this proprietary attitude caused a grave problem. The new comrades coming into the enterprise automatically became second-class workers, wage laborers for the group that had begun the experiment. We were therefore forced to rethink our entire model, not according to the latest book of some bleary-eyed theoretician, but in direct response to a concrete challenge that faced us.

In this way, we came to understand that participation is not maintaining the existing system, in which one person acquires the labor power that others must sell. To continue within that framework was leading us inexorably into a travesty of participation.

Our conceptions matured within a very hostile environment. The Mobile Group of Carbineros (Special Police Force) kept tabs on us as though we were delinquents. And when we went to banks to apply for credit assistance, they consistently denied it because we had nothing but our hands as collateral. It was a deeply instructive lesson about the reality of the capitalist system. We shall never forget it.

We also learned that a single productive unit, a single enterprise managed by its workers, was meaningless in isolation from the rest of the class. That is why we began to create and acquire other production units. And gradually we discovered that participation has to evolve from below. Along the way, we had to create popular democratic slogans and guidelines to eradicate once and for all certain bureaucratic attitudes in comrades who had been encharged with administrative functions.

We also had run-ins with the political party structure. Chileans who actively participate in parties constitute a minority. People sympathize with parties and cluster around them. They identify with certain groups but do not actively enter into them.

This "independent" sector—in quotes because we know they are not neutral—is very important in our country. Political groups do not seem to have understood this—not even those of a popular character. That is why even these latter groups fall into the vices typical of the capitalist system within which they operate. They think of themselves as the masters over the people. The party is an enterprise, the people the workers; and the Administrative Council is the Central Committee or the National Council of the commonwealth which issues communiques and orders to its base. These were facts which clashed head-on with that reality. We were determined that we would not fall into the simplistic error that confuses a political party with the working class, because that party is only one of the organizations of the class.

In our concern with having even the most uneducated of our comrades participate, we discovered that self-management as such does not exist. It does not exist because we depend on something called a market, on something else called the provision of raw materials, and, third, on something called credit. We then came to understand that it was essential to alter radically the Chilean sociopolitical system to allow workers gradually to assume decision-making positions. We realized, on the other hand, that state ownership is not necessarily synonymous with social ownership. The United States, gentlemen, has state enterprise, yet no one would think of calling it a socialist nation!

Our experience has also shown us that central planning is essential. Without it, the risk of precipitating untrammeled competition among various workers' collectives is enormous. We could say, then, that self-management requires central planning.

We discovered something else, too: that the agencies of participation cannot be confused with unions. A union represents class interests. The production committee basically represents efficiency indices. A union, therefore, must always remain autonomous, no matter what system of participation is put into effect.

There are many other things we have discovered along the way over these four years, questions which may seem ridiculous to the technicians, but which have concerned us. I can mention, for example, the problem of including our women in the experiment. Those of us workers who embarked on this venture are enthusiastic about it. We often decided to sacrifice distribution of useful goods in order to reinvest; at other times we have decided to absorb higher costs through greater productivity. How important it was to be able to count on the support and understanding of our women comrades in making decisions of this kind, which have such a direct bearing on the life and well-being of the family.

I believe our experience is especially useful to those who work in the thousands of small and medium-sized enterprises. I wonder if it would not be possible to form complexes of interrelated production units of this kind. There are enterprises that have been abandoned or are poorly administered by their owners. Perhaps they could be used to expand a system whose viability we have proven despite the many difficulties we have had to overcome.

Let me finish this unorganized exposition—for which I excuse myself, since I am a simple worker—with a comment on what Comrade Huepe says. He defined capital as the sacrifice of present consumption and declared himself in favor of society's assuming the responsibility of compensation for that sacrifice. I have my doubts; I do not think that the capital accumulated by Señor Yarur represents that gentleman's sacrifice of much personal consumption. On the other hand, it is truly a sacrifice of consumption for me when I must save so that I can pay my tax quotas. That much I can say with certainty!

43. Principles, Types, and Problems of Direct Democracy in the Kibbutz
[1965]

MENACHEM ROSNER

The principles governing the organization and administration of the kibbutz are not the outcome of an applied theory
or ideology. They have developed gradually out of the daily experience of the kibbutz movement. A desire for self-management
was always present in the movement (the first kibbutz, K'vutsat
Degania, was established as a result of a strike ensuing from disagreement between workers and managers). This desire for self-
management also separates the kibbutz from other types of utopian and religious communities, which in the past either were
headed by a charismatic leader or had an internal organization
that was nondemocratic and centralized.

The limited size of the kibbutz, its homogeneous population,
its simplified agrarian character, and its restricted contact with
the external world have helped in the establishment of a democratic procedure involving all members in management and administration. The institutionalization of these principles of self-
management is still going on. Even today differences can be
found in organizational structure between one kibbutz and another, just as a difference may be observed between the organiza-

Reprinted from *Principles, Types, and Problems of Direct Democracy in the Kibbutz* (Givat Haviva: Center for Social Research on the Kibbutz, 1965), by permission of the author.

tion of a given kibbutz today and its organization in the past. However, there exists a base common to all kibbutzim which enables us to define the general principles characterizing the system of democracy in the kibbutz.

The principles of kibbutz democracy

Democracy in the kibbutz is not only an administrative system in which all members take part in decision-making and in management by electing the kibbutz officials; it is also a system which aims to attain complete identification of the individual with the society. This aim grows out of the voluntary egalitarian and cooperative basis of the kibbutz democracy.

A. *The voluntary basis:* Since membership in the kibbutz is voluntary and each member is free to leave when he wishes, administrative coercion in securing submission to kibbutz decisions is obviated. Only a feeling of cooperation among members secures the observance of decisions contrary to the wishes of one or another individual. Gaining conformity of all members to the decisions of the kibbutz is a crucial problem for kibbutz democracy. A positive correlation can be found between identification with the kibbutz and observance of its decisions.

B. *Cooperation:* Integral cooperation is characteristic of the kibbutz. The kibbutz is a social and organizational structure which embraces all aspects of the lives of its members. This constitutes the source for the norms of active participation by most members in all kibbutz functions and not just in the election of management and in decision-making.

C. *Egalitarianism:* The wish of the kibbutz is to achieve equality in all respects, including power of decision and power to influence decisions. Such equality cannot be achieved if participation is passive and confined to the election of management and to voting. Participation of members in the General Meeting without their all-around participation in kibbutz life does not in itself secure equality.

Kibbutz democracy, therefore, is not based on constitutional rules but is a result of the members' will to identify with the kibbutz. This is expressed in an active, all-around participation in kibbutz life.

The conditions necessary for the attainment of the kibbutz's ideals were dependent on its organic structure. (The concept of "ideals" is used purposely, since the founding members of the kibbutz considered a complete identification of the individual with society to be utopian.) The system of communal social relationships in the kibbutz is of the *Gemeinschaft* type and is based on an all-embracing social contact, which enables public opinion to become the major mechanism for social orientation and pressure. The ideal of identification is expressed in discussions in the General Meeting, which are part of the decision-making process. Voting and majority decisions are not considered sufficient. After a majority decision has been reached, there is still opportunity for further objections and the reopening of discussion.

The small importance given to formal and legal procedure is reflected in the unification of the "powers" (i.e., the legislative, executive, and judicial) in contrast to the usual "separation of powers" in representative democracy. Those taking part in a kibbutz General Meeting (the legislature) are in part identical with those executing its decisions (committee members, heads of different work sections, and other officials of the kibbutz make up 50 percent of kibbutz members). There is a complete absence of formal judicial power in the kibbutz.

The unity of powers is in fact invested in the General Meeting, which, as well as being the legislature, acts at times as a "judiciary" and often takes decisions which normally are the province of the executive power.

Prerequisites for the fulfillment of kibbutz democracy

The philosopher Jean Jacques Rousseau, in his treatise on modern political ideas, stated that Direct Democracy is possible only in a relatively small, agrarian community with a simple way of life and without a complex social and economic structure.

In their beginnings, the kibbutzim fulfilled those requirements. Later developments in the kibbutz created conditions which many socialist thinkers—and also many sociologists—consider essential for the existence of real democracy.

In the light of research done by the American sociologists Lipset, Trow, and Coleman, the following can be said to be the essential social conditions for the existence of real democracy within a voluntary organization or society:

1. A relatively *small scale* for the society or organization, allow-

ing members proximity to the decision-making center and thus awareness of events without the need to resort to formal means of communication.

2. *Awareness* of members about the life of the organization, active interest in the events of the organization, and willingness to take part in the execution of its functions; this awareness is greater the more functions of the organization there are or the more these functions are essential to its members.

3. The existence of conditions for the creation of *nonformalized public opinion,* which will be a mechanism for regulating the organization. Nonformalized public opinion should regulate together with or even in the absence of formalized legislative or supervisory institutions.

4. The existence of a reserve of *potential* cadres, i.e., a large number of members who can take on duties and who have both the personal qualities and the experience necessary for carrying out those duties. Generally, the less specialized the functions and the less the need for specific knowledge to carry them out, the greater will be the reserve of cadres.

5. *Equality* between the living conditions of the officials and those of other members of society. There should be no privileges which will make it advantageous to hold office for long periods. The supposition is, therefore, that a correlation will exist between the equality of all members and the frequent changeover of officials.

The economic, social, and organizational structure of the kibbutz in the past has created the basis for the existence of all the conditions mentioned above. The question we will try to deal with in this paper is the extent to which these conditions exist today in the light of internal changes in the kibbutz movement. We will deal particularly with the question of whether it is possible to predict future developments in the kibbutz and, if so, what they are likely to be.

1. The past (up to the establishment of the State). The number of members in a kibbutz (with very few exceptions) did not exceed 200, even in the oldest, most established kibbutzim. The membership was homogeneous with regard to age, length of residence in the kibbutz, and country of origin. In most kibbutzim, there were still no second-generation members. Today, there are a large number of veteran kibbutzim with a membership of 400 and a population of over 600 or 700 (including those which preserved a small membership on principle). This population is het-

erogeneous with regard to age and country of origin. The greatest change, however, has been in the complexity and density of social relations. There has been a rise in social density and a decline in the visibility of social relations, to use Durkheim's terms.

A similar process of enlargement and increase in complexity and heterogeneity has taken place in the economy of the kibbutz. In this connection, the war brought a real technical revolution. Machinery was introduced into almost all branches of agriculture and services, and industry started to develop in the kibbutz.

2. The degree of awareness of members about general life in the kibbutz is linked with the integral, multifunctional, multi-sided nature of this type of organization. Despite the fact that there has been no change in the basic character of the kibbutz, there are indications of a decline in general awareness.

Awareness is being affected by an increase in the heterogeneity of the population. Different groups in the kibbutz have special problems, and the discussion of these problems does not seem to awaken interest in the other groups of the population. Similarly, specialization in many aspects of kibbutz life—economic, educational, cultural, political—is leading to departmentalization and even greater specialization, and, with this, to an increase in apathy among members over other problems and aspects of kibbutz life. The decline in awareness is intensified when more decisions concerning the individual are transferred from the kibbutz to the individual himself. For instance, an increase in personal consumption is likely to bring a decline in the awareness and activity of members, since general decisions will then affect only limited aspects of the individual's life. Awareness is also influenced by outside agents. Awareness declines when the external society becomes a reference group for members of the kibbutz, and internal cohesion is thus reduced.

3. As mentioned above, in the past nonformal public opinion fulfilled the role of a social regulator. This was possible because of the limited size of the kibbutz society, its integral character, and the type of social relations in it. These social relations were not confined to specific, predetermined patterns. They therefore led to intense contact between members, which created specific personal relationships. The particular and personal approach was also apparent in the interpretation of basic social principles. The tenet "From each according to his ability—to each according to his needs" was interpreted so as to emphasize particular individual abilities and needs. (The fulfillment of this principle has

never been fully achieved.) With the rise in the heterogeneity of the kibbutz population and the increasing separation of different aspects of life, it is doubtful whether public opinion can now fulfill the same social role.

Therefore, a process of institutionalization of social regulation is taking place. This process has two aspects: (a) the number of rules and codes regulating and defining norms of behavior is increasing. Some of these rules are drawn up by the national organizations of the kibbutz movement and some are specific to a given kibbutz. (b) the number of formal institutions regulating different aspects of life is growing as the functions of the kibbutz expand, due to the increasing complexity of the organic structure of the kibbutz.

4. The level of education in the kibbutz has always been above the average for the Jewish population, as a whole. The kibbutz has also been characterized by a high degree of social awareness and by the continual training and retraining of its members. The realization of the various functions of the kibbutz did not require a high degree of specialization, due to the limited size of the kibbutz, the simplicity of its social life, and its narrow field of economic activity. (Economic activity was confined to agriculture, and services were very few due to the low standard of living.) Under these conditions, a certain type of kibbutz official developed—the "synthetic official," i.e., an official who could carry out functions in almost all spheres of kibbutz life. The interchange of duties was not confined to one type of activity, such as economic activity, but one and the same man would carry out functions that were poles apart (for instance, after being chairman of the education committee, the same man could become the treasurer, or, after holding the post of economic director of the kibbutz, a person could become a political functionary).

It is very difficult to measure precisely the changes in the educational level of the members of the kibbutz. There has been an increase in the number of newcomers from wartime Europe and from Middle Eastern countries, and these had a lower educational level than the founding members of the kibbutz. On the other hand, the percentage of second-generation members with twelve-year schooling is rising, and the educational level of these second-generation members is higher than the average level of the founding members. Therefore, we do not consider there to have been any qualitative change in the general educational level of the kibbutz. In contrast, there has been a qualitative change in the level of specialization needed for the realization of the increasing number and variety of kibbutz functions. To carry out some of these functions, specific training in formal educational institutions is necessary. The time required for this training varies from months to years. In the fulfillment of all kibbutz functions, experience gained in performing the actual tasks concerned is becoming increasingly important. This tendency is particularly obvious when we consider the growth of associative kibbutz activity on the regional and national levels.

After postulating the structural conditions necessary for direct democracy, we stated that those conditions were fully realized at the beginning of the kibbutz movement and for a considerable time in its later development. In this light, the ideal of upholding those principles within a modern society seems unusual. But the question is whether the new developments that are altering the necessary conditions for direct democracy can, by causing deviations and distortions, damage the chances of preserving and fulfilling the principles of kibbutz democracy.

We will try to answer this fundamental question by analyzing the three central components of kibbutz democracy: (a) the General Meeting; (b) the organizational structure; (c) the types of participation of members in the various kibbutz activities.

A. The general meeting

This is the crucial, but not the only, expression of direct democracy in the kibbutz. In its regular meeting (at least once a week) it reflects, in its multisided discussions and its variegated agenda, the integral quality of kibbutz life and the unity of the three powers invested in the meeting. The position held by the General Meeting is linked with the specific organizational structure of the kibbutz. The latter is not an executive structure serving one particular function (not solely economic or educational or cultural). The General Meeting does not make distinctions between the three powers and tries to balance all the aspects of kibbutz life in its agenda. The principle of balance has been preserved throughout the history of the kibbutz. The General Meeting, in its integrating role, tries to strike a balance between the principles underlying the different fields of activity (for instance, economic, social, and educational considerations). It also seeks to balance the interests of various social groups or different departments (for instance, between work groups in budgeting for their financial and labor needs) .

The integrative process of the General Meeting is expressed in its practice of free discussion by all sides without a formal time limit. Agreement is often reached without the need for a formal vote. In most cases, the General Meeting fulfills the *executive function* by taking majority decisions in cases of disagreement and by ratifying proposals from the executive departments. The *legislative function* of the General Meeting is reflected in the taking of policy decisions and decisions of principle, which affect various aspects of life, and thus codifying behavior; in the discussion of and voting on budgetary problems; and in the setting of precedents as regards the discussion of various problems.

The *judiciary function* of the General Meeting is expressed primarily in the circumstantial consideration of each case under discussion, and also in the interpretation of previous decisions and accepted codes in each case under consideration.

In addition to the three functions mentioned, the General Meeting fulfills the function of social communication, since all members from all sections of the kibbutz are in attendance. The importance of this function of the General Meeting increases in light of the growing heterogeneity in the kibbutz population and the decreasing density of the means of developing an informal public opinion.

Considering the importance of the General Meeting's functions, it is interesting to find out whether changing conditions have affected the members' participation in it. A survey carried out by the author among members of twenty-four kibbutzim shows a tendency toward a decrease in participation with an increase in the membership of the kibbutz. The findings, however, do not warrant the assumption that the size of membership is a decisive factor in the degree of participation in the General Meeting.

The following table shows the percentages of members attending the General Meeting according to size of kibbutz membership.

No. of Kibbutzim	Size of Membership	Average % of Members Attending	Maximum % of Members Attending	Minimum % of Members Attending
8	Less than 100	55	83	26
9	100–200	53	70	41
7	200 or more	50	65	38

In the same survey, members were asked whether, in their opinion, the General Meeting is fulfilling its executive function. The general feeling among kibbutz members was that it is not. A further analysis of the answers showed that there is a differential appraisal according to field of activity. The most widespread feeling was that the General Meeting is not fulfilling its executive function specifically in the economic field. This can be explained by the greater specialization in economic activity, as compared with other fields. Specialization in one field of economic activity causes a decline in awareness as regards other fields of economic activity. Expansion and specialization in the kibbutz economy made it more convenient for detailed discussion to be carried out within the groups of people concerned with the particular work section, and for most decisions concerning that field of activity to be taken in these groups. Although the decisions are submitted to the General Meeting for ratification, the feeling is growing that this body is not fulfilling its function in the economic field.

Those in the kibbutz movement who are concerned with social policy are worried about this situation and have suggested means for checking further development in this direction. They propose:

(a) a more detailed discussion of economic matters in the General Meeting; they think that proposals brought for ratification should be more detailed, and that clear alternatives emerging from the discussion in the specific committees should be put to the General Meeting;

(b) the introduction of a system of communication using modern techniques for disseminating information to members on questions which are to come up for decision;

(c) the opening of meetings of the specialized economic committees (departments of production) to all members so that they may become a forum for discussion of the economic problems of the kibbutz.

Other proposals concern the development of informal public opinion. It has been suggested that opportunities be created for members to meet informally; for example, various kinds of clubs, study groups, and other cultural groups which would bring together the different social groups in the kibbutz could be established.

B. The organizational structure

The major changes in the organizational structure of the kibbutz have been in the field of subsidiary organizations. The number of institutions with integrative functions has increased. The previously separate economic and social secretariats have been synthesized into a single, unified organization. In its present form, this Secretariat is made up of eight to ten members who are heads of committees representing various aspects of kibbutz life. The economic side is represented by the Economic Secretary, the Treasurer, and the Works Manager; the social side, by the head of the Social Committee which deals with the problems of individual members. Education is represented by the head of the Education Committee, and sometimes the head of the Cultural Committee is also in the Secretariat. The General Secretary heads the Secretariat; his main duty is to coordinate the different fields of activity, in particular, noneconomic activities.

The synthesizing character of the Secretariat is reflected in its structure, which allows equal representation for all sides, different though their functions may be. The meetings of the Secretariat are preparatory to the General Meeting; there the different views can first be put forward, differences smoothed out, and interests—as well as conflicting views—brought together.

The Secretariat has the power of decision on some questions of administration, and problems are brought to the General Meeting only when there is disagreement among Secretariat members or when a kibbutz member objects to its decisions. Questions of principle, however, are always decided by the General Meeting; the Secretariat only prepares proposals.

The functions of the General Secretary and the Economic Secretary have also changed due to the need for integration created by the process of specialization. In both cases, the tendency is toward more general coordination in their work and less intervention by the secretaries in more specialized fields.

In the past, the Economic Secretary was trained to deal with specific agricultural problems in each field of production. Today, both his training and his functions have changed and have increasingly taken a managerial character. Similarly, the General Secretary no longer deals with specific problems of individual members—this is the task of the Social Committee—but shoulders duties that are more on the order of Social Management.

This trend toward integrative functions in the Secretariat should not be assumed to be a trend toward centralization. On the contrary, it is accompanied by a process of decentralization, since many of its functions and powers of decision have been transferred to the numerous specialized committees.

In general, therefore, there has been no deviation from the guiding principles of the kibbutz's organizational structure, principles that are in complete opposition to the principles of bureaucratic organization as defined by Max Weber.

The following is a list of the contradictions between the guiding principles of the two types of organization:

PRINCIPLES OF BUREAUCRATIC ORGANIZATION AS DEFINED BY MAX WEBER	PRINCIPLES OF KIBBUTZ ORGANIZATION
1. Permanency of office.	1. Impermanency of office.
2. The office carries with it impersonal, fixed privileges and duties.	2. The definition of the office is flexible—privileges and duties are not formally fixed and often depend on the personality of the official.
3. A hierarchy of functional authorities is expressed in the authority of the officials.	3. The equal value of all functions is a basic assumption, and no formal hierarchy of authority exists.
4. Nomination of officials is based on formal objective qualifications.	4. Officials are elected, not nominated. Objective qualifications are not decisive; personal qualities are more important in election.
5. The office is a full-time occupation.	5. The office is usually supplementary to the full-time occupation of the official.

Modern theories of organization do not accept the assumptions of rational bureaucratic organization. The tendency today is to vary the type of organization to suit the needs of particular social structures. This change is due to the dysfunction of the bureaucratic system—i.e., its lack of flexibility, its disjunction with the informal social structure, and the danger that arises when procedure takes over from the aims of the office concerned.

The kibbutz organization is not only a functional alternative to the dysfunction of bureaucratic organization, it is a general way of life formed from ideals which negate the principles of bureaucracy.

The interaction between the social structure and the organizational structure of the kibbutz is entirely different from the interaction between the social structure and the organizational structure of a different type of society. While in other societies informal and personal relations between the citizen and the official constitute a possible threat to the smooth and efficient operation of the organization, in the kibbutz it is precisely personal relations, diffused and many-sided, which contribute to its most efficient functioning.

The organizational structure of the kibbutz also differs from other organizational structures in its system of rewards for and supervision over its officials.

Certain of the principles underlying bureaucratic organization are based on the assumption that some officials do not identify with the aims of the organization, and that only strict supervision and sufficient rewards will secure adequate services from the officials. (This gives rise to the bureaucratic hierarchy and the system in which official service is a paid, full-time occupation.)

In contrast, in the kibbutz there is no connection between remuneration and the level of achievement. Supervision is a function of public opinion, and therefore formalized supervision and a power hierarchy are absent.

This difference between the two types of organization is due to the fact that the kibbutz is based on principles of economic equality, while bureaucratic organization is an outcome of the economic relations in the market.

44. The Changing Culture of a Factory [England]

ELLIOTT JAQUES

The continuing effects of history

In order to understand the present situation [in the Glacier Metal Company, London], it is necessary to consider the dynamics of certain outstanding historical events in the life of the organization, events whose definite mark is left on the pattern of the present. There was at first a small metallurgical works in which the alloying of white metal was supreme, and engineering activities relatively unimportant....

By 1935, although the white metal activities had continued unchanged, the new engineering development was stretching to bursting point its boundaries as minor partner in the concern. Radical changes occurred between 1935 and 1940. Engineering became dominant. It swamped the white metal work (which now remains as a small section of the manufacturing shop) and forced sweeping organizational changes. The firm was made into a public company, with the previous owner as Managing Director. He retired in 1938, and was replaced by co-managing directors. One of these was the Works Manager, a "production man" of

Reprinted from *The Changing Culture of a Factory* (London: Routledge & Kegan Paul, 1951), pp. 263–72, 279–80, 298–305, 313–20, 323–26, by permission of the publisher.

long experience, and the other the Sales Manager, a younger man interested both in new technical and administrative methods.

The legal requirements for costing, stock and other financial controls through becoming a public company brought an extension of specialist controls. This trend was further stimulated by the relationship established with an American concern whose managing director was especially interested in advanced costing methods. Accounting, production control, production engineering, and personnel departments were introduced. A special research section was created. And beginnings were made at establishing a formal managerial structure, and stepping up managerial skills by means of training. All this happened during the period when there occurred an open split in the management. This split was precipitated by a difference in technical and social outlook between the co-managing directors. Although the older of the two resigned in 1939, the split remained. The new specialist functions were in the hands of those who were identified as supporting the younger man, who became sole managing director, and who favoured the wider use of specialists. The line managers feared they might be dominated by the others. This fear was reinforced by the fact that greater controlling power was given to the specialists as a means of coping with the large numbers of new and inexperienced supervisors created during the wartime expansion. At the same time, the national emphasis on joint consultation in the engineering industry, combined with the personal interests of the Managing Director, led to the setting up of joint consultation in the firm. This laid the basis for an extension of democratic control. But it also added to the confusion about the functions of the executive, a confusion which had already been exacerbated by the split between the line managers and the specialists. . . .

Executive-consultative confusion

The use by higher management of so-called functional managers, to keep control over the line managers, was reinforced by the use of the joint consultative machinery to by-pass the executive chains and establish direct contact with the workers' representatives. These latter were regarded as a more reliable source of information about shop floor matters than the middle and lower grades of management. The Works Committee and Works Council were set up without the support of the middle management levels. Nevertheless, the meetings between workers and top management made it possible to put into practice, to some extent at least, the principle that people should be able to participate in the decisions that affect them. The existence and growth of the consultative system marked a change in the character of the firm. It established a basis for good relations between workers and management, and for tackling some of the cynicism and despair left over from the confusion of the 1930s. With the development of the *Principles of Organization,* hammered out by the Works Council, the pattern was set of the Council taking part in policy making, while leaving to the management the implementation of policy. At the same time, however, joint consultation had the effect of increasing the sense of loss of authority experienced by the line executives. The shop floor had a channel round them. Instead of supplying executive leadership for the subordinate management grades, top management was getting together with the workers' representatives. The fact that the superintendents, through their committee, had from the beginning been given a seat on the Works Council did not improve the situation. On the contrary, it served to exaggerate the difficulties by giving middle management the feeling that their contact with top management was no closer than that of the workers (if indeed as close) .

The difficulties thrown up by joint consultation arose from unconscious motives which were at play along with the conscious and constructive aspects of the developments. The top management were partly evading their anxiety about facing and working through their relationships with each other and with their subordinates. And the Works Committee representatives were using their relations with higher management, whether cooperative or antagonistic, to avoid having to face their constituents. Both these groups also mirrored larger scale forces in the factory. Everyone desired to avoid stresses in group relationships; and the Works Council provided the lead that was wanted—a lead in flight from dealing with these stresses.

This consultative collusion between the appointed management and the elected staff and workers' representatives was bolstered up by a number of strongly held beliefs. One of these was the general belief in industry that if only the discord between management and workers could be resolved, everything else would come out all right. Another was the belief that irrational or emotional influences could not be at work among people who had reached the level of top management or had become elected representatives. But the beliefs that caused the most argument were those based on ultimate values associated with principles of democratic living. For instance, the view that if people were treated responsibly, they would behave responsibly, was adopted (although individuals differed in the whole-heartedness of their endorsement of such a view) . . . .

The regulation of power

The change in structure of the Works Council completed the differentiation of the executive from the consultative chain, the General Manager being left as the top-level channel of communication between the two systems, with full responsibility for implementing the views of the Council in management, and for placing the views of management before the Council. The Works Council, as an elected body representative of the total factory, acquired policy-making functions as a member of a company-wide policy-making network composed of three groups. These are the Board of Directors, for the company as a whole, and the Works Councils of each of the two main factories. Company policy can now be decided only by unanimous agreement of all three. The way in which this unanimity procedure works in practice is very much a matter of the balance of power between these three groups, and the special interests they represent. Unlike responsibility and authority, which are structurally defined and relatively constant, the relative power of these groups shifts continuously. Before the significance of the unanimity rule can be understood, the sources of power of each of the three bodies must be examined.

Power of the branches of the policy-making network

The present Board of Directors owes much of its power to the fact that a large interest is concentrated in the hands of a few shareholders who consistently supports its policy. Other sources are its special knowledge of the general financial situation, and its own group cohesion. The particular composition of the Glacier Board—five whole-time executives out of a total of seven directors—also affects its power, increasing that attendant upon intimate knowledge of the firm, but lessening that arising from wide outside experience. The presence of the Managing Director and four divisional managers makes it difficult for management to scapegoat the Board; but there is again a loss of power in this same situation, due to the difficulties of keeping roles distinct. . . .

The power of management depends on technical expertise, skill in leadership, the efficiency of operation of the executive communication chain, and the cohesiveness of the management group. The top management of each of the two factories, through the general managers, and finally the Managing Director, have a say in policy making with widespread effect, and the shop floor and junior management can only speak executively through them. This does not necessarily mean that the executives near the top have greater power, this being the matter of how well organized are the lower levels, but it does mean that the higher level managers have access to greater stores of information, and these do confer power.

The power of the elected bodies in carrying out their authority sanctioning task, and in particular the power of the Works Council, which has the authority to participate directly in policy making, derives from the skill of the elected representatives themselves, as well as the degree of organization and cohesiveness of the members of their constituent groups. As a special case, the new Works Committee also acquires powers from its relationship to the trade union movement, the shop stewards being able to get support and advice from union and district officers, as well as direct support from union officers where negotiation is involved.

Power and the principle of unanimity

The question, "Where in such a set-up does the final authority for deciding policy rest when unanimity cannot be reached?" is one that has no absolute answer. Where legal issues are involved and the directors are held responsible at law, the Board of Directors will usually have to make final decisions. Apart from cases of this type, real failure to reach unanimity means that the matter will be decided by power. But whereas the authority and the responsibility of the different bodies are known and defined, their power is constantly undergoing change, and therefore the main weight for final decisions on policy is likely to rest with different bodies at different times. For example, the relative power of the Board of Directors and the trade union leaders under conditions of unemployment and weak union organization will be sharply different from that obtaining under conditions of full employment and strong, coherent trade union organization. It is precisely because power relations may shift, while the authority structure remains unchanged, that the firm's unanimity principle is of such value, for it allows the continuous testing-out and exploration of the power situation by means of constructive discussion, instead of the intermittent testing of power which accompanies executive policies and actions which have not been agreed upon and which when unacceptable lead to a piling up of stress and to explosive outcomes. Not that the unanimity principle automatically solves questions of power relationships; rather is it to be seen as a mechanism for facilitating more constructive relationships and ensuring more realistic compromises when the necessary motivations and skills exist in those concerned.

The unequal distribution of responsibility, authority, and power in the three groups is associated with differences in the value and extent of their respective contributions to policy in particular spheres. On the Board of Directors and the top managements falls the main weight of responsibility for initiating financial and commercial policy and technical development. But proposals in these fields are subject to modification in the light of their effects on factory personnel, as perceived by elected representatives. For example, a programme of technological development which would radically alter methods of production could only be planned by the Board and by higher management in conjunction with the firm's technicians. But it could only be adopted as policy after consultation with, and sanctioning of the plan by, the Works Council in the light of an assessment of possible effects on the firm's personnel. Conversely, on matters such as promotion, methods of payment, status, and other aspects of group relationships, the Works Councils are centrally placed to deal with whatever problems may be thrown up either by the management or by representatives, and to adumbrate principles to deal with them. And such principles would, however, affect financial policy, so that the other members of the policy-making network require to have their say.

The delegation of policy making to a network of bodies, with primary responsibility in various areas falling on different bodies and with final implementation being the subject of unanimous agreement, is a pattern which comes to grips with many real problems. It begins by recognising that members of the Board of Directors for the Works Council may be better equipped by training, position, and experience to deal with some problems than with others. It takes into account the fact that changes in any one region of policy have effects on every other region and, hence, that effective joint consultation means consultation on all matters between all the bodies, though not necessarily in the same order or for the same reason. . . .

The members of the factory recognise that this unanimity rule may lead them into situations of stalemate. But they prefer to maintain it on the grounds that decisions so arrived at have the best chance of being both the most correct and the most acceptable. Their experience is that so long as group relations remain satisfactory, no stalemate occurs. People show themselves to be flexible enough to modify their views. On occasions when stresses between groups appear, the unanimity rule is still useful. Even should a stalemate occur, it is by this means that the unfortunate consequences are avoided of taking decisions without full agreement, for decisions of this kind are usually impossible to carry out successfully.

Significance of the new works council structure

The original two-sided (management-worker) Council reflected the general split in industry between management and workers. But as the Works Council and the consultative machinery generally began to assume a role in the policy-making structure, a two-sided mechanism became confining. The worker-management Council represented directly by election only some 800 of the approximately 1,400 members of the factory. The other 600 were represented by the members of higher management appointed by the General Manager.

In principle at least, the new multi-sided Council lays the basis for an integrative rather than a split approach. The General Manager, representing the total managerial structure and indeed the total interest of the factory, meets with elected representatives of all strata. A structure of this kind provides the opportunity for major issues of policy affecting the whole factory to be considered, and for the decisions taken to be implemented by the General Manager through the executive chain. All the forces sanctioning authority in the factory meet in the Council. The General Manager carries the sanctions from outside given by the Board of Directors. He also carries the executive or task sanctions given by the Managing Director and by the managers and other members of the factory in their working roles. The elected representatives carry the sanctions given by their constituents, and the Works Committee representatives those also of their trade unions. All members carry their own personal interpretation of the sanctions given in the general code of industry and in the unwritten culture of the firm. These forces are all at work in the Council meetings. The work of the meetings continues until a point of equilibrium is found which balances incompatibilities between the needs of the various sections of factory personnel, the demands of the task, and the standards of outside society. The new Works Council structure allows more of the real social forces affecting the factory to impinge directly upon each other than did the previous structure with its more limited representation. . . .

Should a given problem not affect the whole factory, provision has now been made in company policy for sectional consultative meetings between the General Manager and any of the Staff Committees or the Works Committee. Decisions taken at these meetings affect only those concerned, and are subject to review by the Works Council. The new structure is capable, therefore, of taking into account splits such as that between the management and the workers, or between the management and a particular grade of staff, when and as these splits occur, without harm to the multisided character of the Works Council itself in dealing with factorywide affairs. . . .

Factory policy

Within overall company policy, as laid down by unanimous decision of the three bodies composing the policy-making network, the Works Council at the London factory has the power on its own to establish principles governing local practices. Under these arrangements, a central responsibility of elected representatives is to collect and collate significant problems of concern to their constituents so that general principles may be clarified and developed. The function of the management is to run the factory within principles laid down and agreed, and to raise matters of principle which are not clear and have them discussed at the Works Council in order to get sanction for executive action. The management, by virtue of its full-time administrative role, carries the burden of responsibility for maintaining effective relations between the consultative and executive systems.

It is for the management to ensure that it has a sufficiently clear policy within which to work, and to make proposals when it has not. It is also a duty of management to collect the necessary material and information to enable the Works Council to arrive at well-informed decisions. . . .

Confusion about social policy

One of the main difficulties still to be resolved concerns the diffidence, based on suspicion, of delegating to the management the responsibility for investigating problems of social relationships, and for drawing up proposals for principles to govern them. Responsibility for these matters has not yet clearly or consistently been assigned to any particular executive role. It is still left to the Works Council in many instances to take care of the difficulties. As a result, a feeling grew up in the factory that a split existed between social and technical policy, social policy being regarded as having to do with consultation and technical policy with management. The management, for example, were reluctant to regard the structure of joint consultation as a matter on which they were entitled to make recommendations other than as members of the Works Council. To do so in a managerial role would have been regarded as trespassing. No manager had the right to interfere in matters which affected the democratic rights and mechanisms of members of the factory. The present trend, however, is to recognise that joint consultation, along with all other matters of social policy, is as much a responsibility of the management as anything else, and consideration is being given to mechanisms for delegating responsibility for this function. The point of confusion has been that which lies between responsibility, on the one hand, for deciding policy, and, on the other, for planning it and putting it into execution. Clarification of the Works Council's responsibility with regard to the former has allowed responsibility for the latter to be delegated to the management in all matters, including social policy, so that the elected representatives may not be overburdened with carrying out extensive and difficult investigations. The assignment of greater responsibility to the consultative structure, together with the sanctioning of greater authority for it, has in turn made greater demands for efficient and powerful management than have been experienced in the factory before.

45. Joint Management in a Textile Factory [Malta]

GERARD KESTER

The developments at the Drydocks created a climate for more initiative. In Autumn 1971, a textile factory was in a state of liquidation and threatened with closure. The factory was a branch of a larger foreign company and had been in operation for only one year. It had two hundred employees and a relatively large foreign managerial staff. The latter enjoyed high salaries—by Maltese standards—and emoluments such as free company cars and housing facilities. The majority of the shares were in private hands; the Malta Development Corporation (MDC) also had shares in the company and was represented on the Board of Directors.

In consultation with the banks, the MDC and the owners, the unions had tried to find a solution, but without success. On a Friday night in October, the workers received their last wages and faced immediate unemployment. On the same night, the secretary of the textile workers section of the Garment Workers Union called the workers together and proposed that they should continue with production, using the available raw materials to produce garments for the local market. The workers agreed, and volunteered to give up part of their wages, all bonuses and piece rates.

Reprinted from "Towards a Participative Malta" (The Hague: Institute of Social Studies), mimeo, pp. 12–15, by permission of the Institute of Social Studies.

Work started the following Monday without management. Nevertheless, production was kept going and by the sale of garments on the local market as well as the sale of company cars, reduced wages could be paid during the first weeks. The greatest immediate problem was replacement of the managerial staff. At a meeting with the previous management, the managers were asked which of the Maltese supervisors would be the most suitable to take over their own managerial work. These newly assigned managers had to be trained in their new jobs on the spot; they were never fully introduced to managerial work by their superiors, whether in terms of organization or in technical know-how. They now spend their free time reading and studying, trying things out at the factory, working until midnight. Through effective and genuine cooperation between union officials, new managers (who previously, as supervisors, had not been unionized and had maintained a social distance between themselves and the rank and file workers), and the workers to keep production going, impetus in the operation increased. Workers were called together at regular intervals and informed about the results. When it became clear that the unions and the workers were determined to continue, the MDC and the banks became interested, especially when they saw that the company's debts were decreasing significantly due to the fact that overhead costs (foreign managers and their emoluments) had been heavily reduced.

During this period, the Board of Directors of the private company resigned, the general manager was sent on paid leave and, with the consent of the shareholders, decision-making powers were given to a managing committee. This committee is composed of only two people: one officer of the Malta Development Corporation and one trade union official. The MDC representative manages economic matters such as financing and accounting. The union official, secretary of the textile workers section of the GWU, is responsible for social and personnel matters, a function comparable to that of labor director in West Germany. Both men do their managerial work without extra remuneration.

Positive results quite soon became visible. Business has picked up and is now normal, including exports; the MDC and the banks have offered financial assistance and early this year workers were put back to their original wage level. Work relations have undergone substantial change. The former division between management and labor has been replaced by a shared feeling of responsibility by workers, supervisors and union officials, through their success in safeguarding employment and making the enterprise feasible again. The enterprise claims that productivity has increased and that absenteeism and labor turnover have been remarkably low since the new structure was introduced.

One of the most difficult and immediate problems of the enterprise is what to do about the ownership. With its initiative in continuing production, the union intervened on behalf of the workers, but in the final analysis also on behalf of the owners. Company shares are mostly in private hands, but the workers and the GWU evidently feel that if the enterprise should again make a profit, it should not automatically go to the shareholders.

Another problem is the participative structure itself. Participation was introduced with the original objective of safeguarding employment, but it has developed into much more than was foreseen. The union is fully involved in the managerial decision-making process and in the implementation of decisions. Serious problems may soon arise from the role conflict that seems inherent in the position of the union leader cum "labor director": how will he be able to match efficient management and effective representation of workers?

46. The Work Community of Boimondau [France]

CLAIRE BISHOP

Boimondau—the name of this community—was made up of three words: BOI, *boîter* (watch case), MON, *montre* (watch), DAU, Dauphiné (the French province). Boimondau, so they called themselves in order to fool the Germans in 1943—the name sounded just like that of a house in the woods. Before that, it was called Community of Work Marcel Barbu, named for its founder. . . .

How did it all start? Boimondau has already its legend and so has its originator. Yet when all is examined, it seems that a few essential facts can be retained and summed up:

Barbu and his wife, who started the ball rolling, were watch-case makers who knew their trade exceptionally well. So much for the sound technical background.

About the communitarian aspect. Whether or not Barbu knew of past scattered experiences in communitarian colonies which had taken place in previous centuries throughout the world, including America, Boimondau bears little resemblance, if any, to nineteenth-century collectivists (Fourier, Owen, etc.). Barbu and his few companions tackled the problem anew and by themselves. Both economically and ideologically, Boimondau is the result of

Reprinted from *All Things Common* (New York: Harper & Brothers, 1950), pp. 1–37, by permission of the author.

their own discovery, their work and their experience. On the other hand, if Boimondau and other Communities of Work may, by certain of their aspects, remind the student of the kibbutzim or the kolkhozes, it is not because there is imitation or even remote adaptation. But because there is a trend of thought in the air the world over, somewhat perhaps as happened when our modern system replaced feudality. It is one of the reasons why the experience is successful and has multiplied. Barbu acted as a catalyzer; the elements were already present. He crystallized the thoughts of many.

Of his own evolution, Barbu has this to say:

> At home I knew destitution. . . . Then I was taken into an orphanage. . . . Then at the preparatory seminary where I stayed up to the fourth year (fifteen years of age) until I discovered that I did not have the vocation. Then they wanted to stick me in an office. I did not like it. I learned a trade in Paris. I was a young worker. I got a firsthand knowledge of what bosses are worth and also workers. Like everyone else, I was unionized. But soon I understood that I had to look elsewhere. Together, my wife and myself, we decided we would try to build our own business in order to shape our own means of liberation. . . . We sold all our furniture to buy machines. . . . We slept only three or four hours at night in order to stick it out. We had no money, no backing, the banks refused to accept the drafts. That's how I started on my own. . . .

It was not until 1940, after the defeat, that Barbu was able to make a real start toward the liberation he had hankered for since childhood. At that time everything in France was so bad that it seemed everything could and must be reshuffled. It was a time when a man could make a choice, and wanted to make a choice, especially if he had been in the army, where there was no choice at all and where there was only defeat. Barbu tried to find some mechanics in Valence. He could not find any. So he went out in the streets and corralled a barber, a sausagemaker, a waiter, anyone, except specialized industrial workers. The men were all under thirty. He offered to teach them watch-case making, provided they would agree to *search* with him for a setup in which the "distinction between employer and employee would be abolished." The point was the search.

At that time Barbu and his wife (they had then five children) were the only competent workers. The whole outfit was settled in a barn, the only place found for lease, but within two months they started to sell, notwithstanding the fact that the people who supplied the raw materials were so distrustful that they would extend no credit on their bills.

The first and epoch-making discovery was that each worker should be free to tell the other off—"to wash each other's head," as the saying goes in France. At once, this complete freedom of speech between themselves and their employer created a buoyant atmosphere of confidence.

It soon became evident, however, that "telling each other off" led to discussions and a waste of time on the job. So they unanimously set apart a time every week for an informal meeting to iron out differences and conflicts.

But as they were not out just for a better economic setup but a new way of living together, discussions were bound to lead to the disclosure of basic attitudes. "Very soon," says Barbu, "we saw the necessity of a common basis, or what we called, from then on, our common ethics."

This necessity: unless there was a common ethical basis, there was no point to start from together and therefore no possibility of building anything. To find a common ethical basis was not easy, because the two dozen workers now engaged were all different: Catholics, Protestants, materialists, Humanists, atheists, Communists. They all examined their own individual ethics, that is, not what they had been taught by rote, or what was conventionally accepted, but what they, out of their own experiences and thoughts, found necessary.

They discovered that their individual ethics had certain points in common. They took those points and made them the common minimum on which they agreed unanimously. It was not a theoretical, vague declaration. In their foreword they declared:

> There is no danger that our common ethical minimum should be an arbitrary convention, for, in order to determine the points, we rely on life experiences. All our moral principles have been tried in real life, everyday life, everybody's life. . . .

The men pledged themselves to do their best to practice their common ethical minimum in their everyday life. They pledged themselves to each other. Those who had more exacting private ethics pledged themselves to try to live what they believed, but recognized that they had absolutely no right to infringe on the liberties of others. In fact, they all agreed to respect fully the others' convictions or absence of convictions to the extent of never laughing at them or making jokes about it.

To find this ethical concern at the very start of their search for a setup in which the "distinction between employer and employee would be abolished" may seem surprising. It may even appear out of place and, to some people, almost clerical or Sunday-schoolish. Yet, history teaches us that one of the causes of failure of previous communitarian colonies developed out of disagreements which could not be ironed out because no common ethical basis had been originally established. And it seems that one of the reasons for the survival of the early religious communities was precisely that they had a common spiritual basis. It does not imply that the common ethical minimum worked out by the young workers of Boimondau is the only one to be had. In the course of this book we shall see that even in the Communities of Work this ethical minimum occasionally varies. It is true that it does not vary greatly, but it is not in an effort to conform to Boimondau, but because this ethical minimum is universal in character. . . .

"There was unanimity." The common ethical minimum worked out by all was agreed upon by all. It was not a majority vote. Unanimity, as we shall see later, is the only mode of decision recognized by Communities of Work. . . .

The second discovery the men made was that they craved to educate themselves. First they wanted to be able to sing well together, then to polish their French grammar. Then they wanted to read the accounts, etc. They were just ordinary French workers who had left school at the age of thirteen.

In order to make a living they had to produce a specified amount. They figured out that the time saved on production could be used for education. Within three months, they gained nine hours on a 48-hour week. Later they were to triple the production.

So it was that, instead of working to make extra money or profit, they worked in order to better themselves.

Don't we all do it? In one way or another?

But the originality of the Boimondau group was threefold:

They did not work overtime. They worked less time. That is, they speeded up at the machines in order to have extra time. And therefore that time was covered by their pay. So that to the outsider they appeared to be paid for educating themselves. And they were, since to them all human activity is work, as we shall see later.

Then, that time which they had all together contributed to save, they used together too. They did not go out individually to spend in a private way their extra time. The group had earned that extra time as a whole. The time belonged to the group, the Community, not to individuals.

And last but not least, their choice in using that extra time is worth pondering. It was not used for additional material comfort. At the start and unanimously, they did forego, for the time being, material raising of the standard of living for the sake of their intellectual and artistic development. It was their own choice. I am not saying that they were right or wrong. I am merely stating a fact.

As they all knew that after a day's work no one was very keen on going somewhere else to study, they arranged for the teachers to come to the factory and give the lessons there. That is how the system started which I saw working that afternoon in 1946.

It turned out that production and education went hand in hand. The new friendly atmosphere created by all at the start had made possible a speeding up of production, which in turn had made possible the studies. Through it all a climate had been created and the men had thrashed out many questions together. Soon it became evident to all that the new setup had developed through each and all, spiritually and materially. They had created not an organization but an organism. *They* were the organism within which they could live fully. They were a Community. They said: "The Community is a real person composed of all the buddies who are in it, with their wives and children."

Two years had elapsed. They had learned much. They had come of age. All of them (90), including Barbu, agreed that it was time to turn over the means of production to the Community. They took the leap. Barbu simply turned over to the Community the factory that had been created by the work of all. In order to safeguard the dignity of all, it was decided that Barbu would be reimbursed gradually his original layout in money, and that in the event he would want to leave and start a new Community a certain number of machines would be given to him.

The group called themselves a Community of Work for lack of a better word. Community of Work does not mean common living quarters, nor one purse for all. We shall see later that some Communities of Work, called integral Communities, do have common living quarters and one purse. But this is a special feature and not a characteristic of the majority of Communities of Work.

It should also be clear that in a Community of Work, though it is work itself that is common to all, it is not so as an established, ineluctable fact. A Community of Work does not mean plant community, enterprise community. The members might decide to do something else. The work, the plant, the field (there are rural Communities), is but the economic expression of a group of people who wish to search for a way of life better suited to present living conditions and to a fuller expression of the whole man. It is true that there is no Community of Work without work but the work comes second in the title: "We do not start from the plant, from the technical activity of man, but from man himself." I have seen Communities of Work where people wanted to live communitarianly long before they had decided what kind of economic expression, work, they would tackle. The mere agglomeration or juxtaposition of workers in a factory does not make a Community of Work. . . .

In a Community of Work accent is not on acquiring together, but on working together for a collective and personal fulfillment. Of course, "objects" must still be made. Communitarians make them. In our present world, more and more objects are made, through mass production. Communitarians make them that way. They aim at a style of living which, far from relinquishing the advantages of the industrial revolution, is adapted to them. When asked why they get together, people in Communities of Work have different answers which, I found, all amount to this: "We want to be men." Of course? Not at all. Communitarians are very definite and articulate on what it means to be men.

1. In order to live a man's life one has to enjoy the whole fruit of one's labor.

2. One has to be able to educate oneself.

3. One has to pursue a common endeavor within a professional group proportioned to the stature of man (100 families maximum).

4. One has to be actively related to the whole world.

When these requisites are examined one discovers that they amount to a shifting of the center of the problem of living—from making and acquiring "things," to discovering, fostering and developing human relationships. From a civilization of objects to a civilization of persons; better even—a civilization of movement between persons. . . .

That is not all. People who work industrially together are not single entities. In the family, each one, in his own way, is also working and his work has value for the Community. The Community of Work does not comprise only those who work in the factory (men and women) but also the wives and the children at home. The Community of Work is a community of families. The work the wives do at home *is* Work; housekeeping has professional value to the community. In addition wives can also contribute to the Community socially. So, like the industrial producers, they are rated professionally and socially and receive an allotment on their total human value. As for the children, they grow, and that is work too. So they too have to be "paid." They are so paid the moment the physician recognizes conception. A sick person who follows the doctor's instructions is paid. The work of a sick person is to get well. . . .

The countereffort mentioned above is the work performed at the farm. The Community acquired a farm, 235 acres. They did so for several reasons. One of them is never mentioned because I think they are unconscious of it. It is the love for the soil that every Frenchman is born with. What they do mention is the fact that most of them having been in the Resistance, they yearned for the open and camp life. Also that they wanted to raise their own products. Finally, that no man should be entirely divorced from the soil. All, including the wives, have to work on the farm, during the year, three periods of ten days each.

As everyone has a month vacation it means that people work only ten months a year at the factory.

As for unanimity, they say it is the only guarantee of complete freedom for each one. In the parliamentary system the majority rule is an oppression on the minority. It is a primitive way of ruling. First, one authority, the king, then the majority tyranny. The human way is the full agreement. Agreement must be reached. Of course it requires time, thinking, giving up too-personal concepts, etc. Therefore, unanimity cannot be reached spontaneously at the General Assembly. It would be artificial. It is prepared in the groups. It emerges, then, naturally at the General Assembly. If it does not, if there is one dissident voice with a countersuggestion, the motion is not carried out. The whole question is re-examined in groups.

It is surprising to see how comparatively easy is unanimity in a group of people whose interest is common. Obstruction for obstruction's sake would not make sense.

The unanimity principle is one of the chief characteristics of the present-day communitarian movement. It is also one of its aspects most criticized by outsiders, as we shall see later.

Boimondau has been in existence ten years now and is going strong even from a purely industrial aspect. To accomplish this in the midst of a society entirely different in structure, Boimondau has to be something more than a lucky anarchist realization.

People who have experience in industry and with groups of men always ask: "Who directs? If no one does, it won't last long. Nowadays a factory needs technicians, managers, executives. It is no child's, amateur's or dreamer's play." Boimondau is none of them.

The communitarian administrative structure, patiently built by Boimondau people, is the result of their daily experience and thoughts.

Ultimate power rests on the General Assembly, which meets twice a year. Only unanimous decisions bind the Companions (members).

The General Assembly elects a Chief of Community. Unanimous vote only. The Chief is not only the most qualified technically, as a manager should be, he is also "the man who is an example, who educates, who loves, who is selfless, who serves. To obey a so-called Chief without those qualities would be cowardice."

The Chief has all executive power for three years. At the end of this period he may find himself back at the machines.

The Chief has the right of veto against the General Assembly. If the General Assembly does not want to yield, a vote of confidence has to be taken. If confidence is not granted unanimously, the Chief has the choice either to rally to the General Assembly's opinion or to resign.

The General Assembly elects the members of the General Council. The General Council's task is to counsel the Chief of Community. Members are elected for one year. The General Council meets at least every four months. There are seven members plus the Heads of Departments. All decisions have to be taken unanimously.

Within the General Council, section managers and eight members (including two wives) and the Chief of Community form the Council of Direction, which meets weekly.

All responsible positions in the Community, including section managers and foremen, are secured only through "double trust" appointment, that is, the person is proposed by one level and unanimously accepted by the other level. Usually, but not always, candidates are proposed by the higher level and accepted or rejected by the lower. This, say the members, prevents both demagogy and authoritarianism.

All members meet once a week in an Assembly of Contact, which, as the name indicates, aims at keeping everybody abreast of what is happening in the Community and also of keeping in touch with each other.

Neighbor Groups meet periodically. A Neighbor Group is the smallest organism of the Community. Five or six families which do not live too far from each other get together in the evening after supper under the guidance of a Chief of Neighbor Groups chosen according to the principle mentioned above.

In a sense, the Neighbor Group is the most important unit in the Community. It is "leaven" and "lever." It is required to meet at one of the families' homes and at no other place. There, while drinking coffee, all the issues are thrashed out together. Minutes of the meeting are taken down and sent to the Chief of Community, who sums up the minutes of all the Neighbor Groups. Answers to their questions are then given by those who are in charge of the different departments. In that way Neighbor Groups not only ask questions but voice discontent or make suggestions. It is also of course in the Neighbor Groups that people come to know each other best and help each other.

I have perused a number of notebooks of Neighbor Groups. The informality and thoroughness of the minutes make it delightful reading. The penmanship is beautiful, as so often is the case in France. The neatness of the notebooks reflects the care of good workmanship and respect for the reader. All sorts of questions are brought to light, trivial ones and important ones. Except in very few cases, politics is entirely out of the picture. Groups discuss: what is communitarian spirit, gifts, festivals, visitors, marriage, news of everybody. Then comes the discussion of the Theme that has been proposed by the Chief of Community to all Neighbor Groups alike: remuneration, collective savings, countereffort, attitude in case of a general strike, etc. Then are discussed the suggestions to present to the Chief, matters to be brought to his attention. The groups also discuss proposed candidates to various posts of responsibility which makes it easier for the unanimous vote at the General Assembly.

On the level of the Neighbor Groups, much immediate help is constantly practiced: baby sitting, caring for the sick, sharing vegetables grown in one's own little plot, taking charge of children while the mother has a baby, painting an apartment, exchanging books, etc. Anniversaries and national holidays find the members of the group celebrating together. In summer they make it an outing in the country.

The Neighbor Group brings everybody together, including wives and children who, not working at the factory, do not come in everyday contact with the rest of the Community. . . .

The General Assembly elects the members of the Court. A Community of Work is not composed of perfect people, not even of a so-called elite, but of average men and women. So conflicts are bound to arise between them, or between two departments or between a department and a member. It may happen that the Chief of Community cannot iron it out. That is why a Court is necessary. So eight members are elected (unanimous votes, as usual). The Community has no set of laws. Verdict is based on and directed by the Rule, the common ethical minimum, and common sense. The Court does not judge the fault, but the man. Therefore, the same fault may bring different verdicts according to the culprit. What is to be kept in mind by the judges is the common good, on one side, and, on the other, giving the culprit a maximum of chance to make good. The verdict is rendered on unanimous agreement: judges and culprit alike. What is the good of a sanction simply submitted to and not really understood and accepted, say Boimondau people.

The General Assembly elects the members of the Commission of Control. They are members without any other responsibilities who keep an eye on everything and report to the Chief of Community. If something goes wrong and the Commission of Control has not brought it to the attention of the Chief, the Commission is responsible to the same degree as the department at fault. . . .

At Boimondau there are two main sectors: the social sector and the industrial sector. As we shall see later, the social sector is always present in any Community of Work. It is not necessarily so for the industrial sector. At Boimondau the economic expression of the Community is a watch-case factory; therefore, an industrial sector has to exist.

The pattern for the industrial sector is as follows:

Men—maximum 10—form technical teams.

Several teams form a section, a shop.

Several sections form a service.

Members of teams are responsible all together toward the section, several sections toward the service.

Nothing very unusual in this except that one should be aware of what is meant by being responsible at Boimondau. It is not only from a technical point of view, but also from a human point of view:

At different levels the responsibilities are human and not only technical. Thus the heads of services, teams or sections have to create, within the professional activities, the most favorable atmosphere for a production made to serve man and not to dominate him.

The social department deals with all activities other than technical ones. The social department is not made up of outsiders who devote their lives to that question, but of the members themselves who form the different social teams and are responsible for them. As we have already seen, 6, 7, 8, 9 hours of the working week are devoted to the development of the whole man, and paid like professional hours. For extra hours, a certain number of points are allotted. All members, including wives, are expected to carry on their spiritual, intellectual, artistic and physical development. In that respect reading the monthly review of Boimondau, *Le Lien,* is enlightening. Reports and commentaries on everything: football matches (competition with outside teams) , photographic displays, visits to art exhibits, cooking recipes, ecumenical gatherings, reviews of musical performances such as Loewenguth Quartet, appreciation of films, lectures on Marxism, basketball scores, discussion on conscientious objectors, accounts of days at the farm, reports on what America has to teach, passages from St. Thomas of Aquinas regarding money, reviews of books such as Louis Bromfield's *Pleasant Valley* and Sartre's *Dirty Hands,* etc. Sometimes the members also indulge in "taking each other for a ride" with humor but without malice. It is all lively, gay, strong. A resilient spirit of good will permeates it all. *Le Lien* is a candid picture of people who have said "yes" to life, and this with a maximum of consciousness. . . .

I have talked about Boimondau with people who said: "It sounds too good to be true. But granting that it is Boimondau must have a long list of people eager to join. How do they do the hiring?"

First, they do it as in any other factory in France: individual persons present themselves, or some of the members of Boimondau present someone they know.

The candidate is interviewed by the Chief of Community. If

he is already a qualified worker a place is found for him so far as is possible in keeping with his technical capacities. He is also interviewed as man to man: his reasons for applying at Boimondau, etc. If he is not a qualified worker, he is put through standard tests.

He then enters as a salaried worker for a minimum of three months. He takes part in all social activities and he studies the Rule.

At the end of three months he may ask to be received as a postulant. If he is not accepted, he has to leave. The trying-out period is not renewable.

If he is accepted, he starts his novitiate, which lasts at least one year. During that period he is not a salaried worker. He is remunerated according to his total human value, he is present at all activities, including the General Assembly, but cannot vote.

At the end of the second period his marks are examined, his candidacy is discussed in the Neighbor Groups, the General Council questions him on the Rule and his understanding of it. If he is not accepted unanimously, another period of training is offered him. This is extremely rare because usually one who has made good for at least fifteen months is ready to be received into the Community.

The pledge of the Companion upon his entering the Community has already been studied here.

Every three months the General Council examines everybody and decides whether he is still worthy of his status as a Companion.

Wives of Companions can become Companions too by going through the same three grades.

Within the Companions themselves there are the Productive Companions and the Family Companions. Productive Companion men and women are directly engaged in the economic expression of the Community. The Family Companions are wives, not working in the industrial sector. All members, Productive and Family Companions alike, vote in the General Assembly. Children, apprentices and postulants can voice their opinions, but do not vote. In case of sanctions, man and wife face the Court together, the fault being always considered the joint responsibility of both.

We have now to examine from a business point of view the system adopted by Boimondau, and its commercial results.

Definition of assets runs as follows:

> Resources of the Community are constituted by the fruit of the sale of factory products, farm products, rendering of services to people or communities outside our own Community, artistic performances, etc.

Business transactions are carried out according to the following principle:

> Capitalism as the theory of the reproduction of money is done away with. Members of the Community pledge themselves not to claim interest in any form whatsoever.

Boimondau makes it very clear that its objective is not the suppression of capitalism. Capitalism does disappear in the new setting because it is simply dissolved. It is a result, not an end. Communities of Work do not want to despoil owners. They reimburse them gradually. But the reimbursed stockholders receive no dividends. "Money does not make money" any more; it is "dead work" and "abusive appropriation of collective savings."

PART II

Social and Political Philosophy

Introduction

1. Philosophical Foundations of the Idea of Self-management

MIHAILO MARKOVIĆ

Most economic, sociological, or political texts on self-management take for granted certain basic theoretical assumptions about its meaning, its desirability, and its feasibility.

These assumptions should be examined, clarified, and evaluated within the framework of a critical social philosophy which differs from pure, speculative philosophy insofar as it concentrates on the field of concrete historical possibilities, and also differs from positive, specialized science insofar as it does not remain satisfied with a mere description of the opportunities actually given but also explores the hidden potential of the historical situation. Critical social theory of self-management tends, therefore, to build up a synthesis of experience and wisdom, of theory and practice, of explanation of the given present forms of social reality and insight into qualitative future social change.

Such a theory explores the following three crucial problems:

1. What is the meaning of the concept of self-management in contrast to related ideas such as workers' participation, workers' control, direct democracy, decentralization?

2. What are the more basic philosophical principles which can justify the view that self-management is a desirable form of social organization?

3. Is the idea of self-management really feasible in modern industrial society? Is it a mere utopian dream or are there certain

specifiable historical conditions under which it could be practically implemented and give rise to a rational and efficient social system?

1

The term *self-management* is currently used in a very indiscriminate way, covering a number of different social structures which have not yet fully eliminated old authoritarian and hierarchical relationships or which contain new autonomous, equitable relationships in an incomplete, not yet fully developed form.

Workers' control is by all means an important, progressive objective in a class society. And yet it may only contribute to preventing undesirable decisions; it is still far from determining a positive policy in enterprises and local communities.

Workers' participation is also a progressive demand that has been gaining more and more ground in the international labor movement. And yet this is a broad, vague demand, and in various forms could be accepted by the ruling class without really affecting the general social framework of a capitalist society, for workers might be given the right to participate only in decision-making on some matters of secondary importance; they might be in a minority in a given body of management; they might be allowed only advisory or consultative functions and not the right to make decisions; finally, they might be denied access to information and left in the position of merely endorsing decisions that have been prepared by others and presented without any real alternatives.

Dictatorship of the proletariat, which in Marx's theory referred to a transition period of the "withering away" of the state and of increasing democratization, is nowadays associated with the existence of a strong, centralized, authoritarian state which is actually in the hands of a political bureaucracy and which uses the phrases *the power of soviets* or *workers' state* in order to conceal and mystify the really oppressive nature of social relationships.

Participatory democracy refers to a social form in which the freedom of citizens is not reduced to an occasional election of representatives who rule "in the name of the people" but involves the right of direct participation in decision-making. This is surely more than the classical liberal conception of democracy, which turns out to be rule by consent of a silent majority that can be easily manipulated. It is also more than mere "participation" because it specifies that what is in question here is not any insignificant participation but participation in government. It is less than what the concept of self-management implies, however, because it is not clear, first, whether this form of democracy embraces the economic sphere in addition to the political one, and, second, whether the totality of social power will stay in the hands of the people or whether a considerable part of it might remain a monopoly of a center of alienated economic and political power.

Finally, the idea of self-management should not be confused with the idea of a mere *decentralization*. An atomized, disintegrated society lacking the necessary coordination and conscious regulation would be at the mercy of blind, alienated social forces. Self-management is surely not the absence of any management or conscious direction within the society as a whole in all matters of common interest (such as general policy of economic development, communications and transportation, health service, social security, education, macro projects of general social importance in science and culture).

Self-management cannot be reduced to *direct democracy*. If it is to be an integral form of organization of the whole society and not only the organizational form of enterprises and local communities (which would then require the existence of the classical state), self-management involves not only an immediate commitment at the level of social micro structure but also *delegation* of social power at the level of the macro structure. In contrast to the "people's representatives" who constitute the apparatus of the classical democratic state, the delegates who constitute the self-managing organs of the global society (the republic, the federation) are not professional politicians; they must be elected on a rotating basis and must not be granted any material privileges.

*   *   *

The idea of self-management rests on a more general philosophical principle—that of *self-determination*.

Self-determination is a process in which conscious practical activity of human individuals becomes one of the necessary and sufficient conditions of individual and group life. This is a process contrary to *external* determination, i.e., a process in which the necessary and sufficient conditions of the life of some human individuals are exclusively factors outside their control and independent of their consciousness and will. To be sure, self-determination is always conditioned by a given social situation, the level of

technology, the given structure of production, the nature of political institutions, the level of culture, the existing tradition, and
habits of human behavior. However, it is essential for self-determination: (1) that all these external objective conditions constitute only the framework of possibilities of a certain course of
events, and that subjective choice and conscious human activity determine which of these possibilities will be realized; (2)
that the subjective choice be autonomous, genuinely free, and not
heteronomous and compulsory. This means that the subject, by
his own activity, creates a new condition of the process, instead of
merely repeating time and again an act to which he is compelled or for which he is programmed. This act need not be arbitrary and groundless; it should be an act of self-realization, of
the actualization of basic human capacities, of the satisfaction of
genuine human needs.

This active role in the course of events, this creation of new
conditions instead of mechanical reproduction according to the
laws of the system and inherited instincts, this extension of the
framework of possibilities instead of permanently remaining
within that framework, is a specific power of men, characteristic
of every human individual, present at least in the form of a latent
disposition.

Under certain social conditions, this power can be *alienated*. It
will be concentrated in the hands of a privileged social group and
become its monopoly. Alienation is a consequence of: (1) the
professional division of labor; (2) the accumulation of the surplus product; (3) the creation of institutions whose function is to
take care of common social interests; (4) increasing mediation
between individual needs and the needs of the whole society.

Political and economic alienation involves a process of social
polarization which, on the one pole, transforms a conscious, potentially creative subject into an object, into a member of a reified, oppressed, and exploited mass, and, on the other pole, transforms a normal, limited, and fragile human subject into an authority, into a mystified entity that has supernatural power and
control over human lives.

Such a critical analysis leads to the question of what social conditions are necessary in order that the life of individuals and communities be less and less reified, less and less contingent upon external authority, and more and more self-determined. There are
four such basic conditions.

The first such condition is negative: coordination and direction of social processes must no longer be in the hands of any institution that enjoys a monopoly of economic and political power (such as capital, the state with its coercive apparatus, and the party with its bureaucracy, hierarchy of power, and ideological manipulation). People themselves must decide on all matters of common interest, and this is possible only if the society is organized as a federation of councils composed of nonprofessional, nonalienated representatives of the people at all levels of social structure: in the enterprises and local communities, in the regions and whole branches of activity, and, finally, in the society as a whole.

The second condition of self-determination is reliable knowledge of the situation, of its scarcities and limitations, of the existing trends, of the conflicts to be resolved, of the alternative possibilities of further development. Freedom is incompatible with ignorance or biased perception of reality. The right to make decisions without previous access to information is a mere formality: self-determination becomes a façade behind which a real manipulation by others, by political bureaucracy and technocracy, takes place. Therefore, a genuine self-determination presupposes the formation of critical study groups at all levels of social decision-making, from the local community and enterprise to the federation as a whole.

The third condition of self-determination is the existence of a powerful, democratic public opinion. The genuine general will of the people can be formed only through open communication, free expression of critical opinions, and dialogue. It is clear, then, that any monopoly over the mass media (either by big business, or the church, or the state, or the party) must be dismantled. Such a monopoly enables a ruling elite to manipulate the rest of the population, to create artificial needs, to impose its ideology, and to construe its selfish particular interests as the general ones. Therefore the mass media must be free and genuinely socialized.

The fourth condition of self-determination is the discovery of the true *self* of the community, the development of consciousness about real general needs of the people. This condition is basic and most difficult to achieve. Only with great effort and in some crucial situations does an individual, nation, or class reach a full sense of self-identity. Therefore, most of what passes under the name of freedom in contemporary society is only an illusory freedom: mere opportunity of choice among two or more alternatives. But alternatives are often imposed, choice is arbitrary, and, even when it has been guided by a consistent criterion of evaluation, this criterion is hardly ever authentic, based on a critical, enlightened examination of one's real needs and one's long-range interests. This condition clearly presupposes a universal humanist point of view, and practically implies creation of a new socialist culture and a humanist revolution of all education. Leading the individual to discover himself, his own specific powers and potential capacities, teaching him how to develop them and use them as a socialized human being that cares about the needs of other individuals, would have to become the primary task of a new humanist education.

The preceding analysis clearly indicates that the transition from reification and external determination to freedom and self-determination is a matter of a whole epoch.

Existing forms of self-management, seen in this broad historical perspective, are surely of great revolutionary importance, but they should be regarded as only the initial steps. With general material and cultural development, many other steps would have to be made, many present limitations would have to be overcome. Thus, the organs of the classical state (in the sense of an instrument of class rule) would have to be replaced by the organs of self-management composed of the delegates of workers' collectives and territorial communities. Planning of production and social development would have to be a synthesis of the decision-making in decentralized, autonomous units of the social micro structure and the democratic centers of the macro structure. The market economy, with its production for profit, would have to be gradually replaced by production for genuine human needs. With further technological advance, productivity of work will quickly increase, while, at the same time, present-day hunger for consumer goods will be replaced by entirely different aspirations. The present-day overstressed concern about production and management will naturally tend to diminish. Self-determination in various other aspects of free and creative praxis will naturally gain in importance.

2

In the preceding analysis, it was assumed that a model of society based on self-determination (the special case of which in the economic and political sphere is self-management) is superior to any authoritarian (strongly or moderately) social model. This is a challenge not only to totalitarianism (of the fascist, bureaucratic, or technocratic variety), whose intellectual and moral position is so weak that it must disguise itself behind a pseudorevolutionary, populist ideology, but also to liberalism, which reduces human emancipation to political liberation only, and even in that narrow sphere reduces human freedom to a set of liberties and rights of the individual citizen confronted with the permanently indispensable state. The state remains always an inevitable external authority. As it is out of the question that human individuals and various social groups could freely organize themselves and freely coordinate the efforts that are necessary in order to take care of general social interests, they will, time and again, have to consent to the rule of a privileged, powerful minority. On the other hand, labor remains always the essential part of a "healthy" human life, no matter how much the productivity of work increases. If law and order within a stable state and maximization of material production remain the basic pillars of the human society, then an alternative to the earlier described social form based on self-management would be a computerized consumer's society in which an increase of comfort and entertainment would remain the essential aspiration of the greatest part of humankind.

This liberalist model of society has a well-known philosophical, ideological, and religious background. Toil is an inescapable part of the human predicament. It is both a healthy outlet for human energy and a means to conquer nature. The coercive function of the state is necessary in order to curb the evil, aggressive, selfish drives in human nature and to provide peace and security.

What, then, is the philosophical background of the model of socialist self-management? The basic philosophical ideas, developed by Karl Marx and some of his followers, are the following:

1. Man is essentially a being of free, creative activity, of *praxis*.

2. Under the conditions of class society, human potential is wasted; man is *alienated*.

3. Commodity production and political life controlled and dominated by the state are two essential forms of alienation (alienated labor and alienated politics) .

4. Ruling classes have a vested interest in the preservation of alienation; therefore, human emancipation and full realization of the human potential can be achieved only through a revolutionary transformation of the whole economic and political structure and the introduction of self-management.

*   *   *

This entire analysis rests on a concept of human nature that holds that beneath a vast variety of manifested, observable features of human behavior in history is revealed a permanent potential capacity of man to act in an imaginative, creative way, to produce ever new objects and forms of social life, not only to change in such a way his surroundings but to evolve himself. Man is often inert and passive; he occasionally manifests a strong irrational drive to destroy; and, in general, he has many conflicting latent dispositions (to be independent and free but also to escape responsibility; to belong to a social community but also to pursue selfish private goals; to live in peace and security but also to compete and be aggressive, etc.). These latent dispositions are empirically testable in the sense that they can be brought to life and observed when appropriate conditions are created. Some of them are responsible for great achievements of human history and are worthy of being reinforced; some of them have led to great disasters or long periods of decay and stagnation and should be modified and overcome.

The capacity for *praxis* is taken to be the essential characteristic of men precisely because it was and remains the necessary and sufficient condition of human history. In all real historical moments, moments of novelty, individuals and whole large collectives acted in a specifically human way which is distinguished from the behavior of animals in the following respects:

1. Specifically human activity, praxis, involves a conscious, purposeful change of objects. This change is not repetitious, it introduces a novelty. Man rebels against any form of limitation, be it from the outer world or from within himself. Novelty is essentially the overcoming of the limitation.

2. Praxis is the objectification of all the wealth of the best human potential capacities and powers. It is an activity which is a goal in itself and free in the positive sense of a genuine self-realization. Therefore, it is profoundly pleasurable for its own sake, no matter how much effort and energy it might require.

3. While it involves self-affirmation, praxis also mediates between one individual and another and establishes a *social relation* between them. In the process of praxis, an individual is immediately aware that through his activity and his product he satisfies the needs of other individuals, enriches their life, indirectly becomes part of them. Thus, through praxis an individual becomes a *social being*.

4. Finally, praxis is universal in the sense that by constant learning man is able to incorporate in his activity the modes of action and production of all other living beings and all other nations and civilizations.

These potential characteristics of a specifically human, free, and creative activity very rarely come to expression under the conditions of modern industrial production and modern political life.

The work of the vast majority of human beings, due to a series of historical conditions, does not have a specifically human character and may be described as a tremendous waste of human potential, as *alienated labor.*

When the necessity for an increase in the productivity of labor results in the division of labor, in the partition of society into professional groups, in the polarization of physical and intellectual workers and of managers and employees, in the crumbling and atomizing of the entire working process into individual phases, and, finally, in the creation of operations around which the whole life of individuals or groups of workers may sometimes be fixed, the entire structure of human work disintegrates and an acute gap between its constituent elements appears: the product no longer has its determined producer and the producer loses all connection with the object he produced.

This is a *two-sided* externalization (*Entäusserung*), for the product not only escapes from the control of its creator, but it also begins to act like an independent power which treats its maker as an object, as a thing to be used.[1] This phenomenon is possible because behind the object there is another man (the capitalist) who uses it to transform the producer into a thing (the labor force). The human qualities of the labor force are completely irrelevant except for one: this is a special kind of commodity which can produce other commodities, and which needs for its upkeep and reproduction a smaller amount of objectified work (in the form of wages) than the amount of objectified work (the value of the product) which it creates. This two-sided externalization, which in essence is not a relation of a man to the

---

1. "Die Entäusserung des Arbeiters in seinem Produkt hat die Bedentung nicht nur dass seine Arbeit zu einem Gegenstand, zu seiner äusseren Existenz wird, sondern dass sie ausser ihn unabhängig, frei von ihm existert und eine selbstständige Macht ihm gegenüber wird," in Karl Marx and Friedrich Engels, *Historisch-kritische Gesamtausgabe* (Berlin: Marx-Engels Institute, 1932) , Vol. 3, p. 83.

natural object, but rather a specific relationship of a man toward the other man, is alienation.[2]

Marx did not discover the idea of alienated labor; it can be found in Hegel's early works. However, Marx reopened a problem which Hegel had fictively solved and closed. He gave it a real historical perspective within the framework of a general humanistic philosophical vision. While working on *Grundrisse der Kritik der politischen Oekonomie,* and in his first draft of *Capital,* Marx rarely used the term *alienation* itself, but the conceptual structure expressed therein was the basis for Marx's entire critique of political economy.

Marx's critical position in *Capital* can only be understood in the light of his hypothesis of true human community and true production where each man both "affirms himself and the other man."

The analysis of labor in *Capital* is the starting point for the explanation and criticism of capitalist society, and of any other society which is based on commodity production. The character of labor is contradictory. What Marx in his earlier works called "alienated labor" is now placed under the term "abstract labor." Only abstract labor creates exchange value and only it has a socially acknowledged importance. However, man's labor is here totally crippled, deprived of everything personal, free, creative, spontaneous, or human, and reduced to being a simple supplement to machines. The only socially acknowledged characteristic of that labor will be its quantity, and this will be judged on the market and will receive its abstract objective form—money. The fetishism of commodities, the mysticism of the merchandise world are the concepts by which, within the sphere of economics, Marx expresses the same structure of productive relations which he termed in his earlier works "alienated labor." Again the point is, as Marx says in *Capital,* that "their [the commodity producers'], own historical movement takes the form of the movement of things under whose control they happen to be placed, instead of having control over them."[3] The conclusion which Marx draws from his analyses of the production of relative surplus value re-

2. "Durch die wechselseitige Entäusserung oder Entfremdung des Privateigentums, ist das Privateigentum selbst in die Bestimmung des Entäusserung Privateigentums geraten," Marx and Engels, *Historisch-kritische Gesamtausgabe,* Vol. 3, p. 538.

3. Karl Marx, *Das Kapital,* in Karl Marx and Friedrich Engels, *Werke* (Berlin, 1961) , Vol. 1, p. 89.

produces, in condensed form, all of the elements of his criticism of alienated labor in early writings.

"Within the capitalist system, all methods for increasing social productive forces are carried out at the expense of the individual worker; all means for developing production degenerate into means for the exploitation of and rule over the producer. They make of the worker a cripple, a semi-man; they reduce him to the common equipment of a machine, destroy the last remains of appeal in his work, transforming it into a real torture. They alienate from the worker the intellectual possibilities of the process of labor to the degree to which science is included as an independent force. They deform the conditions under which he works, subject him in the process of labor to a disgusting and pedantic despotism, transform his entire life into working hours, and throw his wife and his child under the juggernaut's wheel of capital."[4]

In his *Economic and Philosophical Manuscripts*,[5] Marx distinguished four types of alienation of the worker:

1) alienation from the product of labor, which becomes an independent blind power;

2) alienation from the production itself, which becomes compulsive and routine and loses any traits of creativity (which, among other things, implies production according to the laws of beauty) ;

3) alienation from the human generic being, for whom conscious, free, and productive labor is characteristic;

4) alienation from the other man, because satisfaction of another's needs, supplementing another's being, cease to be the prime motive of production.

All of these aspects of alienation can be found in *Capital*.

The fetish character of commodities lies precisely in the fact that "the social characteristics of their own work seem to people to be characteristics which objectively belong to the products of labor themselves, to be properties which those things have by nature." Hence, "social relationships among people assume for them a phantasmagorical form of the relationships among things."

---

4. Ibid., p. 674.

5. Karl Marx, *Economic and Philosophical Manuscripts*, in Erich Fromm, *Marx's Concept of Man* (New York, 1961) , pp. 93–103; also in *Writings of the Young Marx*, L. Easton and K. Guddat, eds. and trans. (New York, 1967) , pp. 287–96.

This reification of human relations springs from specific characteristics of labor which produces commodities. Labor can take on the character of a commodity only "when various specific cases of work are reduced to a common character which they all have as the expenditure of working capacity, as human labor in the abstract." This abstract labor ceases to be a need and fulfillment of the human being and becomes the mere necessary means of its subsistence. "The accumulation of wealth at one end is at the same time the accumulation of poverty, hard labor, slavery, ignorance, growing bestiality, and moral decline at the other, that is, on the part of the class which brings forth its own product in the shape of capital."[6]

The alienation of the producer from the other man stems from the simple fact that the purpose of the work is no longer the satisfaction of another's needs but rather the possibility of transforming labor into money—the general and impersonal form of objectified labor. The drastic forms of alienation among people arise as a consequence of the competition, exploitation, and despotism to which the worker is submitted. In order to increase production and at the same time to prevent a decline in the profit rate, it becomes necessary to squeeze out from the worker an increasingly large amount of unpaid work.[7] Hence, the necessity for the most efficient manipulation of workers possible and the need for an increase in the degree of the exploitation of labor.

Criticism of alienated labor, therefore, is present both in *Capital* and in all earlier works. One who loses sight of this criticism also loses the possibility of understanding the deepest meaning of Marx's message and opens himself up to the dangerous illusion that many historical problems have been already resolved when all that has been realized are some preconditions and all that has been achieved are some first steps toward their resolution.

Marx carefully explained in his earlier writings that *private property is not the cause but the consequence of alienated labor*, just as gods are originally the consequence, not the cause, of religious alienation. Only later does conditioning become reciprocal. In the society which Marx calls "primitive," "nonreflective communism," "man's personality is negated in every sphere"; the entire world of culture and civilization is negated and regresses to-

---

6. Marx, *Das Kapital*, Vol. 1, Chap. 23, p. 675.

7. Ibid., Vol. 3, Chap. 14, Sec. 1.

ward the unnatural simplicity of the poor and wantless individual, who has not only not surpassed private property, but has not yet even attained it.[8] In this kind of society, Marx says, "the community is only a community of *work* and of *equality of wages* paid with communal capital by the community as universal capitalist."[9]

That is why Marx felt that the basic question was that of the *nature of labor* rather than the question of private property. "In speaking of private property, one believes oneself to be dealing with something external to mankind. But in speaking of labor, one deals directly with mankind itself. This new formulation of the problem already contains its solution."[10]

The solution, therefore, is to abolish those relations into which the worker comes during the process of his labor, to abolish the situation in which he becomes only one of the commodities in the reified world of commodities. The essence of exploitation lies in the fact that accumulated, objectified labor—that is, capital—rules over live work and appropriates the value it creates, which is greater than the value of the labor force itself. Marx expressed this major thesis of his in *Capital*, in the following concise manner: "The rule of capital over the worker is merely the rule of things over man, of dead over live labor."[11]

The specific historical form which enabled the appropriation of objectified labor in Marx's time was the disposal of capital on the basis of private ownership of the means of production. This specific feature clouded over the generality of its content, and it is no wonder that to many Marxists it seemed, and still seems, that the possibility that exploitation may exist in a society in which private enterprises have been nationalized is a *contradictio in adjecto*. Nevertheless, it is obvious that private ownership of the means of production is not the only social institution which allows for the disposal of objectified labor. First, in a market economy during the transitional period, this institution can be the monopolistic position of individual collectives which enables them to sell their commodities above their value. Such collectives,

---

8. Marx, *Economic and Philosophical Manuscripts*, in Fromm, *Marx's Concept of Man*, p. 108.

9. Ibid., p. 125.

10. Ibid., p. 126.

11. *Marx-Engels Archiv* (Moscow, 1933), p. 68.

in fact, appear on the market as collective capitalists and collective exploiters. (Needless to say, within the process of internal distribution, it is assured that this appropriated surplus of value will never reach the pockets of the producers themselves, but rather will find its way into the bureaucratic and technocratic elements of the enterprise.) Second, it can be a monopoly over decision-making in a statist system. To the degree to which a bureaucracy exists and takes control of the disposal of objectified labor into its own hands, rewarding itself with various privileges, there is no doubt that this is only another form of appropriating the surplus value created by the working class.

The only way definitely to abolish exploitation is to create the conditions which will prevent objectified labor from ruling over live labor, in which, above all, the right to *dispose of objectified labor will be given to the producers themselves.*

*   *   *

Alienation in the field of material production entails a corresponding form of alienation in the field of public, social life, the state, and politics: politics is separated from economics, and society is divided into two opposite spheres. One is *civil society,* with all the egoism of the concrete owner of commodities, with all its envy, greed for private possession, and indifference toward the true needs of others. The other sphere is that of the *political society* of the abstract citizen, which in an illusory way personifies within itself the general interest of the community.

Kant and Hegel outlined two basic but contrary concepts of the state and law. Kant's liberal concept starts from the real, empirically given society, characterized by the market and the mutual competition among egotistic individuals, and attempts to reconcile the general interest and freedom of the individual in a negative manner, by demanding restriction of the self-initiative and arbitrariness of the individual. Hegel correctly perceived that simple common coexistence and mutual restriction of selfish individuals does not constitute a true human community. He therefore tried to transcend this negative relationship of one individual with the next, seen as his limit, by the assumption of a rational citizen and a rational community in which the individual relates positively to the social whole and, through it, to the other individual. However, Hegel himself remained within the framework of the limited horizon of bourgeois society, conceiving rationality as an abstract identification of the subjective spirit of the individual with the objective spirit of the state. The state as the personification of ideal human community is a pure abstraction which fictively transcends the existing empirical reality of bourgeois society.

In his criticism of Hegel's philosophy of law, Marx properly observed that: (a) such a reduction of a concrete possible human community to an abstraction of the state (the moment of the objective spirit), along with reduction of a concrete, historically given individual to an abstraction of the citizen, takes the form of alienation, and (b) this alienation in thought is the result of alienation in reality itself. The picture of the modern state imagined by the Germans was possible only because the state abstracts itself from true people and fulfills the total man in only an imaginary way.[12]

Contrary to civil society, in which there is *bellum omnium contra omnes* and in which only intersecting and mutually contradictory *separate* interests come to expression, in the political state the state-in-general appears as a necessary supplement, and in Hegel's conception it "exists *an sich* and *für sich.*" The state, then, is an alienated universal and necessarily entails the formalism of the state, namely, bureaucracy. Bureaucracy attempts to affirm general interest as something special, *beside and above all other private and special interests.*[13] In that way it presents itself as an alienated social power which treats the world as a mere object of its activity.[14] On the other hand, the state and bureaucracy are necessary supplements to the crumbling world of the owners of commodities, who all follow only their special and private goals; the state also supports a special interest but creates the illusion of its generality. "General interest can be maintained in the face of special interest only as something 'particular' inasmuch as the particular in the face of the general is maintained as something general."[15]

Needless to say, this dualism between the bureaucratized state and special private interests was impossible to resolve by identify-

---

12. Karl Marx, "Kritik der Hegelschen Rechtsphilosophie," in Marx and Engels, *Werke,* Vol. 1, p. 384-85.

13. Ibid., p. 297.

14. Ibid., p. 250.

15. Ibid., p. 248.

ing these contradictions in an imaginary way, within the framework of abstract thought.

"The abolition of bureaucracy," says Marx, "is possible only when general interest becomes reality," and when "special interest really becomes *general* interest."[16] And that is only possible when the individual man begins to live, work, and relate to his fellow man in a human way. "Only when man ceases to separate his *forces propres* as a social power from himself in the form of political power, only then will human emancipation be achieved."[17]

Marx explained this conception more clearly in *Grundrisse*. Here he compares political with religious alienation; in both cases, man projects his general human generic characteristics and needs either onto an out-of-this-world being or onto the state. Both are a necessary supplement to the incomplete social reality and can wither away only when man liberates himself from the idiocy of tying his entire life to one calling or to wage labor.

Marx shows in *Capital* that all the basic rights guaranteed by the state to its citizens have a formal and alienated character. *Freedom* is essentially the citizen's right to dispose of his commodity. *Equality* is in reality merely the application of the principle of equality to the exchange of commodity.[18] Everyone looks out for himself and not for the other. General good can only be realized "behind the back of the individual" by the "invisible hand," as Adam Smith says. For Marx, the question is how to strive for the general goals of the community consciously and freely, in the most rational and most human way possible. For that, the state is no longer necessary. "Freedom consists in transforming the state from an organ which dominates society into an organ which is completely subordinate to it, and even at the present, the forms of the state are more or less free to the degree that they limit the freedom of the state."[19]

In his early work *The Poverty of Philosophy,* Marx offered the theory that "in the process of its development the working class will replace the old civil society with an association which excludes classes and their contradictions. Then there will no longer

---

16. Ibid., p. 250.

17. Karl Marx, "Zur Judenfrage," in Marx and Engels, *Historisch-kritische Gesamtausgabe,* Vol. 1, Part 1, p. 599.

18. Karl Marx, *Das Kapital,* popular edition (Berlin, 1947), Vol. 1, p. 184.

19. Karl Marx, "Kritik des Gothaer Programms," in Marx and Engels, *Werke,* Vol. 19, p. 27.

be political rule in the traditional sense, because political rule is precisely the official expression for the class contradictions in civil society."[20] In *The Communist Manifesto,* Marx says that achieving democracy is the first step in the workers' revolution. The new state will be nothing more than "the proletariat organized as the ruling class."[21] Marx's conception of the fate of the state during the revolution is particularly clear in his analysis of the experiences of the Paris Commune. He talks throughout of "destroying state rule," of "smashing" it, of its being "superfluous." With enthusiasm he accepts two "infallible means," as Engels calls them, for preventing bureaucratism. First, "the Commune appointed for its officials persons elected by the general vote, persons who are directly responsible and at any time replaceable by their electors." Second, "public office, whether it concerns high or low positions, had to be performed for worker's wages."[22] For the first time in history, if only for a short period, the state was replaced by self-management.

In his "Paris Manuscripts" of 1844, the road to overcoming alienated labor was not yet clear to Marx. He makes only a rough draft here of the general vision of a society in which all individuals develop freely and realize themselves as complete personalities. Social relationships are no longer those of envy, competition, abuse, or mutual indifference, but rather relations in which the individual, while fulfilling the needs of the next man, and fulfilling and enriching his being, directly experiences his own affirmation and self-realization as a man.

Marx gives a concrete historical dimension to this general vision of transcending alienated labor in his *Grundrisse.* It was entirely clear to Marx that new, more humane relations of production will occur only in an advanced society, in the production relations which, thanks to scientific and technological progress, have already become universal, no matter how reified. Only when man is no longer directly governed by people but by abstract forces, by reified social laws, will the possibility be created to

20. Karl Marx, *The Poverty of Philosophy,* in Marx and Engels, *Historisch-kritische Gesamtausgabe,* Vol. 4, p. 182.

21. Karl Marx and Friedrich Engels, *The Communist Manifesto,* in *The Marx-Engels Reader,* R. C. Tucker, ed. (New York, 1972), p. 353.

22. Karl Marx, "Address to the General Council of the International Workers' Union Concerning the Civil War in France," in Marx and Engels, *Werke,* Vol. 17, p. 339.

bring these reified conditions of existence under communal social control.

In *Capital,* Marx's solution for the problem of alienation of labor is quite clearly outlined, for example, in the discussion on the fetishism of commodities. "The form of the process of social life, i.e., of the process of material production, will cast off from itself the mystical foggy veil only when the product of freely associated people is under their conscious, planned control. But this requires such a material basis and such a set of material conditions which in themselves are the wild product of a long and painful history of development."[23] One should particularly underline that famous passage in the third volume of *Capital* where Marx says:

> Freedom in the field of material production cannot consist of anything else but the fact that socialized men, associated producers, regulate their interchange with nature rationally, bring it under their common control, instead of being ruled by it as by some blind power; that they accomplish their task with the least expenditure of energy and under conditions most adequate to their human nature and most worthy of it.[24]

All basic elements of self-management are already given here:

1. The regulation of the process of labor should be left in the hands of the workers themselves; it cannot remain the monopoly of any special profession of managers who concern themselves with that only and who, as the only historical subjects, will manipulate all other people like objects.

2. Producers must be associated, and that association must be free. Self-management is not, therefore, a synonym for the atomization and disintegration of society, as some of its opponents like to represent it and as it may appear in practice when mistakenly understood. Self-management assumes integration, and this integration must be free and voluntary.

3. The control of production carried out by the associated producers must be conscious and planned; the exchange with nature must be regulated in a rational manner and not abandoned to the rule of blind powers. Self-management, therefore, assumes constant direction, the elimination of uncontrolled economic

23. Marx, *Das Kapital,* Vol. 1, Chap. 1, Sec. 4.

24. Ibid., Vol. 3, Chap. 48, Sec. 2.

forces. That presupposes the development of culture and science, and a clear understanding of the goals of development.

4. This communal control and direction of material production should engage as little human energy as possible, for managing things—and above all people—cannot be a goal in itself, but only a means for securing truly free, creative, and spontaneous activity.

5. The kind of self-management which Marx had in mind is possible only with a relatively high degree of social development. According to him, it requires the kind of material basis which is the result of the "long and painful history of development." However, if something is ever to achieve a developed form, it must *start* to develop in time. That is why Marx investigated so seriously and with such interest the experience of the Paris Commune and derived conclusions from it for the practice of the workers' movement. That is why history will certainly justify the efforts in Yugoslavia to begin with the introduction of the initial forms of self-management, even if in unripe conditions.

6. Still, in observing the conditions under which the exchange with nature is to take place, Marx does not consider the greatest success and efficiency, the greatest increase in power over nature, the greatest material wealth, as the most important things. For him, it is of greatest importance to carry out this process under those conditions which are the *most adequate and the most worthy of the human nature of the worker.*

Marx concludes the third volume of *Capital* with the same humanist ideas which he expounded in his early writings, especially *Economic and Philosophical Manuscripts.*

Thus, self-management is far more than one among several alternative principles of economic organization and economic decision-making.

It is a necessary condition of a new, genuinely socialist society; it is the form of socialist democracy and radical human emancipation.

3

What most critics of self-management try to challenge is not so much its desirability as its feasibility.

The most customary objection against self-management is that such a system is incompatible with the demands of technological efficiency and rationality in a complex modern industrial society. The argument is: self-management is a noble humanitarian idea, but it cannot be brought to life because workers and ordinary citizens are not educated enough to run a modern economy and a modern state. Professional experts are needed to do the job. In modern society, it is much more important that decisions be taken by the persons who are appropriately equipped for that function by necessary technical and other knowledge and skill than by persons who are just elected in the hope that they will best express the needs of the people. Consequently, self-management is either a utopian scheme or it must be reduced to a rather limited participation of workers in the decision-making process.

There are two ways in which a humanist philosopher might challenge the very idea of efficiency.

First, he might argue that, beyond a certain high level of technological, economic, and cultural development, efficiency will begin to lose its importance. After all, efficiency in its present-day meaning is ability to produce a desired result, to perform well a certain defined role in the social division of labor. In a highly developed future society, automata will increasingly replace man in routine physical and intellectual operations. As "production of specified, desired results" and "performance of well-defined roles" are typical routine activities, it would follow that man will let computers be efficient instead of himself, and he will engage more and more in the production of unique, beautiful objects, and in playing new, surprising roles not defined in advance. In other words, he will engage in praxis, and in praxis the question of efficiency either does not arise at all, or is of secondary importance.

Second, it might be argued that the concept of efficiency is devoid of any humanist meaning. It appears to be value free and ideologically neutral. On closer scrutiny, however, it turns out to be ideologically loaded and encourages certain harmful and dangerous attitudes toward nature and existing society. Maximum efficiency in conquering and controlling natural surroundings means a dangerously growing rate of waste of scarce material resources and available forms of energy. Maximum efficiency in running present-day social organizations and institutions means full-scale endorsement of their inhuman, degrading practices. For unjust systems, efficiency really is their best chance of survival.

Under given assumptions, this critique is perfectly sound. In a highly developed future society, both material production and the maximization of efficiency will become social goals of secondary importance. But they are still the primary concern of every present-day society. Man will liberate himself from too well defined and ordered roles in material production and will be able to afford to relax about efficiency only when he masters it, when he catches hold of it to such an extent that he will be able to relegate it to machines.

And, even then, there is a sense of the term *efficiency* which will always be associated with achievement of goals of human activity, whatever these goals might be.

This leads us to the second argument. From the fact that "efficiency" is a neutral concept, it does follow that it could be—and, as a matter of fact, is—associated with all kinds of wasteful, irrational, and inhuman practices. But it also follows that its meaning would be entirely different in relation to progressive and rational human goals. After all, no theory and no program of social change is possible without some neutral concepts. There is an element of neutrality in most concepts, including self-management. There is no guarantee that self-mangement will always, in itself, make people happier, more rational, less alienated. It is only part of a complex project—not the absolute.

*   *   *

With these qualifications in mind, one must take quite seriously the problem of compatibility of self-management with efficiency. While dozens of countries average one hundred dollars of national income per capita or even less, while there is still poverty among large segments of the population even in Europe and North America, while human beings still spend their best life energy in boring, technical work, further increase of efficiency is a necessary condition of human liberation and possible self-realization.

Human liberation is certainly inconceivable without the right of every individual to participate in social decision-making. But is it really the case that full, meaningful participation of each citizen destroys efficiency?

This does not happen if the following three groups of conditions are satisfied:

1. The first group follows analytically from the very concept of integral self-management. Workers' councils in the enterprises and the councils of local communities are not isolated atoms but elements of a whole network at different levels (from the territorial point of view: local–regional–federative; from the profes-

sional point of view: basic unit–the whole enterprise–the branch–
the community of all producers).

Any individual has direct decision-making power in the basic
units where he works and where he lives, and, in addition, he has
an indirect decision-making power at higher levels through his
delegates (freely elected, serving on a rotating basis, always replaceable, responsible to him). Any unit has all necessary autonomy and responsibility for the decision-making on matters of its
specific concern. But there must also be a readiness to cooperate
and harmonize interests with other units of the system. On the
other hand, higher-level organs of self-management must have
maximum possible understanding for the particular interest of
each subsystem. They are vastly different from the organs of the
state insofar as they are not instruments of any ruling elite, they
do not oppress, and they tend to reduce interference to a minimum. But in matters of common interest, after a certain policy
has been widely discussed and accepted, its decisions must be binding. Otherwise, social life would lack a minimum of necessary
organization and coordination, and would tend to disintegrate.

2. Another group of conditions follows from the general characteristics of self-determination discussed above. Organs of self-
management operate in an area characterized by the following features: mass media of communication are free and contribute to
the creation of a genuinely democratic public opinion; political
parties in the classical sense are absent, but there is a plurality of
various other forms of nonauthoritarian and nonmanipulative
political organizations; and there is an ongoing process of education and raising of the socialist consciousness of all individuals.

3. The third group of conditions under which the principles of
participatory democracy and efficiency would be reconciled derives from the analysis of the basic stages of the process of decision-making and of different kinds of knowledge and competence
needed. Each rational technical decision presupposes (a) a critical analysis of the situation (including scrutiny of the effectiveness of policies adopted in the past), and (b) a long-range program of development, a set of basic goals of the organization,
with respect to which all concrete technical decisions would constitute the means. In other words, there are three distinct necessary functions in the process of rational decision-making: One is
fact-finding, analytic, informative. Another is governing, political.
The third is technical, managerial. Accordingly, there are three
distinct kinds of knowledge relative to these functions: factual,

theoretical knowledge (*know that*) ; knowledge of the basic needs of people in a certain situation (*know what* is good and just to do) ; technical knowledge of the ways in which basic decisions can most effectively be realized (*know how*). Thus, in addition to the organ of self-management composed of wise, experienced persons who understand the basic needs at a given moment (who know what could and should be done), there must be, on the one hand, a group of analysts who critically study the implementation of adopted programs and the changes in external and internal factors, and, on the other hand, the technical management, composed of people who "know how," who elaborate concrete alternative policy proposals and who try to bring to life decisions of the organ of self-management in the most efficient possible way.

In this complex structure, the technocratic tendencies are the main danger for self-management. (To be sure, while there is still a state and a ruling party, much greater danger comes from political bureaucracy. However, we are discussing here a model of highly developed, integrated self-management in which the functions of the traditional state and authoritarian party have been taken over by the central organs of self-management.) A permanent source of technocratic tendencies lies in the fact that it is the managers who hold the executive power, who usually have better access to data, and who, therefore, might try to manipulate the self-managing council. Excessive power of the managers, the executives, is dangerous because their understanding of social needs might be very limited and their scale of values very biased, giving priority to typically instrumental values of growth, expansion, and order. Contrary to a common prejudice that modern society requires the rule of experts, the truth seems to be that experts are the least qualified candidates for good, wise, rational rulers, precisely because they are only experts and their rationality is only technical.

Self-management has at least three powerful potential devices to resist manipulation by the technostructure: (1) independent access of the self-management organ to data; (2) the iron rule that the management must always prepare its proposals for the organ of self-management in the form of alternatives among which to choose; (3) the right of the self-management organ to elect, reelect, or replace the manager.

The organ of self-management must have its own informative and analytic service and must not depend on the manager. Otherwise, it will be at the mercy of the half-truths produced by the management whenever the latter is interested in having its own particular point of view adopted.

The organ of self-management must, time and again, assert its right of freely taking a decision after carefully examining other possible alternatives. Once it is reduced to an institution that merely votes on the proposals prepared by the management, it clearly becomes a victim of manipulation.

In order to keep the balance and to be able to assert its rights, the organ of self-management must have the power of rotating the manager. There is no real danger that a "primitive," "ignorant" workers' council will fire a good, efficient manager. In the experience of Yugoslav self-management, if the workers' council ever fires a manager, it is either because he is utterly incompetent or because he is too authoritarian (or both). The real danger is rather that the workers use this right too rarely or too late, after considerable damage has already been done, and the enterprise operates with heavy losses. This reluctance to react promptly indicates that what jeopardizes the efficiency of production in socialism is too little, rather than too much, workers' participation.

A developed self-management has the historical chance to overcome both wasteful and irrational models of contemporary efficiency: one imposed by capital and the market, the other dictated by the authoritarian political machine.

2. Alienated Labor

KARL MARX

The worker becomes all the poorer the more wealth he produces, the more his production increases in power and range. The worker becomes an ever cheaper commodity the more commodities he creates. With the *increasing value* of the world of things proceeds in direct proportion the *devaluation* of the world of men. Labor produces not only commodities: it produces itself and the worker as a *commodity*—and does so in the proportion in which it produces commodities generally.

This fact expresses merely that the object which labor produces —labor's product—confronts it as *something alien, as a power independent* of the producer. The product of labor is labor which has been congealed in an object, which has become material: it is the *objectification* of labor. Labor's realization is its objectification. In the conditions dealt with by political economy this realization of labor appears as *loss of reality* for the workers; objectification as *loss of object* and *object-bondage;* appropriation as *estrangement,* as *alienation.*

So much does labor's realization appear as loss of reality that the worker loses reality to the point of starving to death. So much does objectification appear as loss of the object that the worker is

Reprinted from *Economic and Philosophic Manuscripts of 1844* (Moscow: Foreign Languages Publishing House, 1959), pp. 69-82, 98-105.

robbed of the objects most necessary not only for his life but for his work. Indeed, labor itself becomes an object which he can get hold of only with the greatest effort and with the most irregular interruptions. So much does the appropriation of the object appear as alienation that the more objects the worker produces the fewer can he possess and the more he falls under the domination of his product, capital.

All these consequences are contained in the definition that the worker is related to the *product of his labor* as to an *alien* object. For on this premise it is clear that the more the worker spends himself, the more powerful the alien objective world becomes which he creates over against himself, the poorer he himself—his inner world—becomes, the loss belongs to him as his own. It is the same in religion. The more man puts into God, the less he retains in himself. The worker puts his life into the object; but now his life no longer belongs to him but to the object. Hence, the greater this activity, the greater is the worker's lack of objects. Whatever the product of his labor is, he is not. Therefore the greater this product, the less is he himself. The *alienation* of the worker in his product means not only that his labor becomes an object, an *external* existence, but that it exists *outside him*, independently, as something alien to him, and that it becomes a power on its own confronting him; it means that the life which he has conferred on the object confronts him as something hostile and alien.

Let us now look more closely at the *objectification,* at the production of the worker; and therein at the *estrangement,* the *loss* of the object, his product.

The worker can create nothing without *nature,* without the *sensuous external world.* It is the material on which his labor is manifested, in which it is active, from which and by means of which it produces.

But just as nature provides labor with the *means of life* in the sense that labor cannot *live* without objects on which to operate, on the other hand, it also provides the *means of life* in the more restricted sense—i.e., the means for the physical subsistence of the *worker* himself.

Thus the more the worker by his labor *appropriates* the external world, sensuous nature, the more he deprives himself of *means of life* in the double respect: first, that the sensuous external world more and more ceases to be an object belonging to his labor—to be his labor's *means of life;* and secondly, that it more and more ceases to be *means of life* in the immediate sense, means for the physical subsistence of the worker.

Thus in this double respect the worker becomes a slave of his object, first, in that he receives an *object of labor*, i.e., in that he receives *work;* and secondly, in that he receives *means of subsistence.* Therefore, it enables him to exist, first, as a *worker;* and, second, as a physical *subject.* The extremity of this bondage is that it is only as a *worker* that he continues to maintain himself as a *physical subject,* and that it is only as a *physical subject* that he is a *worker.* . . .

Political economy conceals the alienation inherent in the nature of labor by not considering the direct relationship between the worker (labor) *and production.* It is true that labor produces for the rich wonderful things—but for the worker it produces privation. It produces palaces—but for the worker, hovels. It produces beauty—but for the worker, deformity. It replaces labor by machines—but some of the workers it throws back to a barbarous type of labor, and the other workers it turns into machines. It produces intelligence—but for the worker, idiocy, cretinism.

The direct relationship of labor to its product is the relationship of the worker to the objects of his production. The relationship of the man of means to the objects of production and to production itself is only a *consequence* of this first relationship— and confirms it.

When we ask, then, what is the essential relationship of labor we are asking about the relationship of the *worker* to production.

Till now we have been considering the estrangement, the alienation of the worker only in one of its aspects, i.e., the worker's *relationship to the products of his labor.* But the alienation is manifested not only in the result but in the *act of production—* within the *producing activity* itself. How would the worker come to face the product of his activity as a stranger, were it not that in the very act of production he was estranging himself from himself? The product is after all but the summary of the activity, of production. If then the product of labor is alienation, production itself must be active alienation, the alienation of activity, the activity of alienation. In the estrangement of the object of labor is merely summarized the estrangement, the alienation, in the activity of labor itself.

What, then, constitutes the alienation of labor?

First, the fact that labor is *external* to the worker, i.e., it does not belong to his essential being; that in his work, therefore, he does not affirm himself but denies himself, does not feel content but unhappy, does not develop freely his physical and mental energy but mortifies his body and ruins his mind. The worker therefore only feels himself outside his work, and in his work feels outside himself. He is at home when he is not working, and when he is working he is not at home. His labor is therefore not voluntary, but coerced; it is *forced labor*. It is therefore not the satisfaction of a need; it is merely a *means* to satisfy needs external to it. Its alien character emerges clearly in the fact that as soon as no physical or other compulsion exists, labor is shunned like the plague. External labor, labor in which man alienates himself, is a labor of self-sacrifice, of mortification. Lastly, the external character of labor for the worker appears in the fact that it is not his own, but someone else's, that it does not belong to him, that in it he belongs, not to himself, but to another. Just as in religion the spontaneous activity of the human imagination, of the human brain and the human heart, operates independently of the individual—that is, operates on him as an alien, divine or diabolical activity—in the same way the worker's activity is not his spontaneous activity. It belongs to another; it is the loss of his self.

As a result, therefore, man (the worker) no longer feels himself to be freely active in any but his animal functions—eating, drinking, procreating, or at most in his dwelling and in dressing-up, etc.; and in his human functions he no longer feels himself to be anything but an animal. What is animal becomes human and what is human becomes animal.

Certainly eating, drinking, procreating, etc., are also genuinely human functions. But in the abstraction which separates them from the sphere of all other human activity and turns them into sole and ultimate ends, they are animal.

We have considered the act of alienating practical human activity, labor, in two of its aspects: (1) The relation of the worker to the *product of labor* as an alien object exercising power over him. This relation is at the same time the relation to the sensuous external world, to the objects of nature as an alien world antagonistically opposed to him. (2) The relation of labor to the *act of production* within the *labor* process. This relation is the relation of the worker to his own activity as an alien activity not belonging to him; it is activity as suffering, strength as weakness, begetting as emasculation, the worker's *own* physical and mental energy, his personal life or what is life other than activity—as an activity which is turned against him, neither depends on nor belongs to him. Here we have self-alienation, as we had previously the alienation of the *thing*.

We have yet a third aspect of *alienated labor* to deduce from the two already considered.

Man is a species being, not only because in practice and in theory he adopts the species as his object (his own as well as those of other things), but—and this is only another way of expressing it—also because he treats himself as the actual, living species; because he treats himself as a *universal* and therefore a free being.

The universality of man is in practice manifested precisely in the universality which makes all nature his *inorganic* body—both inasmuch as nature is (1) his direct means of life, and (2) the material, the object, and the instrument of his life-activity. Nature is man's *inorganic body*—nature, that is, insofar as it is not itself human body. Man *lives* on nature—means that nature is his *body,* with which he must remain in continuous intercourse if he is not to die. That man's physical and spiritual life is linked to nature means simply that nature is linked to itself, for man is a part of nature.

In alienating from man (1) nature, and (2) himself, his own active functions, his life-activity, alienated labor alienates the *species* from man. It turns for him the *life of the species* into a means of individual life. First it estranges the life of the species and individual life, and secondly it makes individual life in its abstract form the purpose of the life of the species, likewise in its abstract and alienated form.

For in the first place labor, *life-activity, productive life* itself, appears to man merely as a *means* of satisfying a need—the need to maintain the physical existence. Yet the productive life is the life of the species. It is life-engendering life. The whole character of a species—its generic character—is contained in the character of its life-activity; and free, conscious activity is man's generic character. Life itself appears only as a *means to life*.

The animal is immediately identical with its life-activity. It does not distinguish itself from it. It is *its life-activity*. Man makes his life-activity itself the object of his will and of his consciousness. He has conscious life-activity. It is not a determination with which he directly merges. Conscious life-activity directly distinguishes man from animal life-activity. It is just because of this that he is a generic being. Or it is only because he is a generic being that he is a Conscious Being, i.e., that his own life is an object for him. Only because of that is his activity free activity. Alienated labor reverses this relationship, so that it is just because man is a conscious being that he makes his life activity, his *essential* being, a mere means to his *existence*.

In creating an *objective world* by his practical activity, in *working-up* inorganic nature, man proves himself a conscious species being, i.e., as a being that treats the species as its own essential being, or that treats itself as a species being. Admittedly animals also produce. They build themselves nests, dwellings, like the bees, beavers, ants, etc. But an animal only produces what it immediately needs for itself or its young. It produces one-sidedly, whilst man produces universally. It produces only under the dominion of immediate physical need, whilst man produces even when he is free from physical need and only truly produces in freedom therefrom. An animal produces only itself, whilst man reproduces the whole of nature. An animal's product belongs immediately to its physical body, whilst man freely confronts his product. An animal forms things in accordance with the standard and the need of the species to which it belongs, whilst man knows how to produce in accordance with the standard of every species, and knows how to apply everywhere the inherent standard to the object. Man therefore also forms things in accordance with the laws of beauty.

It is just in the working-up of the objective world, therefore, that man first really proves himself to be a *species being*. This production is his active species life. Through and because of this production, nature appears as *his* work and his reality. The object of labor is, therefore, the *objectification of man's species life:* For he duplicates himself not only, as in consciousness, intellectually, but also actively, in reality, and therefore he contemplates himself in a world that he has created. In tearing away from man the object of his production, therefore, alienated labor tears from him his *species life,* his real species objectivity, and transforms his advantage over animals into the disadvantage that his inorganic body, nature, is taken from him.

Similarly, in degrading spontaneous activity, free activity, to a means, alienated labor makes man's species life a means to his physical existence.

The consciousness which man has of his species is thus transformed by alienation in such a way that the species life becomes for him a means.

Alienated labor turns thus:

(3) *Man's species being*, both nature and his spiritual species property, into a being *alien* to him, into a *means* to his *individual existence*. It alienates man's own body from him, as it does external nature and his spiritual essence, his *human* being.

(4) An immediate consequence of the fact that man is alienated from the product of his labor, from his life-activity, from his species being is the *alienation of man* from *man*. If a man is confronted by himself, he is confronted by the *other* man. What applies to a man's relation to his work, to the product of his labor and to himself, also holds of a man's relation to the other man, and to the other man's labor and object of labor.

In fact, the proposition that man's species nature is alienated from him means that one man is alienated from the other, as each of them is from man's essential nature.

The alienation of man, and in fact every relationship in which man stands to himself, is first realized and expressed in the relationship in which a man stands to other men.

Hence within the relationship of alienated labor each man views the other in accordance with the standard and the position in which he finds himself as a worker. . . .

If the product of labor is alien to me, if it confronts me as an alien power, to whom, then, does it belong? . . .

The *alien* being, to whom labor and the product of labor belongs, in whose service labor is done and for whose benefit the product of labor is provided, can only be *man* himself.

If the product of labor does not belong to the worker, if it confronts him as an alien power, this can only be because it belongs to some *other man than the worker*. If the worker's activity is a torment to him, to another it must be *delight* and his life's joy. Not the gods, not nature, but only man himself can be this alien power over man.

We must bear in mind the above-stated proposition that man's relation to himself only becomes *objective* and *real* for him through his relation to the other man. Thus, if the product of his labor, his labor *objectified*, is for him an *alien*, hostile, powerful object independent of him, then his position towards it is such that someone else is master of this object, someone who is alien, hostile, powerful, and independent of him. If his own activity is to him an unfree activity, then he is treating it as activity performed in the service, under the domination, the coercion and the yoke of another man. . . .

Through *estranged, alienated labor,* then, the worker produces the relationship to this labor of a man alien to labor and standing outside it. The relationship of the worker to labor engenders the relation to it of the capitalist, or whatever one chooses to call the master of labor. *Private property* is thus the product, the result, the necessary consequence, of *alienated labor,* of the external relation of the worker to nature and to himself.

Private property thus results by analysis from the concept of alienated labor—i.e., of alienated man.

We also understand, therefore, that *wages* and *private property* are identical: where the product, the object of labor pays for labor itself, the wage is but a necessary consequence of labor's alienation, for after all in the wage of labor, labor does not appear as an end in itself but as the servant of the wage. We shall develop this point later, and meanwhile will only deduce some conclusions.

A *forcing-up of wages* (disregarding all other difficulties, including the fact that it would only be by force, too, that the higher wages, being an anomaly, could be maintained) would therefore be nothing but *better payment for the slave,* and would not conquer either for the worker or for labor their human status and dignity.

Indeed, even the *equality of wages* demanded by Proudhon only transforms the relationship of the present-day worker to his labor into the relationship of all men to labor. Society is then conceived as an abstract capitalist.

Wages are a direct consequence of alienated labor, and alienated labor is the direct cause of private property. The downfall of the one aspect must therefore mean the downfall of the other.

. . . From the relationship of alienated labor to private property it further follows that the emancipation of society from private property, etc., from servitude, is expressed in the *political* form of the *emancipation of the workers*; not that *their* emancipation alone was at stake but because the emancipation of the workers contains universal human emancipation—and it contains this, because the whole of human servitude is involved in the relation of the worker to production, and every relation of servitude is but a modification and consequence of this relation. . . .

The transcendence of self-alienation follows the same course as self-alienation. *Private property* is first considered only in its objective aspect—but nevertheless with labor as its essence. Its form of existence is therefore *capital,* which is to be annulled "as such"

(Proudhon). Or a *particular form* of labor—labor levelled down, parcelled, and therefore unfree—is conceived as the source of private property's *perniciousness* and of its existence in alienation from men. Finally, *communism* is the *positive* expression of annulled private property—at first as *universal* private property. By embracing this relation as a *whole*, communism is:

(1) In its first form only a *generalization* and *consummation* of this relationship. It shows itself as such in a twofold form: on the one hand, the dominion of *material* property bulks so large that it wants to destroy *everything* which is not capable of being possessed by all as *private property*. It wants to abstract *by force* from talent, etc. For it the sole purpose of life and existence is direct, physical *possession*. The category of *laborer* is not done away with, but extended to all men. The relationship of private property persists as the relationship of the community to the world of things. Finally, this movement of counterposing universal private property to private property finds expression in the bestial form of counterposing to *marriage* (certainly a *form of exclusive private property*) the *community of women*, in which a woman becomes a piece of *communal* and *common* property. It may be said that this idea of the *community of women* gives away the *secret* of this as yet completely crude and thoughtless communism. Just as the woman passes from marriage to general prostitution, so the entire world of wealth (that is, of man's objective substance) passes from the relationship of exclusive marriage with the owner of private property to a state of universal prostitution with the community. In negating the *personality* of man in every sphere, this type of communism is really nothing but the logical expression of private property, which is this negation. General *envy* constituting itself as a power is the disguise in which *avarice* re-establishes itself and satisfies itself, only in *another* way. The thoughts of every piece of private property—inherent in each piece as such—are *at least* turned against all *wealthier* private property in the form of envy and the urge to reduce to a common level, so that this envy and urge even constitute the essence of competition. The crude communism is only the consummation of this envy and of this levelling-down proceeding from the *preconceived* minimum. It has a *definite, limited* standard. How little this annulment of private property is really an appropriation is in fact proved by the abstract negation of the entire world of culture and civilization, the regression to the *unnatural* simplicity of the *poor and undemanding* man who

has not only failed to go beyond private property, but has not yet even attained to it.

The community is only a community of *labor,* and an equality of *wages* paid out by the communal capital—the *community* as the universal capitalist. Both sides of the relationship are raised to an *imagined* universality—*labor* as a state in which every person is put, and capital as the acknowledged universality and power of the community.

In the approach to *woman* as the spoil and handmaid of communal lust is expressed the infinite degradation in which man exists for himself, for the secret of this approach has its *unambiguous,* decisive, *plain* and undisguised expression in the relation of *man* to *woman* and in the manner in which the *direct* and *natural* procreative relationship is conceived. The direct, natural and necessary relation of person to person is the *relation of man to woman.* In this *natural* relationship of the sexes man's relation to nature is immediately his relation to man, just as his relation to man is immediately his relation to nature—his own *natural* function. In this relationship therefore, is *sensuously manifested,* reduced to an observable *fact,* the extent to which the human essence has become nature to man, or to which nature has to him become the human essence of man. From this relationship one can therefore judge man's whole level of development. It follows from the character of this relationship how much *man as a species being, as man,* has come to be himself and to comprehend himself; the relation of man to woman is *the most natural* relation of human being to human being. It therefore reveals the extent to which man's *natural* behavior has become *human,* or the extent to which the *human* essence in him has become a *natural* essence—the extent to which his *human nature* has come to be *nature to him.* In this relationship is revealed, too, the extent to which man's *need* has become a *human* need; the extent to which, therefore, the *other* person as a person has become for him a need—the extent to which he in his individual existence is at the same time a social being. The first positive annulment of private property—*crude* communism—is thus merely one *form* in which the vileness of private property, which wants to set itself up as the *positive community, comes to the surface.*

(2) Communism (a) of a political nature still—democratic or despotic; (b) with the annulment of the state yet still incomplete, and being still affected by private property (i.e., by the

alienation of man). In both forms communism already knows itself to be re-integration or return of man to himself, the transcendence of human self-alienation; but since it has not yet grasped the positive essence of private property, and just as little the *human* nature of need, it remains captive to it and infected by it. It has, indeed, grasped its concept, but not its essence.

(3) Communism as the *positive* transcendence of *private property*, of *human self-alienation*, and therefore as the real *appropriation of the human* essence by and for man; communism therefore as the complete return of man to himself as a *social* (i.e., human) being—a return become conscious, and accomplished within the entire wealth of previous development. This communism, as fully-developed naturalism, equals humanism, and as fully-developed humanism equals naturalism; it is the *genuine* resolution of the conflict between man and nature and between man and man—the true resolution of the strife between existence and essence, between objectification and self-confirmation, between freedom and necessity, between the individual and the species. Communism is the riddle of history solved, and it knows itself to be this solution.

The entire movement of history is, therefore, both its *actual* act of genesis (the birth act of its empirical existence) and also for its thinking consciousness the *comprehended* and *known* process of its *coming-to-be.* . . .

The positive transcendence of *private property* as the appropriation of *human* life is, therefore, the positive transcendence of all alienation—that is to say, the return of man from religion, family, state, etc., to his *human*, i.e., *social* mode of existence. . . .

Social activity and social consumption exist by no means *only* in the form of some *directly* communal activity and directly *communal* consumption, although *communal* activity and *communal* consumption—i.e., activity and consumption which are manifested and directly confirmed in *real association* with other men —will occur wherever such a *direct* expression of sociality stems from the true character of the activity's content and is adequate to the nature of consumption.

But again when I am active *scientifically,* etc.—when I am engaged in activity which I can seldom perform in direct community with others—then I am *social,* because I am active as a *man.* Not only is the material of my activity given to me as a social product (as is even the language in which the thinker is active):

my *own* existence *is* social activity, and therefore that which I make of myself I make of myself for society and with the consciousness of myself as a social being. . . .

What is to be avoided above all is the re-establishing of "Society" as an abstraction *vis-à-vis* the individual. The individual is the *social being*. His life, even if it may not appear in the direct form of a communal life carried out together with others—is therefore an expression and confirmation of *social life*. Man's individual and species life are not *different*, however much—and this is inevitable—the mode of existence of the individual is a more *particular*, or more *general* mode of the life of the species, or the life of the species is a more *particular* or more *general* individual life.

3. The Human "Relevance" of Marx's Concept of Alienation

GAJO PETROVIĆ

Marx's thesis that modern man and modern society are self-alienated is not only a pure "thesis" but at the same time a call to change existing man and society. And this is not a call for any kind of change whatever. If modern man and society are basically self-alienated, this means that the fulfillment of man and the realization of a truly human society are impossible without their revolutionary transformation.

If we were to characterize existing man and society simply as insufficiently humane, then a solution could be found in the gradual further development of humaneness. But if it is a basically inhumane, self-alienated society, such gradual change cannot help. Radical revolutionary change of the existing class society and man is necessary. Thus the "concept" of alienation is simultaneously a call for the revolutionary transformation of the world.

Some think that dealienation could be accomplished on the individual level without any sort of change of the social structure or of "external conditions" through internal moral revolution or the application of certain medical-psychiatric therapies. Others think that dealienation can be carried out only on the social level by the transformation of the social structure, primarily by changes in the sphere of the economy, after which corresponding

Reprinted from *Mogućnost čovjeka* (Zagreb: Razlog, 1969), pp. 69–71. Translated by Helen Kramer.

changes in all other spheres of life will automatically follow. But alienation is a phenomenon that is encountered both in the individual person and in human society, and it does not dominate only this or that aspect of man's life, but the whole man. Hence, the way toward dealienation does not lead across only the transformation of the external conditions of man's existence or only change in his "interior." The dealienation of social relations is the precondition for the full development of unalienated, free human personalities, and free personalities are the necessary precondition for the dealienation of social relations. There is no theoretical way out of this theoretical circle. The only way out is revolutionary social practice by which people, changing social relations, also change their own nature.

The question of the decisive or essential sphere of human dealienation is justified only if we do not forget that the difference between the essential and inessential is very relevant. Perhaps the most fundamental form of man's self-alienation is the split of his activity into various "spheres" in external interpersonal relationships. In accordance with this, we can say that the essential sphere of dealienation is not some separate sphere but the "sphere" of relations among spheres, the "sphere" of the struggle for overcoming man's split into mutually opposed spheres.

This does not mean that the existing difference among spheres should be ignored or denied. In all of past history the decisive role in the interaction of different spheres ultimately belonged to the economic sphere. Hence, the struggle for the dealienation of that sphere has particular importance. It should not be thought, however, that the struggle for dealienation in other spheres has no importance. It is also necessary to avoid the illusion that it is possible to carry out dealienation of the economic sphere while remaining only within the framework of that sphere.

The problem of the dealienation of economic life cannot be solved by the abolition of private ownership. The transformation of private ownership into state ownership (whether "capitalistic" or "socialistic" state ownership) does not introduce an essential change in the position of the working man, the producer. The dealienation of economic life requires also the abolition of state ownership, its transformation into truly social ownership, and that can be attained only by organizing all of social life on the basis of the self-government of the direct producers.

But if producers' self-government is the necessary condition for the dealienation of the economic "sphere" of man's life, it alone is not sufficient. Producers' self-government does not lead automatically to the dealienation of consumption; neither is it sufficient for the dealienation of production. Some forms of alienation in production have their root in the nature of modern means of production and in the organization of the process of production, and they cannot be eliminated only by a change in the form of managing production. Some forms of the struggle for dealienation have already been found and verified; others are still to be discovered and tested.

4. Alienation and Power

HERBERT GINTIS

Alienation appears on many levels. Most of these can be explained in terms of *social roles*. A social role is a "slot" that people fit into, carrying with it characteristic duties and obligations, defined by institutionalized expectations as to the behavior of the role-occupant. "Butcher," "baker," "worker," "soldier," "capitalist," "lover," "husband," "community member"—all these are social roles. The nature of these roles and their availability to the individual are quite as important as the distribution of material goods and power in assessing the value of a social system. Alienation occurs because the roles open to individuals do not satisfy their immediate needs in terms of their interpersonal activities in family, community, and work, and their requirements for healthy personal psychic development. Thus we center on the role-concept to emphasize the inherently *social* nature of alienation. To be alienated is to be separated in concrete and specific ways from "things" important to well-being, but these "things" are not physical objects or natural resources, but types of collaboration with others, with society, and with nature. These "things" are social roles.

The structure of roles at a point in time, and the way they

Reprinted from *Review of Radical Political Economics,* 4, No. 5 (Fall 1972): 6–11, 24–27, by permission of the publisher.

change and develop over time, depend on criteria and priorities required by basic social and economic institutions. This is not an obvious assertion, and its truth can only be ascertained through specific examples to be presented below. But its truth allows us a particularly simple *causal* explanation of alienation under capitalism: alienation arises when the institutionally-patterned social criteria determining the structure and development of an important social role are *essentially independent of individual needs.*

Our discussion of social roles takes us some distance in understanding alienation as a social rather than purely psychological phenomenon. An individual's welfare depends on the constellation of social roles available to him as worker, community member, and citizen, as well as the material goods and services that enable him to act to the limit of his capacities in these roles. Thus, for instance, an individual's alienation from his work is due to the fact that the social criteria explicitly or implicitly used to determine the value of his work do not take into consideration his personal needs. Yet the source of the "gap" between individual needs and social roles remains to be analyzed. This depends in turn on who has *power* to determine social roles.

How are social roles determined? What is the relative *power* of various social forces in choosing from the set of potential social roles, those which will actually be available? We can think of two broad types of power: *institutional* and *political.*

Institutional decisions are those where outcomes are determined by impersonal forces outside the control of any group of individuals. All the decision-mechanisms of this type that we shall treat are market-mechanisms, where the price of a commodity or factor of production (land, labor, capital) is determined by the "impersonal" forces of supply and demand. Very few outcomes in modern society are the result of purely institutional decision-mechanisms. An example would be the price of a perfectly homogeneous commodity supplied by a large number of small producers, and demanded by a large number of individual consumers (e.g., the market for table salt). Nevertheless, the prices of most goods and services are determined on a market over which individual producers and consumers have only limited control. Hence our analysis of power and alienation will emphasize the overriding power of institutional decision-mechanisms. For, as we shall see, they provide the structured environment within which political decision-mechanisms operate, and they strongly affect—if not essentially determine—the actual decisions reached concerning

the pattern and distribution of essential social roles and resources.

By a political decision-mechanism we mean one in which the
outcome is determined by the direct, consciously applied power
of a group of individuals. There are two types of political power
that are important for our analysis of alienation. On the one
hand, there is *state* power—legislative and state-administrative.
Examples of social outcomes determined by legislative decision-
mechanisms are tax schedules, minimum wage laws, zoning regulations, and the size of the military budget. Examples in the domain of state-administrative decisions are the setting of postage
rates, the choice of military technology, and the President's decision to send troops to Vietnam.

On the other hand, there are important decisions which are
definitely political in the sense of being consciously made by either one or several individuals, but are not state decisions. For example, the owners and managers of a firm *decide* what is to be
produced and with what technologies and work-roles, although
their decisions are powerfully circumscribed by the firm's institutional environment. Similarly, the wage structure in General Mo-
tors is determined by collective bargaining, again a political decision-mechanism, however constrained by its institutional context.
We shall call this form of "political" power *private-administrative*. Thus private-administrative decision-mechanisms determine,
although only in the most immediate sense, the structure of
work-roles, the direction of technological development, the use of
natural resources, and the pattern of community land-use and development. All are effected and implemented by those who own
capital, land, and have some control over production.

The shape of society at a point in time, and the way it changes
over time depends on institutional power, state power, private-administrative power, and how they interrelate. We shall see that
available social roles and the forms of social interaction in the
most important areas of life are determined *outside* the area of
state decision-making.

The distribution of income, the prices of factors of production,
the historical development of technology, the organization of
work activities, the structure and development of communities,
are all basically directed through the impersonal operation of
market institutions and private-administrative control. In fact, we
shall argue that, given the backdrop of economic institutions
(markets and private-administrative decision-mechanisms), the

latitude of state power for autonomous, effective decision-making is severely limited.

What about the relative power of institutional and private-administrative decision-mechanisms? We should note that *both* forms are involved in most private economic decisions. For instance, while wages are determined basically by the supply and demand for different types of labor (institutional decision), they are also affected by union-management negotiations, as well as racial and sexual discrimination (private-administrative decision). Similarly, while a capitalist can decide the technologies to be used and the work-roles he uses to apply them, his decision will be closely affected by the prices of capital goods and various types of labor—all determined by essentially institutional decision-mechanisms.

Thus the real question is not *which* decisions are primarily institutional and *which* are basically private-administrative. Rather, we must ask: What is the *latitude* of private-administrative power in the determination of any particular outcome? Here, we shall see that for the most important decisions that affect our daily lives, this latitude is rather minimal. The small capitalist in a perfect market for a homogeneous commodity in fact has no latitude at all. The prices of his factors of production, as well as the price of his product and its quality, are determined by the market (institutional power). The work-roles he chooses must be those that minimize his costs, or else he will lose money and go out of business. Such producers merely *ratify* and *implement* decisions really made in the sphere of institutional power. Oligopolistic producers do indeed have some independent latitude—they can control both price and quality of output to some extent, and to some degree the demand for their product through advertising and political lobbying (e.g., the so-called "defense" industries). Nevertheless, even here the latitude of their administrative power is highly circumscribed. For they must grow and maximize profits to satisfy their owners and stockholders. This is most strikingly seen in collective bargaining, which is a private-administrative decision-mechanism having quite limited power to alter the market-determined wage rate. Workers can only bargain over "excess" profit—what is left over *after* interest, dividends, taxes. management wages, and raw materials costs are deducted from total revenue. Moreover, since the corporation requires these "excess" profits for the expansion without which its position on the stock market would seriously deteriorate, wage increases must be

followed either by unemployment in the industry, or price increases which hurt consumers. The latitude that corporate directors have does not include the ability to permit a rise in the share
of labor significantly above that determined by the market in
labor (an institutional decision-mechanism). We shall see that
the latitude of private-administrative power is in other social
spheres equally limited.

Thus institutional power lies at the base of all of social life and
social development. It is the context within which both state
power and private-administrative power must be analyzed. The
importance cannot be overemphasized, because it cuts counter to
our most immediate political experience. We *experience* the war
in Vietnam—an inherently political decision—while the most important aspects of the capitalist domination of poor countries are
effected through the normal operation of international commodity, factor, and financial markets. We *observe* the political battle
over tax rates, minimum wage legislation, income redistribution,
and welfare programs—all determined by political decision-mechanisms—while the fact that the income distribution is basically
determined by supply and demand of privately owned factors of
production is so immediate, it remains unnoticed. We *observe*
collective bargaining—again a political decision-mechanism—
when in fact the level of wages is determined largely by market
mechanisms, and the institutional context within which the wage
bargain is fought sets the determining limits of its outcome. And
so on.

This observation sheds light on the problem of alienation. We
have already argued that alienation is not merely a psychological
problem, and hence cannot be cured by purely individual means
(drugs or psychiatrists). We now see that alienation is an *institutional* problem, not merely political. In this sense it is a *problem
of everyday life*, not of political struggle divorced from the immediate day-to-day concerns of individuals. Nor could it be otherwise, for, as we shall sketch below, the application of political
power—however "progressively realigned"—is severely delimited
by the institutional contexts within which it works. To change
the course of historical development requires a change in economic institutions at their base—in everyday life.

The liberal theory of the state, in contrast, views state decision-making as the guiding force in social development, insofar as
technology itself does not determine outcomes. Thus such eco-

nomic problems as inequality, poverty, ecological destruction, alienation, and the like, are either seen as inevitable or due to *political mismanagement* and can be cured by a turnover of political representatives. Whether this mismanagement is due to the "backward ideas" of political leaders, or that they have "vested interests" in the status quo, or that they are controlled by large corporations and congressional lobbies, or that government is simply an unwieldy and unresponsive bureaucracy, the solution is the same: elect "progressives" who will respond to the people's needs. We shall see, however, that since the real guiding force in social development is the set of economic institutions, the political power to cure social problems is quite limited, unless the state (i.e., political activity) attacks, destroys, and replaces basic capitalist economic institutions at their root. Thus even if perfect democracy were achieved in the state sphere, the major contours of people's lives would be determined by processes beyond their control.

The state is really a dependent force, whose main function is to preserve, in as pure a form as is feasible, the basic capitalist institutions which determine social development. The growth of the state is due to several conditions: (a) basic economic institutions have functioned less perfectly over time, so increasing intervention to "shore them up" has been necessary; (b) conflicts between various groups of capitalists have become increasingly severe, requiring more and more legislative mediation; (c) more and more state palliatives have been necessary to avoid the "politicization" of workers and citizens over intolerable social conditions; and (d) certain services necessary to the expansion of capital (e.g., roads, education, the military) can only be supplied by the state. In all cases, state power is a dependent and conditionally applied power.

But if the operation of the state depends on capitalist economic institutions, then the study of institutional decision-making becomes central. This is in turn captured in the theory of alienation. *A decision-mechanism will be termed "alienated" when the criteria—implicit or explicit—according to which it determines outcomes are substantially independent from the needs of individuals whom the outcome affects.* Hence the consequences of decisions made according to these criteria will only by accident serve the needs of affected individuals. Insofar as this is true we shall say that the individuals are alienated from the social object (be it a physical object, a social role, another individual, an element of culture, the natural environment, or their own personalities) which is the outcome of the decision-mechanism.

We shall argue that the basic institutional decision-mechanisms of capitalism are alienated. Since political decision-mechanisms —even within their rigidly circumscribed sphere of effective action—must conform to the dictates of the capitalist institutional environment, they are alienated as well. Hence the course of history within capitalism is itself a series of alienated outcomes. . . .

Alienation from self and culture

Alienation from work-activities and community are the basis of the individual's estrangement from all aspects of social life.

According to this explanation, alienation is a form of deprivation—deprivation from important social roles. But this deprivation holds deep personal implications because *individual psychic development is controlled by social experience.* Just as "individuals develop through their social relations of production" and hence become incomplete individuals when alienated from their work-activities, so individuals develop through their roles relating to community, product, and other individuals. When deprived of these formative influences in healthy forms, they become "self-alienated." To continue a metaphor, society may alienate a man's psyche as much as a pick-pocket his wallet. We are alienated from ourselves when we are not what we really could be—when we cannot love, play, run, work, spiritualize, relate, create, empathize, aid, as much as our potential allows.

Self-alienation in this sense is often seen as a personal rather than social problem, and the "afflicted" troop to counselors and psychiatrists (and drugs) in search of themselves. But the social base of even this most intimate form of alienation lies in the deprivation of growth-conducive social environments and relationships, and its cure is accordingly *social.* When one grows up alienated from others, he cannot love or relate; alienated from work, he cannot create; from community, he cannot mature as a social being. Dominant economic institutions, especially markets in labor, land, and capital, and their control by individuals making decisions on the basis of profit rather than human need, provide unrewarding social roles. Hence psychic growth is thwarted, much as vitamin deprivation inhibits physical development.

Individuals become alienated from themselves for yet another reason. To produce workers with the proper ideologies, values, and personalities to participate effectively in alienated social roles requires special attention on the part of those institutions which regulate the development of youth. Thus communications media, especially advertising, instill materialist values which hold meaningful work and community of no importance in comparison with individual consumption. They depersonalize and objectivize interpersonal, intersexual, interracial, and international relations, reducing them to brute power, competition, and ruse, by equating the individual's success as lover, worker, or community member with what he possesses in the form of goods or status.

Similarly schools, by mirroring the impersonal and competitive relations of community and the bureaucratic-authoritarian aspects of alienated work, thwart the development of true initiative, independence, and creativity in their charges. Thus they attempt to produce docile, unimaginative workers fitting the needs of hierarchical commodity production. The media and the schools are alienating, but are not the true culprits—they merely serve an economic mechanism which shapes community and work in patterns alien to human needs.

Nevertheless, the educational system warrants special attention in any analysis of alienation. For it is the educational system that is turning out cultural and political revolutionaries, as well as disaffected and unhappy workers. Why are schools beginning to fail in producing properly alienated workers? There are many reasons for this, and we shall discuss only several of the most important.

First, there has been an important qualitative shift in the composition of the work in modern corporate, bureaucratic capitalism. Most important, the middle class and the capitalist class no longer coincide as in the days of early entrepreneurial capitalism. Indeed they scarcely overlap. The vast majority of middle class people today are workers, in the sense that they sell their labor at a market and have no control over production. The social technology of corporate capitalism has reduced the bourgeoisie to the middle strata of the labor force. Students, who are by and large of middle class background, are thus *future members of the working class,* and their political actions must be viewed in this light. Moreover, long-term trends in occupational structure exhibit a shift away from the traditional blue-collar manufacturing stratum, toward the white-collar corporate-bureaucratic (clerical, secretarial, sales, administrative, and technical) and service (teacher, government worker, postman, policeman, soldier) strata. Hence the political views of students will be increasingly transferable to the working class as time goes on.

But the student movement is especially important because of the *special position* of education in relation to the modern capitalist economy. Bureaucratic order in production requires *an increasing period of socialization of labor* for the occupational roles the worker must assume. Educational institutions—high schools, junior colleges, and universities—are among the instruments of this socialization process. The schooling process—a basic formative influence on individual personality—is progressively reduced to its functional role in instilling the psychological requisites of an adequate alienated labor force. Men become "alienated from themselves" in the sense that their personal development is geared to the requirements of an economic system whose needs are based on criteria independent of human values.

It is assumed by liberal and radical alike that the purpose of schooling is primarily intellectual. Schools produce "good workers" by supplying individuals with the cognitive and psychomotor skills to operate in an increasingly "technological" work-environment. This is in large part false. In fact, *one cannot account for the contribution of schooling to worker earnings in terms of the concrete cognitive attainments of students.* Given the number of years of schooling an individual has attained, additional information as to his IQ or actual cognitive achievement (reading and mathematical facility, logical reasoning, etc.) have virtually no value in prediction of eventual income or position in the status-hierarchy of production. Cognitive development is associated with occupational status only through their common association with level of educational attainment. There is little direct causal connection.[1]

In fact, schooling contributes to the generation of an adequate labor force through the *inculcation of a "bureaucratic mentality" in students.*[2] This enables them to function properly in alienated work-environments; i.e., by directing the *emotional development*

---

1. For empirical support, see Herbert Gintis, "Education, Technology, and the Characteristics of Worker Productivity," *American Economic Review,* May 1971.
2. Ibid.

of a future worker. Since an increasing proportion—nowadays a large majority—of workers pass through this process of "psychic bureaucratization," *the development of a counter-culture negating the bureaucratic mentality is a necessary instrument in the emergence of working class consciousness.*

The Marxist principle that socialism can result only from the political activity of a working class conscious of itself as an oppressed class, remains essentially correct today. However, psychic conditioning as student is an essential and increasingly time- and energy-consuming segment of every worker's life. Education serves the production of alienated labor. Contradictions in the educational system are quickly transformed to factories and offices themselves.[3] A breakdown in the educational system produces "imperfectly socialized" workers—workers who enter the labor force in unalienated form, and hence incapable of, and unwilling to, submit to the meaninglessness and oppressiveness of bureaucratic order and hierarchical control. These are the revolutionary labor organizers of the future.

However, there have developed important contradictions within the educational system. First, schools perform their function *only insofar as they operate as objectively repressive institutions.* The "liberated" school cannot produce adequate workers, and education is *productive* only insofar as it is *repressive.* The otherwise astute analyses of such commentarists as Paul Goodman, George Leonard, Charles Silberman, John Holt, and Edgar Z. Friedenberg falter precisely on this point. The seeming "irrationalities" of formal education are in fact highly functional to the operation of capitalism. First, the *social relations* of education mirror the social relations of hierarchical control in alienated production. Firm authority lines (administration, teacher, student), emphasis on precise rule-conformity in punctuality, interpersonal relations and teacher-dominance, and the treatment of fellow students as competitors rather than cooperators ("cooperation in task performance," as Robert Dreeben notes, "is known in school circles as cheating") are of course obvious examples. More important, perhaps, is that the motivation and reward structure of

---

3. A "contradiction" is a process wherein the normal operation of a social system produces a condition which tends to undermine normal operation itself. Dialectical social analysis holds that social change takes place because a social system creates, through its internal contradictions, the conditions for its own breakdown. Hence the study of history becomes the study of developing contradictions in a society.

schooling mirrors that of alienated labor. Just as the worker on the job is not motivated by the subjective value of his work or the goal of that process—the object or service produced—so the student must learn to be motivated by external reward in the form of grades. Second, the *content of grading* is in itself repressive and conducive only to the development of alienated and bureaucratic mentality. Discipline, subordination to authority, and suppression of affective and creative modes of personality response are required of all strata in the labor force under bureaucratic conditions. Empirical investigation shows these traits are in themselves rewarded in terms of higher grades—in both high school and college—independent of their actual contribution to cognitive achievement.[4] Schooling impedes the development of the liberated individual by direct penalization of the liberated act, and not irrationally, but in the service of the economic system.

4. Gintis, op. cit.

5. The Problem of Reification

JOACHIM ISRAEL

The background to the theory
of reification

In our society it is an empirical fact that within an enterprise the right to decide was located in the owner of capital and in those persons appointed by him as the administrators of the enterprise. This empirical fact rests upon notions of a normative nature which prescribe that the right to make decisions is a part of the function of ownership. Those who own capital ought to determine how it is used.

Assume that one substituted this normative principle with another, for example, that those who work in an enterprise *ought* to have the right to make decisions, whereas the owners of capital are only guaranteed reasonable gain. A social system which is built upon such normative principles will naturally give rise to different empirical facts as far as the conditions of power within an enterprise and probably also within society in general are concerned. Many value premises could be quoted which form the basis of social facts. For example, the existing sex-role divisions and

the behavior of men and women in our society builds upon these
values. Or take the existing system of social stratification, which is
assumed to rest upon the value of an individual's work for the
functioning of the society. In this case one must ask what is
meant by the value of an individual's work, and what is meant by
the functioning of society? Marx attempts to reveal that that
which stands out as empirical fact (or as "natural law") can, in
fact, be referred to certain categories and social relations which
are intimately connected to certain values. The distinction between that which "stands out as real" and that "which is real" has
no metaphysical meaning. . . .

From fetishism of commodities
to reification

In Marx's theories the market system, in particular the
form it assumes in capitalist society—especially during the period
when it was still characterized by Manchester liberalism—is the
social origin of the fetishism of commodities. This system is characterized by the fact that use-value is substituted by exchange-
value, that human relations between individuals are substituted
by object relations between buyer and seller. This is true both
with regard to commodities and with regard to labor power.
Labor power is transformed into a commodity and therefore into
an object. The producers become differentiated from their products, which do not belong to them and which emerge as impersonal things. Lukács goes a step further. He relates the fetishism
of commodities to other social conditions, particularly to the development of bureaucracy and its functioning. As mentioned earlier, he had been a student of Max Weber's and now used Weber's theories about bureaucracy and rationality to supplement
Marx's theory of the fetishism of commodities. Therefore the theory of reification can be said to be built upon a synthesis of some
of Marx's and some of Weber's thoughts. Max Weber points
out how modern capitalism cannot function without formal rationality and calculation, how bureaucracy is the power system
which, from the point of view of formal rationality, is the most
effective one, and how other institutions are affected by this development. In particular, he mentions the legal system and how it
becomes rationalized and bureaucratized. This leads to the fact

that it loses any arbitrariness it may possess, and makes possible accurate predictions concerning its method of functioning.

Lukács's reasoning goes something like this. A market system leads to the fact that the commodity form gains a universal function. This means that *qualitatively* different things are considered as being in principle *similar* with regard to *quantity*. (Half a bottle of whisky is the same as half an hour's work or the pay received for this work.) To achieve such a similarity function, one must measure work performance very exactly. This is accomplished by time studies. (Lukács says that by means of these studies "the rational mechanization penetrates deeply into the worker's soul.") In its turn, that is one of the preconditions for the division of labor, which, as a consequence, transforms labor into abstract though rational, partial operations. Central to this development is the possibility of calculating and accounting for all work behavior. The consequence is that from the point of view of the producer the labor process is no longer a unified, continuous process, but a repetition of partial operations. The worker's own individual characteristics soon become seen as sources of error in a production which otherwise functions in a rational and accountable way.

Man becomes a mechanical part of a mechanical system. One of the consequences is that social contacts in the labor process diminish, as the individual is transformed into an isolated atom.

However, atomization and isolation are only one side of the problem. They correspond to a regularity in the social structure, a regularity which, in Lukács's view, is for the first time in history extended over all types of life manifestations. Thus, we have two tendencies: on the one hand, the individual's isolation and atomization; on the other hand, his total dependence on society and its mechanisms. Atomization results in the individual's being more easily ruled and manipulated.

Lukács asserts that the phenomenon of reification is often recognized, but that it is not placed in relation to existing economic conditions. It is from these economic conditions, namely, the capitalist mode of production, that they originate [*sic*]. Among other things, this is because the capitalist mode of production affects all social phenomena. "Thus the capitalist development has created a legal system which corresponds to its needs and which is fitted to its structure." The same is true of the structure of the state, and, as a main witness for this, Lukács refers again to Weber's comparison between state bureaucracy and the bureaucracy existing in private enterprise.

It is notable that in this description Lukács himself used a "reified" language, when maintaining that "the capitalist development" has created its own institutions and organizations. One might get the impression that not man but an impersonal power had created certain human institutions.

This depends on the fact that Marxist theory denied that "capitalists" are the cause of certain social conditions, for example, exploitation. It is "a capitalist system" which gives rise to these conditions, the capitalists themselves being the prisoners of the system, since seen from this point of view the system possesses its own laws, independent of the desires of individuals.

Bureaucracy is part of the institutions and organizations created by the capitalist development. It is related to the process of division of labor in industry. Within bureaucracy there occur formal rationalization and systematic division of function, which leads to the fact that all questions are considered in the light of strict, formal, and rational principles. This leads to the formalizing of human relations. In fact, Lukács asserts that total submission to the "system of object-relations" is a precondition for bureaucracy's functioning. Bureaucrats themselves feel that it is not only their duty to submit themselves to the rule of the bureaucratic organization, but also a matter of honor, i.e., a moral duty.

"The transformation of the commodity-relation into a ghostlike reification is not, therefore, complete when all objects of need-satisfaction become commodities. It influences the total structure of the human consciousness: the abilities and capabilities of man are no longer closely knit into an organic unit in the individual, but appear as 'objects' which man 'owns' and 'sells' in the same way as the things in the world around him."

In Lukács's analysis, much more strongly than in the theories of Marx, the point is made that the theory of reification means criticism not only of the capitalist mode of production but also of industrialization, rationalization, and bureaucratization, even though Lukács considers the latter phenomena to be a consequence of capitalism. How much more realistic and even to a certain extent more visionary, Weber's assumption emerges today, i.e., that no socialist society which wishes to have an effectively functioning apparatus of production can do so without formal rationality and bureaucracy.

The central problem, therefore, is not, for instance, how one is able to avoid the development of a bureaucracy, but how one is able to control this bureaucracy in such a way that it does not become dictatorial or despotic and that, in exerting its power, it does not become independent of those in whose service it was originally created. The concept of reification is useful and therefore important in such an analysis.

The process of reification

What is reification?

In an essay on reification Lucien Goldmann *exemplifies* the process of reification following the Marxian analysis of commodity and commodity relations. Take the owner of a factory, Goldmann proposes. In order to produce, he has to buy machinery and raw material and hire labor. He then starts the production process, and finally he tries to sell his products. At two points of the production process he is confronted with a market: (1) before he can produce, i.e., when he has to buy the material and the machinery necessary for the production as well as when he has to hire his workers; (2) when he wants to sell the finished products.

The traditional producer and capitalist (not the "mature corporation" described by Galbraith) is confronted with the market "on which events appear as the result of blind laws, being independent of his personal will. These events are ruled by the price, i.e., by objective characteristics of things. Thus the market economy obscures one of life's most essential areas—the economy—the historical and human character of social life. Man is transformed into a passive element. He is ascribed to the role of an on-looker in a drama, which is continuously renewed before his eyes and in which *dead things are really active elements."* (My italics.)

Probably an economist would argue that today the notion of a market's functioning in a completely blind manner, i.e., regulated only by supply and demand without social planning or governmental or private interference, is a myth. It is a notion which does not correspond to reality. In a mixed economy of the Swedish type, price mechanisms are controlled in different ways. In a society in which large corporations dominate, these corporations actively try to regulate and control market mechanisms. In societies with a planned economy, on the other hand, there is a tendency to introduce price mechanisms into the economy.

At present I do not wish to discuss the relevance of objections which can be raised against Goldmann's description, important as such objections may be. Instead I wish to analyze his exemplification of the process of reification.

In the first place there exist certain *social processes,* which are anchored in definite social conditions. The processes concern the "behavior" of objects—dead things—in a market situation. As commodities, their exchange-value, being perceived as an objective characteristic of these things, determines their "movements."

Second, there are *cognitive processes,* an experience of the social processes leading to a motion that man has surrendered to blind powers beyond his control.

Third, there exists a certain relation between the *social processes* and the *cognitive* ones. The cognitive processes are assumed to occur under conditions whereby it is impossible for an individual to reveal and to understand the "true" nature of the social processes, namely, that commodity relations veil relations between human beings.

There are two problems: (1) Is the description of market conditions correct in the sense that man is exposed to powers beyond his control? (2) Independent of the correctness of the actual social conditions, is man able to experience the fact that he is exposed to blind powers?

Let us start with the second question, to which the answer is apparently in the affirmative. Certain types of magical thinking can be used as an example. There is sufficient material from folklore to show that man is perceived as being exposed to powerful nonhuman entities, which direct him and force him to act independent of his own will.

However, magical thinking can also be characterized by anthropomorphism, i.e., a tendency to ascribe human characteristics to dead things such as plants and other objects found in nature, as well as to living objects, e.g., certain animals, which then rule man. Therefore, if reification is a tendency to ascribe to nonhuman objects the ability to rule man, then there seems to be some similarity to magical thinking (or to religious, as Marx also points out in his analysis of commodity relations). Thus reified thinking is correspondent to anthropomorphism. This may give us a hint as to how we can delimit reification as a cognitive process.

So far we have discussed the problem on a "pretheoretical level," a level on which knowledge is arranged and ordered in a way which differs from the systematic classifications and the specific modes of thinking which characterize the "theoretical" or "scientific" level. Thus "pretheoretical" knowledge partly builds upon preconditions which differ from scientific ones and therefore may lead to other explanations. Also, in our society knowledge can be divided into "prescientific" and "scientific." The "prescientific" level comprises the ways in which people construct their social reality, which then influences their behavior, as well as these commonsense explanations of facts and events, which are used when scientific explanations are unavailable or unknown. Prescientific thinking can be characterized in different ways. For example, there may be attempts to establish causal relations between two or more factors, which in fact relate in a statistical covariation only. It may concern the establishment of causal relations when such relations do not or cannot occur. A third example of such thinking is the drawing of wrong conclusions from facts or erroneous generalizations either from correct or incorrect relationships.

It is apparent that on the prescientific level many notions exist which can be classified as "reified." Take, for example, notions that the individual is powerless, that he totally lacks the possibility of influencing society and consequently his own fate, but that instead he is exposed to uncontrollable, impersonal forces. Notions of powerlessness can be classified as reified notions to the extent that the forces to which an individual perceives himself as subordinate are not really human powers or are not perceived as such.

6. Address of the Central Committee to the League of Communists [1850]

KARL MARX AND FRIEDRICH ENGELS

During the struggle and after the struggle, the workers must at every opportunity put forward their own demands alongside the demands of the bourgeois democrats. They must exact guarantees for the workers as soon as the bourgeois democrats are prepared to take the government into their hands. They must if necessary force these guarantees and in general contrive to oblige the new governments to make all the concessions and all the promises possible; this is the surest means of winning compromises. They must strive to subdue the inebriation of triumph and infatuation with the new state of things, the consequence of all victories won in the street, while judging the situation calmly and dispassionately and assuming an undisguised distrust of the new government. Alongside the new official administrations they must establish at the same time their own revolutionary worker governments, whether in the form of local boards or local councils, whether by workers' clubs or committees, in such a way that the bourgeois democratic governments not only immediately lose the workers' support but feel watched and menaced by authorities having behind them the whole mass of workers. In a word, as soon as the victory is won, the distrust of the proletariat must be turned no longer against the defeated reactionary party but against its former allies, against the party that wants to exploit the common victory alone.

Translated by Helen Kramer.

7. Necessity and Freedom

KARL MARX

The realm of freedom actually begins only where labor which is determined by necessity and mundane considerations ceases; thus in the very nature of things it lies beyond the sphere of actual material production. Just as the savage must wrestle with Nature to satisfy his wants, so must civilized man, and he must do so in all social formations and under all possible modes of production. With his development this realm of physical necessity expands as a result of his wants; but, at the same time, the forces of production which satisfy these wants also increase. Freedom in this field can only consist in socialized men, the associated producers, rationally regulating their interchange with Nature, bringing it under their common control, instead of being ruled by it as by the blind forces of Nature; and achieving this with the least expenditure of energy and under conditions most favorable to, and worthy of, their human nature. But it nonetheless still remains a realm of necessity. Beyond it begins that development of human energy which is an end in itself, the true realm of freedom—which, however, can blossom forth only with this realm of necessity as its basis. The shortening of the working day is its basic prerequisite.

Reprinted from *Capital,* Vol. 3 (Moscow: Foreign Languages Publishing House, 1959), pp. 799–800.

8. Power and Humanism

LUCIEN GOLDMANN

There is no abstract and universal socialism, nor any particular criterion that authorizes one to say *always and everywhere* that this or that society is or is not socialist. Neither the nationalization of the means of production nor the professions of faith of this or that government suffices to affirm it in a well-founded way. Socialism assumes, above all, social relations that permit people to live as much as possible in accordance with their aspirations, under conditions of optimal conformity between the relations of production and the circumstances that allow the praxis of the great majority of the society's members. In this connection, it must be added—and Marx sufficiently stressed it himself—that the richer the society, the easier is this conformity to achieve, so that it is difficult to imagine a really socialist society without a very high development of the productive forces.

For the same reasons, I cannot agree with those who claim that it is useless to speak of organizational capitalism or of capitalist technocratic society, since it is always capitalist societies that are involved.

The question is not posed in order to make a moral judgment; it is not a matter of having more or less antipathy or sympathy for one or the other of these social forms, but of elaborating operational concepts that enable us to understand the nature of social reality and to formulate a theory of it. Marx was able to speak of *capitalism* without particular specification, for he had before him only a single fundamental capitalist structure—liberal competitive capitalism—with, of course, diverse modalities in each country. But from the beginning of the century, faced with a fundamental structure in which the mechanisms of market regulation were transformed by the development of finance capital, monopolies, and trusts, the Marxist thinkers Hilferding, Lenin, and Trotsky were obliged to create a new operational concept, that of imperialism. Of course none of these theoreticians ever lost sight of the fact that finance capital is a form of capital and that imperialism is a form of capitalism. But this general concept no longer sufficed once two fundamental forms of the capitalist structure were recognized—forms that had to be distinguished.

Fifty or sixty years later, we find ourselves confronting a new range of transformations of capitalist society that obliges us to create, alongside the concepts of liberal capitalism and imperialism, a third concept: organizational capitalism, or technocratic society (the terminology is still not consecrated). We must not forget, of course, that we are always dealing with capitalist societies for which the fundamental concepts of exploitation, alienation, and surplus value continue to be valid. Nonetheless, this introduction of a new concept is necessary to understand the *concrete* nature and the *actual* functions of exploitation, alienation, and surplus value, as well as a whole series of contemporary phenomena.

Let us return to the idea that people—that is to say, social groups—tend to establish as strong a correspondence as possible between the productive forces and the relations of production. This indicates that the problem of the relations between these two aspects of social life is still posed and will be posed for a long time, not only in the capitalist world but also in the societies that call themselves socialist. And since all tension between the technical conditions of work and the social relations existing at a given moment has led in the past to the creation of social groups oriented toward a reorganization of these relations—that is to say, to the formation of social classes—the problem will continue to be posed in a similar manner in the societies of today. The urgent task is to perceive concretely the specific forms of these phenomena.

As to the problem of the relations between political power and humanism, it is not a matter of searching for a total and definitive identification of the two elements, the means of establishing a true and durable humanist political power, or of admitting their radical opposition by affirming that power is always inhumane and humanism a moral attitude deprived of political realism. Rather, it is necessary to explore the nature of the moments when, in the actual history of people, power and humanism were most reconciled, and, conversely, those moments when they entered resolutely into conflict. Ultimately, this is, it seems to me, the only positive and scientific approach to the problem of alienation.

Now, the response to the first of these questions depends on two parameters: first, the maximum *possible* development of the productive forces at the moment of the analysis; second, the relation between the real level of the development of the productive forces and the existing production relations.

If we take our examples from societies in the past, on which agreement will be easier to establish among Marxist inquirers or those close to Marxism, I think that we will all concur that, during a very long period of the history of humanity, division into classes was necessary: on the one hand, in order to master nature to the greatest degree possible and to assure the continued improvement of this mastery, and, on the other, to insure men the possibility of living better and better within the society. But once this extremely general statement is made, one must ask in each case whether the concrete form of the division into classes corresponds to the greatest possible degree of mastery over nature or has already become oppressive, in that privileged groups defend structures that no longer correspond to the optimum of interpersonal relations and of the development of the productive forces. In a case of the first type, there is doubtless no ideal situation conforming to a spiritualistic and abstract moralism, but rather an optimal situation in the relations between political power and what one might call humanism; it is, in historical study, the only possible meaning of the concept of nonalienation. In a case of the second type, power becomes necessarily oppressive, engendering alienation, and humanism falls to the side of the opposition forces oriented toward the overthrow of power and the transformation of the social order. . . .

Marx viewed the future in terms of alternatives: either a political revolution preliminary to complete takeover of economic and social control and followed by a profound overthrow on these two levels, or barbarism and total alienation; and of these alternatives, the first possibility, the proletarian revolution, was by far the more probable.

Today, a century after the appearance of *Capital,* we find ourselves at the very outset before a working class that has—slowly, no doubt, but nevertheless quite progressively—raised its standard of living, and this has prevented the development in Western Europe (except for very brief periods) of powerful revolutionary political organizations. While Lenin explained reformism as due to the existence of a worker aristocracy, one must take into account the fact that it is not a minority but a great majority of the working class in England, Germany, France, and the United States which has constituted this aristocracy in relation to the rest of the world. This is one of the most important factors explaining the essentially reformist character of the German Social Democratic Party before the war as well as the German and French Communist parties since at least 1924 or 1925; and this is true in spite of the fact that a superficially revolutionary ideology had become more and more scholastic. This reformism, linked among other things to the organization of the working class and to trade union gains, was—and still is—a *reformism integrated* into capitalist society, a reformism which proposes to introduce into the latter a certain number of modifications—no doubt important but nonetheless secondary—which do not at all menace capitalism as such, and whose *real* action is not at all oriented toward a profound changing of the social order. In short, the political and trade union organizations of the working class pose the problem of surpassing capitalism in words only and not at all in their real actions.

Now, what is called the new working class, or the new middle, salaried strata, is in an essentially different situation. No doubt the problem of the standard of living is completely knocked down here; improvement in living conditions is becoming evident and, for these strata, pauperization could be defended only with difficulty, even by the most dogmatic doctrinaires. In addition, the problem of alienation is being modified from top to bottom. The Frankfurt school, Adorno, and especially Marcuse have shown us in some remarkable works the stultification, the narrowing of the intellectual horizon, the disappearance of all critical and creative dimensions of consciousness, which menace these strata to the extent that they passively accept the advantages offered to them by organizational capitalism. A highly administered society, which extends this administration to culture to the point of suffocating it and causing it to disappear, for nothing is more contrary to culture than administration; the absolute and passive consumer, earning his living as a simple performer* in order to provide himself with gadgets; the Club Méditerranée of thought —that is the great menace forming on the horizon. For the external constraint of fascism and the concentration camps, something more subtle and more dangerous is substituted: stultification, brainwashing, corruption by income, vacations, the action of the mass media, and advertising.

It should be recognized that during an entire period extending from around 1950 to 1968, this process of integration seemed to succeed effectively. It was during this time that some sociological theories were developed which, though radically opposed to one another in their value judgments, nonetheless affirmed the same thing and transformed a transitory situation into a historic period. Enchanted by the birth of "positive" (that is to say, integrated) thinking, Raymond Aron and Daniel Bell sang the hymn of the end of ideology; with the melancholy consciousness that culture was in its death throes, David Riesman announced the end of inner direction; with the apocalyptic consciousness of the prophet who sees the coming of the end of the world, Herbert Marcuse cried out the coming of that monster, one-dimensional man. At the same time, elsewhere in France a theory which was presented as scientific although it was in reality highly ideological, and which, along with the ideas of Althusser, penetrated even Marxist thought, announced the disappearance of the subject, of man, and of History, and the coming of a "knowledge" reserved to an elite completely separated from the masses by the "epistemological gap" between "ideology" and "uncivilized thought," on the one hand, and "Science," on the other.

On the economic and social level, what were the characteristics of the technocratic society, as it established itself in the Western world, that engendered these ideologies?

First of all, progressive establishment of self-regulating mechanisms and economic planning. From there, considerable decrease of persons of note and progressive diminution of the social weight of unskilled workers, the former workers in chains; increase in a new stratum of relatively well paid specialists enjoying a growing income and more and more having a decisive importance in the

---

*One who merely carries out decisions made by others—*Trans.*

production process; but also—the major phenomenon—progressive concentration of decisions in the hands of a relatively restricted group of individuals, notably of planners (I shall call them *technocrats,* linking this word not so much to the idea of technique as to that of decision, and opposing it to the word *technician;* there are thus technocrats of the economy, of politics, of education, of advertising, of leisure, etc.) ; finally, a counterpart to the development of technocracy, the reduction of specialized technicians—of the new middle, salaried strata—to the level of simple performers. I shall not stress the intellectual narrowing and the suppression of the critical dimension that this transformation has entailed—Marcuse and the Frankfurt school have done it with sufficient brilliance.

Is it necessary from this to accept the conclusions—catastrophic for man and culture—of the apologists for capitalism, of the prophets of the Apocalypse, of the theologians of antihuman scholasticism? Is it necessary to side with Raymond Aron, Daniel Bell, Herbert Marcuse, Claude Lévi-Strauss, or Roland Barthes? I do not believe so. Social reality is much more complex than it appears to all these theoreticians who confuse a relatively brief period of transition with a historic period or with a fundamental and "ahistoric" law of humanity.

First of all, while it may be true that a generation which had already known—directly or through the intermediary of their parents—the uncertainty and anguish of the years 1929–1945 first reacted to the improved standard of living with enthusiasm for the security and well-being offered by the new technocratic society, matters had to be and are being modified as this evolution is pursued. Security and income allowing a decent standard of living are becoming natural things that continue by themselves.

A still more notable phenomenon is that, with every increase in income, the following increase must lose some of its value for consciousness. A second automobile is less important than the first, a third much less important than the second. The difference between the possession of one or of two suits is enormous, but it diminishes considerably between the sixth and seventh, etc. It is thus very probable—and this constitutes a real possibility for socialist action—that the increase in the standard of living will lose its weight as an integrating factor and that, parallel to this, exclusion from all participation in decision-making, the status of simple performer, will become a frustration more and more difficult to support; and all the more so since there is here a virtual contradiction—which will continue to grow—between, on the one hand, university education and the increase of knowledge that demands specialization, and, on the other, the narrowing of the intellectual horizon and the absence of all interest—not only social and political, but even organizational—in the investment policy of the enterprise, which implies adaptation to technocratic society. The most important product underlying the image of integrated organizational capitalism—which I once called the illiterate specialist and professor—contains an internal contradiction which threatens to explode violently in the course of historic evolution. However, to the extent that the consciousness of the middle, salaried strata becomes oriented more and more toward not quantitative but qualitative demands, toward exacting participation in decision-making and, at the extreme, forcing an entirely democratic management of the enterprise, the perspective of the evolution of the industrial societies toward socialism is both renewed and profoundly modified.

Now, this stratum is tending to become, at the same time, the most important numerically in the new society—a social group whose individuals, hardly replaceable in view of their qualifications, are situated at the nerve center of all social organization; its orientation therefore has every chance of becoming decisive for the evolution of society. Self-government was first launched by Yugoslav socialists and was born of the need to provide an infrastructure expressing their critical attitude toward the centralist and bureaucratic socialism of the USSR; it was, and still is, very difficult to implement in a country in the process of industrialization (owing to, among other things, the backwardness of the peasant strata and certain worker strata that have just left the peasantry). The idea of self-government spread like a flame in the West in May 1968. Today it is, if not accepted—and the fierce resistance of the French Communist Party and the General Confederation of Labor suffice to make this acceptance impossible—at the very least discussed by tens of thousands of young people and workers who had never heard of it before, and it is becoming in this perspective the principal and perhaps only concrete form that can take a socialist orientation in the advanced industrial societies.

The traditional Marxist sketch of a proletariat which, lacking any possibility of acquiring important social and economic positions within capitalist society, could reach socialism only by a political revolution, a conquest of the state prior to all fundamental reform of the economic structure, is profoundly modified. Qualitative conquests oriented toward the control of production and self-management no longer necessarily presuppose a prior conquest of the machinery of state, and the march toward socialism will probably take a road analogous to that followed in the development of the bourgeoisie within feudal society; namely, a gradual acquisition of economic and social power, marked by sometimes very sharp conflicts, followed by a revolutionary acquisition (England, France) or reformist acquisition (Italy, Germany) of political power.

It is doubtless a question of a reformist orientation, but a reformism essentially different from that which characterized the previous period in the history of capitalism. The latter was oriented toward the improvement of the existing social structure; this time —as in the case of the ultimately reformist struggle of the bourgeoisie against feudal society—it is a reformism oriented toward a radical change of structures, that is to say, a revolutionary reformism. . . .

To conclude on the dilemma of power and humanism: in the former problems of the workers' movement and Marxist thought, the hierarchy and discipline of the dominant classes, which organized and perpetuated exploitation, required an organized, centralized, and hierarchical defense along the same lines on the part of the oppressed classes and human values. The struggle was between two camps that both took on organizational structures approaching the military structure of traditional armies formed, above all, of infantry troops. Two things, however, struck me in the movement of May 1968, and notably in the student movement: the radical refusal of all organization and all discipline, and the consummate demand for liberty and spontaneity—a refusal and a spontaneity that went to the pathological when some Action Committees refused to keep the same secretary in both the morning and the afternoon, which prevented all continuity and did not even allow the keeping of minutes. All that was, of course, absurd and condemned to ineffectiveness. What is important, nevertheless, is to ascertain if we are confronted with an infantile mentality or, on the contrary, with a still confused but essentially justified reaction against the discipline and hierarchical character of organizations no longer corresponding to the new society in the course of establishing itself. The answer depends on the existence of new forces in the course of development, oriented at the same time toward liberty, democracy, and the socialist transformation of society. The hope of democratization of the workers' movement could in reality be based only on the fact that it now finds itself in a new world, confronting a new set of problems.

It could be realized that discipline and organization are, in effect, the same in an infantry corps and in an airplane crew or any other technically advanced body. . . . Little by little technical progress requires replacement of hierarchy by cooperation, of authority by comradeship. . . .

There remains the most fundamental, and no doubt most difficult, problem: that of the forms of organization of a truly socialist movement in contemporary industrial societies.

It is evident that no realistic and valid program confronting this problem has appeared in the West during the last several years, and that this constitutes the most important weakness of the European Left. Although between 1916 and 1925 Lenin, Lukács, and Gramsci, independently of each other, rediscovered dialectical thought and the necessity of basing the comprehension of society and socialist action on the forces within the societies that they were fighting, their analysis remained basically at the philosophic level; although after World War II the Yugoslav socialists, Trentin and Foa in Italy, and later Mallet in France discovered this internal social force being born with the second industrial revolution in the new working class and its program based on the concept of self-government, all that they could affirm on the organizational level was the probability—which is constantly being confirmed—of an increased political function for the trade unions and self-management bodies in relation to that of parties. In the advanced capitalist societies, the problem still remains of developing new forms of organization capable of uniting democracy and internal liberty with effectiveness in the struggle against the dominant classes.

I have no recipe to offer on this point. Nevertheless, I once read a comment in a work of Trotsky that seemed extremely interesting: the author asked himself why the proletariat needed centralized and disciplined organizations in its struggle, while the bourgeoisie succeeded with the revolution in France with a much more loose and decentralized organization of clubs and sections; and he replied—justly, it seems to me—that the bourgeoisie, already possessing economic and social power, had acquired the mental frameworks, the class consciousness, that spontaneously oriented its action in a revolutionary direction. There is in reality a dialectical relationship between spontaneity and discipline that makes the latter less necessary as the former is more developed.

At the root of the positions of the old Marxists, from Kautsky to Lenin and from Bebel to Stalin, was the intuition—and often the conviction—of the absence of all revolutionary spontaneity in the working class, an absence that had to be compensated for by hierarchic and disciplined organization. But if the new working class succeeds by its action in conquering positions of control in production even within capitalist society, it will find itself in a situation analogous to that of the bourgeoisie before 1789. The exercise of these economic and social functions will entail a psychological and intellectual formation sufficient to allow a considerable increase of spontaneity and democracy in the organizations to come, which the theoreticians must discover from future historic experience, as their predecessors formerly discovered the trade unions in the West or the soviets in Russia.

The future forms of organization, in order to be functional and effective, will no doubt have to rid themselves of all that was untimely, irresponsible, and exaggerated in the enthusiasm and radicalism of the students of 1968. There nonetheless remains their rejection of hierarchy and bureaucratic discipline—these two characteristics of the workers' movement of the last decades. Their consummate demand for liberty and spontaneity contained in germ, and in a no doubt anticipatory form, a profound and powerful intuition of the modern world being born and of the forms that will probably be taken by humanist values, the organization of the struggle for socialism, and power structures. In that alone, the students of May 1968 were in advance of the bureaucratic consciousness of the defenders of antecedent structures that have been oppressive and are being surpassed by history.

9. Escape from Freedom

ERICH FROMM

What then is the meaning of freedom for modern Man?
He has become free from the external bonds that would prevent him from doing and thinking as he sees fit. He would be free
to act according to his own will, if he knew what he wanted,
thought, and felt. But he does not know. He conforms to anony-
mous authorities and adopts a self which is not his. The more he
does this, the more powerless he feels, the more he is forced to
conform. In spite of a veneer of optimism and initiative, modern
man is overcome by a profound feeling of powerlessness which
makes him gaze toward approaching catastrophes as though he
were paralyzed.

Looked at superficially, people appear to function well enough
in economic and social life; yet it would be dangerous to overlook
the deepseated unhappiness behind that comforting veneer. If life
loses its meaning because it is not lived, man becomes desperate.
People do not die quietly from psychic starvation either. If we
look only at the economic needs as far as the "normal" person is
concerned, if we do not see the unconscious suffering of the average automatized person, then we fail to see the danger that threatens our culture from its human basis: the readiness to accept any

ideology and any leader, if only he promises excitement and offers a political structure and symbols which allegedly give meaning and order to an individual's life. The despair of the human automaton is fertile soil for the political purposes of Fascism.

Freedom and spontaneity

So far this book has dealt with one aspect of freedom: the powerlessness and insecurity of the isolated individual in modern society who has become free from all bonds that once gave meaning and security to life. We have seen that the individual cannot bear this isolation; as an isolated being he is utterly helpless in comparison with the world outside and therefore deeply afraid of it; and because of his isolation, the unity of the world has broken down for him and he has lost any point of orientation. He is therefore overcome by doubts concerning himself, the meaning of life, and eventually any principle according to which he can direct his actions. Both helplessness and doubt paralyze life, and in order to live man tries to escape from freedom, negative freedom. He is driven into new bondage. This bondage is different from the primary bonds, from which, though dominated by authorities or the social group, he was not entirely separated. The escape does not restore his lost security, but only helps him to forget his self as a separate entity. He finds new and fragile security at the expense of sacrificing the integrity of his individual self. He chooses to lose his self since he cannot bear to be alone. Thus freedom—as freedom from—leads into new bondage.

Does our analysis lend itself to the conclusion that there is an inevitable circle that leads from freedom into new dependence? Does freedom from all primary ties make the individual so alone and isolated that inevitably he must escape into new bondage? Are *independence* and freedom identical with *isolation* and fear? Or is there a state of positive freedom in which the individual exists as an independent self and yet is not isolated but united with the world, with other men, and nature?

We believe that there is a positive answer, that the process of growing freedom does not constitute a vicious circle, and that man can be free and yet not alone, critical and yet not filled with doubts, independent and yet an integral part of mankind. This freedom man can attain by the realization of his self, by being himself. What is realization of the self? Idealistic philosophers have believed that self-realization can be achieved by intellectual insight alone. They have insisted upon splitting human personality, so that man's nature may be suppressed and guarded by his reason. The result of this split, however, has been that not only the emotional life of man but also his intellectual faculties have been crippled. Reason, by becoming a guard set to watch its prisoner, nature, has become a prisoner itself; and thus both sides of human personality, reason and emotion, were crippled. We believe that the realization of the self is accomplished not only by an act of thinking but also by the realization of man's total personality, by the active expression of his emotional and intellectual potentialities. These potentialities are present in everybody; they become real only to the extent to which they are expressed. In other words, *positive freedom consists in the spontaneous activity of the total, integrated personality.*

We approach here one of the most difficult problems of psychology: the problem of spontaneity. An attempt to discuss this problem adequately would require another volume. However, on the basis of what we have said so far, it is possible to arrive at an understanding of the essential quality of spontaneous activity by means of contrast. Spontaneous activity is not compulsive activity, to which the individual is driven by his isolation and powerlessness; it is not the activity of the automaton, which is the uncritical adoption of patterns suggested from the outside. Spontaneous activity is free activity of the self and implies, psychologically, what the Latin root of the word, *sponte,* means literally: of one's free will. By activity we do not mean "doing something," but the quality of creative activity that can operate in one's emotional, intellectual, and sensuous experiences and in one's will as well. One premise for this spontaneity is the acceptance of the total personality and the elimination of the split between "reason" and "nature"; for only if man does not repress essential parts of his self, only if he has become transparent to himself, and only if the different spheres of life have reached a fundamental integration, is spontaneous activity possible.

While spontaneity is a relatively rare phenomenon in our culture, we are not entirely devoid of it. In order to help in the understanding of this point I should like to remind the reader of some instances where we all catch a glimpse of spontaneity.

In the first place, we know of individuals who are—or have been—spontaneous, whose thinking, feeling, and acting were the expression of their selves and not of an automaton. These individuals are mostly known to us as artists. As a matter of fact, the artist can be defined as an individual who can express himself spontaneously. If this were the definition of an artist—Balzac defined him just in that way—then certain philosophers and scientists have to be called artists too, while others are as different from them as an old-fashioned photographer from a creative painter. There are other individuals who, though lacking the ability—or perhaps merely the training—for expressing themselves in an objective medium as the artist does, possess the same spontaneity. The position of the artist is vulnerable, though, for it is really only the successful artist whose individuality or spontaneity is respected; if he does not succeed in selling the art, he remains to his contemporaries a crank, a "neurotic." The artist in this matter is in a similar position to that of the revolutionary throughout history. The successful revolutionary is a statesman, the unsuccessful one a criminal.

Small children offer another instance of spontaneity. They have an ability to feel and think that which is really *theirs;* this spontaneity shows in what they say and think, in the feelings that are expressed in their faces. If one asks what makes for the attraction small children have for most people I believe that, aside from sentimental and conventional reasons, the answer must be that it is this very quality of spontaneity. It appeals profoundly to everyone who is not so dead himself that he has lost the ability to perceive it. As a matter of fact, there is nothing more attractive and convincing than spontaneity whether it is to be found in a child, in an artist, or in those individuals who cannot thus be grouped according to age or profession.

Most of us can observe at least moments of our own spontaneity which are at the same time moments of genuine happiness. Whether it be the fresh and spontaneous perception of a landscape, or the dawning of some truth as the result of our thinking, or a sensuous pleasure that is not stereotyped, or the welling up of love for another person—in these moments we all know what a spontaneous act is and may have some vision of what human life could be if these experiences were not such rare and uncultivated occurrences.

Why is spontaneous activity the answer to the problem of freedom? We have said that negative freedom by itself makes the individual an isolated being, whose relationship to the world is distant and distrustful and whose self is weak and constantly threatened. Spontaneous activity is the one way in which man can overcome the terror of aloneness without sacrificing the integrity of his self; for in the spontaneous realization of the self man unites himself anew with the world—with man, nature, and himself. Love is the foremost component of such spontaneity; not love as the dissolution of the self in another person, not love as the possession of another person, but love as spontaneous affirmation of others, as the union of the individual with others on the basis of the preservation of the individual self. The dynamic quality of love lies in this very polarity: that it springs from the need of overcoming separateness, that it leads to oneness—and yet that individuality is not eliminated. Work is the other component; not work as a compulsive activity in order to escape aloneness, not work as a relationship to nature which is partly one of dominating her, partly one of worship of and enslavement by the very products of man's hands, but work as creation in which man becomes one with nature in the act of creation. What holds true of love and work holds true of all spontaneous action, whether it be the realization of sensuous pleasure or participation in the political life of the community. It affirms the individuality of the self and at the same time it unites the self with man and nature. The basic dichotomy that is inherent in freedom—the birth of individuality and the pain of aloneness—is dissolved on a higher plane by man's spontaneous action.

In all spontaneous activity the individual embraces the world. Not only does his individual self remain intact; it becomes stronger and more solidified. *For the self is as strong as it is active.* There is no genuine strength in possession as such, neither of material property nor of mental qualities like emotions or thoughts. There is also no strength in use and manipulation of objects; what we use is not ours simply because we use it. Ours is only that to which we are genuinely related by our creative activity, be it a person or an inanimate object. Only those qualities that result from our spontaneous activity give strength to the self and thereby form the basis of its integrity. The inability to act spontaneously, to express what one genuinely feels and thinks, and the resulting necessity to present a pseudo self to others and oneself, are the root of the feeling of inferiority and weakness. Whether or not we are aware of it, there is nothing of which we are more ashamed than of not being ourselves, and there is nothing that gives us greater pride and happiness than to think, to feel, and to say what is ours.

This implies that what matters is the activity as such, the pro-

cess and not the result. In our culture the emphasis is just the reverse. We produce not for a concrete satisfaction but for the abstract purpose of selling our commodity; we feel that we can acquire everything material or immaterial by buying it, and thus
things become ours independently of any creative effort of our
own in relation to them. In the same way we regard our personal
qualities and the result of our efforts as commodities that can be
sold for money, prestige, and power. The emphasis thus shifts
from the present satisfaction of creative activity to the value of
the finished product. Thereby man misses the only satisfaction
that can give him real happiness—the experience of the activity
of the present moment—and chases after a phantom that leaves
him disappointed as soon as he believes he has caught it—the illusory happiness called success.

If the individual realizes his self by spontaneous activity and
thus relates himself to the world, he ceases to be an isolated atom;
he and the world become part of one structuralized whole; he has
his rightful place, and thereby his doubt concerning himself and
the meaning of life disappears. This doubt sprang from his separateness and from the thwarting of life; when he can live, neither
compulsively nor automatically but spontaneously, the doubt disappears. He is aware of himself as an active and creative individual and recognizes that *there is only one meaning of life: the act
of living itself.*

If the individual overcomes the basic doubt concerning himself
and his place in life, if he is related to the world by embracing it
in the act of spontaneous living, he gains strength as an individual and he gains security. This security, however, differs from the
security that characterizes the preindividualist state in the same
way in which the new relatedness to the world differs from that of
the primary ties. The new security is not rooted in the protection
which the individual has from a higher power outside of himself;
neither is it a security in which the tragic quality of life is eliminated. The new security is dynamic; it is not based on protection,
but on man's spontaneous activity. It is the security acquired each
moment by man's spontaneous activity. It is security that only
freedom can give, that needs no illusions because it has eliminated those conditions that necessitate illusions.

Positive freedom as the realization of the self implies the full
affirmation of the uniqueness of the individual. Men are born
equal but they are also born different. The basis of this difference
is the inherited equipment, physiological and mental, with which

they start life, to which is added the particular constellation of circumstances and experiences that they meet with. This individual basis of the personality is as little identical with any other as two organisms are ever identical physically. The genuine growth of the self is always a growth on this particular basis; it is an organic growth, the unfolding of a nucleus that is peculiar for this one person and only for him. The development of the automaton, in contrast, is not an organic growth. The growth of the basis of the self is blocked and a pseudo self is superimposed upon this self, which is—as we have seen—essentially the incorporation of extraneous patterns of thinking and feeling. Organic growth is possible only under the condition of supreme respect for the peculiarity of the self of other persons as well as of our own self. This respect for and cultivation of the uniqueness of the self is the most valuable achievement of human culture and it is this very achievement that is in danger today.

The uniqueness of the self in no way contradicts the principle of equality. The thesis that men are born equal implies that they all share the same fundamental human qualities, that they share the basic fate of human beings, that they all have the same inalienable claim on freedom and happiness. It furthermore means that their relationship is one of solidarity, not one of domination-submission. What the concept of equality does not mean is that all men are alike. Such a concept of equality is derived from the role that the individual plays in his economic activities today. In the relation between the man who buys and the one who sells, the concrete differences of personality are eliminated. In this situation only one thing matters, that the one has something to sell and the other has money to buy it. In economic life one man is not different from another; as real persons they are, and the cultivation of their uniqueness is the essence of individuality.

Positive freedom also implies the principle that there is no higher power than this unique individual self, that man is the center and purpose of his life; that the growth and realization of man's individuality is an end that can never be subordinated to purposes which are supposed to have greater dignity. This interpretation may arouse serious objections. Does it not postulate unbridled egotism? Is it not the negation of the idea of sacrifice for an ideal? Would its acceptance not lead to anarchy? These questions have actually already been answered, partly explicitly, partly implicitly, during our previous discussion. However, they are too important for us not to make another attempt to clarify the answers and to avoid misunderstanding.

To say that man should not be subject to anything higher than himself does not deny the dignity of ideals. On the contrary, it is the strongest affirmation of ideals. It forces us, however, to a critical analysis of what an ideal is. One is generally apt today to assume that an ideal is any aim whose achievement does not imply material gain, anything for which a person is ready to sacrifice egotistical ends. This is a purely psychological—and for that matter relativistic—concept of an ideal. From this subjectivist viewpoint a Fascist, who is driven by the desire to subordinate himself to a higher power and at the same time to overpower other people, has an ideal just as much as the man who fights for human equality and freedom. On this basis the problem of ideals can never be solved.

We must recognize the difference between genuine and fictitious ideals, which is just as fundamental a difference as that between truth and falsehood. All genuine ideals have one thing in common: they express the desire for something which is not yet accomplished but which is desirable for the purposes of the growth and happiness of the individual. We may not always know what serves this end, we may disagree about the function of this or that ideal in terms of human development, but this is no reason for a relativism which says that we cannot know what furthers life or what blocks it. We are not always sure which food is healthy and which is not, yet we do not conclude that we have no way whatsoever of recognizing poison. In the same way we can know, if we want to, what is poisonous for mental life. We know that poverty, intimidation, isolation, are directed *against* life; that everything that serves freedom and furthers the courage and strength to be oneself is *for* life. What is good or bad for man is not a metaphysical question, but an empirical one that can be answered on the basis of an analysis of man's nature and the effect which certain conditions have on him. . . .

Obviously, one of the greatest difficulties in the establishment of the conditions for the realization of democracy lies in the contradiction between a planned economy and the active co-operation of each individual. A planned economy of the scope of any big industrial system requires a great deal of centralization and, as a consequence, a bureaucracy to administer this centralized machine. On the other hand, the active control and co-operation by each individual and by the smallest units of the whole system requires a great amount of decentralization. Unless planning from the top is blended with active participation from below, unless the stream of social life continuously flows from below upwards, a planned economy will lead to renewed manipulation of the people. To solve this problem of combining centralization with decentralization is one of the major tasks of society. But it is certainly no less soluble than the technical problems we have already solved and which have brought us an almost complete mastery over nature. It is to be solved, however, only if we clearly recognize the necessity of doing so and if we have faith in the people, in their capacity to take care of their real interests as human beings.

In a way it is again the problem of individual initiative with which we are confronted. Individual initiative was one of the great stimuli both of the economic system and also of personal development under liberal capitalism. But there are two qualifications: it developed only selected qualities of man, his will and rationality, while leaving him otherwise subordinate to economic goals. It was a principle that functioned best in a highly individualized and competitive phase of capitalism which had room for countless independent economic units. Today this space has narrowed down. Only a small number can exercise individual initiative. If we want to realize this principle today and enlarge it so that the whole personality becomes free, it will be possible only on the basis of the rational and concerted effort of a society as a whole, and by an amount of decentralization which can guarantee real, genuine, active co-operation and control by the smallest units of the system.

Only if man masters society and subordinates the economic machine to the purposes of human happiness and only if he actively participates in the social process, can he overcome what now drives him into despair—his aloneness and his feeling of powerlessness. Man does not suffer so much from poverty today as he suffers from the fact that he has become a cog in a large machine, an automaton, that his life has become empty and lost its meaning. The victory over all kinds of authoritarian systems will be possible only if democracy does not retreat but takes the offensive and proceeds to realize what has been its aim in the minds of those who fought for freedom throughout the last centuries. It will triumph over the forces of nihilism only if it can imbue people with a faith that is the strongest the human mind is capable of, the faith in life and in truth, and in freedom as the active and spontaneous realization of the individual self.

10. Order and Freedom

LJUBOMIR TADIĆ

The starting point and guidelines for determining a clear attitude of socialism toward the state and bureaucracy are given in Marx's criticism of the state and bourgeois society, and in the historic struggle of the proletariat for the "winning of democracy." But, at the same time, disagreements and wrong roads begin here as well.

Marx's criticism of political representation and bureaucracy begins with the criticism of Hegel's political philosophy. . . . Hegel sees in bureaucracy that "general class" in which lie the "consciousness of the state and the most outstanding education," the class that represents the "main pillar of the state." He defines the state as the "reality of the common idea," the *realization of freedom,* and considers the bureaucracy to be the class that insures the linking of general and special interests; its hierarchy and responsibility, combined with "control from below," are sufficient guarantees for the prevention of arbitrariness and abuse of power. Marx considers this view of Hegel's unfounded because of Hegel's characterization of the state as the realization of freedom. But Marx also criticizes Hegel's proposition that the idea of freedom is realized in the modern state. . . .

In his criticism of Hegel's philosophy of the state, Marx dem-

Reprinted from *Poredak i sloboda* (Belgrade: Kultura, 1967) , pp. 112–19, 258–63. Translated by Helen Kramer.

onstrates the *dialectic* character of the state. He implicitly adopts Hegel's thesis that the state (more precisely, the community) is that *whole,* that place where personal freedom can alone be realized; he considers . . . that Hegel precisely describes the essence of the modern state. However, for Marx the essence of the modern state is not the essence of the state in the sense of a community in which there exists "substantial unity" of the people and the state, of special and general interests. He shows that the alienation of the modern state from man arises at that moment when the "general business," as well as engagement in it, become a *monopoly.*

Reason and freedom are realized only when the state laws, as a human work, are truly the free product of man and not the special monopoly of administrators, the bureaucracy. In other words, freedom is possible only when man is truly the subject, the *creator,* of his own fate, and not a mere *object* over which power is exercised. . . . The historical process in the development of modern society led to the separation of the state from bourgeois society. And it is precisely on that separation that the origin of bureaucracy is based. . . .

In world literature, it is difficult to find better, more complete, and more profound characterizations of the phenomenon of bureaucracy than those which Marx gave in his *Critique of Hegel's Philosophy of State Law.* They strike the very essence of bureaucracy as a modern social phenomenon, regardless of the color of the political flag under which it is hidden. But the greatest value of Marx's analysis lies in its revealing the *spiritual* structure of that phenomenon whose manifestations are directly present in our time and are daily confirmed in countless examples. Let us consider several of the most important characteristics:

1. The true goal of the state appears to the bureaucracy as a goal *against* the state.

2. The bureaucracy considers itself to be the ultimate, final goal of the state; the state's goals are transformed into the bureaucracy's goals, or bureaucratic goals are transformed into the state's goals.

3. The bureaucracy is a circle from which no one can depart.

4. The bureaucracy is an imaginary state beside the real state; it is the spiritualism of the state.

5. The bureaucracy possesses the essence of the state, the spiritual essence of society. This is its *private property.*

6. Under the rule of the bureaucracy, everything receives double significance—real and bureaucratic; this is true even for

knowledge and will: there are real and bureaucratic knowledge and will.

7. The general spirit of bureaucracy is *secret,* a mystery maintained internally only by hierarchy and externally as a closed corporation. An open spirit of the state, as well as public opinion, seem to the bureaucracy as the *betrayal* of its mystery. Hence true science appears to the bureaucracy to be without content, for it considers its own imaginary knowledge as the essential.

8. *Authority* is the principle of bureaucratic knowledge, and the deification of authority a bureaucratic conviction. In the bureaucracy itself, spiritualism is transformed into a crude materialism of subordination and passive obedience, into a *mechanism* of rigid formal activity, of ready-made principles, views, and traditions. For the individual bureaucrat, the state goal is transformed into his private goal, into a pursuit of ranks, the progress of his career. Bureaucracy therefore aims at making life as material as possible.

9. With the true state, the bureaucracy acts in a Jesuitical way. Since knowledge is the opposite of this Jesuitism, it becomes intentional Jesuitism.

10. The crude spiritualism of the bureaucracy is shown in the fact that it wants to *do everything,* views the world as the mere object of its activity, and transforms will into a *causa prima.*

11. In bureaucracy, the state interest becomes a special private goal opposed to other private goals.

In the cited characteristics of bureaucracy, Marx shows the most negative consequences that emerge from the birth of the "political state." Here in bureaucracy general interests are reduced to meaninglessness, drown, and disappear in the mud of the egoism of infected private interests. The spirit of bureaucracy sets all human relations upside down and degrades them to a simple illusion: the true goals of the state, on the one hand, become goals against the state, and, on the other, are transformed into the private goals of the bureaucracy, into its usurpatory private property and monopoly with all the traits of that institution (*usus, fructus, et abusus*) , into a source and means for acquiring privileges.

From the sociological standpoint, as a "separate, closed society within the state," bureaucracy resembles a peculiar feudal institution of the estate type, an institution very close to corporations and guilds.

The spiritual and organizational structure of bureaucracy is bipolar. It is the product of the capitalist mechanism, on the one hand, and directly similar to church and Jesuitical organization, on the other. Bureaucracy is a peculiar emanation of the scholastic-theological spirit on wordly terrain (*la république prêtre*, as Marx says). That spirit emerges out of its profane-spiritual position. Hence bureaucracy, like the church hierarchy, is closely connected with *dogmatism*, which is its "symbol of faith." The permanent conflict of bureaucracy with true science results from slavish ties to the dogmatic truth of authority which is not subject to any sort of examination, in contrast to the authority of truth used by science. The instinctive hatred of bureaucracy for every objectively based knowledge results from its servile position, which is always oriented to a crudely materialistic goal: the acquisition of a career and higher rank in the hierarchy. Hence, since as early as Napoleon's time, bureaucracy has been known for persecution of the intelligentsia and for its subjectivistic and ideological connection with personal interests—the criterion by which it measures and judges everything.

Marx's characterizations of bureaucracy also show its *voluntaristic* trait. To wish to "do everything" is one of the most basic, vulgarly optimistic traits of bureaucratic voluntarism and subjectivism. As in all voluntarism, bureaucratic activity manifests itself as *fictive* activity: since there are no real goals, it fabricates imaginary goals *as though* they are real goals. Therefore trying to transfer its own structure to all human relations and to make them the object of arbitrary modeling, it leaves behind itself everywhere arbitrariness and spiritual wasteland. The result is total dehumanization.

Since in its own activity it turns in a vicious circle, hung up between its own illusions about how the world ought to look and a social reality which denies those illusions, bureaucracy is forced to weave a mystical aureole about its activity. This serves as a veil behind which it hides and justifies its spiritual nakedness and its otherwise fictive existence. Hence bureaucracy makes use of the deceptive formula of the protector of "higher interests," and in the name of "reasons of state" excludes every serious form of public criticism and public opinion except that on which it has its own stamp. Therefore, Marx also says, public opinion and real control seem to the bureaucracy as "betrayal of its mystery," of its imaginery raison d'être. Public opinion is transformed into an offense against its enlightenment, and there is thus created a psychosis of permanent state of siege in which the human spirit must "live." It is natural that in such a climate, in spite of total "orga-nizedness," sheer disorganization and unprincipledness, a feeling of being lost, spiritual apathy, boredom, and tedium prevail. Vol-untarism here goes hand in hand with fatalism.

In contrast to Hegel and many contemporary writers who "re-alistically" and "wisely" seek an out within the framework of the existing political relations and therefore inevitably find them-selves constantly at starting positions, Marx tries to show how a true solution of the problem cannot be reached within the frame-work of the "political state" nor, to use Weberian terminology in a somewhat modified sense, through the devising of an "ideal type of bureaucracy." For Marx, all these are obviously only pal-liatives. Hence, he also refutes Hegel's assertion that bureaucratic hierarchy is a means of preventing arbitrariness and the abuse of power. Marx indeed poses the decisive question: *where is the pro-tection against the hierarchy itself?* For precisely hierarchy is the "main abuse." Marx finds a principled solution in the type of de-mocracy in which man would be treated not as an object but as a true subject. Here the negative designation of politics in Marx, which is reserved for the modern state and relations in it, makes way for a positive concept of politics, the real humanization of human relations. Only in that sense is it possible to comprehend Marx's idea of the "reclaiming of the state" and "true democ-racy" in which "the *formal* principle is simultaneously also the *material* principle," a real reconciliation of the state and the peo-ple. The carrier of that reconciliation is neither Rousseau's petite bourgeoisie nor Hegel's bureaucracy, but the *proletariat*. This real social force has the greatest understanding of the general in-terests, for it is not infected by private-ownership egoism nor con-cerned with the perpetuation of its rule: "When the proletariat is victorious, it by no means becomes an absolute side of society, for it wins only in abolishing itself and its contradiction." Accord-ingly, the idea of "classless society" and the "withering away of the state" is nothing other than the teaching of the possibility of human emancipation by means of the reclaiming of the commu-nity, through the intermediary of a class of contemporary society which stands closest to that idea.

For socialism as socialism, there is not and cannot be a solution to the problem of bureaucracy based on the abstract, political state, for bureaucracy is its necessary product. To say that bu-reaucracy is necessary in socialism is therefore possible only under the assumption of a definite acceptance of the political state under the name of the "dictatorship of the proletariat" and "socialist democracy." Then every criticism of bureaucracy ends *on the ground of the very bureaucracy* and, by the very nature of things, remains illusory and impotent. In the final analysis, there is no radical solution, for in the best of cases it is possible to achieve only "correction" of the work of the bureaucratic apparatus and "greasing" of the state mechanism; a true *surpassing* of this historic category cannot be achieved. Even the thesis that in socialism "all are bureaucrats, so no one will be a bureaucrat" is precisely in this line. Marx therefore rightly criticizes Hegel when the latter assumes that every citizen can become a state official: "Every Catholic has the possibility of becoming a priest. But is the priesthood therefore less opposed to the Catholic as an alien power? The fact that everyone has the possibility of acquiring the right of *another* sphere shows only that *his own* sphere is not the reality of this right." The possibility that every citizen can become a state official shows that the official class is far from being a "general class," the class of the general interests. On the contrary, both before and after that, bureaucracy remains "alien power," the "other sphere," and not the citizen's own sphere.

Here there is an analogy with the equal right of all citizens to acquire property. To "deserve" the right of property and to actually be an owner are two different things. Right *as right* gives only the *formal* possibility of ownership and nothing more. The *factual* property relation is a privilege. The passive right to vote in a representative state offers all citizens the *formal* possibility of being elected to all state organs. However, everyone knows very well that in such a system rule is also the privilege of those engaged in politics as a profession. This phenomenon is nothing other than the reflex of the fundamental relation of private property on the political terrain.

The working class begins its struggle for a new, socialist society not only by the act of socializing the means of production but also by the socialization of public functions, by the *abolition of political professionalism,* i.e., by the uniform abolition of monopoly of private property both in economics and in politics. But this is only the first condition of constituting socialism counter to bourgeois society. In order to avoid remaining imprisoned within the framework of the fetishistic structure of capitalist society, and consequently being wagged as its tail without principles, the working class must take new steps and begin new undertakings.

The idea of *workers' councils* which has arisen in all socialist revolutions and in the resistance to bureaucratic dictatorship of the Stalinist type represents the essential negation of political forms of the old society. It expresses the first act in transforming the possibility of socialism into reality, the rising of proletarian consciousness from the domain of the old world, the germ of the future, the clearing of the horizon.

What workers' councils represent potentially, however, should be distinguished from what they are. For even today, workers' councils are seeking themselves. Sometimes they look backward, asking themselves whether they are only a better organization of work than the capitalist mode or *something more* than that. In that painful hesitation between today and tomorrow is hidden one of the most difficult problems of contemporary socialism. In many countries, the bourgeoisie has disappeared as the ruling social force, but that alienated condition which characterizes bourgeois society has not disappeared. The rule of commodities and money which produces and reproduces bourgeois objectivism, the rule of facts, the state, law, and "realism" in politics, has not, therefore, disappeared. On the other hand, the history of the workers' movement from the October Revolution onward shows the multiplied danger of counterrevolution, substantially greater than that which Engels foresaw in his *Anti-Dühring*. The danger not only comes from the classical bourgeois source, but also arises on "domestic" soil. Stalinism as an *international* phenomenon showed with sufficient clarity that *bureaucratic counterrevolution* is at least as dangerous for socialism as is bourgeois counterrevolution. The "strange" metamorphosis of the "minister" into the master has shown its deformed face in socialism as well.

In socialism, bureaucracy arises, generally speaking, when there is *uncritical confidence of the proletariat in the state* and its instruments, when the proletariat looks backward and accepts "tested" and "reliable" tools of authority which, in fact, ought to be superseded. What is more, even when it is in principle conscious of the danger of bureaucracy and of the state apparatus but considers that their abolition should be postponed for "tomorrow" because its first task is to devote itself to "creative work," the proletariat misses the historic chance of carrying out the necessary radical destruction of the product of the old society without which there is no socialism. . . .

If socialist society is historically called upon to achieve a higher form of democracy than bourgeois society, then for the attainment of this goal a more developed form of a democratic public in which there will be no contradictions between form and content is essential. But since socialism does not begin its existence outside the course of history, it is also absolutely essential for it critically to assimilate the best democratic inheritance of past epochs. In the category of public opinion, it must therefore differentiate its *concept* from its *ideological* distortion, to which Hegel already directed attention in his *Philosophy of Right*. Socialism must furthermore distinguish two dimensions clearly manifested historically in the function of publicity: *critical* and *manipulative*. Since in the ambivalent structure of public opinion two intentions are hidden—the intention of wisdom (the politics of truth and freedom) and the intention of reification (passive resonance and fictive freedom) —socialist society is forced to make a critical choice here as well. It must surpass the ideological, manipulative and reified function of public opinion in order to be able, by opting for its true, critical, and intellectual function, to carry out the *rehabilitation* of a democratic public, which is one of the decisive points at which socialism begins to distinguish itself in principle from previous class systems.

All the elements cited are implied in Marx's conception of socialist society, i.e., in the concept of socialist society as the antithesis of capitalism. The private sphere of capitalism, or bourgeois society itself in relation to its political abstraction (the state) , by means of its public opinion, exercises indirect control over public affairs, for the state is only the "business board" of private owners in which their average interests are reflected in an "ideal independence of particular elements of bourgeois life." Hence, the liberal bourgeois *constitutional state* is only the *res publica* of private owners and entrepreneurs, regardless of the fact that it (ideologically) represents and conceives of itself as a republic of all citizens without differences. It can do so insofar as, in its revolutionary declaration, it confuses freedom with the private autonomy of entrepreneurs and man with the bourgeois. Marx, however, sees through this "false consciousness," this illusion of the private owner about himself, his republic, and public opinion, and critically teaches that the very concept of the public means real accessibility of all public affairs to all citizens, without class discrimination. This basic idea is implied in political liberalism itself, but it is covered by an ideological veil which should be torn aside. Political liberalism obligates its government: (1) to seek truth through *discussion;* (2) to conduct this search *publicly,* before the eyes of its citizens; and (3) through *freedom of the press,* to induce the citizens themselves to seek this truth and tell it to the government.

If the ideological confusion of the public with the public of private owners is eliminated—i.e., if the identity of the bourgeois and man is replaced by the identity of man and the citizen in a republic of free citizens and producers, whose natural basis is not private property over the means of production, and in which public affairs are not the object of private oligarchic or bureaucratic usurpation—then what is the socialist public other than the mutual "seeking of truth" through public discussion, freedom of the press, and scholarship? It is in just such a *spiritual* atmosphere that "public authority loses its political character."

And indeed, Marx conceives the role of a democratic public precisely in this way, beginning with his earliest works when he was still engaged in journalism.

In the *Rheinische Zeitung,* No. 135, May 15, 1842, Marx wrote an ode to freedom of the press, sharply opposing himself to the then unscrupulous censorship of the German regime: "A free press is everywhere the open eye of the national spirit, the embodied confidence of the people in itself, the verbal bond that ties the individual to the state and the world, the incorporated culture which transforms material struggles into spiritual struggles and idealizes their crude materialized form. It is the heedless confession of a people before itself, and confession, as is known, has liberating power. It is the spiritual mirror in which the people observe themselves, and self-observation is the first condition of wisdom. It is the spirit of the state which can be carried into every hut, cheaper than material gas. It is versatile, the most modern and all-knowing. It is the ideal world which always originates in the real world and flows into it again, giving life, as an ever richer spirit."

Since lack of freedom is a "true deadly danger for man," Marx warns the censorial potentates of a simple truth that has been consciously repressed innumerable times: "Bear in mind that the advantages of freedom of the press cannot be enjoyed without toleration of its inconveniences. There are no roses without thorns!" A censured, unfree press is easily recognized by its attributes: hypocrisy, characterlessness, castrated language, and dog's tail wagging.

Is there anything more natural than that in a socialist society, more than in any other society, the press and other sources of information must become a free tribune in which progressive—and, in Marx's sense, unideologized—social consciousness comes to expression? And in order for them to become that, they must be neither the monopoly of anyone nor the expression of particular interests.

The same principles hold for all organizations in socialist society. In opposition to the bourgeois political parties and public opinion described earlier, a class workers' party of the Marxist type is conceived, and through it also socialist democracy.

This party cannot look upon the popular masses as an amorphous crowd that fatalistically submits itself to the active leaders. The primary task of socialism lies in the political activization of the people, of democratic public opinion. In this, the role of the proletarian party also essentially changes in contrast to that of all bourgeois political parties. Its goal is not to organize the masses to follow it blindly, but to be the concrete *intermediary between man and history*. The workers' party must decisively break with the traditional views according to which the proletariat represents spiritual poverty, a riffraff. It endeavors to draw the former observer of action, action which took place outside of and beyond him, into the historical process and make him the creative agent of social events. The Communist Party, in that sense, has no separate interests whatever from the people and class but is the *conscious mobilizer of the collective will*, by which are united consciousness and spontaneity, theory and practice.

An essential need of the workers' movement, therefore, is social criticism, which the proletariat rigorously applies to itself as well, in the form of self-criticism. In that sense, the role of the public, the widest political democracy, and freedom of initiative, assembly, and the press become second nature in a socialist society. The latter must continue where the revolutionary bourgeoisie stopped in the struggle with feudalism, decisively breaking with the usurpatory tradition which replaces the rule of the people with the authority of hierarchy and an "elite," and a democratic public with bureaucratic secretiveness. Socialist society may not permit its institutions to ossify things that escape human control. Marx's criticism of the bourgeois parliament as a "chatter house" does not constitute a demand that the national representatives cease to talk and discuss, so that the government's decisions will be accepted in advance by acclamation, but rather that *empty* verbal contention be replaced by *substantive* discussion and critical solution of social problems, before the eyes and under the control of the public. The right of recall of national representatives is an instrument of democratic activism and control by public opinion.

With the elimination of the confusion of freedom of criticism with freedom of enterprise, there must flow a parallel process of eliminating arbitrariness and subjectivism and their replacement by objectivity (not objectivism!), which is characteristic of dialectical science.

The crystallization of the progressive class consciousness of the proletariat and its transformation into the penetrating force of organized political will cannot be achieved by uniformity and dull simplification, according to which the only goal is *simple political effectiveness* of a blindly disciplined membership, but by the democratic enactment of political decisions from the bottom up, from the widest sources of the mass movement. In a word, the formulation of revolutionary political theory and the transition to political action are possible only through the close connection of the party organization with the popular mass, with its currents and interests, which can be attained only by the decisive elimination of all sectarianism and narrow party interests.

Accordingly, we can designate public opinion in a socialist society as the qualified, competent, and articulate judgment of the working people about the general affairs of the community, and in that sense it is the enduring, essential, ideational precondition of socialist democracy. The qualifiedness and competence of public opinion here arise from the role of its *subjects* in the production of material and spiritual *goods* (not commodities), i.e., from the unified position of the citizen as producer and manager, subject and object at the same time. In that way, public opinion becomes the *ideational basis of socialist self-government,* the consciousness of the working people *(the people without drones)* about itself.

11. Socialism and Self-management

MIHAILO MARKOVIĆ

Eight decades after the Paris Commune and Marx's analysis of its experiences, the socialist movement has revived the forgotten idea of self-management. It has thus retrieved its soul, its deeply human values, and its universal historical meaning just at the moment when it already seemed that in the West its time had run out and that all that was left to it was the practice and theory of a specific way of industrializing the underdeveloped countries. For, not only does *democratic* Socialism and a society based on self-management mean the radical negation and, in its most extreme fulfillment, the radical humanization of contemporary Capitalism, but furthermore it is a necessary means for the further development of existing embryonic forms of post-capitalistic society.

But the rediscovery and decisive affirmation of the principle of self-management have met bitter resistance from many who regard themselves as followers of Marx and builders of Socialism. Part of the explanation must be sought in the economic and social conditions of certain countries in which the socialist transformation of society has already begun. Real self-management presupposes the existence of a reasonable number of rational, socialized, and human persons who understand the major aim of the

Reprinted from *Praxis,* No. 2–3 (1964) , 178–95.

social process, persons who are themselves alive to the relative in-
terlinking of personal, group, and general interests and who base
their activities on ideals of general human significance. An undeveloped, predominantly rural society does not have enough of
such people, and moreover does not have all the preconditions for
producing them relatively rapidly. Thus it cannot avoid that
phase in its development in which an elite, at best a genuinely
revolutionary elite, through the maximum mobilization of the
masses—and using compulsion—creates all the necessary preconditions, i.e., industry, a working class, an intelligentsia, schooling,
mass culture. In the absence of these preconditions, self-management could come to mean only general disintegration. However,
the critical question is: will this elite, when these preconditions
are realized, find within itself the moral strength and consistency
to voluntarily pass to the basic element of the socialist revolution,
i.e., the realization of self-management, and consequently the
gradual setting aside of itself as a power elite (this does not mean
that it cannot permanently remain as an elite of the mind—if it
has a powerful mind)? Or will several decades of intense concentration of power in its hands so change its social nature that this
elite will identify itself with socialism and wish to cling permanently to its political and material privileges, and to remain
permanently not only the mind but the iron hand of the historic
process?

Thus a political factor of resistance to self-management joins
the economic and social ones. This factor is the existence of a political structure for which a greater or lesser degree of *bureaucratization and political alienation* is characteristic.

Different attitudes to self-management are directly conditioned
not only by the degree of economic and social development but
also by the degree of bureaucratization of the given social community. So, for example, China today could not in general have
self-management because of the immaturity of its social and economic conditions. The question does pose itself, however: Should
it not normally have self-management in its program, in its perspective, as an aim which, although belonging to the future, nevertheless also gives meaning to the movement at the present time?
In connection with this, then, the question also arises of taking
the first steps to begin even now the introduction of workers'
self-management, be it only in the very biggest and strongest economic units. The whole issue seems to be controversial. While
there are important elements of self-government and autonomous,

decentralized decision-making in communes and counties, the theory of the withering away of the state and the Party, and of self-government is now falling under suspicion as revisionist.

In the Soviet Union all the objective conditions necessary to begin the realization of self-management have already long existed. However, self-management in the Soviet Union is still regarded with characteristic caution and only in most recent times has it been possible to study it and experiment with it to a very limited extent.

Yugoslavia may claim the historic credit of having reintroduced the idea of self-management and begun its practical realization. Does it, however, follow from this fact that in Yugoslavia there is no bureaucracy or, if there is, that it is an insignificant social force? Unfortunately it does not follow. And despite the significance which is given to self-management in official theory and in public, it is not as well developed as it could be, it is constantly thwarted and checked by bureaucratic elements, its material basis is still conspicuously feeble, and, what is more significant, it is still always understood as an institution which exists in *addition* to the state: an institution which embraces only *local* organs of social power. This means that social self-management with us has not yet been fully realized and also that its full meaning is very often not properly understood. To explain this meaning is to explain the philosophical and political assumptions of social self-management and above all the concepts of political alienation and bureaucracy.

1. Political alienation under socialism

Under *politics* in the widest sense of the word I understand all those human activities of decision making and realization whereby important, public, social processes are regulated and directed. Marx was right in regarding politics in class society as a sphere of alienation. As a partial sphere of social activity and consciousness, isolated from morality, science, philosophy, very much conditioned by the particular position and interests of the class concerned, politics had become one of the forms of practice in which every individual person permanently missed the real possibilities of an authentic, rich human life.

But what of politics after the abolition of the ruling class of capitalist society? While the revolutionary process of abolishing the political and economic power of the bourgeoisie is going on, important changes are taking place. The state apparatus of the old society is being destroyed from its very foundation, civic parties disappear, politics gains great significance owing to the fact that economics and science, culture and art become the object of the revolutionary, centralized regulation and direction. In addition, what is particularly important, very considerable sections of the people become politically active, take part directly in the process of transformation of the old society, or at least there is a lively feeling that the course of events depends on their attitude.

But then, as time passes, following the successful revolutionary encounter with the one-time ruling class, an ever clearer tendency appears to concentrate the majority of decisions concerning all key social questions in the hands of a limited group of rulers. Indeed, they take decisions in the name of others, often with their consent and not infrequently with their real or potential support. But as soon as such a sharp division has been completed in a society into those who are permanently political *subjects* and who make decisions and implement them, and those who are political *objects* and who are called on only to agree with the decisions made and to behave in agreement with them, it is not difficult to discover all the essential forms of political alienation. They are:

1. Man loses control over political institutions: the state, the party, etc., institutions which he has created and which function in his name. Thence his feeling of power lessens: he is not part of the political process and has no influence on the course of events. Political occurrences, including those when his active participation is called for—as is the case with elections—lose their meaning, for there is no real choice and his vote has no real part to play. For this reason politics ceases to offer any really intellectual or emotional satisfaction—the point is reached where people begin to withdraw and become apathetic. In such a situation there is moral degradation and a lowering of the standard of political behavior of those who still find it useful for themselves to engage in politics. Now often fear, greed, craving for success become the primary motives of political activity.

2. Man alienates himself in a bureaucratic society from other people no matter whether he falls within the group of those who rule or of those who are ruled. In the first case, there develops within the man an explicitly inhuman feeling for hierarchy, for social status: in choosing those with whom he wishes to have

closer relationships he is guided primarily not by *what a man is* but by *what position he has.* In the second case the politically apathetic individual in a society in which all politics is decided by other people, and in which his own rise and fall to a very large extent depend on how he is thought of in powerful political institutions, will often be tempted to play various roles which do not suit him, suspecting that others do the same. In this atmosphere of mistrust, insincerity, artificiality, many potentially human and intimate relationships between people die before they really begin to develop. In the drastic circumstances of a bureaucratic society (in the time of Stalin) the individual had at times to hide his political opinions even from members of his own family.

3. In a bureaucratic society political activity ceases to be *creative* activity. Thus a man who involves himself in politics alienates himself from one of his essential needs and from one of the essential possibilities of a really human way of his existence. Discussion of things about which conclusions have been previously prepared, elections of candidates already decided on in advance, criticism which—most certainly—will not have the slightest effect and which is in fact only part of a clearly defined ritual—all this gives political activity a purely manifestational character, turns it into a routine and empty formalism. It is for this reason that nowhere are there so many cliches, so many stereotypes, nowhere so much spiritual emptiness and boredom as in the functioning of a bureaucratized political apparatus.

4. Finally, all these conditions often lead to a complete split between the way in which man politically exists and his authentic potential being. We find one form of this conflict in those who are aware of their degradation and who know that their opportunist or bureaucratic existence is far below the level of what they *can* be and of what they *should* be.

A second form of the loss of the true Self is to be found in Caesaristic political structures. The history of Socialism will record that such structures often appeared in the initial bureaucratic phases of Socialism. Social psychologists have explained the nature of the process which we are dealing with here. A feeling of insecurity—which can be objectively historically conditioned or can be created or supported by bolstering propaganda—leads to powerful affective identification of the mass with the leader and to their readiness to follow him blindly, fanatically. In this way, one arrives at the point of a clear-cut regression and depersonalization of the individual. Instead of growing progressively and becoming more individualized, the individual forgets himself, his needs and his potentialities, his living projects; he frees himself from personal responsibility and becomes an element of the mass which completely uncritically and irrationally adapts itself to the mood of the leader.

This analysis shows that in post-capitalist society which evolves towards Socialism powerful and drastic forms of political alienation are possible to the extent to which the revolutionary elite turns itself into a bureaucracy, and to the extent to which a division of people into political subjects and political objects occurs.

The time has now come to explain the concept of bureaucracy which has been assumed in the foregoing exposition.

2. The essence of bureaucracy

This is a notion which in its application to the society of a transition period has undoubtedly undergone a degree of generalization. In a capitalist society, bureaucracy is the apparatus of the expert, of the executor, and to a greater or lesser extent it can be identified with the social group which constitutes the state apparatus and wields executive power. Both Marx and Lenin—the former in his analysis of the civil war in France, the latter more particularly in his later writings—were very much aware of the danger that, following successful political revolutions, a new bureaucracy forms itself from the ranks of the leaders of the victorious working class. However, after the death of Lenin, Stalin very soon shifted the meaning of the term: from then on "bureaucratic" came to be used only for the definitely cold, superior, routine, formalistic relationship of some functionaries towards ordinary people and towards their problems.

Not until the criticism of Stalinism was the problem of bureaucracy as the problem of a social group that has taken all political power as a monopoly into its own hands again put on the agenda. But all the maze of different, more or less revolutionary opinions which we call criticism of Stalinism had weaknesses of their own. First of all, the very concept of bureaucracy was never really explained in a satisfactory way—very often there appears to have been no attempt at all to analyze it. In addition, bureaucracy and bureaucratic tendencies are often discussed with much heat by those who are themselves, to a marked degree, bureaucrats: so that one not infrequently gains the impression that bureaucracy has become a phantom force against which everybody is striving but which it is quite impossible to locate.

On the other hand, in widening the concept of bureaucracy it is possible to go so far in the other direction that it sometimes becomes identified with any social group which guides and regulates the social processes. In this sense, it has been stated that politics itself gives birth to bureaucracy and that bureaucracy is necessarily connected with the existence of the function of centralized planning in society. Here the ideas of *politics, centralization,* and *planning* are treated in a very non-dialectical way. In a developed socialist society, governing and directing functions will have to exist, and this exactly from the viewpoint of the whole, at the level of the central social organs. Without this it would be impossible to grasp the idea of that rational control which Marx speaks of as a vital characteristic of the transition period.

People who perform these governing functions do not fall by virtue *of this itself* into bureaucracy—in this sense we can distinguish the politics of self-management and bureaucratic politics. In reality, *political bureaucracy is a permanent and coherent social group which occupies itself professionally with politics, which has escaped the control of the masses, and which, thanks to unlimited power in the distribution of the past, embodied labor, secures lesser or greater material privileges to itself.* Each of these three conditions is *necessary* but all taken together constitute a *sufficient* condition for the existence of bureaucracy.

1. The professionalization of politics is the first step towards the creation of an isolated, closed, and, in relation to the rest of society, a very coherent social stratum. In this sense bureaucracy is that social stratum which longs to hold permanently to the principle of *partiality* which in the process of revolution had already begun to be surpassed. After the destruction of the bourgeoisie as a class, all the social strata except the bureaucracy are interested in making sure that political activity is general public life open to all, and that it should be moral, just, philosophically thought out, scientifically based, in other words, that instead of being a particular, partial sphere of social consciousness and activity it becomes a *moment* of integral rational and human practice. Bureaucracy is the material bearer of the isolation and partiality of politics, and this is why it resists so bitterly all tendencies to supersede traditional professional politics as a sphere of alienation.

2. The process of withdrawal and isolation of the bureaucracy from the masses in whose name it rules lies in the fact that elections become a pure form, that the bureaucracy transforms responsibility to the electors into responsibility to party forums and that the electors lose power to replace their representatives for the simple reason that they are atomized, isolated one from another, and, as individual units, quite powerless. In all the key economic and political processes in such a society, the greatest number of people find themselves permanently in the position of the *objects* of history. They are the mass which gives necessary, material energy to the realization of the apparently collective will mediated by the bureaucracy. Indeed under such circumstances the bureaucracy is the sole historic subject. Far from being that part of the proletariat in which the collective will of the proletariat arrives at a self-conscious and practical fulfillment, the bureaucracy ensures that the proletariat and the mass of society accept its personal will as its own and thus become instruments of its practical realization. This is the highest form of "cunning subtlety of mind": people, who normally have their own purpose, act towards things as if they were things themselves, in order to fulfill an exterior bureaucratic purpose. This is the highest and most subtle form of reification: never have people been so successfully manipulated—thanks, among other things, to the extraordinary technical perfection of the mass media of communication and the intensification of all forms and methods of propaganda—and never have so few people been aware that they are being treated as things. Because of this bureaucracy is the bearer of the principle of *reification* in a society which has already begun to create essential preconditions for its surpassing in the sphere of politics.

3. Bureaucracy has full monopoly in deciding on the distribution and use of the past embodied labor. It usually uses this monopoly in order to secure for itself various material privileges. And this does not happen by chance, although history has shown us individual cases of utter modesty and ascetism. As a social stratum the bureaucracy recruits its members from the ranks of people who no longer have any humanistic ideals and whose human needs have remained very undeveloped. The need to possess social power is the fundamental life need of the bureaucrat. But power demands, among other things, an unlimited disposal of things. The most expensive car, the most stylish furniture, etc., all these things are to the bureaucrat, above all, symbols of his social

status, of the degree of his power. Having originally developed very indirectly, the impulse to private disposal and even ownership can become the dominant motive in the second generation of bureaucrats. What was at the beginning a typically ideological attitude—an attempt to rationalize and justify the relationship of exploitation which at first was not yet clear even to the bureaucrat himself—later became a clearly cynical and hypocritical attitude: one no longer believes one's own words but uses them for pragmatic reasons—in order deliberately to conceal truth. So it becomes evident that in order to supersede exploitation it is not sufficient merely to destroy the private ownership of the means of production. As long as relatively undeveloped productive powers and relative material shortages produce the impulse for the possession of ever better material goods, and as long as a particular social group has a monopoly of decision making on embodied labor, it is possible for that group to use a considerable part of the surplus value for its own personal appetites and not for the general social needs. So bureaucracy is the bearer of the principle of *exploitation* in a society in which all other exploitatory social groups have been abolished.

The concept of bureaucracy which has been given here is a theoretical one. In a simplified way it designates a developed, full, final form of something which in reality is found in varying degrees of growth or which possesses only some of the above-mentioned characteristics. Therefore, when we are concerned with the concrete empirical reality of a given country, we shall need to speak sometimes of the *tendency* towards bureaucratization and of the fact that certain individuals are bureaucrats to the degree to which their behavior corresponds to the above-mentioned patterns.

It would be wrong to *identify* bureaucracy with a stratum of professional politicians in a socialist society. There are also bureaucrats among the leaders and organizers in the fields of economics, science, and art. In addition, there are politicians who contribute to surpassing bureaucracy by the progressive realization of a system of self-management, just as there are some political leaders in whom the revolutionary and the bureaucrat are locked in combat.

On the other hand, there is no reason to differentiate strictly between political leadership and bureaucracy as only the executive apparatus of government. Under certain social conditions, which have been specified in the foregoing exposition, the notion of bureaucracy must be applied in such a way as to embrace both.

3. The meaning of self-management

Self-management is the dialectical negation of so-called state socialism with its inherent tendencies towards bureaucratization.

However, self-management cannot be reduced to its initial historical forms which at present exist in Yugoslavia. This means, first of all, that it cannot be limited only to production relations at the level of the enterprise and to the local organs of social power. The complete and definite surpassing of bureaucracy is possible only when self-management reaches the top: when the central organs of the state are converted into organs of self-management. Secondly, even if self-management is primarily an economic and political phenomenon, it is not only that. This is a concept which embraces the whole social life, which has a range of technical, social, psychological, and cultural presuppositions and consequences. Behind it stands a radically different, new concept of society and of man, a whole new structure of philosophical assumptions, radically opposed to that by which bureaucracy tries to rationalize its existence.

We can begin an explicit formulation of this philosophical structure with an analysis of the concept of self-management itself.

Self-management means that the functions of directing social processes are no longer performed by forces outside the mass of society, opposed to it, but are in the hands of the very same people who produce, who create social life in all its forms. Self-management means the supersession of the *permanent* and fixed division of society into the subjects and the objects of history, into rulers and executors, into the cunning social mind and its physical instruments in human form.

The idea of management which has been used here means, in the context of Marx's humanistic thought, *rational* and *revolutionary* management. It is *rational* in the sense that it is based on an objective critical analysis of existing reality, on a knowledge of the real possibilities of its change, on a choice of those real possibilities which are optimal in relation to the given end.

The fundamental end which serves as the main criterion of rational decision making in the process of management is the *aboli-*

tion of all forms of human oppression and poverty and the freeing of every individual for a full, rich life in a really human community. This aim is *revolutionary,* and so is the whole of management, which takes on its meaning in relation to this aim. The concern is not, however, with any "total revolution" in an absolute historical meaning of the word. The aim is fully determined historically by the given forms of human needs and human wants. It is "fundamental" or "ultimate" only in relation to the given historical epoch. However, being aware of this and knowing the real situation in society at a given historical moment are sufficient to allow us to determine the next practical steps and to give a revolutionary impetus to our practice.

Of course self-management does not mean that every individual takes part *directly* in management at all levels. Such direct self-management is possible only in the basic social organizations —enterprises, communes, cultural institutions, etc. Self-management means that the functions of management in the broader social organizations are performed in turn by competent, freely elected individuals who factually express the interests of the people and whose functions cannot bring them, even temporarily, any material privileges, any superior status in society—nothing but confidence, respect, and love. In a society in which self-management is growing, the criterion of the *personal abilities* of the candidate—his mind, his knowledge, his moral integrity, his skill— is increasingly expressed. In bureaucratic society the function of ruling has endowed definite authority. Here people must first win authority in order to get the honor of performing a political function.

Such a view of rational and revolutionary self-management implies a radical reappraisal of the concept of politics. Not only is politics no longer the concern of a single personal profession— it is no longer an isolated, partial, social activity. The gradual abolition of practicism, of frequent amorality, of the improvisatory character of politics now begins to take place. Politics is being given an awareness of the basic revolutionary aims by humanistic philosophy—politics is now becoming *philosophical.* Knowledge of the real situation and tendencies of change is provided by science—politics is becoming *scientific.* In order to apply means which are adequate to ends, political behavior must conform to defined moral norms, which for their part, correspond to basic accepted human values—politics is now becoming *moral.* It is also beginning to become an *art—sui generis—*for there is no reason why in this field, beauty, nobility, and a feeling of dignity should not be preferred to greyness of thought and rawness of behavior.

Such a process of the totalization of social consciousness is parallel with the process of the simultaneous individualization and socialization of man. Both of them presuppose a technically highly developed and rich society in which the elementary material needs of people are satisfied, in which genuine culture has come within the reach of all, and in which there exist sufficiently strong forces which, in the name of a critical and humanistic self-consciousness, unceasingly lay down the demand for the dialectical supersession of every existing historical form.

It is an irony of history that self-management first began to be realized in a relatively backward semi-rural country and not in the highly developed and relatively rich social communities of the West. From this it follows that, on the one hand, self-management in Yugoslavia will not be fully realized and its forms be fulfilled by the corresponding content for a long time. On the other hand, this paradox may be explained by the absence of a powerful critical humanistic conscious force in the West, such as would be able to lead the whole of society to the realization of its optimal historical possibilities.

What is essential for Marxist theory is the thesis of the *objective possibility of self-management* and not of its necessary realization. The very idea of self-management presupposes that people themselves are the creators of history in given conditions, i.e., in the objectively determined framework of possibilities. In this way, the idea of self-management presupposes an open, activist interpretation of history in which the artificial gap between law and contingency, necessity and freedom has been overcome. The philosophy of bureaucracy is essentially different in this respect. Bureaucracy advocates voluntarism when the question is of the future and absolute determinism when the question is of the past. As it itself does not have scientific knowledge, as it does not even have sufficient confidence in the scientist, and finally as the most rational decisions, most adequate to the expected course of things, would often be against its own interests, the bureaucracy does not even try to justify rationally its projects for the future, but at best, gives them the necessary authority by quoting the texts of the classics. But this is why it gives an aura of necessity to everything that happened in the past. In both cases the key concept of *real possibility* has no meaning. History is being taken as a linear process in which bureaucracy never has any chance of going wrong.

But if history is an open and multilinear process in which nothing is completely provided for in advance, we are faced with the question: cannot perhaps self-management lead to chaos and disintegration, to a predominance of change, to a bad and irrational solution of the key questions of society? Such a course is not only a possibility but a necessity—in the opinion of a bureaucrat. From this comes his historical responsibility for the further course of building Socialism. From this there follows not only a lack of confidence in the intelligentsia but also an aristocratic attitude towards the working class and towards people in general. Whenever it speaks of the people, bureaucracy regards them basically as a primitive, backward mass, which without its rule would become quite savage and destroy all that has been gained by revolution. In the last analysis it would seem to follow from this that the building of Socialism is a type of enforced happiness, in which the man who is making someone happy never stops speaking in the name of the man who is made happy.

The notion of social self-management presupposes a fundamentally different conception of man. In the framework of a philosophy whose method is dialectic, this conception can hardly have anything in common with empty rhetorical romantic idealizations of man. Man is a contradictory creature and in his present-day behavior opposing tendencies appear: of creativeness and destructiveness, of sociability and non-sociability, of rationality and of irrationality, etc. However, in certain historical conditions, for which a high degree of material and spiritual culture of the mass is characteristic, sociability, rationality, and creativeness predominate in man. Hence the conviction that in a society of self-management, development, in spite of all particular and temporary irrationalities and possible individual eruptions of bestiality, will as a whole tend to bring to life the optimal human possibilities of the epoch. In any case there is no reason to think that some self-appointed guardian of the general interest can be superior in relation to the total mental power of the society whose interests these are.

Finally, one of the most essential differences in the philosophical assumptions of bureaucracy and self-management is their respective attitudes toward dialectics. Bureaucracy often makes use of the formulae of dialectics. Apart from this it makes considerable efforts to give an appearance of permanent dialectical movement and perfection to the society which it controls. It makes use of a vast amount of activity in thinking out new social forms, new institutional frameworks, new programs. These forms and institutions are changed even before they have been properly tried; programs are "surpassed" even before they can be realized in practice. This pseudo-dialectics goes together with a very decisive denial of dialectics in all essential things. Dialectic unity of the different is made into "monopolithic unity." Contradictions are denied and concealed. Philosophers, scientists, and artists are expected, above all, to confirm the present state, to look for the positive in it. Public criticism is usually treated as a kind of petty bourgeois confusion, and is often frustrated in the most brutal way.

In complete contrast to this situation, self-management presupposes dialectics to such an extent that it could be regarded as political dialectics in practice. Self-management is only a special form of self-movement; thus the struggle of different tendencies, opinions, and projects is presupposed, although in a highly developed society all these tensions and conflicts gain a more humane form and resolve themselves in a more humane way. So we are concerned with a society which is pluralistic, in which there are many different groups and communities but in which the degree of socialization has advanced so far, in which certain values are already so widely accepted, that there is no longer any need for any force to be used in preserving its integrity. Public social criticism is now the most efficient means of surpassing the limitations of every existing social form.

Bureaucracy has so far been rather successful in the struggle against the dialectical method of explaining the contemporary historical process. It has achieved this by the formalization and dehumanization of dialectics, by linking it primarily with the natural sciences.

However, bureaucracy is powerless against dialectics as an objective structure of the historical process itself. The struggle of bureaucracy to maintain its privileged status in post-capitalist society is at the same time a preparation of the conditions for its disappearance. In order to hold on to the illusion that it speaks in the name of the progressive forces of society it transforms into the most important *aim* of the revolutionary movement what should be the *means* of its realization—industrialization, an increase of production, material prosperity. While leading to various deformations, this process step by step will inevitably be creating a state of society in which bureaucracy will lose even its last *raison d'être*.

With the definitive abolition of bureaucracy and the relationships of class society of which it is the bearer (political partialization, reification, and exploitation) the first great phase of the transition period is becoming completed. The historical form of society which follows is the system of self-management.

4. Self-management as a historical process

When we understand social self-management in the totality of its moments it becomes clear that its introduction really is a fundamental social revolution and also that it must be construed as a long-lasting historical process and not just as the act of a minute.

In Yugoslavia it was first introduced at the level of the enterprise, then it was gradually widened to include all working organizations and social institutions. However, at the level of the central organs we have just begun to take important transitional measures which will open the way to self-management. . . .

In this way it is characteristic of our self-management that, first, it is still rather incomplete, not yet built to the top and, secondly, that in Yugoslavia, because of relative backwardness in the technical, economic, political, and cultural fields, the forms of self-management so far introduced have not yet gained their full content. A strong insistence on institutional frameworks, statutes, and regulations carries the threat of laying too much emphasis on the formalistic element.

However, be this as it may, with all its imperfections self-management in Yugoslavia has an enormous historical significance not only for that country and not only for the socialist world, but for mankind in general. It is the beginning of the establishment of totally new human relationships, the beginning of a radical change in the status of the worker, the beginning of the fundamental liberation of the individual in general. (In connection with this: Marxist criticism of contemporary forms of Socialism is not simply negation, is not exclusively an expression of dissatisfaction with the present in the name of "chimerical ideals of the distant future." It is, *inter alia* and above all, criticism in the name of the origin of the human future in the present. It is criticism from the point of view of a consistently developed social self-management.)

In order to assess in a more concrete way the present position and future prospects of social self-management, it is necessary to take into account its essential objective preconditions. The gradual realization of these preconditions creates the possibility for a fuller development of self-management.

The first group of preconditions is of a *technical* character. Contemporary machine technology is to an increasing extent changing the condition of the worker in production. He is slowly ceasing to be a mere fragment of the machine and to an ever greater extent is becoming an active element in a very complicated system. The effect of automation is particularly revolutionary: in addition to the fact that automation is freeing vast amounts of time for non-productive activity, it is leading to the abolition of the differences between the physical worker and the "white-collar worker"; it is integrating the producer into a whole united production process and awakening in him an interest in the efficient functioning of the enterprise as a whole. This increase of interest in a more efficient operation of the production process as a whole is conditioned, among other things, by the fact that the idea of the individual effect of work and the idea of the productivity of an isolated individual lose all meaning. The work of an individual can no longer be measured—he is only a moment in the effect of the work of the whole collective. So, the fact that the technological process has been revolutionized, on the one hand, compels the individual producer to take an increasing interest in the effect of the work of the whole collective and, on the other hand, equips him with increasing competence to assess the work of the enterprise and to take a more active part in all decision making about it. In this way the worker is becoming a natural ally of the technical intelligentsia: in capitalism—in the struggle against the bourgeoisie, which completely loses its reason for existence; and in the transition period—against the political bureaucracy which in the new conditions becomes increasingly incompetent and wasteful.

The second group of conditions is of an *economic* character and is concerned, above all, with the level of economic development. Self-management can grow successfully only in a relatively rich society and one in which the elementary needs of the people have already been satisfied, and in which each individual has reached such a degree of economic security that he does not have to worry about possible economic repercussion in the event of his social involvement. In a poor and backward society there is not much to decide freely about. If "the national cake" is too small and the pressure on it too large, strict centralization and firm planning, which of course leaves very little room for the initiative of the mass, will be needed.

The third group of conditions is of a *political* character. When the state and party apparatus take decisive economic, cadre, and other decisions and fix the details of the framework within which the decision taking of the organs of self-management should occur, self-management is but an ideological fiction with hardly any connection with real social relationships. The development of self-management is nothing but another name for the withering away of the state. In addition, it presupposes a transformation of the revolutionary party of the classical type into an organization whose fundamental aim is: the growth of socialist consciousness, the activization of the masses to realize the optimal objectively given historical possibilities of the country at a given period of time. A party whose leading bodies concern themselves first and foremost with ruling as such will inevitably become bureaucratized and fail in its most fundamental tasks. The withering away of the state and the change in the character of the party means a simultaneous wide democratization of all forms of social life, the growth of political freedoms, the destruction of any monopoly in using mass means of communication, the creation of all the conditions necessary for public social criticism.

Finally, the fourth group of conditions is of a *cultural* character. Only educated, cultivated workers, conscious of their historical role, can successfully take part in the management of social processes. It is therefore necessary to develop a genuine culture of the masses (as distinct from the so-called "mass culture," which in reality is a substitute for culture). Therefore it is necessary that the social community be sufficiently developed economically in order to be able to put aside significant resources for the development of culture. In addition, it is essential that within society and acting as a significant and active force there should be a humanistic, revolutionary intelligentsia which elaborates revolutionary theory and to an increasing extent makes the working class aware of its historical position and its historical possibilities.

5. Contradictions in the present system of self-management in Yugoslavia

Many of the conditions mentioned above have not yet reached a great measure of realization in Yugoslavia. For this reason, in discussing the Yugoslav experience one can speak only of the initial steps in fulfilling the system of social self-management.

In spite of this it is sometimes possible to hear it said that self-management is being forced along too much, and that it ought to be limited to some extent. The problem here, at best, is of misunderstanding or incomplete understanding of the nature of self-management. There is indeed a tendency to excessive forcing of the institutional forms of self-management, but that should not be confused with the real growth of self-management. On the other hand, there are many who confuse self-management with decentralization. Tendencies of excessive decentralization really lead to the disintegration of the global society. However, the further development of self-management means the dialectical surpassing of the centralism-decentralization opposition by forming central (federal and republican) organs of self-management. Consequently, the difficulties which occur as a result of decentralization can be correctly explained as the lack of development of self-management.

A more careful analysis of this lack of development reveals the following contradictions:

1. The contradiction of self-management and the state. Our present social system is characterized by efforts to find a temporary equilibrium between two disparate elements: the state, the political form which as a form has been inherited from class society, and self-management, the political form of the new socialist society. . . . The existence of the state in general, especially so strong a state, automatically generates bureaucratic tendencies, which are by their nature tendencies to resist the further development of self-management, tendencies to preserve it in its present embryonic and limited forms. Bureaucracy sees a possibility for its own survival in finding a kind of balance between the state and local self-management: the state to continue to hold the power of decision on basic instruments and proportions of global society, while within the framework the state itself defines, to leave a certain amount of scope for the initiative of workers' collectives. In addition, the compromise which bureaucracy is prepared to offer includes purely material concessions: somewhat greater financial means to dispose of. This is of course very significant but much more important things are at stake: that the state organs should continue to transform themselves into the organs of self-management. And this means: the further deprofessionalization of political functions, real election, and rotation of the office of representative of the working people—and in connection with this, a progressive lessening of the power of the executive ap-

paratus of the government, the abolition of all material privileges, and a system of rewarding the discharge of political functions as for every other type of highly qualified and creative work.

In this way, the contradiction of state and self-management will be resolved in Yugoslavia by a gradual surpassing of the state and its replacement by the organs of self-management.

2. Self-management and rational direction. When self-management is adopted only at the level of the local organs, and direction is understood as strictly bureaucratic planning from the center, these two essential principles of socialist society interpreted in such a way will give rise to an unsolvable contradiction. The authority and discipline which the plan forces seem to exclude initiative and the freedom of the individual and the collective. The independent decision making of the local organs of self-management seems to bring a certain amount of disorder which is incompatible with planning.

However, this contradiction will be gradually eliminated to the extent that self-management extends itself to the central organs of society and to the extent that centralized planning is debureaucratized and brought into harmony with decentralized planning. The possible objective foundation of this harmonizing is twofold. It is possible to arrive at optimal decisions which would satisfy both the interests of particular collectives and the interest of society as a whole, first, on the basis of generally accepted scientific knowledge about the real situation in society and about objective tendencies of further changes, and secondly, on the basis of generally accepted aims and values, which the society as a whole and every single collective are trying to realize. This harmony obviously presupposes, on the one hand, a high degree of development of the social sciences and their application to the process of planning, and, on the other hand, a high degree of education, culture, and socialist consciousness in the collective and in the individual producer.

3. In a relatively backward milieu, in conditions of economic shortages and in collectives which are insufficiently developed politically and culturally, one arrives at a contradiction of self-management and local bureaucratic tendencies. Bureaucratic cliques are formed, which are composed of technical leaders and the functionaries of political institutions and organizations (the League of Communists, the trade union, the state organs) and sometimes include leading activists of the workers' councils and which usurp all power in the enterprise or in the local govern-

ment [opština]. The members of these cliques misuse their functions and their influence to gain full control of decision making and, not infrequently, to gain definite material privileges for themselves and their friends. This leads to a further process of passivization and demobilization of the masses—and sometimes to a deep demoralization of the collective. Of course, in such a situation one must take sharp measures against such petty bureaucrats of unlimited power-lust, who tend to brutally suppress all resistance and criticism within the framework of the collective. In such cases a stronger control and a more decisive element of intervention by higher-level organs of self-management is necessary. However, this is very far from an ideal solution. No measures from outside can have decisive effects merely on their own. What is needed is growth of internal progressive forces. This means in the first place that the working class should raise itself professionally, politically, and culturally, that within itself it should develop an awareness of its social role and of the necessity of its struggle against all forms of bureaucracy. This implies that it is essential to make maximum efforts, far greater than hitherto, to have the working class schooled and thoroughly educated, to have its initiative in the organs of social self-management stimulated in every possible way. This presupposes, in addition to other things, the growth of an atmosphere of free public criticism and a greater insistence on the moral and legal responsibility of each individual and especially the ruler.

4. Finally, in Yugoslav society the beginnings of the introduction of self-management coincide with a strong insistence on material stimuli, on the role of the market as a regulator of production, on free functioning of economic laws. In connection with this we come to the following question: how to reconcile self-management with market relations, which have been taken over, with considerable modifications, from class society. This really is an objective contradiction. At the basis of self-management is the principle of the freedom of man, the principle of the initiative of the subject which, in the last analysis, leads to the creation of important human values. At the basis of a market economy is the principle of economic necessity, the principle of activity to obtain an ever greater income.

It is true that the initial forms of workers' self-management with a substantial increase of the initiative of the worker cannot be realized without developing and satisfying his material interests, and this condition cannot be fulfilled if there is no competition between the enterprises on the market and a greater role for the market in the regulation of production. But, on the other hand, were market relations to remain *permanently,* without significant corrections, a gradual degeneration of self-management into a certain type of capitalist system of cooperatives would be possible. If the value of an enterprise is *permanently* assessed *only* on the basis of success in realizing income, and if the whole system came for a long time to rest on the idea that the fundamental interest of the worker is the acquisition of ever greater wages and personal incomes, then this would have deep and lasting consequences on the prevailing morality in such a society. The type of people who would be created by a society under such conditions would not essentially differ from the type of people created by capitalism. Society would be made up of people whose entire motivation to action is directed by the single desire to acquire and possess material goods. These are the majority of people who strive to *have,* and not to *be* as much as possible. In this way the same spiritual pauperism would in fact be maintained which is characteristic of capitalist society and the destruction of which is, according to Marx, one of the aims of communism.

The attitude taken here does not imply a rather naive belief that the laws of commodity production and distribution can be eliminated or superseded at will. In our present historical conditions it is really possible only to control them to a certain extent, and to correct them by preventing growth of concealed forms of exploitation, of serious inequalities, of any other kind of inhuman relationship among various social groups.

The contradiction of self-management and market economic relations will be gradually solved in the future by surpassing the motive of earnings and possessions as the universal motive of human activity. But this is possible only to the extent that the society frees itself from material wants and shortages, that there grows within all its members needs of a higher order, such as: the need for creative activity, for political involvement, for culture and art, for knowledge, for sincere, human relationships with other people. In such conditions material stimuli lose their primary importance. Apart from this, socialist society is confronted with the problem of finding effective methods for measuring the value of work other than the price of products on the market. The price certainly is, or could be, an indicator of the quantity of the live work of the producer, but it is also conditioned by a series of other factors which it is quite impossible to isolate. The socialist society will also have to arrive at better methods of assessing social needs than deductions on the basis of demand on the market.

From the foregoing analysis of certain key contradictions in Yugoslav society the conclusion follows that the further development of social self-management is the necessary way of creating a really socialist society, and that for this development the essential preconditions are: the withering away of the state, the gradual transformation of the central state organs into organs of self-management, the raising of the cultural and political level of the working class and the elimination of local bureaucratic cliques, and finally the gradual supersession of market relations and unilaterally material motivation in the process of productive activity.

12. Critique of the Gotha Program

KARL MARX

What we have to deal with here is a communist society, not as it has *developed* on its own foundations, but, on the contrary, just as it *emerges* from capitalist society; which is thus in every respect, economically, morally and intellectually, still stamped with the birth marks of the old society from whose womb it emerges. Accordingly, the individual producer receives back from society—after the deductions have been made—exactly what he gives to it. What he has given to it is his individual quantum of labor. For example, the social working day consists of the sum of the individual hours of work; the individual labor time of the individual producer is the part of the social working day contributed by him, his share in it. He receives a certificate from society that he has furnished such and such an amount of labor (after deducting his labor for the common funds), and with this certificate he draws from the social stock of means of consumption as much as costs the same amount of labor. The same amount of labor which he has given to society in one form he receives back in another.

Here obviously the same principle prevails as that which regulates the exchange of commodities, as far as this is exchange of

Reprinted from Karl Marx and Friedrich Engels, *Selected Works* (New York: International Publishers, 1968), pp. 323–25, 330–31, by permission of the publisher.

equal values. Content and form are changed, because under the altered circumstances no one can give anything except his labor, and because, on the other hand, nothing can pass to the ownership of individuals except individual means of consumption. But, as far as the distribution of the latter among the individual producers is concerned, the same principle prevails as in the exchange of commodity-equivalents: a given amount of labor in one form is exchanged for an equal amount of labor in another form.

Hence, *equal right* here is still in principle—*bourgeois right*, although principle and practice are no longer at loggerheads, while the exchange of equivalents in commodity exchange only exists on *the average* and not in the individual case.

In spite of this advance, this *equal right* is still constantly stigmatized by a bourgeois limitation. The right of the producers is *proportional* to the labor they supply; the equality consists in the fact that measurement is made with an *equal standard,* labor.

But one man is superior to another physically or mentally and so supplies more labor in the same time, or can labor for a longer time; and labor, to serve as a measure, must be defined by its duration or intensity, otherwise it ceases to be a standard of measurement. This *equal* right is an unequal right for unequal labor. It recognizes no class differences, because everyone is only a worker like everyone else; but it tacitly recognizes unequal individual endowment and thus productive capacity as natural privileges. *It is, therefore, a right of inequality, in its content, like every right.* Right by its very nature can consist only in the application of an equal standard; but unequal individuals (and they would not be different individuals if they were not unequal) are measurable only by an equal standard insofar as they are brought under an equal point of view, are taken from one *definite* side only, for instance, in the present case, are regarded *only as workers* and nothing more is seen in them, everything else being ignored. Further, one worker is married, another not; one has more children than another, and so on and so forth. Thus, with an equal performance of labor, and hence an equal share in the social consumption fund, one will in fact receive more than another, one will be richer than another, and so on. To avoid all these defects, right instead of being equal would have to be unequal.

But these defects are inevitable in the first phase of communist society as it is when it has just emerged after prolonged birth pangs from capitalist society. Right can never be higher than the

economic structure of society and its cultural development conditioned thereby.

In a higher phase of communist society, after the enslaving
subordination of the individual to the division of labor, and
therewith also the antithesis between mental and physical labor,
has vanished; after labor has become not only a means of life but
life's prime want; after the productive forces have also increased
with the all-round development of the individual, and all the
springs of co-operative wealth flow more abundantly—only then
can the narrow horizon of bourgeois right be crossed in its entirety and society inscribe on its banners: From each according to
his ability, to each according to his needs! . . .

Free state—what is this?

It is by no means the aim of the workers, who have got rid of
the narrow mentality of humble subjects, to set the state free. In
the German Empire the "state" is almost as "free" as in Russia.
Freedom consists in converting the state from an organ superimposed upon society into one completely subordinate to it, and
today, too, the forms of state are more free or less free to the extent that they restrict the "freedom of the state."

The German workers' party—at least if it adopts the program
—shows that its socialist ideas are not even skin-deep; in that, instead of treating existing society (and this holds good for any future one) as the *basis* of the existing state (or of the future state
in the case of future society), it treats the state rather as an independent entity that possesses its own *intellectual, ethical and libertarian bases.*

And what of the riotous misuse which the program makes of
the words *present-day state, present-day society,* and of the still
more riotous misconception it creates in regard to the state to
which it addresses its demands?

"Present-day society" is capitalist society, which exists in all civilized countries, more or less free from medieval admixture, more
or less modified by the particular historical development of each
country, more or less developed. On the other hand, the "present-day state" changes with a country's frontier. It is different in
the Prusso-German Empire from what it is in Switzerland, and
different in England from what it is in the United States. The
"present-day state" is, therefore, a fiction.

Nevertheless, the different states of the different civilized countries, in spite of their motley diversity of form, all have this in
common, that they are based on modern bourgeois society, only

one more or less capitalistically developed. They have, therefore, also certain essential characteristics in common. In this sense it is possible to speak of the "present-day states," in contrast with the future, in which its present root, bourgeois society, will have died off.

The question then arises: what transformation will the state undergo in communist society? In other words, what social functions will remain in existence there that are analogous to present state functions? This question can only be answered scientifically, and one does not get a flea-hop nearer to the problem by a thousandfold combination of the word *people* with the word *state*.

Between capitalist and communist society lies the period of the revolutionary transformation of the one into the other. Corresponding to this is also a political transition period in which the state can be nothing but the *revolutionary dictatorship of the proletariat*.

13. New Humanism: A Manifesto

M. N. ROY

No political philosophy nor a scheme of social reconstruction can have more than a very limited revolutionary significance if it dismisses the concept of individual freedom as an empty abstraction. A political system and an economic experiment, which subordinate the man of flesh and blood to an abstract collective ego, cannot possibly be the suitable means for the attainment of the goal of freedom. It is absurd to argue that negation of freedom is the road to freedom. The purpose of all rational human endeavor, collective as well as individual, should be the attainment of freedom in ever larger measure, and freedom is real only as individual freedom.

A new world of freedom will not result automatically from an economic reorganization of society. Nor does freedom necessarily follow from the capture of political power by a party claiming to represent the oppressed and exploited classes. The abolition of private property, State ownership of the means of production, and planned economy do not by themselves end exploitation of labor, nor lead to an equal distribution of wealth. By disregarding individual freedom on the pleas of taking the fullest advantage of technology, of efficiency and collective effort, planned economy defeats its own purpose. Instead of ushering in a higher

Reprinted from *New Humanism: A Manifesto* (Radical Democratic Party, 1947), pp. 53–56, 59–61.

form of democracy on the basis of economic equality and social justice, it may establish a political dictatorship. Economic democracy is no more possible in the absence of political democracy than the latter is in the absence of the former. That consideration should be borne in mind by those who make a fetish of economic planning.

The crucial question is: planning for what? It is assumed that planned economy will guarantee the greatest good to the greatest number; in other words, it will mean equal distribution of wealth—establish social justice. In that case, it should be possible to reconcile planning with freedom. If modern technological trends preclude such reconciliation, then they should be curbed so as to be more amenable to human welfare. Machine should not be the Frankenstein of modern civilization. Created by man, it must subserve man's purpose—contribute to his freedom.

Dictatorship of any form, however plausible may be the pretext for it, is excluded by the Radical-Humanist perspective of social evolution. Politics cannot be divorced from ethics without jeopardizing the cherished ideal of freedom. It is an empirical truth that immoral means necessarily corrupt the end. In the Soviet Union, proletarian dictatorship promises to be a permanent institution. It has become identical with Communism. The means have become the end. The State does not hold out any hope of withering away. If a socialist society has been established in the Soviet Union, then, the period of transition has passed, and dictatorship must disappear. But so long as no other party is allowed to exist, or the party of the proletariat does not disappear with dictatorship, it is idle to say that a higher form of democracy has been established.

The practice of Western Democracy is equally disappointing. Traditional democratic Socialism, therefore, also does not inspire any confidence of success. Democracy must reorientate itself. It must revert to the humanist tradition. It must not be limited by the counting of heads, particularly when the heads have not the opportunity to raise themselves with sovereign dignity. Formal parliamentarism must be replaced by actual democratic practice. . . .

The people can have a hand in the government only when a pyramidal structure of the State will be raised on a foundation of organized local democracies. The primary function of these latter will be to make individual citizens fully conscious of their sovereign right and enable them to exercise the right intelligently and conscientiously. The broad basis of the democratic State, coinciding with the entire society, will be composed of a network of political schools, so to say. The right of recall and referendum will enable organized local democracies to wield a direct and effective control of the entire State machinery. They alone will have the right to nominate candidates for election. Democracy will be placed above parties. Individual men will have the chance of being recognized, on their merit. Party loyalty and party patronage or other forms of nepotism will no longer eclipse intellectual independence, moral integrity and detached wisdom.

In other words, what is suggested is creation of conditions under which democracy can be possible. In the first place, there must be a conscious and integrated effort to stimulate amongst the people the urge for freedom, the desire to rely upon themselves and to be the makers of their destiny, the spirit of free thinking, and the will never to submit to any external authority by exchanging their freedom for the security of slaves. A new Renaissance, based on rationalism, individualism and cosmopolitan Humanism, is essential for democracy to be realized and made capable of defending itself.

Such an atmosphere will foster intellectual independence dedicated to the cause of making human values triumph. Moral excellence alone can mold a community together without sacrificing the individual on the altar of the collective ego, be it of the nation or a class. Men and women, possessed of that great virtue, will command the respect of an intelligent public, and be recognized as the leaders of society. Demagogy will be placed under a heavy discount. Democratic practice will not be reduced to periodical elections. People will no longer be mere "masses."

14. The Production-Relations Basis of Self-management

ANDRIJA KREŠIĆ

Various opponents and adherents of self-management can be found in Yugoslavia. Thus, in the motley company of the political right wing, self-management is considered an anarchistic social experiment, already rather largely compromised by disorder in the economy and politics and doomed to die—slowly and quietly or suddenly and spectacularly, but surely to die. Such a fate for self-management is prophesied most often by those of deposed politics, whether adherents of bourgeois ideals and white regimes or followers of red rule of the firm hand. The protagonists of the prevailing policy and the holders of present power consider self-management to be their revolutionary merit and programmatic goal, but in practice they zealously dose it so that it does not exceed the bounds prescribed by its authors. Left of this position, social self-government in our country is believed to be only *in statu nascendi,* and much is still considered necessary for it to become the dominant characteristic of the social order. To some, it appears normal that underage self-management must be led, but others hold that it will remain juvenile, in spite of its years, as long as it has guardians.

The state-political order or the regulation of so-called public life in Yugoslavia changed after the war in the direction of decen-

Reprinted from *Praxis,* 6(1971): 827–33. Translated by Helen Kramer.

tralization of power and political liberalization; state domination over social wealth was maintained by various methods. At first the very centralized governmental authority managed *directly* by planning the economy and society as a whole, until striking economic disproportions and other irrational consequences of state monopoly and the subjectivism (arbitrariness) of the political hierarchy became evident. Then came the gradual freeing of so-called objective economic laws from political dictation, or the reorientation to a free market economy, along with the cautious affirmation of parliamentary democracy in a decentralized state. The state continues to direct and to find its raison d'être in the economy; it does not function exclusively as a *direct* economic decision-maker, however, but increasingly acts as an external *intermediary* which determines by law the general framework of economic activity, although it sometimes also intervenes more directly (for example, when cyclical crises of the market economy arise or when receivership is employed).

Self-management of enterprises and institutions is established by law. This state standardization of self-management includes not only the external relations (rights and obligations) of the enterprise but also essential internal relations. The enterprise actually adopts its by laws itself, but these must conform to the law and are subject to the approval of the government authority. Self-management, accordingly, is a priori subject to government control or limited by law. Limited self-management is rather like a square circle, for it is not self-limitation by a broad social interest. Hence, what is involved here is, in fact, more a certain participation of workers in management together with the state, which remains the stronger participant. Otherwise, the already common phenomenon of strikes in enterprises and institutions could not be understood. A terminological quid pro quo cannot always help the state to hide its responsibility for the position of the workers, and class instinct can aid the workers to guess precisely a fundamental truth: namely, *workers' self-management under the tutelage of the state cannot be a new production relation in which exploitation of the workers is no longer known.*

Unconscious as well as conscious apologists for etatism hinder the emancipation of self-management by presenting the state itself as social self-government. It is not simply a matter of so-called national self-government in the form of the national state. An attempt was made to reform the more or less classical parliament as the highest organ of government, and separate chambers of work communities were established in it. These chambers are by no means supreme workers' councils, however, for they do not grow naturally as such out of the uniform organization of work. Although the representatives in the cited chambers are not, as a rule, professional politicians, their electoral body is composed for the sole act of election and empowers them for the entire mandate. It is still more significant that these chambers are not equal in responsibilities to classical parliamentary houses. Accordingly, the very organization of the parliament as the author of laws obviously confirms state domination over social self-government or limited worker participation in state management.

Self-government by definition negates every external, foreign, or alienated control, as well as every etatism (despotic and democratic, national and supranational, prerevolutionary and postrevolutionary).

State domination over self-management means its stagnation, degeneration, and compromise, so that all the economic, social, and political mistakes of the state are loaded onto the weak back of self-management. The only revolutionary escape from this social crisis is a decisive turnabout of the very relation of domination; that is, the establishment of entire social self-government as a new and dominant *production relation* and the transformation of the state into a subordinated service of self-government.

On the basis of everyday experience, it may appear to us that the abolition of state mediation in social life would open the way to general anarchy. Indeed, the abolition of some organ of state authority sometimes leads to misfortunes because a self-governing way of practicing that authority does not exist or is not sufficiently prepared so that it can be at least as efficient as the state way.

Today the so-called social contract is recommended as a nonstate way of harmonizing interests, especially in the economic sphere as a corrective of various anomalies of the market economy. However, the very recommendation assumes the disharmony of interests, means therapy more than prevention, and, in the economic sphere, represents noneconomic intervention.

The question is posed of the possibility, in principle, of self-regulation of social life, i.e., without any state mediation and without danger of anarchy. Can the basic preconditions for such a solution be found and freed in economics?

It is necessary to consider consistently the position, which is at least verbally acknowledged by all, that self-management is a *new production relation,* and to draw all the practical consequences of that position.

According to this determination, self-management is above all the *organization of the sphere of work,* and especially of modern social labor. Therefore, it is a matter, first, of society as a *uniform work association.* If we recall a famous text of Marx, it is a matter of the associated producers rationally regulating their interchange with nature, bringing it under their common control, instead of being ruled by it as by the blind forces of nature, and achieving this with the least expenditure of energy and under conditions most favorable to and worthy of their human nature.

Even at the beginning of this reflection on social self-government, essential differences appear between the conception presented here and various conceptions of self-government according to the territorial principle (for example, communal self-government and a federation of these communes) or according to the principle of blood relationship (for example, the family cooperative [*zadruga*] as primary). We consider social self-government to be an organization of society according to the *production principle,* and thus acknowledge that the social order is primarily a *mode of production and reproduction of social life.*

The order of a self-governing society of labor should not be conceived as a certain nonexisting condition that is still to come and that possibly has its original models in past history or even prehistory. What is involved is to free the existing, *real* associated labor of every external force and allow the workers themselves to perform it in harmony with their human needs and possibilities. The prototype for the physiognomy of self-governing society as the self-production of the total labor force can be an ordinary factory anywhere, but without a private owner or director in the capacity of a state agent.

In factory workshops, parts are produced and assembled into a final product. The relations between workshops, as well as within a workshop, are dictated by technology and the functional division of operations. It is essential to observe that the nature of these internal relations is *production directly for use.* In other words, here the mediation of the factory owner or the state or the autonomous market for goods is entirely superfluous. The quality and quantity of the product of each workshop is fixed in advance or planned by the production needs of the other workshops, by their orders, so to speak.

According to the historical logic of the development of labor, it can be assumed that the final factory product was once produced by one craftsman performing the operations of later workshops one after the other. On the other hand, the activity of each individual workshop can be carried out in an independent specialized factory. While workshops produce directly for use, however, an independent factory produces for the so-called free market or for the state according to the state plan of production. The direct relationship of production and use is now broken; between them has been interposed an intermediary that dictates the conditions of work, alienating them from the workers.

Modern production, by its own force of technological-economic rationalization, pushes out external interference, and, by various means, direct linking or integration of isolated units of economic activity again appears. This is, naturally, on a significantly higher level of the historical development of labor, and the new integral subject or unit of labor is collective. Specialized factories enter into complex production organisms, *mutually completing each other* like the organs of a living body and renewing in principle the *directness* of interworkshop relations. Rational integration is the condition and basic need of a modern economy, a need which cannot be completely satisfied so long as it does not include the *whole economy and all areas of labor.* This "natural drive" of the economy must be comprehended and accelerated so that it will be freed of all noneconomic obstacles to integration.

The production process from the natural raw material to the final consumer good tends to constitute itself into a unified, productive organism, breaking the fetters about various sectors of labor, establishing unmediated relations between industry and agriculture, the economy in the narrow sense, and science, education, culture, health, etc., by the force of the interest that each individual subject of integration holds for its other partners. For example, the tobacco industry is directly interested in getting a higher quality and quantity of tobacco for the same price and is very concerned with more productive labor of the cultivators who produce tobacco. The tobacco producers have the same interest in the fertilizer and implements industry, seed producers, etc.; and the tobacco manufacturers, in the producers of cigarette paper. Why should not all these sectors of production join in a production community in which the mutual interest is observed and directly satisfied? Similar mutual interest and rational need for merging can be found, for example, among a clothing factory, weaving mill, spinning mill, livestock farm, wool processing enterprise, pasture cultivators, and livestock feed producers. Each of these sectors of industrial and agricultural production can be independent and produce for the market, where they compete with other producers, not knowing in advance whether they will succeed, maintain themselves, or fail. They can each produce separately, in keeping with a state plan, for the state, which distributes their products according to its own interest. However, only in their "natural" economic-technical merging can production sectors be the measure and law for themselves alone, produce according to mutual needs, and avoid the waste of human labor. In such a community, direct measurement of labors of different intensities is carried out and the realization of the principle "to each according to his work" becomes possible. According to the same logic of the production and reproduction of human life in society, the *direct* mutual supply and demand between the economy in the narrow sense and education or health, etc., can be determined. Workers in the economy have an interest in raising their qualifications, improving their work training, and educating their children. Hence, they join together in a united work community with educators and with schools of various types and levels. In such a *production commune,* the school also participates equally in the creation and distribution of material goods; that is, it raises the productivity of workers just as science raises the productivity of the means of production. In principle, the association of medicine with other spheres of work is a similar matter. In this new social status, medical work also directly participates in production along with other types of work, and when it is thus directly motivated, then it is not in its interest to have as much illness as possible but to have as much health as possible, and hence a maximally productive labor force, and health activity becomes primarily preventive medicine. And so forth.

In short, every human product is really the product of social labor—a social, and not private or state, product. Accordingly, only social ownership, which is not identical to national or group ownership, is suitable to the social nature of the production of human goods. And it alone is suitable to human nature. The man-producer himself is a social product, the product of social labor. He is created by his parents and arrives in the world as only raw material, the mere material of a man. As manpower, i.e., as a mechanic, engineer, writer, or actor, he is the product of educational, medical, literary, and many other labors.

From all this, it follows that a real self-governing commune is possible as a *productive commune* and not primarily and necessarily as a territorial community of citizens. Our present-day township is a *state* jurisdiction which finds its raison d'être in *mediation* among *various* spheres of social labor in *one* territory, *separating* some from others by its mediation. Separation does violence to the social nature of work, and the township makes use of the power of state laws and organs for the regulation of social relations. Modern work creates the real preconditions for the creation of communities of *work* (production communes) regardless of territory. With modern means of communication, spatial distance becomes practically irrelevant as a factor of separation. For example, the identity of interests of tobacco factories in Sarajevo, Mostar, Niš, Skopje, Zagreb, etc., is today already more tangible than the interests connecting, for example, producers of coal and producers of tobacco who touch geographically. Accordingly, in the historical view, especially with respect to the development of the productive force of labor, every exaggerated insistence on territorial boundaries is conservative.

The formation of a social whole, in contrast to state constitutionalism, is carried out "from below," by the transformation of social labor "by itself" into social labor "for itself" and by the line of realizing true social ownership. By this formation, there is established a unified *economic* system of the country which is simultaneously the country's *political* system. The organized social self-government of the workers is itself the lawmaker. The law or norm of social behavior is no longer that forced or skillfully manipulated accommodation to an a priori reason of state, but is that *subsequent* generalization or statement of the "common denominator" in various self-governing environments. The norm which is thus proclaimed by an organ of social self-government (from the council in the enterprise to the congress of workers' councils or the supreme workers' council) acquires the true authority of law by some suitable type of social ratification. By such organization of society, the epochal slogan of the workers' movement—"All power to the workers' councils"—which until today has nowhere become empirically dominant, would finally be implemented. Accelerated progress of work and human life would be liberated, and the basic driving force would be the natural need of workers to produce as much as possible with the least possible expenditure of manpower. (If someone still wants competition on the commodity market as a stimulus to material development, for consolation the world capital market will still long re-

main in operation.) Instead of the surplus of labor time for alienation and the surplus of workers, a surplus of time for workers
would appear.

It is clear in and of itself that self-government as a method of
liberating the working class (in the modern sense of the word)
can be only the affair of the working class itself. No one else, even
if he originates from its bosom, can, in the name of that class,
consistently carry out its class liberation—neither the workers'
state nor the workers' political party, regardless of the merits of
these institutions in the struggle for class liberation.

In our country, the League of Communists is with reason identified as the leading force of society. The leading role of the Communist Party of Yugoslavia (or LCY) from the creation of the
new Yugoslavia until the present is an undoubted historic fact.
Likewise, in our country self-government is described as a new
type of society that has been introduced and that still must be
built up. How does one agree with the other?

Both practically and logically, they doubtless do not agree at all
if the LCY is considered as a classical political avant-garde of the
proletariat of the Leninist-Comintern type, and if, on the other
hand, workers' self-government is understood as the authentic economic and political liberation of the proletariat. Parties of the
type mentioned above can be very effective in destroying bourgeois rule and its socioeconomic foundations, and subsequently
building up their own state authority (either directly or indirectly) with the socioeconomic bases of its stability. Viewed historically, this is, to be sure, incomparably more than the seizure
of power by one party (or coalition of parties) from another. But
the social self-government of workers involves not some *change* of
power but the *abolition* of *every* external compulsion over associated labor, the *self-rule* of the associated workers, the self-conscious act of the whole working class which can be mediated by
no one, which no one can replace if it is to remain what it is by
its very concept.

Accordingly, it is time to begin to speak of the leading role of
the working class and only of that leading role in society.

It is certain, however, that a substantial part of that class, even
a majority of workers, are not allowed by the conditions of life up
to now and the manipulation of their class interest to raise themselves to a consciousness of their historic interest and to corresponding revolutionary engagement. It is certain, at the same
time, that in a *modern* working class (in which the number of

manual workers is falling and the number of intellectual workers is increasing) there are workers who are capable of that. They can also observe the repressive nature of a contemporary "consumer society" of abundance and already dispute it in various ways. Such workers inevitably also appear in our country as the first partisans of class emancipation in the sense of workers' self-government. These tested worker partisans today are, in fact, communist revolutionaries, regardless of whether or not they possess a Party card. If this is so factually, then only such workers can be considered formally communists. Other workers can elect them as their *representatives,* and they are communists only if they are *workers* who enjoy that confidence and only as long as they enjoy it. Communist-worker representatives are the revolutionary elite of their class; in our country they are the masters of workers' self-government, which means, *eo ipso,* that they by no means assume for themselves that class act, but qualify other *workers* for it *in their* experience of self-government. A child cannot go into life on his own feet as long as his mother walks instead of him (carrying him in her stomach or her arms) —she must let him walk independently. Thus, the working class can be the author in the building of social self-government as a new production relation and social order without exploitation of the workers, and its authorship alone is certain.

15. The Theoretical Foundation of the Idea of Self-government

PREDRAG VRANICKI

Viewed historically, mankind has barely taken the first steps in the realization of a new human community, that community which hovered before the eyes of many great humanists and entire movements that, drawn by the utopian vision of a new world, were ready for the greatest exertions, self-denial, and sacrifices. Mankind has also followed a progressive path up to this time. Not even the greatest skepticism regarding the methods employed can deny man's achievements in all spheres of his culture, scholarship, consciousness, and even morality. It cannot be concealed, however, that this entire ascent was paid for with innumerable victims, much suffering, and the deprivation of entire strata and classes of their rights. More humane relations among people were even established by inhumane methods, and thus the vision of the humane became a historical constant of the world up to now.

Today we know that this dissension in mankind—which always expressed the existential interests of individual classes, whether they could coincide with objective historical possibilities or not —has only in the present day reached that level which allows its overcoming. Marx's basic vision of this humanism was the over-

Reprinted from *Teorija i praksa samoupravljanja u Jugoslaviji* (Belgrade: Radnička štampa, 1972) , pp. 136–48. Translated by Helen Kramer.

coming of class dissension through the "self-government of the producers," that type of social organization which would be the germ cell of the abolition of power alienated from man, of political hierarchies and bureaucracy. And when, fifty years ago, at the end of the first world dance of death, the European workers' movement began to open a new chapter of history, the basic demand and idea on its revolutionary banner was "All power to the councils!"

Whether these took the form of Lenin's soviets, the German and Austrian *Räte,* or Gramsci's *consigli,* mankind was on the threshold of a new historical era. A single word, a single thought—council—united in itself all the sufferings, all the hopes, all the revolutionary strivings of innumerable nameless generations, as well as all the wrath of the enslaved and exploited. Just as the ideas of freedom of ownership, equality before the law, and equality were the symbols of the bourgeois world, the idea of councils became the symbol of the overcoming of bourgeois civilization—the symbol of a world without private ownership of the means of production, without classes and exploitation, without the state and political hierarchies, without national hatred and extermination.

As with every other great historical idea, however, this was no mere reflection of a historical situation already created, but its anticipation. To achieve this goal, it was necessary for reality itself to aim toward it, historical reality which was still divided, undeveloped, contradictory, and often unforeseeable. And that meant that reality could resist, which it did—and not only in its bourgeois but also in its socialist forms!

While from time to time the bourgeois world reckoned with this idea by force, and with the aid of the social democrats, Lenin's soviets gradually lost their original authenticity in a statist socialism.

Thus, throughout three decades of the history of the workers' movement and socialism, these fundamental ideas of Marxian socialism stood in "oblivion." The idea of workers' councils and workers' self-management appeared to have vanished from the historical stage and the claims of the working class. The fetishized "socialist state" was, to a substantial degree, imposed on the workers' movement as the model of socialism. The working masses remained as nothing but masses, for the agent of history and of socialist development was someone else—higher authorities who ruled in their name. These authorities, the party-etatist bureaucracy, disposed of the entire surplus labor of the masses; determined the norms of their conduct, their freedom of mobility, and even their assignment to jobs; and limited the right of protest, proclaiming every protest as an antisocialist and antinational act, without rendering account to anyone.

It is not at all surprising that this etatist bureaucratic hierarchy, in its omnipotence, was horrified and deeply offended when the renaissance of the idea of soviets and workers' self-management appeared in a wing of the socialist movement.

A new historical conflict began—a conflict for a more developed model of socialism that would be closer to Marx's visions and assumption. The apparent dimensions of that conflict are more or less known; but its essential dimensions, much less so. An entire ideology was called into question: the ideology of a single road to socialism; the ideology of the state and Party as the basic driving force of socialist development as well as the basic arbiter in all social questions, from political to cultural and artistic; the ideology of one style of life, work, art, and philosophy; the ideology of inviolable spheres (in this case, political) that were exempted from all dialectical criticism since for them the dialectics of negativity no longer held; the ideology of Marxist dialectics that toward the outside was to be a devastating critique of the bourgeoisie, but from within an obedient apology for every political proclamation; the ideology of inflexible centralism in Party and economic life, etc.

The basic idea, which burrowed like a historic mole in this wasteland of dogmatism (everywhere, including in Yugoslavia), was and is the idea of councils, the idea of self-management. The category of negativity that was thrown out of Stalin's system of seven characteristics stubbornly pleaded for its historic right. And no one could or will be able to take it away, for it was and will be an essential aspect of the historic process, an essential lever for overcoming the historically limited and anachronistic. Thus, not only is the working class in the modern world the historic negation of bourgeois society and the bourgeoisie as a class, but likewise *self-government of the working class and of the working man is the negation of the bureaucratic-statist structure of the initial stage of socialism.*

The above criticism of Stalinist ideology actually involved a criticism of *ideological consciousness* in the true Marxist sense. One's own ideas and practice were equated with socialism in general. One's own political pragmatism, which was capable even of assuming monstrous forms, was raised to a principle. The category of the special, of the specific, completely disappeared from dialectical and Marxist perception of the historical process—all because of an inability to comprehend the world in its complexity and to regard one's own case merely as a special case, on a specific historical basis and in particular historical relations, and not as a paradigm for all more or less developed situations.

Thus a historical conflict arose with respect to more advanced conditions of socialist development: on what should the basic accent be placed in that development? In what should the germs of a more developed communist world be seen? In the political forms of socialist society (state and Party) or in the self-governing organization of the working class and of socialist society in general? In the anticipation of the withering away of political forms and the strengthening of self-governing forms which are *eo ipso* also the negation of the political, or in the strengthening of the political sphere?

The idea of workers' councils, workers' and social self-government, was sharply attacked as anarchosyndicalism, a return to capitalism, right opportunism, etc., as though it were something that, until then, had not existed at all in Marxist theory and practice, as though it were not, in fact, the continuation of an interrupted historical dialogue and historical practice that concerned the most essential factors of the new historical relations. Hence the discussion of this problem cannot begin with 1950, when that important historical turnabout was made in Yugoslav practice; it has lasted, although with the interruptions noted above, from the moment of the birth of Marx's conception of man, history, and socialism until today.

The question is posed concretely: which historical conception emerges from Marx's, Engels's, and Lenin's philosophical and theoretical analyses and positions—the conception of self-governing socialism or of statist socialism? Which of these conceptions is the expression of a consistent Marxist solution of the socialist problem, and which is the expression of political opportunism and pragmatism?

The answer cannot be found in any individual quotation, but rather in an overall Marxist perception of historical problems, and particularly the problems of bourgeois society and its surmounting.

History for Marx is no sort of occurrence external to man, but his own work. The creation of history and the creation of man is a simultaneous and unified process. The level of the development of man's consciousness depends on the level of man's historical practice. The levels of development of the human community, and thus of man's consciousness, depend on its material existence, as Marx had already shown brilliantly in his youth. Changing man, therefore, is no contemplative or educational work, but the result of man's material and revolutionary historical practice. . . .

The category of historical practice is therefore a fundamental category of Marx's philosophical interpretation of man and history. But to Marx it was likewise clear that every historical process until now, although always a totality, was divided and split within itself. In past history, in view of the still low levels of man's development, the embodiment of man [in his products or creations—*Tr*.] meant that in a certain organization of social relations and production—in the system of private ownership and classes—the object was opposed to man. The object possessed an independent existence and became the property of another who stood opposed as an independent force, often as an alienated group, class, authority, or mystery.

Thus, the system of private ownership and class division led to crucial and tragic splits, not only in society but in the historical agent himself—man. Instead of fulfilling man's all-around possibilities, a large part of mankind is reduced to an ordinary means of production and politics; the interests of individual groups and classes were imposed on man as general interests to which he was existentially subject and dependent; a system of rule and power was built which was imposed on others as an external and unlimited power; and this economic and political alienation, which in bourgeois society was based on the wage relation and the bureaucratized rule of the state, was accompanied by various ideological alienations of partialized existence and similar consciousnesses of the masses deprived of rights.

The partialization of man was not only the consequence of life-long binding to physical activity alone, which was also caused by the low level of economic and social development in general; it was the consequence as well of his social rejection and separation from participation in ruling the social community. Privileged groups and classes had the privilege of rule. To the working man, the sphere of rule remained the sphere of the unattainable and mysterious. And instead of experiencing and conceiving history as his creation, he saw it as completely opaque, alien, external— which only allowed the further fetishization of his consciousness.

In these briefly presented philosophical perceptions of man's being and the phenomenon of the historical lies also the source of Marx's conception of the necessity of overcoming these forms of man's alienation and of the conception of the all-around development of the human being, the human personality. In his early works, as well as in the later *Outlines* and *Capital*, Marx gave a fundamental analysis of the economic structure of bourgeois society, of the rule of capital as the basis of economic—as well as political—alienation, and of the creation of fetishized consciousness as the consequence of these relations. He also clearly showed how this relation acts to limit the versatility of the human being, alienating man from his essence, from production as the basis of his historic existence, transforming his work into torment, stunting his possibilities, etc. That a partial, limited historical activity necessarily led to the limiting and partialization of man's personality is only the consequence of this limited and alienated relation.

Hence, Marx, at the same time that he proclaimed the general humanistic position that criticism of religion results in the teaching that man is the highest being for man and in the overthrow of all relations in which man is humiliated, persecuted, abandoned, and despised, also pleaded for the surmounting of modern class society by the struggle of the proletariat for new social relations. But precisely for all the reasons cited above, Marx's vision is not the renewed establishment either of a new *class* society or of a *political* society, but rather their surmounting, so that the dignity of the human is established, so that man by his total historical engagement will truly feel himself the real and sole demiurge of his historical world and life.

Stalinism neither had nor has these philosophic dimensions. The mechanistically conceived conception of historical determinism was to have served it pragmatically as a justification of every political step as the only possible and historically determined one. Stalin's philosophical theory of subject and object reduced the subject ultimately to one who reflects an objective historical process to which, in the best of cases, he can only adapt himself. Initiative remains only to the avant-garde and, ultimately, to the very political summit; thus, in both theory and practice, regardless of references to the masses, there was created within socialism one of the most radical conceptions of an elite, one that was also consistently put into practice. How much such a conception and practice contradict the genuine Marxist and socialist intention needs no special emphasis. . . .

We have already shown how Marx's vision of history and of man is consistently based on the idea of the necessity of surmounting the society of the wage relation, and thus also its political expression, the state. The free development of individuals—and they are the basis of history—could be realized if the separation of society into the rulers and the ruled were abolished, if class division of labor were abolished, and if the many-sided engagement of man in his historical process were realized. This historical engagement, historical many-sided practice, was and remained for Marx and Marxism the basis, the medium, for man's development of the wholeness of his being, of emancipation from fetishistic ideas that only fettered his individual and social action. Hence, one of the basic assumptions for all great Marxists was that socialism—immediately at its beginning—declares war on all those institutions that replaced the working man, that ruled in his name, that in the course of history alienated him, and in relation to which he was in constant dependence and subordination. And the first and basic institution with such powerful prerogatives was, and is, the *state*.

The state is a special, historical form of social organization—above all a form of force, oppression, and bureaucracy, regardless of the fact that the state both earlier and today performs a number of general social functions without which society cannot survive. But society can also perform these functions without such an organization. No matter how essential the state is to the working class in the very beginnings of the revolution, it is essential, in the views of Marx, Engels, and Lenin, as well as of the majority of the more important Marxists, only in the form of its own abolition. For it was clear to all that the state is such a concentration of power and force that even in socialism it can easily become a force over the working class itself. Hence, in the well-known discussion about the trade unions, Lenin was strongly against nationalization of the unions and in favor of as great as possible independence for them, so that precisely as an organization of the working class they would protect that same class against the eventual abuses of its own state. Only later, in Stalin's totalitarian conception of socialism, did the trade unions, as well as other organizations, become merely transmission belts of the omnipotent bureaucratic statist center. . . .

There is no doubt that at the base of the Marxist interpretation of socialist development lies the conception of the *necessity of the withering away of the state as early as the first phase of communism,* that is, under socialism. The question is posed as to what the other side of that process is. It is well known that Marx, until the Paris Commune, did not have a solution to this problem. Only the historic creativity of the Paris communards gave Marx the basic elements for conceiving the process of surmounting the state organization of society. "The Paris Commune was, of course, to serve as a model to all the great industrial centers of France. Once the communal regime was established in Paris and the secondary centers, the old centralized government would have to give way to the self-government of the producers in the provinces as well" (Karl Marx, *The Civil War in France*).

Marx's basic preoccupation with the solution to the historic problem of the political and economic emancipation of the working class finds in these perceptions an organizational solution. Regardless of how essential the state is in the first moments of the revolutionary process, the accent is not on that political sphere but on the "self-government of the producers," workers' councils that become the basis of a new social structure and community. . . .

That Lenin, both before and after the revolution, saw the *basis of the new proletarian state, as well as the basis of its withering away,* to lie in the soviets—and that means in self-government foremost of the working class—is known from a number of his lesser writings after the revolution. That was still the period of armed revolution, when it was necessary to think of the new state of the working class, when it had to be strengthened and when truly iron discipline of both the proletariat and the Party was necessary to resist the counterrevolution. Hence, in Lenin's writings of that period, there also necessarily appears the problem of strengthening the state, but neither as an organism that is separate and stands over the people nor without those social preconditions that will also be the basis of its withering away.

At that time the proletariat needed the state, but the state so "arranged that it could immediately wither away and must wither away." And this "arrangement" that will enable the state to wither away immediately is not the transfer of all economic and political power to a state bureaucracy, but the inclusion in administration (not only of the state) of as many of the masses as possible through workers', soldiers', and peasants' soviets and their deputies. "The socialist state," wrote Lenin at the beginning of 1918, "can arise only as a network of producer-consumer communes which conscientiously keep records of their production and consumption, economize with labor, constantly raise their productivity, and thereby achieve the possibility of shortening the work day to seven hours, six hours, and still less."[1] And somewhat further: "Every factory, every village represents a producer-consumer commune, which has the right and duty to apply in its own way the general soviet laws ('in its own way' not in the sense of their violation, but in the sense of the diversity of forms of their implementation), to solve in its own way the problem of records of production and the distribution of the output. Under capitalism this was the 'private affair' of the individual capitalist, the large landowner, the kulak. Under soviet rule this is not a private affair, but the most important state work."[2]

Lenin, therefore, even in the most difficult days of the existence of the young Soviet Republic when the hardest concrete problems of organizing the new rule were posed, approached matters concretely and on the basis of principle. Self-government of the producers, workers' councils as the organization of communes, were to concern themselves not only with the organization of production but also with "records of production and distribution of output." The new organization of soviets, whose members he explicitly maintained dare not transform themselves into "parliamentarians" or "bureaucrats," was for Lenin a new type of democracy, proletarian in nature, which is a "higher type of democracy, a break with its bourgeois distortion, the transition toward socialist democracy and the conditions in which the state can begin to wither away."[3] The organization of soviets in the initial period was the foundation of the new state, but simultaneously also the basis and condition of its withering away: soviets to which increasing rights and jurisdictions were to be gradually transferred, economic above all, but also many of a social nature. . . .

Lenin was not able to further strengthen and develop this conception because of the civil war, the practically complete disappearance of the old working class in that war, the destruction and backwardness of the country, and the too brief time still left to him. His successors conceived the whole problem one-sidedly and developed it in the direction of strengthening just that sphere which Lenin considered temporary and, at the same time, dangerous for socialism—the state, bureaucratic sphere. The

---

1. V. I. Lenin, "Naredni zadaci sovjetske vlasti" [The Next Tasks of Soviet Power], in *Izabrana djela*, Vol. II, Book 1 (Zagreb, 1950), p. 329.

2. Ibid., p. 333.

3. Ibid., p. 343.

etatist conception of socialism won a complete victory over that of self-government in a certain historical period.

In Lenin's time, the idea of workers' councils, especially under the influence of the new experience of the Russian Revolution, was conceived as the herald of a new era, of historically new social relations. A. Gramsci, G. Lukács, K. Korsch, and many others perceived in that conception the historical innovation that was to replace bourgeois relations.

It is necessary to cite at least the ideas of the great Italian Marxist and founder of the Communist Party of Italy, Antonio Gramsci, who, like Lenin and under his influence, saw the basis of the dictatorship of the proletariat to lie in neither the trade unions nor the Party, but in workers' councils, in which the working class feels itself as producer and not wage laborer. "The dictatorship of the proletariat can be formed into a type of organization specific to the activity of producers, and not wage laborers, the slaves of capital. The factory council is the first cell of this organization. Since all the branches of labor are represented in the council in accordance with the contribution that each occupation and each branch of labor gives to the manufacture of the object that the factory produces for the community, the institution is class, social."[4]

Gramsci very perceptively felt that the key to the problem lies here, that only such a social basis will make it possible to surmount the wage relation, and thus also economic and political alienation, which can exist in the relation of the working class both toward the capitalists and the bourgeois state and toward the state in socialism, insofar as the latter becomes independent and takes over from the working class those functions without which the working class is deprived of its economic and social power (taking away and disposing of the surplus labor, retaining power over investment, preventing the democratic and proletarian right of free recall of delegates, etc.). Hence, for Gramsci, "the factory council and system of factory councils try out and discover at the first level of jurisdiction the new positions that the working class has in the field of production, give the working class consciousness of its own present value, of its real function, its responsibility, its future. The working class draws conclusions from the sum of positive experiences that people personally accumulate as individuals, acquires the psychology and character of

4. A. Gramsci, *Ordine nuovo*, September 11, 1919.

the ruling class, and organizes itself as such; that is, creates a political soviet and introduces its dictatorship."[5] For all these reasons, Gramsci considers that the creation of workers' councils in the factory "represents a great historical event, the beginning of a new era in the history of the human race."[6]

These are, in briefest outline, the theoretical bases of the conception of self-government. This conception, as we have seen, emerges from the specifically Marxian interpretation of history, man, the alienation of man in modern society, and the overcoming of that alienation and of the entire bourgeois society by socialist development. The conception of workers' and social self-government is the logical and necessary consequence of conceiving man as a historical being of practice, as a polyvalent being who, in class relations up to now and in alienated labor, has experienced various partializations and deformations, which on this level of historical development can be gradually overcome by socialism. The conception is this coming of man to himself from the alienated spheres of the economy (private ownership, wage relation), politics (the state, hierarchy, bureaucracy), and ideology (various mystifications), to the possibility of surmounting all these alienated spheres by taking into his hands his own historical fate. For all these reasons, this conception marks the profoundest conceiving of humanity at this stage of historical development.

Although there were individual Marxists who never abandoned this conception, for an entire three decades in the workers' movement, this idea, this fateful concept of human emancipation, was entirely suppressed and even proscribed. Hence, the year 1950, when the position of workers' self-management was proclaimed and legally adopted as the basic and main line of development of Yugoslav socialism, is a new milestone of history. A historic dialogue and practice were again established on a mass level, and no longer only on an individual level.

The first years of this new historic practice, which after so many decades had the effect of a real historic innovation, already called into question the whole Stalinist, statist conception of socialism. Only from this perspective did all those phenomena which so discredited international socialism finally become clear.

Only by the conception of workers' councils, of workers' and

---

5. *Ordine nuovo,* February 14, 1920.

6. *Ordine nuovo,* June 5, 1920.

social self-government, was it possible to understand and reject the undialectic division of the first phase of communism from the second, of so-called socialism from communism. It was shown that the conception of socialism as a system in which the supreme arbitration, supreme authority, control, disposal of surplus labor, etc., are given to a political jurisdiction in which state ownership and all that follows from it dominates, is only an apology for an etatist practice and, accordingly, a historic mystification. Not one of the founders of Marxism conceived of any historic period of socialism in which the state, the state bureaucracy, would dominate, in which social hierarchies would reach so much power and opaqueness. Each of them conceived of that first phase of communism as communism (regardless of whether they called it socialism) in which precisely these separated and hierarchical spheres would immediately begin to wither away. All of them, therefore, conceived of socialism as a transitional and contradictory period in which both state and self-government forms historically intertwine, while the latter must ultimately gain the victory if the construction of new bureaucratic-technocratic leviathans is to be avoided. . . .

Higher levels of socialist development, and thus also further revolutionary perspectives, can unfold only on the line of the transition of state ownership into social ownership by the development of self-government relations. Whether these processes will be carried out faster or slower with respect to the development of democratic relations, with a multiparty or a one-party system, etc., are not essential questions of socialism, although they are not unimportant. Private ownership of the means of production and the indirect democracy of the multiparty system are, historically viewed, the axis of bourgeois society. Self-government and direct democracy, which means the withering away and surmounting of the political, the parliamentary, and the bureaucratic, is the historic axis of socialism, those germs, elements, and relations that essentially designate a historic innovation.

The creation of a new historic personality is not an educational act—and least of all with the sort of literature, press, and ideology that exist in the world today. Although the importance of the cultural sphere in forming consciousness and the essential cultural shape of the new personality is not underestimated, the essential precondition of that innovation is the realization of the historic right of the working class and the working man to overcome at this stage of social development all those historical institutions that thought and ruled instead of him, and most of all against him, and to gradually achieve that society in which control will cease to exist as a political function—that is, control of people—and become general social control—control of things.

16. Between Ideals and Reality

SVETOZAR STOJANOVIĆ

Socialist self-government should be constructed as an *integral* social system. This means, first, that it must embrace *all parts* of society, and second, that in addition to the self-government of individual elements, it must be seen as the self-government of society *as a whole*. This assumes the convergence of self-governing elements into a complete self-governing society. In any other case, Marx's belief in the subordination of social processes to the "power of united individuals" and the hope he placed in the "free association of producers" would prove to be utopian.

Concrete proportions between the autonomy of self-governing groups and the influence of a self-governing society over them, of course, depend upon concrete circumstances and an evaluation of them. Yet one thing is clear in advance, at least theoretically: Any monopoly achieved by individual groups, even if disguised as self-governing autonomy, cannot be socialist in character. Social self-government as a macro-phenomenon is certainly inconceivable without self-government on the micro-level. But social self-government is not the *same* as group self-government.

Yet, the ideologists of group self-government take Marx's idea of "freely associated labor" and the "free association of the produc-

From *Between Ideals and Reality: A Critique of Socialism and Its Future* by Svetozar Stojanović, translated by Gerson S. Sher. Copyright © 1973 by Oxford University Press, Inc. Reprinted by permission.

ers" to denote a cluster of completely autonomous, mutually unconnected and conflicting groups.

Yugoslav Marxist theory is absolutely correct when it opposes
self-government to statism. More recent development, however,
has exposed contradictions within self-government itself: between
social and group-particularistic self-government. It is not enough
to speak simply of social self-government on the one hand, and of
abuses of social self-government on the other. It is time to turn
our attention more decisively to the tendency of individual self-
governing groups to exploit and threaten other self-governing
groups and thus society as a whole.

Thus fragmented, the working class naturally displays egoism
and particularism. Only in a system of integral self-government
will it fully manifest its social character, solidarity, and universality. Only horizontally and vertically integrated self-government
will enable the working class to become the dominant social
force. Self-government based exclusively upon groups will reinforce the power of the state rather than negating it, contrary to
the claims of its protagonists. So long as integration, coordination, regulation, and planning are not inherent in self-government, these functions will have to be performed by an alienated
part of the society—the state. When there is no real community, a
surrogate for it is indispensable. The Yugoslav experience shows
that the state can easily manipulate atomized self-government.
Mired in the framework of self-governing groups, the working
class cannot make its way onto the political stage to pose questions concerning the total distribution of surplus value. So long
as this is the case, the burden of economic reform will fall most
heavily by far upon the shoulders of the working class.

The theoretical background of group-particularist self-government is created by the illusion that social self-government is
equivalent to complete *decentralization* and the naive belief that
it is possible to realize *absolutely direct* self-government. As a result of this conception massive networks (the railroads, the postal
services, the power supply systems, and so on) have been intentionally fragmented and the dimensions of production organizations and institutions artificially limited. Territorial entities,
above all the communes, are seen as complete and closed units.
Local autonomy has developed as local autarchy.

We should supplement this picture by mentioning the aversion
of group-particularistic self-government to all binding *general social* standards and regulations, a consequence of the view that

they threaten the rights of self-governing groups. The process of the "withering away of the state" is primitively understood as the renunciation of general norms, and not as the transformation of the nature of the agent of these norms, and thus of their content. It is indeed strange that people in Yugoslavia are astonished by the fact that unconnected and mutually opposed self-governing groups do not spontaneously observe certain general standards when such standards are neither formulated nor binding. The theoretical inspiration for the tendency described here must be sought in Proudhon rather than in Marx.

It was inevitable that this state of affairs should come into conflict with the indispensability of technical, technological, organizational, and financial integration and cooperation. Adherents of statism skillfully took advantage of this tendency, using it as proof that self-government limits the development of the forces of production. Campaigns of artificial disintegration have yielded to campaigns of forced integration, which of course were not capable of improving the situation. Permanent revolution is hardly the same thing as permanent improvisation. Only more recently has an organized movement developed for voluntary and at the same time studied integration.

Our system's official theorists claim that along the path to self-government integration Yugoslavia *had to* pass through a period of excessive decentralization and disintegration. But what about the opposite thesis, i.e., that it was possible from the very beginning to introduce self-government adapted to large systems and massive enterprises and institutions? Actually, the waste of time, energy, and money that resulted was not dictated by any sort of inevitability, but rather by the mistakes of those who had theoretically conceptualized such a path of development.

In Yugoslav political jargon, frequent use is made of the expression "our self-governing, self-managing society." But this is only an ideological veil which social and scientific criticism has still failed to reject. Even a superficial glance at the real centers of social power in our country can show that a "self-governing, self-managing *society*" exists only in ideology, while a vivid dualism exists in practice—self-managing *groups* in the base and a rather strong statist structure above them. Only with the socioeconomic reform have the first serious signs of vertical social integration on the basis of self-management appeared.

The development of social self-government as an integral system assumes, of course, an essential alteration of the sociopolitical structure to the very top—the constitution of vertical associations of self-managing groups, the outgrowth of representative organs of self-government from below, the placing of all state organs, including the military and the police, under their control, a fundamental democratization of the political organizations, and above all of the League of Communists, and so on. This task has all the more importance as the initiation of self-management in 1950 proceeded from a decision of the party and state summit and the main break-throughs in the development of self-government to this very day have largely depended upon the outcome of ideological-political conflicts within that summit. Thus the entire "scheme" of self-government was constructed from without, from above, and was moreover uniform—proceeding from the economic sphere—for all spheres of society. However, the self-governors should themselves conceptualize the manner in which they will make decisions within their groups.

The struggle against statist tendencies should be conceived as much more profound and complex than it is ordinarily believed to be. The classical statism of the state organs is clearly visible. Yet it tries to disguise itself: The state organs do subordinate themselves to representative bodies, but only so that these bodies may remain the transmission belts for the leadership of the ruling political party.

As is well known, the Marxist thesis about the withering away of the state, even in its practical elaboration in Yugoslavia, is held in great skepticism in certain leftist circles in the world. This is not surprising, as contemporary social democracy, together with the greater part of the communist movement in power, possesses a statist conception of socialism. In both cases socialism is held to be based upon the state—on the one hand, upon the "welfare state," and on the other, upon the state "of all the people." Social democracy, of course, cultivates the tradition of multiparty liberalism, while the communist movement relies upon one-party monopoly.

But responsibility for this skeptical attitude toward the thesis of the withering away of the state must be sought on the Yugoslav side as well. We should admit that we do not have a developed *theory* about the withering away of the state. A metaphor cannot cover up huge theoretical vacuums for long. What is more, in some writings—even at times in practice—the withering away of the state is identified with disorganization.

Great illusions are also sown by people who *reduce* the problem of the state in socialism to its withering away. Whatever we may take this concept to mean, it is clear that the process will fill an entire epoch. Whenever society is unable to take over certain state functions, the statists take a maximalist posture in order to make their positions secure, posing the alternatives as either the withering away of the state or the untainted monopoly of the state. But this is a false dilemma, since there is something else which is certainly realizable in principle: *all* state organs should and can be subordinated, even at this very moment, to organs of social self-government.

What is the relationship between self-government and ownership? Can we speak of *social* ownership if social self-government is reduced to group self-government?

Social ownership, as distinguished from private ownership, is a very complex phenomenon which has given social scientists a great deal of difficulty. For the time being it might be better to speak of the socialization of ownership rather than of social ownership as a reality. After all, Marx spoke of the process of the "positive supersession of private property." In Yugoslavia, this process began with the nationalization of private property. For a long time yet to come the state will inevitably have a certain role to play in the disposition and control of ownership. But leaving the state aside for the moment, social ownership implies a certain degree of group decision-making and group disposition of property. Because of one factor—the state—and another—self-governing groups—there is a constant tendency for social ownership to be reduced to statist or group ownership. These are, in fact, two types of particularistic, group ownership. Thus, it is pure illusion to think that group self-governing particularism can really be transcended by statist "universalism."

Only to the extent that true social self-government exists is it possible to speak of truly social ownership. No other type of ownership presupposes democracy. Since concrete social subjects must have the right to dispose of social property to a certain degree, the danger will always exist that they will reduce this property to group property (i.e., property of either the state or self-governing groups). It is necessary, on the one hand, for social property to be brought as close as possible to individuals and groups, to become concretized; while on the other hand, it is at the same time necessary for the narrow and monopolistic disposition of that property to be transcended. The concrete universal is continually menaced by particularism as well as by abstraction. The most powerful

self-governing groups can betray a tendency to extort those decisions from the state and representative organs which would further their own particular interests. The concept of social ownership, just as the concept of social self-government itself, reflects
basic social contradictions.

Group ownership and group self-government, on the one hand,
demand state ownership and government by the state on the
other. Society could not function if state ownership did not set
strict limits to group self-governing ownership.

In these passages we have not been engaging in purely abstract
theoretical speculation, but in a statement of real tendencies in
our society. The danger that social self-government may be reduced to group self-government is based upon the factual treatment of social ownership as group ownership. Besides the statist
myth of social ownership, there are also other forms of group
ownership which masquerade as social ownership.

What else is the complete closing off of individual self-governing groups—with respect to cadres, organization, and distribution
—than the monopolization of one sector of social property?
Group-particularistic self-government is favorable for mediocri-
ties. For a capable, unemployed person who cannot penetrate
such groups in order to replace an incapable one, ownership proclaimed to be social cannot be truly social. This also holds for the
enterprise which has invested a sizeable portion of its income into
the modernization of one section of its plant and then finds that
this section, standing on its right of self-management, does not
want to contribute to the modernization of the other sections. In
apportioning their income, some self-governing groups behave according to the principles of group ownership and group self-government, but when they go bankrupt on the market expect help
from the larger community, invoking the principles of social
ownership and social self-government.

The danger presented by group ownership and group self-government is not very discernible in an economy composed of small
enterprises. But how much autonomy in the distribution of income can a self-governing society allow a working collective composed of a few dozen workers in a highly automated plant in
which it has invested huge resources?

Some theorists claim that in such cases the problem is one of a
conflict between the nature of decision-making and the nature of
ownership. But they are slaves of the legal fiction of social ownership. Ownership is not a metaphysical entity which exists inde-

pendently of decision-making and control. In the instances cited above, individual groups dispose of social property in a largely monopolistic manner. Thus one can at the very best speak of the danger of the constitution of group property. For society as a whole it is of relatively minor importance whether it is entire self-governing groups or only oligarchic groups within them that behave toward ownership in this manner. Although I believe that it is most often the latter that do so, I cannot follow the glorifiers of group self-government, who a priori exclude the first possibility and reduce the entire problem to so-called decentralized oligarchy.

In Yugoslavia alienation in socialism is treated exclusively as a consequence of statism. Yet alienation can appear in self-government as well, not only because of the activity of oligarchic groups, but also because of the behavior of *entire self-governing groups* toward society. Alienation of the means and products of labor from society can be accomplished by individual self-governing groups as well. In the final analysis, it is all the same to society whether it loses control over the means and products of labor to the state or to some self-governing groups. After all, alienation resulting from group-particularistic self-government cannot exist without its complement—statist alienation. Moreover, alienation, as a rule, is accompanied by reification: certain self-governing groups treat the other members of society as means and things. . . .

Social self-government is a necessary, but not a sufficient condition for the construction of socialist community. Who it is that makes decisions and the content of these decisions are matters of equal importance. The quality of decisions should be evaluated from the standpoint of the development of socialist community. In Yugoslavia, however, there is a strong tendency bordering closely on fetishism to treat self-government and self-management as values in themselves. As if the socialist character of decisions is ensured by the fact that they are made by organs of self-management. Some people, again, only extol self-management in their words, but in fact think that the League of Communists ought to treat it as its own transmission belt.

One of the consequences of an uncritical attitude toward self-government is the confusion of self-management with day-to-day management. (I do not wish to address myself here to the contrary phenomenon—about which enough has already been written—that the managerial organs of enterprises and institutions reduce workers' self-management to an empty form.) When democratic bodies omnipotently meddle in operative leadership then, of course, there is neither true self-management nor professional and responsible leadership. It is not at all surprising that such groups do not even contemplate making use of modern achievements in leadership and management, and that the degree of working hierarchy and discipline demanded by any modern society, self-governing society included, is absent. In order to preserve its own position and to compromise workers' self-management, the politocracy rejects (as technocratic) any proposals that boundaries be drawn between workers' self-management and operative management. This shows how even the slogan of "unlimited workers' self-management" can be so cynically abused as to reduce it to the absurd.

Obsessions with production and consumption threaten the prospects of socialism in any country which seeks to emerge rapidly from a state of backwardness. Are there not many people in Yugoslavia who reduce the problems of socialism, directly or indirectly, to problems of production and distribution, and who reduce workers' self-management to the relations of production alone? In this respect, two phases have characterized the development of our society since the revolution: the first was permeated by a sort of production-oriented socialism with exaggerated emphasis on investment and production to the neglect of consumption. More recently, however, one can discern a tendency toward a sort of "consumer socialism."

A poor socialist society must concentrate upon the creation of material abundance. But we should keep in mind that material wealth, which ought to be a means, can take the place of the basic goal, i.e., human wealth. *Homo economicus*—mastered by the pursuit of material goods rather than of human existence—jeopardizes the development of *homo humanus* and his community.

The path of socialist community does not circumvent people's interests, not even their material interests. But socialist community cannot be achieved, either, by means of their absolutization. How, then, can personal and group interests be stimulated without threatening the sense of socialist community? While after the revolution the category of "interest" was almost completely proscribed, in Yugoslavia today one hears more and more reference made to interests alone. However, socialist community is not based upon naked interests. In it serious concern, solidarity, and the devotion of each person to the interests of all are indispensable, even when the individual has to sacrifice to this end certain group and personal interests.

If all life were reduced to the pursuit of money and mutual competition, then such a society, even though bearing the title "socialist," would not have the right to make reference to Marx. Would it not display the very same hierarchy of values which he so severely criticized in bourgeois society? In no essential respect would the man who lives in such a society be any different from Marx's *homo duplex*—the egoistic individual and group on the one hand, and the abstract citizen on the other. It is of minor importance that instead of capitalists there are self-governing groups, when the latter themselves behave as "collective capitalists." For the person who is thrown onto the street by such a group acting in the interests of its own income, the difference is only one of terminology.

In order to become wealthy, socialist society must handsomely reward knowledge, professionalism, and high productivity. But how are we to prevent the gradual formation of an ever more wealthy and powerful elite which will be in a position to prevent a further lessening of social differences when it becomes materially possible for it to do so? How are we to preserve in the meantime the deposit of revolutionary-egalitarian consciousness? Will not the attitude of the revolutionary vanguard toward social inequality change radically in the process? What, in this respect, will be the nature of the new generations upon whom the continuity of the revolution will depend? All these are questions and warnings which Marxists and revolutionaries ought to express before it is too late.

After the lively discussions and practical vacillations that culminated in the New Economic Policy (NEP), the Bolshevik Party decided upon extreme centralization and a distributive economic model. This choice was one of the fateful factors in establishing the basis for primitive-politocratic statism. It was once again confirmed that the mode of production determines the nature of the entire social system. Among the Bolsheviks the view was victorious that rapid industrialization imperatively demands complete state centralization of accumulation. They came to the conviction that socialism is irreconcilable with market economy.

Without going into the question of whether this belief was based upon the authentic Marx or not, one thing should be emphasized as indisputable: in order for social products to lose their character as commodities, it is necessary, according to Marx, that they exist in abundance. But here was a society of *scarcity* which wanted to abolish market economy. The result was statism, not socialism. The state planners and the distributive apparatus became alienated from society and began to take the lion's share of social production for itself. This economic and sociopolitical model later became a paradigm for an entire group of countries.

The choice of the nonmarket economic model after the revolution was also undoubtedly motivated by the desire to avoid the irrationality of anarchic and wasteful market competition by means of strict state planning. However, statist subjectivism and voluntarism have produced results no less irrational.

Without a commodity-money economy today there cannot be any rapid progress toward material abundance. There is still no better way in which to determine the *material* needs of the population and on this basis to produce real "use values." The otherwise noble wish to eliminate the mediation of "exchange values" at the very beginning of socialism has resulted in production for stockpiles rather than for use.

The market can diagnose and cure many "infantile disorders" and shatter many economic myths constructed by statism. It can reveal, for example, that beneath full employment there is only pseudoemployment, or that an extraordinary rate of economic growth can to a certain degree mean accumulation of unused stock. Behind the façade of economic dynamism the market can reveal the harmful investment errors of the politocracy, which has tried to erect monuments to itself in the form of so-called political factories. In a word, the market can unmask parasitism and introduce effective selection and stimulation.

In the absence of the pressure of real market competition, self-managing collectives in Yugoslavia used to react rather indifferently to the use-values of their products. Moreover, their economic interests were not such as to induce them toward mutual integration. Self-government is threatened not only by statism, but also by a utopian picture of human nature, on the basis of which people naively expect that self-managing groups will produce rationally at any given moment, without any competition whatsoever. In a system without competition, solidarity is shattered by its opposite—parasitism.

In order to preserve a given society's socialist character, however, the market must be placed within the framework of serious planning, regulation, and coordination. Otherwise, economics and morality will continue to react *antagonistically* upon each other, economics pulling in the direction of egoism, and morality in the direction of solidarity. Without rational control of economic tendencies by the associated producers, socialism in Marx's sense is out of the question. However, neither in theory nor in practice has an economic model yet been discovered which might synthesize self-management, the market, and planning.

John Maynard Keynes was among the first to perceive that bourgeois economic thought was the victim of two major errors: (1) that the economy can successfully regulate itself by means of the market mechanism; and (2) that an uncontrolled market ensures the maximum utilization of economic potentials. Thus, Yugoslav anarcho-liberals who *glorify* the market in socialism are provincially repeating the mistakes of pre-Keynesian bourgeois economics. In place of the demolished myth of statist de-alienation, they are constructing a myth of de-alienation through the uncontrolled market. But the idea of socialist community is as irreconcilable with servitude to the blind forces of the market as it is with statist alienation.

So long as it exists, the market will try to impose itself over society as the supreme regulator and criterion of human relations so that it may thereby restore the economic basis of bourgeois society. It is generally recognized that the market reacts mainly to the existing level of demand and that it also creates artificial and even harmful demands. It thus comes into conflict with the mission of socialist community, which seeks to humanize existing need and develop new, human needs. This notwithstanding, the "socialist" anarcho-liberals persistently attack Marxists who assert that humanism and the money-commodity economy often come into conflict.

This conflict is quite obvious in culture, although the market could reveal some parasites here as well. Yugoslav experience only confirms what we already know from capitalism—that individual groups (self-governing, now) can use the market to encourage the most uncultured of needs and make quite a bit of money in the process. It is indisputable that capitalist civilization still dictates our structure of needs and consumption to a considerable degree. This has been the source of much confusion over the question of the proper criteria of socialism. Even the every concept of the standard of living is increasingly reduced to a material standard, rather than being seen as a human standard.

In Yugoslavia there are theorists and practitioners who advocate simply transferring market principles to the field of culture. But socialism, if understood in a Marxist sense, should orient itself toward the *gradual* elimination of cultural values from the list of commodities. Statism has replaced the rule of *homo eco-nomicus,* so characteristic of bourgeois society, with the domination of *homo politicus.* In the name of socialism the anarcho-liberals want to transcend *homo politicus* only to rehabilitate *homo economicus.* Actually, both are equally pernicious for socialist culture.

The quality of socialist society depends to a large degree upon the manner in which the consumer is educated. In our country quite a bit has been said about the association of producers, but all too little about the association of consumers. In contrast to group-particularistic self-government, in a system of *integral* social self-government it is possible for needs to be democratically hierarchicalized, for priorities to be established and for means to exist to educate and satisfy the most human of needs. A theory of such needs, which for its part would assume the further development of Marxist anthropology and axiology, would make further elaboration of the theory of socialist community possible.

17. Self-government and Planning

MIHAILO MARKOVIĆ

One of the basic problems, if not *the* basic problem, of Yugoslav society and of contemporary socialism in general is how to insure the guidance of the entire society under conditions of social self-government, how to insure that society as a whole moves with full consciousness of where it is going and what the general goals are that it ought to attain, while every collective, township, and republic retains the right freely to orient itself and move toward its own special goals; how to provide for the rationality of the whole process and at the same time the spontaneity of its individual parts; how to reconcile the discipline that all planning from the center imposes, no matter how elastic it may be, with the initiative and freedom of individuals and collectives, without which there would be no sense in even speaking of workers' and social self-government.

We find ourselves before an undoubted contradiction. This is not one of those subjectively construed contradictions that are the result of confusion and inconsistency in thinking, or, in the best case, of the imprecision of concepts. Here we are dealing with a real, objective, dialectic contradiction, for two essential requirements of socialist society, two of its undoubted values, are in conflict.

Reprinted from *Humanizam i dijalektika* (Belgrade: Prosveta, 1967), pp. 373–97. Translated by Helen Kramer.

1. The contradiction of guidance and self-government

On the one hand, one of the essential limitations of capitalism that should be surmounted by the arising of socialism is its haphazard, anarchic character. Socialism is a more *rational* society since on the macro level, within the framework of the whole social community, and not only on the micro level, within the framework of the separate enterprise, it enables the control of material processes, the anticipation of future events, timely intervention, regulation, acceleration, deceleration, and so forth. Socialism is a more *humane* society: man is not only an individual but also a social being. As a social being, he cannot but strive for society as a whole to exist under conditions worthy of man. This means with clear, critical consciousness of the situation in which man finds himself and of the real possibilities for further change. And this by itself implies the possibility of choice among objectively conditioned alternatives and the possibility of organized, harmonized activity to achieve that alternative that best corresponds to the needs of society. In a society in which there are no such possibilities, neither is there true freedom of the individual, no matter how much he may have the illusion that he is free. . . .

A society in which haphazardness prevails, which lacks planning, is similar to unconscious nature. It is still far from being a humanized society.

On the other hand, the concept of social self-government was introduced in our country precisely as a counterweight to the tendency of strict planning from the center. The forms of planning applied until then by socialist practice disclosed some essential inadequacies; moreover, they manifested the dangers that every planning necessarily carries in itself. Modern society is not a Greek polis, in which all citizens could be members of the assembly and directly participate in making decisions. Hence, someone has to guide in the name of the whole mass of society. That someone can always very easily form into a separate, privileged social stratum. As we have had opportunities to convince ourselves in the history of socialism up to now, this possibility is very often transformed into reality. In modern, mass, highly organized society, therefore, every guidance carries in itself the danger of strengthening the degree of bureaucratization of society. The other side of the coin is the passivization of the direct producers and their maintenance in the position of unfree, inert beings, lacking rights and transformed into a "pendant of the machine," into a fragment of man. . . .

The only way for an ordinary person from the mass to be transformed from an object into a conscious, interested subject, from a doer into an initiator, from a hand into a brain and will, is his active inclusion in various organs of self-government. In that way not only is the initiative of the broadest masses developed, the productivity of labor increased, and the power of the bureaucracy reduced, but only then do some vital forms of man's alienation begin to be abolished: the product of his labor ceases to be completely alien to him; production becomes something more than a mechanical, forcefully imposed activity; cooperation in self-governing bodies necessarily causes a greater degree of mutual communication and solidarity. To the extent that man is not only a social but also an individual being, and a being of a particular collective, it is illusory to speak of his freedom if social self-government in one of its possible forms has not been realized.

To be sure, the individual's acquisition of the right of decision-making does not at all guarantee that he will decide in the general social interest, or even in his own, personal interest, for he must be rather rational to judge his interest correctly. Moreover, there is no assurance that the behavior of people in the organs of self-government will completely coincide with what they think to be their own personal interest; their behavior will often be conformist, but in this case not so much in relation to the general social centers of power as in relation to local microcenters of powers, in the enterprise and in the commune. Accordingly, social self-government latently bears within itself not only the dangers of individualism and particularism, which sharply clash with general social interests, but still greater dangers of the mass creation of small bureaucratic cliques, which are small only in relation to the number of members in them and to the spatial and temporal ranges of power, and precisely because of that can be terribly effective in their antisocial impact. By that alone, social self-government necessarily draws after itself certain forms of haphazardness and anarchy, which socialist society cannot and ought not to tolerate.

Hence, both guidance and social self-government are necessary conditions of socialism. But, simultaneously, they also carry with them certain phenomena that are mutually exclusive.

Up to now, practice has still not succeeded in solving this contradiction. . . .

4. The conditions for guiding social development in Yugoslavia

By abolishing the bourgeoisie as a class and nationalizing the means of production, socialism acquired the historical possibility of the unlimited gradual mastery of blind social forces and of the unlimited progressive humanization of social life. The forms of planning in the development of socialism up to now led also, however, to certain negative experiences, ambiguities, and resistances. To the extent that social ownership of the means of production is manifested as state ownership and political power is concentrated in state organs, planning will be the administrative, external, compulsory imposition of goals and tasks, which reduces to a minimum the initiative, freedom, and dignity of the individual producer. On the other hand, true rational guidance is lacking if objective, unbiased, concrete information about the state of society is not provided, if political decision-making does not rely on that information, if the more remote as well as the more immediate goals and needs of social development are not clearly defined, if the necessary attention is not devoted to the development of the methodology and techniques of planning, and if society does not provide mechanisms for bringing the most capable, professionally competent revolutionary cadres into leading positions.

The problem of guiding social development is posed in our country in very complex and contradictory conditions. We introduced self-management and thus also in practice began the process of the withering away of the state. But we still have a very powerful state and a very great concentration of economic and political power in central social institutions. Our parliaments, especially the federal and republican parliaments, have a hybrid, contradictory character. They are gradually becoming organs of self-government to the extent that in them are introduced more and more working people who are elected democratically, who perform their leadership functions temporarily, and who are compensated for them as for every other creative, highly skilled labor, without any rights to permanent enjoyment of some privileged social status. On the other hand, the parliaments are still organs of the state to the extent to which the executive councils and administrative organs, by their pressure and authority inherited from the past, succeed in exercising a decisive influence—a situa-

tion which results in the violation of the principles of the public-
ness of all activities and the democracy of all elections and decision-making, the substitution of hierarchy for relations of equality, and the replacement of the force of argument by the force of
power, and persuasion by compulsion.

Second, we not only abolished private ownership of the means
of production but we made very important steps in transforming
state ownership into truly social ownership. However, a substantial part of social property is still alienated in specific ways and
does not serve the satisfaction of real general social interests; on
the one hand, because of its disposal in an unsuitable way by the
state administration, or influential individuals in it, and, on the
other, because of particularism, regionalism, and nationalism that
come to expression when sociopolitical organizations place the interests of their township, province, or republic in the forefront.
Such forms of alienation of social property lead to the partial
elimination of those exceptionally favorable historical possibilities of rational guidance that the socialist revolution created.

Third, we have a hybrid economic system, which factually rests
on both the principle of profitable operation, of the freeing of
the laws of market economy, and, at the same time, the principle
of continual administrative intervention not only with the aim of
preventing anarchy and excessively large disproportions but also
with essentially noneconomic objectives—political, humanitarian, and others. There are incomparably more of these administrative interventions than permitted by the Constitution, the decisions of Party forums, the existing political-legal documents,
and, in general, the prevailing political-economic theory. Since it
is an unrecognized and, in large part, unknown force, administrative intervention is smuggled into the system in a haphazard,
uncontrolled, insufficiently rational form and has a doubly negative effect: fettering the operation of the market, it creates many
artificial, economically unjustified relations and smothers the
freedom and initiative of individual work organizations, which
makes it similar to the statist structure of planning except that
the effects are substantially less in this direction; on the other
hand, since such administrative intervention is not sufficiently
thought out, scientifically based, and coordinated for the long
run, it contributes from time to time to the creation of still
greater disproportions and anarchy than those that the market
economy alone would have brought. In this situation, we have

obvious contradictions between theory and practice. On the one hand, parallel with verbal advocacy of freer operation of the laws of a market economy go far greater interventions in the course of economic trends than would be necessary if they were based more on solid economic analyses; parallel with verbal advocacy of allowing the organs of self-management to decide net investment go measures that practically prevent the strengthening of the material base of the self-management organs; parallel with sharp condemnations of statism and statist tendencies goes maintenance of greater state power than is necessary; parallel with demands that, because of destatization, the state budget should be decreased go rapidly growing federal and republican budgets. On the other hand, those who maintain that, in fact, we do not have and cannot have a *purely* market economy, that in every socialist society, there must be a minimum of intervention of the central political institutions, provided that these are genuinely democratic organs of true self-government, are accused of advocating statism and returning to the administrative period! It is difficult to say where the boundary lies here between cynicism and the typically ideological inability to perceive reality.

The fourth characteristic of the conditions under which the problem of guidance is posed in our country is the evident contradiction between the *role* that every individual direct producer should have in a system of self-management and his *real opportunity* of playing that role. Self-management assumes a *rational* producer, who not only knows his work and enterprise well but is capable of judging its long-run interests, of harmonizing them with the general interests of the overall society and of judging which means are most adequate for their realization. Such a degree of rationality presupposes literacy, general culture, and political and professional education. In this respect, however, the situation in our society is worrisome: not only is the tempo of progress in making our working people literate and cultured highly unsatisfactory, but in some areas we are stagnating and even retrogressing. Such failure in this area, which can have far-reaching consequences, is to a large extent the result of a completely insupportable and harmful conception according to which education and culture should be maintained as much as possible by those who consume this type of commodity. Such reasoning is nothing but the distant echo of the long-surpassed liberal capitalism of the nineteenth century. It is clear, however, that it would be absurd if a society built its existence on a condition such as the rationality of the direct producer and yet did nothing to fulfill that condition to as great a degree as possible.

5. The role of science in guiding social development

The guidance of social development must be based on scientific analyses and forecasts. In socialism it has become a commonplace that decision-making about social questions must rest on scientific knowledge (hence the name of the doctrine—scientific socialism). Unfortunately, in the majority of socialist countries, the social sciences are very undeveloped and lag greatly behind the natural and technical sciences. Instead of being required to offer reliable, empirically based knowledge about the true condition of society, its systematic tendencies, its real possibilities, and alternatives of further change, these sciences are often viewed as having primarily an ideological and propaganda function. In recent years in our country we have made a powerful turnabout toward empirical research. Unfortunately, the omissions of the preceding period are still revenging themselves on us, and we still do not have available satisfactory knowledge about many key problems of our society.

Another mistake is perhaps even more serious, because we still have not even perceived it completely.

Planning today can no longer even be imagined without the application of theoretical, methodological, and technical knowledge from a whole series of very exact disciplines that were developed in the West after the Second World War, and that are encompassed by the common name of *operations research* or *management science*. The subject of this science is, briefly, the scientific preparation of decisions, the calculation of the most optimal solutions in a given situation when the objectives to be met are known and the available means are limited. . . .

We, unfortunately, are undertaking nothing, or at least nothing in an organized way. There are individuals who have by chance learned something about this complex of sciences and, on personal initiative, work on some problems. But all this amounts to very little and, taken as a whole, is unsatisfactory. We have neither the corresponding instruction, nor the research work, nor a policy of creating personnel, nor application in practice. We are therefore threatened with the danger of lagging severely behind not only the more developed capitalist countries but also the socialist countries, who, thanks to a great concentration of resources and redoubled efforts, usually succeed in catching up to the West in all the exact disciplines in which they trailed at the time of the Second World War.

In the near future, the conviction will surely ripen in our country that conscious interventions aimed at guiding social processes do not tolerate improvisation and guessing, that they must be far more exactly planned. Then perhaps we will discover that the insufficient development of the necessary expert personnel is one of the main limiting factors.

6. Levels and forms of guidance

To be successful and maximally rational, guidance must be carried out on all levels of the social structure. Those who insist on the importance of planning in socialism need not deny the possibilities of planning also on the level of the work organization, township, and province. To the extent to which the personnel and other preconditions for it exist, it is certain that in a self-management system (in which the laws of the market operate with relative freedom) collectives have a strong interest in operating as successfully as possible and, to accomplish this, in sufficiently acquainting themselves with all factors relevant for the successful forecasting and regulation of production and sale on the market. Generalized, a priori disbelief in such possibilities would in practice truly mean the supporting of bureaucratic tendencies and would imply a simple return to the methods of administrative socialism.

But likewise it is naive, to put it mildly, to think that rational guidance of overall social processes can be achieved by the spontaneous harmonization of individual local and regional plans, or by spontaneous vertical linking. Not only must one planning organization avoid negating the freedom of decision of others, but all organizations together, directly or indirectly, must set certain general frameworks to their freedom of planning, that is, establish certain general objectives that should be achieved in a given time interval. Hence some democratically formed central institutions —in fact, central organs of self-government—are indispensable for the setting of such general objectives and the determination of the means and mechanisms for their fulfillment.

Should the general social plan be only a forecast or also an obligation? If we wish to discuss planning seriously, such a question hardly makes sense. The very concept of planning implies some sort of *practice* that is to be guided, and not some purely *theoretical* interest in finding out and anticipating the course of some process. Thus forecasting is just the assumption of the plan and not the plan itself.

To forecast a certain direction of movement means to decide in favor of it on the basis of our needs and long-run objectives. The question is raised: why should we decide in favor of one possible direction of movement if we do not intend to truly engage ourselves for its realization? Why should we call a plan something that is purely a forecast, simply a nonobligatory reflection on the future and not also the chosen course of action? Or, why should we, in the theoretical phase, decide in favor of one alternative and then, in practice, do something entirely different?

The only consistent position would be the total rejection of the plan—both as an obligation and as a forecast, on the level of the federation and of the republic as well as on local levels. If it is considered unimportant to define in advance where society as a whole will find itself tomorrow, it appears that elementary consistency would require that the same principle also be applied to every individual part of society. Guidance is not something that would be (in and of itself alone) valuable in one area of human life and dangerous in another. In fact, this is one of the essential characteristics of the structure of human practice.

To the extent to which man is *free,* he strives to participate in shaping his future; therefore, among the various real possibilities of the future course, he chooses that which most corresponds to his needs.

To the extent to which man is an *active, creative* being, he does not satisfy himself with only the contemplation of the future possibilities but engages himself in the practical realization of a selected objective.

Finally, to the extent that man is a *social* being, communicating, cooperating, and sharing with others certain needs and values, he is ready also to strive for supraindividual goals, even for those that do not satisfy his personal needs but are indirect values for him because they satisfy the needs of other people for whom he cares.

Only thus is guidance possible not only in personal and family life but also in the life of broader social communities. But the reverse is also true: a man who is interested only in guidance in his own immediate setting shows by this that he is not a sufficiently social being, or that he is not conscious of the inseparable connection of personal and social interest.

7. The bearers of social guidance

Nevertheless, a person can accept guidance as a general value—and hence also accept it where the society as a whole is concerned—yet have reservations about it because of the real danger that the social group that is its bearer may alienate itself from society and oppose itself to society as a tyrannical external force.

Hence, one of the most important questions in connection with guidance of overall social development is: who should carry out this function, and how can possible abuses be avoided?

The experience of the socialist countries has clearly shown that social guidance on the part of state organs inevitably leads to the creation of a very powerful political bureaucracy. Insofar as this bureaucracy is educated, well informed, and willing to rely on the technical intelligentsia and utilize the accomplishments of science, such planning can be relatively effective and can even insure the relatively rapid growth of the material base of society; but it will also lead to great economic losses, passivize the direct producers and maintain them in the position of wage laborers, and create insupportably large social differences.

To give over the function of guidance into the hands of experts would lead to another variant of bureaucracy—technocracy. The technical bureaucracy, because of its greater competence and expertise in controlling social processes, would perhaps show a greater degree of efficiency; but it would also show a greater disregard of political, social, and all other human values.

The only completely satisfactory solution is found in a system of self-government. The supreme organs of self-government should assume full responsibility for defining general social objectives and the instruments for their attainment. To be sure, such defining could be considered rational only if it takes into account, on the one hand, the *long-run objectives of the whole epoch* (the elimination of all hidden forms of exploitation, the overcoming of social differences between social groups and regional differences between the more and less developed areas, the achievement of material welfare, social solidarity, etc.) and, on the other, the *real condition of society, the systematic tendencies of its change, the plans of lower sociopolitical organizations, etc.*

Science should play an important multiple role in the formation of such an overall plan—by precise definition of objectives, elaboration of alternative policies that will lead to these objectives, examination of the effectiveness of the adopted policy, preparation of measures for modifying the given policy when in practice it shows itself less successful than was expected, detailed elaboration of short-run plans, continuous control of their implementation, continuous sounding of public opinion, etc. To be sure, *decisions on the choice* among alternatives ought to be made by the highest political self-government body, the parliament. These decisions would naturally be obligatory; they would constitute the legal framework within which the decision-making of the self-government organs at all other levels would take place. However, these decisions would not be imposed by raw force on the part of some alien power external to society, as is the case under bureaucratic conditions. The essential difference lies in the democratic way in which, after many preliminary studies and discussions, the overall plan is adopted. . . .

At the present time, for our society it would be a step toward a higher degree of democracy, toward the elimination of some disproportions and instabilities, and even toward the freer operation of the laws of the market, if the numerous uncoordinated, insufficiently organized interventions on the part of individuals and individual organs of the state apparatus, which under present conditions are difficult to avoid and prevent, were replaced by carefully prepared, scientifically based, overall regulation of the basic instruments of further social development by the highest, most authoritative, and most democratically elected political institutions of our society.

The following conclusion can be drawn from all the foregoing: the contradiction before which we find ourselves cannot be surpassed by the simple negation of one part of it, as some think today. Guidance cannot be reduced to nonobligatory forecasting of the future course of things, for then it is not guidance at all. On the other hand, neither can this contradiction be surpassed by negating or essentially limiting the principle of self-government, for this is not only one of the key achievements of our revolution, but, in general, it is the precondition of that humanization of society conceived by Marx. Of course, models of society could be built on only one or the other principle, but they would inevitably lead to a series of undesired phenomena, some of the most fundamental of which have been cited. Accordingly, the only solution is to surpass this contradiction by bringing about a certain change in the character of planning, on the one hand, and self-government, on the other, by decisively debureaucratizing guidance by the central organs and insuring that the self-government of local organs is much more rational and more in the spirit of socialism.

Only such a solution is in accord with the basic principles that were propounded by Marx and in whose name we began this grandiose revolutionary transformation of our society.

Notes on the Editors

BRANKO HORVAT was born in Yugoslavia in 1928. As a youth he participated in the Partisan Liberation War. He received D.Sc. and Ph.D. degrees from the University of Zagreb and the University of Manchester. He is a member of the League of Communists of Yugoslavia. Professor Horvat was founder of the Institute of Economic Sciences in Belgrade and of the journal *Economic Analysis*. His numerous publications include *Towards a Theory of Planned Economy*.

MIHAILO MARKOVIĆ was born in Yugoslavia in 1923. He served as an officer in the Yugoslav Partisan Army. He received Ph.D. degrees from the University of Belgrade and the University of London and currently is Professor of Philosophy and Director of the Institute of Philosophy, University of Belgrade. Dr. Marković is the author of numerous philosophical studies, including *From Affluence to Praxis: Philosophy and Social Criticism*.

RUDI SUPEK was born in Yugoslavia in 1913. He participated in the Resistance Movement in France in 1941–1945. He is Professor of Sociology at the University of Zagreb. Dr. Supek is co-editor of the journal *Praxis* and author of many books, including *Power and Socialism*.

88